Imperial Muslims

To the People of Aden.
May their suffering soon come to an end.

Imperial Muslims

Islam, Community and Authority
in the Indian Ocean, 1839–1937

Scott S. Reese

EDINBURGH
University Press

Edinburgh University Press is one of the leading university presses in the UK. We publish academic books and journals in our selected subject areas across the humanities and social sciences, combining cutting-edge scholarship with high editorial and production values to produce academic works of lasting importance. For more information visit our website: edinburghuniversitypress.com

© Scott S. Reese, 2018

Edinburgh University Press Ltd
The Tun—Holyrood Road
12 (2f) Jackson's Entry
Edinburgh EH8 8PJ

Typeset in 10.5/12.5 Times New Roman by
IDSUK (DataConnection) Ltd

A CIP record for this book is available from the British Library

ISBN 978 0 7486 9765 6 (hardback)
ISBN 978 0 7486 9766 3 (webready PDF)
ISBN 978 1 4744 3252 8 (epub)

The right of Scott S. Reese to be identifiedasauthorofthisworkhasbeenassertedin accordance with the Copyright, Designs and Patents Act 1988 and the Copyright and Related Rights Regulations 2003 (SI No. 2498).

Contents

	Acknowledgments	vii
	Map 1 British Aden	x
	Map 2 The Indian Ocean and its commercial routes	xi
	Map 3 Yemen in the nineteenth century	xii
	Introduction: A Community of Muslims	1
1.	Hanuman's Tunnel: Collapsing the Space between Hind and Arabia in the Arab Imaginary	17
2.	Aden, the Company and Indian Ocean Interests	40
3.	Claims to Community: Mosques, Cemeteries and the Universe	64
4.	"The Qadi is not a Judge": The Qadi's Courts, Community and Authority	79
5.	"An Innocent Amusement": Marginality, Spirit Possession and the Moral Community	109
6.	Scripturalism, Sufism and the Limits of Defining Public Religiosity	138
	Conclusions	162
	Notes	168
	Bibliography	196
	Index	206

Acknowledgments

Looking back, it seems almost inevitable that I would write a book on Aden, to many an—undeservedly—obscure colonial outpost in Southern Arabia. But it was hardly a direct path. Nearly thirty years ago I was returning from my first extended period living and working in the Middle East when I passed through London in the hope of looking at various graduate programs. I had occasion to meet Professor Michael Twaddle at the Institute of Commonwealth Studies. Having an interest in both Islam and the British Empire, but not wishing to work in the "traditional" Middle East I asked him how these two may be combined. Among other things, he noted the dearth of scholarship on Aden and that something quite interesting might be done there. Given that this was 1989 and Aden was still the capital of the People's Democratic Republic of Yemen (PDRY), I didn't give his suggestion much thought. I went on to do my Ph.D. research on Sufism in Somalia. Fast forward to 2001 and a chance encounter with a librarian from the University of Washington at a meeting of the Middle East Studies Association. He was an Adeni Somali who regaled me with fascinating stories of Aden's patron saint, Sayyid Abu Bakr Aydarus. I was intrigued, but, again, I was working on other projects and filed this encounter away as interesting, but not really part of my research agenda. Finally, two years later, I was in London for a month, ostensibly to study a Sufi text with a Somali scholar resident in Britain. As luck would have it, he could find little time for me and so I was left at a loose end with four weeks to kill. Largely out of boredom, I went to the India Office Library looking for references to Somali religious scholars. What I found were the Aden residency records and their unbelievably textured accounts of daily life in the Settlement that form much of this book's core. I finally took the hint.

Even so, this is a book with an inordinately long gestation period. After finally deciding that the fates wanted me to write a book on the Muslim community in Aden it is a project that has been beset by delays. While conducting the preliminary research for *Imperial Muslims*, I was also completing my first book *Renewers of the Age*. A near fatal bout of endocarditis (a bacterial infection of the aortic valve) and, later, open heart surgery delayed the project even further. Instability in Yemen made trips to the region at first difficult and then impossible. In other words, there are many reasons why this book should have never seen the light of day. I can only aver that its ultimate publication is due to the fact that Sharif Aydarus and the other *awliya'* of Aden wished it to be so. I can only hope that they will not be displeased.

Saintly assistance aside, a project of this length naturally accrues many debts—professional, personal and institutional. I am enormously grateful to those institutions who have funded my work in various ways. These include my home institution,

Northern Arizona University (NAU), as well as the American Philosophical Society, the British Academy and the American Institute for Yemeni Studies, all of whom provided fellowships for research in the UK and Yemen. A summer fellowship from the Zentrum Moderner Orient (the Centre for Modern Oriental Studies) provided a welcome two-month period in Berlin where I carried out critical work resulting in Chapter 6 of this book. A term spent as the Buffett Visiting Professor of International Studies at Northwestern University enabled me to flesh out much of Chapter 5 on spirit possession. I must also thank the staff of the British Library, especially the India Office Library reading room, who proved ever ready to assist my inquiries.

In addition to financial support, I am grateful to the many institutions who provided me with opportunities to preview my work in various venues, ranging from large public lectures to small dedicated symposia. In addition to Northwestern, I must thank Samira Shaykh and Tony Stewart, who invited me to present an early draft of Chapter 4 at the Muslims Negotiating Modernities workshop held at Vanderbilt University in Nashville, Tennessee. The chapter on Zar and Tamburra was presented at several venues in London and the US, including the Ifriqiyya Colloquium at Columbia University, the University of Florida's African Studies Baraza, and the School of Middle Eastern & North African Studies at the University of Arizona. Versions of Chapter 1 were presented at public talks at the University of Pennsylvania's South Asia Regional Studies (SARS) South Asia Series and the NYU Abu Dhabi (NYUAD) Institute in New York City. The ability to present so much of this work to colleagues prior to publication was invaluable and has, it is hoped, strengthened the work overall.

Of course, I have also incurred a great many personal debts over the course of this project. Far more colleagues agreed to read all or portions of the manuscript than I had any right to expect. Among this legion of indulgent friends and colleagues are Çemil Aydın, Anne Bang, Janice Boddy, Jamal Elias, Michael Gilsenan, Jon Glassman, Nile Green, Brannon Ingram, Kai Kresse, Henri Lauziere, Mandana Limbert, Adeline Masquelier, Nate Mathews, Anne Meneley, Brink Messick, Flagg Miller, Terje Ostebo, Thanos Petouris, Maurice Pomeranz, Sebastian Prange, Keren Weitzberg, Luise White and John Willis. I must extend special thanks to Erin Pettigrew and Terenjit Sevea, without whose insights into the "unseen" would have meant this being a much less interesting book. For help tracking down a number of difficult texts and Qur'anic passages I would like to thank Alan Godlas "bibilographer extraordinaire," Bruce Lawrence and Ebrahim Moosa. A special thanks goes to Carl Ernst, whose encouragement and advice over the years have been essential in my development as a scholar. Thank you for all of your help and insights. Any shortcomings of the book are, of course, entirely my own.

Among the many who have offered their friendship and support over the years, I would like to mention Gabeba Baderoon, Felicitas Becker, Ned Bertz, Anne Betteridge, Rahma Bevalaar, Fahad Bishara, Joel Cabrita, Lee Cassanelli, Dick Eaton, Britta Frede, Ulrike Freitag, Bruce Hall, Sean Hannretta, Joe Hill, Matt Hopper, Rita Koryan, Michael Laffan, Robert Launay, Mara Leichtman, Scott Lucas, Thomas "Dodie" McDow, Pedro Machado, Marc Matera, Gordon "Mac" McMullan,

Maha Nasser, Fallou Ngom, James Onley, Caroline Osella, Marit Ostebo, Carl Petry, Ali Karjoo Ravary, David Robinson, Kaya Sahin, Rüdiger Seesemann, Omnia El Shakry, Heather Sharkey, Rebecca Shereikis, Edward Simpson, Elke Stockreiter, Lakhshmi Subramaniam, Eric Tagliacozzo, Muhammad Sani Umar, Jessica Winegar and Ipek Yosmaoglu.

I must also thank many of my dear colleagues at NAU who have been a source of great support and friendship over the years. Thanks to Sanjam Ahluwalia, Jason BeDuhn, Joe Boles, Alexandra Carpino, Susan Deeds, Tim Darby, Paul and Ruth Donnelly, Paul Dutton, Zsuzsanna Gulacsi, Aly Jordan, Sanjay Joshi, Cynthia Kosso, Bjorn Krondorfer, John Leung, George Lubick, Michael Rulon, Linda Sargent-Wood, Anne Scott, Bruce Sullivan and Rick Tillman. Special thanks to my Chair, Professor Derek Heng, for both his friendship and support as I've struggled to complete this project. I would also be remiss if I did not acknowledge the incredible patience of my long-suffering spouse, Marilya, our kids Svea and Kai, and my parents William and Dixie Reese. The joys of family life are always a welcome distraction from what, if one is not careful, can become an all-consuming obsession.

I would also like to thank the editorial staff of Edinburgh University Press (EUP), especially Nicola Ramsey, Ersev Ersoy and Rebecca Mackenzie, who have made this a relatively painless process.

Last but certainly not least, I must thank those most closely associated with Yemen and Aden for all of their help in completing this project. In Aden, I would like to thank the volunteer staff of the Hambala Centre whose small, but incredibly unique, library collection made this a much more nuanced book. Also, my gratitude goes out to the staffs of the University of Aden as well as the National Library who graciously welcomed me into their midst and made every effort to make my time there productive. There are also many individual Aden "hands" without whose help I could not have completed this book. In particular, Adel Aulaqi in London has been a constant source of inspiration and generosity in helping me make contact with various people and gain access to numerous sources. Thanos Petouris arranged for me to give a talk in London to the British Yemen Society as well as provided introductions to a number of useful contacts. It was also due to his penchant for rummaging through people's attics that I found out about the "lost" Hamza Luqman typescript discussed in Chapter 1. Maher Luqman, of Jeddah, and his sister Huda Wildy, two surviving children of Muhammad Ali Luqman, were unstinting in their efforts to assure my access to their late father's writings. Again, without their help, this book would be far less rich. Similarly, Dr. Shihab Ghanem was indispensable in helping me develop basic biographies for the Luqman brothers. Shelagh Weir needs thanking for her bottomless hospitality and more than one Sunday lunch that turned into drinks and dinner as well. It is always a joy to sit at her table and talk of all things Yemen. Finally, two dear friends who did not live to see the publication of this book, John Shipman and Leilah Ingrams. Both these incredible and generous individuals were instrumental in bringing this work to fruition. This was in part a result of their encyclopedic knowledge of Yemen but it was more so due to their great generosity of heart and willingness to assist someone they hardly knew. I miss them both.

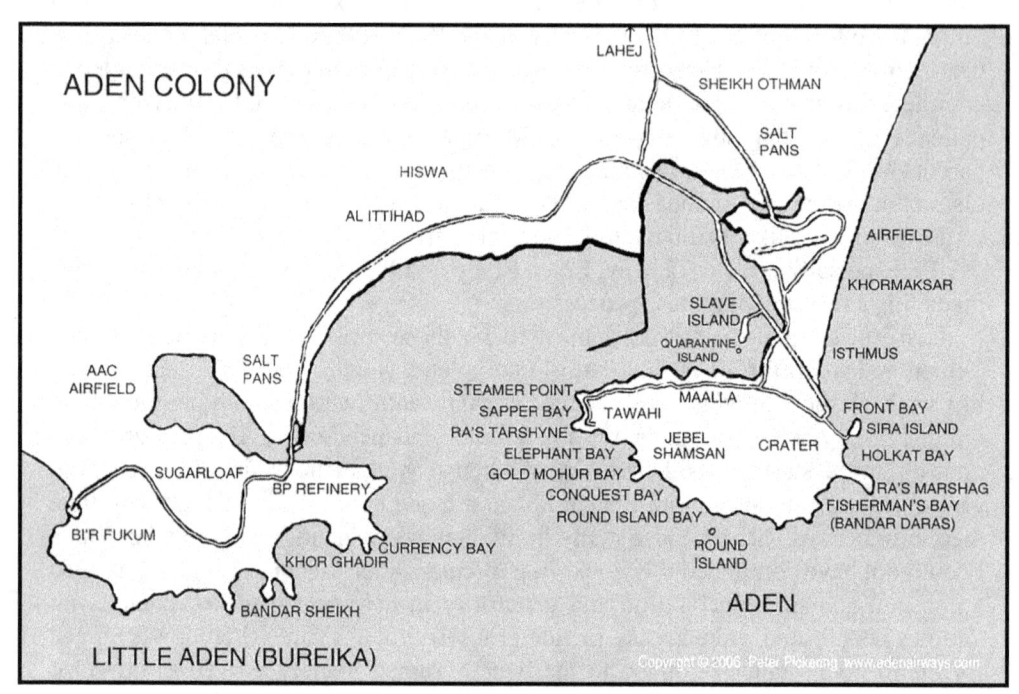

Map 1 British Aden

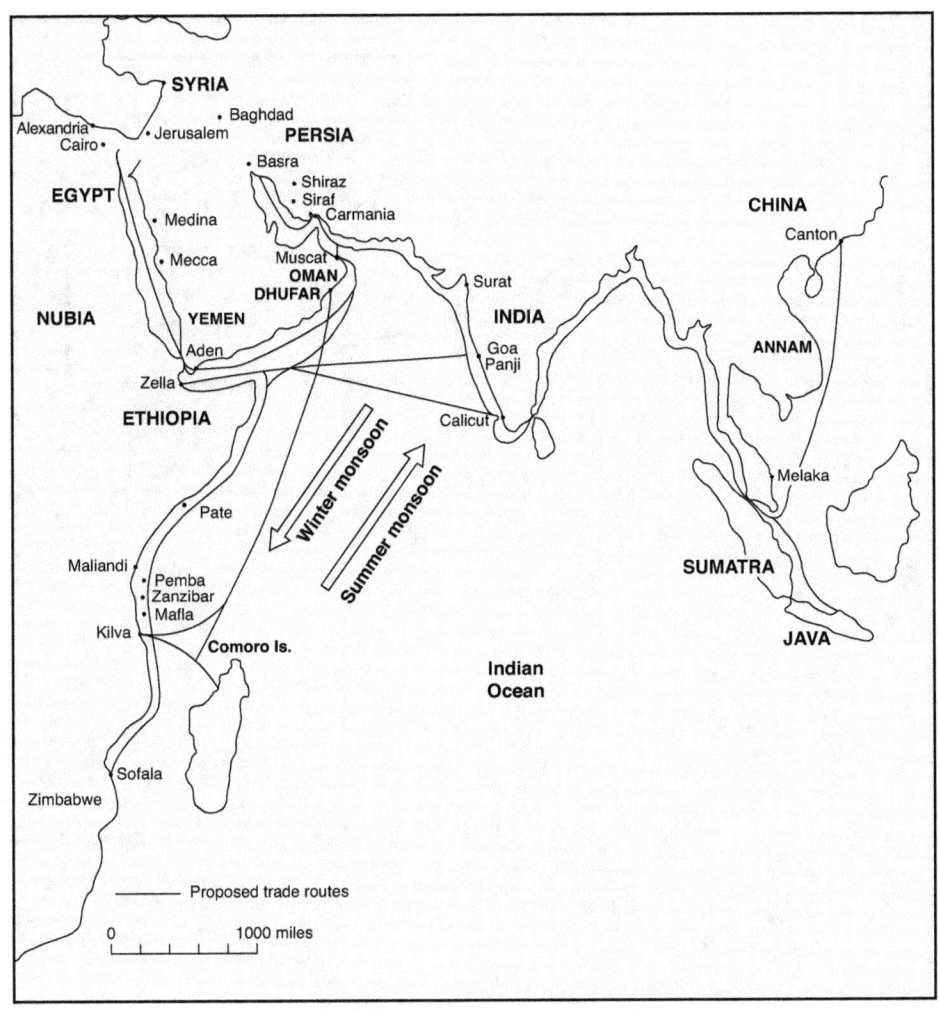

Map 2 The Indian Ocean and its commercial routes

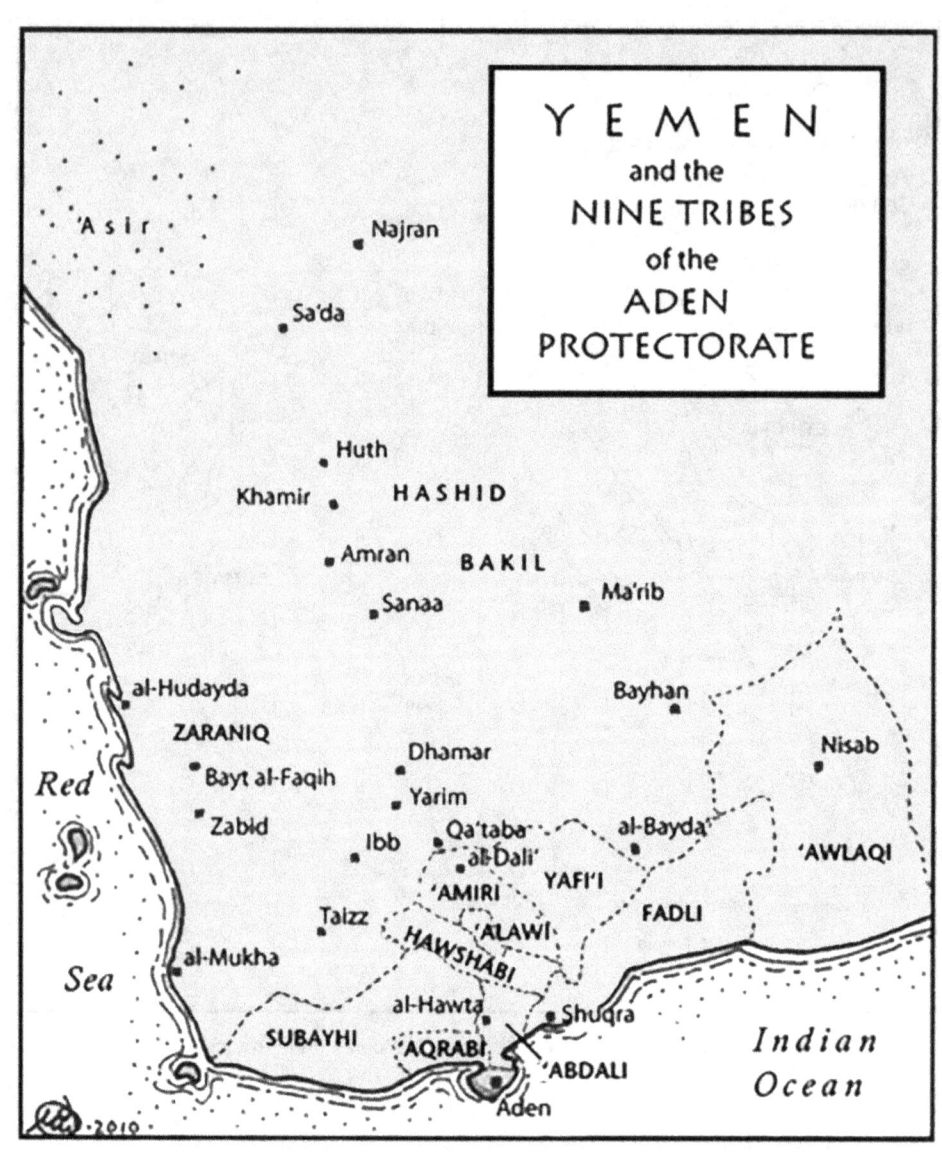

Map 3 Yemen in the nineteenth century

Introduction: A Community of Muslims

In late 1910, Sharifa Aliyya bint Ali, the sister of the Adeni saint Sayyid Hashim al-Bahr—and a pious, saintly woman in her own right—was gravely ill and at death's door. Looking to the not too distant future, the district Qadi, Umar bin Abdullah Sharaf and "other notables of Aden," petitioned British officials for permission to bury the *waliyya* next to her brother within the same shrine. Residency bureaucrats decided that, although there was a strict ban on burials in residential areas, an exception should be granted in this particular instance. As long as she was properly entombed, they noted, there would be nothing unsanitary about the interment and it would "give great satisfaction to the Mohamedan [*sic*] community." More importantly, "the burial of the lady here would probably increase the popularity of the yearly *ziyara* [the festival associated with her brother]" and would in all likelihood be a boon to local merchants.[1]

The collection of Arab, Indian and Somali merchants petitioning for the Sharifa's burial next to her brother would not have disagreed. They were well aware of the economic benefits of the annual festivals.[2] Their motives in this case, however, were not entirely pecuniary. Sharifa Aliyya was as sanctified as her brother. While permission to bury her next to him would save them the added expense of building a separate domed tomb, as a "pious and sacred woman" who was "cherished," the petitioners also hoped they and the faithful would derive "the benefit of her blessing," from the grave.[3]

By the time of this episode, in the opening decade of the twentieth century, Britain was a global empire. But what is often less recognized by lay persons and scholars alike is that by the end of the Victorian age, the British Empire was, demographically at any rate, arguably the largest Muslim state in the world. As Cemil Aydin notes, by the conclusion of Queen Victoria's reign her government ruled over nearly 40 percent of the globe's Muslim population.[4] As such, British authorities and Muslim subjects intersected on a daily basis in the course of the Empire's administration and thus the interest of imperial authorities in the burial arrangements of a local holy woman should come as little surprise. This vignette, however, also provides a window on to the lives of Muslims and the communities they constructed under the aegis of imperial rule.

The notables who lodged this petition were permanent residents of the British Settlement of Aden, but hailed from across the Indian Ocean. As such, one important element that connected them was their imperial subjecthood. The lives of all Aden's residents were shaped by the pervasive colonial state. They arrived in Aden as the result of imperial design and need; their movements, their personal, political and religious associations, along with their economic and domestic activities were subject to the colonial surveillance regime and their civil lives were regulated by the Indian Penal Code. The Muslims of Aden were, in this sense, quintessential subjects of the Empire. Their ability to find common footing as a community, however, was not premised solely on their imperial subjecthood. While Muslims in Aden may find common cause in either their opposition to, or accommodation of, the system that governed them, they were bound together by more positive forces: their faith. The importance of faith as a social bond among the believers of Aden is frequently evident through relatively concrete, or at least observable, institutions, such as mosques, shrines and Sufi orders. In other instances, it can be found in more ineffable concepts such as the *baraka* (blessings) of a deceased holy woman. *Imperial Muslims* explores the dynamics of these relationships within the context of colonial Aden during the nineteenth and twentieth centuries.

Located in Southern Arabia near the mouth of the Red Sea, at the time of its incorporation into the Empire in 1839, Aden was home to only a few hundred people. While it was a port with a long and storied history, by the nineteenth century it had fallen on very hard times. That changed with the advent of the colonial moment. Aden emerged as a critical transportation and communications hub within Britain's Indian Ocean Empire, attracting thousands of new residents. While the town counted Hindus, Jews, Parsis and Christians among these, the vast majority were Muslim. Developing a corporate identity that was quite distinct, this was a community whose fabric was woven from threads that ran across the western Indian Ocean. Throughout the colonial period these people portrayed themselves as a unified group, "the Muslims of Aden."

A great deal has been written about the networks created by Britain's post-Napoleonic Indian Ocean Empire. Most have focused on the political, legal or economic consequences of empire, devoting far less attention to the personal and social. This book examines the development of a local community within the spaces created by imperial rule from the mid-nineteenth century to the eve of the Second World War.[5] It explores how individuals from widely disparate backgrounds brought together by the networks of empire created a cohesive community utilizing various aspects of their shared faith. On the one hand, this study concerns itself with the use of discrete religious institutions—including mosques, tombs, pious endowments and the law—to delineate the parameters of community. However, it goes beyond these "observable" bodies to explore how an Islamic ontology and shared concepts of the universe, along with the "agency" of the unseen (*al-ghayb*), manifest in concepts such as *baraka*, similarly shaped the communal lives of believers within the confines of imperial rule.

Muslims and the imperial context

The impact of the British Empire on the Indian Ocean and Islamic societies has been heavily studied. Over the last decade historians have written about the nature of Britain's presence in the Indian Ocean, characterizing it as a complex web of economic and political power.⁶ Among the most notable are Sugata Bose and Thomas Metcalf, whose approaches are primarily structural in nature, concerned with the administrative, economic and political effects of Britain's Indian colony on its wider Imperial realm. David Lambert and Alan Lester have noted in their book *Colonial Lives across the Empire* that, while such forces certainly played an important role in shaping empire, the communities that emerged from this process were created through the intersection of multiple trajectories of "people, objects, texts and ideas."⁷ While excellent works of scholarship, these and others focus largely on the political, economic and legalistic consequences of empire.⁸ Few address the social consequences inherent in Britain's creation of what was effectively an Indian Ocean empire that brought literally millions of subjects under a single political umbrella for the first time in the modern era.⁹ None examines the impact of empire on the region's single largest confessional community: Muslims.

Scholars of Islam, as opposed to historians of empire, *have* devoted a great deal of attention to the impact of nineteenth- and twentieth-century colonialism on Muslim societies. Much of this has focused largely on the highest levels of religious discourse and the notion of religious reform.¹⁰ Qasim Zaman's writings on the evolution of reformist thought in the late colonial period and Samira Haj's work on Muhammad Abduh have greatly enhanced our understanding of Islamic reform within the colonial context.¹¹ They demonstrate that, while informed by widespread ideals of religious scripturalism current within the "Islamic international," specific reformist ideas were always shaped by local conditions and concerns. More significantly, scholars such as Haj and Talal Asad argue persuasively that rather than a simple reaction to a monolithic Western imperialism, modern Muslim reformist discourse must be understood as only one element in an evolving discursive tradition concerning correct belief and practice embedded in a variety of historically contingent institutions, practices and forms of power within particular communities and contexts.¹² This is undoubtedly an important insight, however, focus on the shaping of the highest levels of debate has led to a preoccupation with Islamic reform movements.¹³ In doing so, other aspects of Muslim spirituality and society that were also responding to colonial rule via the discursive tradition are left underexamined.

Imperial Muslims seeks to remedy what is frankly a critical gap in our understanding of Muslims under colonial rule in a number of ways. The case of Aden entails the examination of a community that was actually created by the so-called colonial moment rather than simply shaped by it. As such, it allows us to explore how individuals, drawn together from enormously diverse geographic, cultural and social backgrounds, actually managed the everyday realities of living together. It also provides insight into how empire itself facilitated the emergence of what were effectively new communities created in part through the movement of ideas and people—as well as imperial design—leading to the rise of new social contexts, constructs and novel constellations of authority. Reformist discourse and the imperial milieu form important parts of this book, but they are only elements of a larger story.

The local community of believers was defined by many other commonalities, including veneration of the saints, spirit possession cults (with varying levels of attachment to the Islamic multiverse) and a shared ontological understanding of the universe.[14] Such metaphysical common ground provided many venues for individuals to create bonds with one another. But, as we shall see, it also afforded avenues to connect with Aden itself as a node in a wider sacred geography. As a result, the study of Aden affords an opportunity to expand our understanding of "discursive tradition" and its role in shaping the lives of believers.

Aden: An imperial community

There were probably few spots in Britain's empire where as many intellectual and social trajectories intersected to shape a new community as Aden (Singapore and Zanzibar being two others). The modern port of Aden was very much a colonial creation. While founded by the Romans in the first century CE, when troops of the East India Company occupied the town in 1839 it was home to a modest population of 800 residents. By the 1849 census it had grown to more than 12,000 and it stood at more than 19,000 by the 1870s and more than 51,000 by the 1930s. As one official pointed out in an early census, these were likely conservative numbers as they did not count the garrison—including camp followers; more transient populations, such as day laborers, merchants and pilgrims; or those who otherwise often actively sought not to be counted.[15] The overwhelming majority of these residents were Muslims. Of the 19,000 plus inhabitants of the port in 1872, more than 16,500 were Muslim; in 1931 of the town's approximately 51,000 residents more than 42,000 were members of the '*umma*'—the community of believers. Jews formed the largest minority, never more than 10 per cent of the whole, followed by Hindus who number 854 men, women and children in 1871 and nearly 1,600 by 1931. Parsis and "native" Christians never accounted for more than a few hundred.[16]

This Muslim community was also one of the most ethnically heterogeneous in the Empire, including Arabs, Indians, Somalis and other East Africans, who may be Sunni, Shi'i or Isma'ili. A precise break down of believers in Aden by ethnicity and geographic origin for much of this period is problematic due to the varying, and often imprecise, categories used across the various censuses. For instance, in the 1872 census while Indian Muslims could be identified by categories that made religious distinctions readily apparent—such as Syed, Memon, Borah and Khojah—there were no such markers to distinguish between Muslim and non-Muslim African residents of Aden. The categories used in 1931 are even less helpful, as communities were identified only by language, which makes determining exact numbers of Indian versus African or Arab Muslims in Aden nearly impossible.

While exact figures cannot be arrived at, it is clear that the community of believers in Aden was drawn from across the Indian Ocean littoral. In 1849, for instance, well over half of the town's approximately 12,000 residents could be identified as Muslim. Of these, more than 3,800 were classified as "Natives of

Arabia"; there were also nearly 2,100 Somalis, and at least 360 Indians identified as Muslim. There were also up to 150 Egyptians, most of whom were deserters from Muhammad Ali's army who until recently had occupied much of Yemen's Red Sea coast.[17] In addition, there were 231 assorted "Sidis," "Dankalis," "Massawans" and "Nubians," the majority of whom were at least nominal members of the faith, recorded as permanent residents. More important than any numerical data, however, are the copious and diverse names in the archival record of Muslims taking an active role in public life. Muslims of South Asian origin with names like Luqman and Khan or Africans with geographic *nisba*s, such as Ishaaqi, al-Sudani or al-Swahili, are as likely to appear in the official record as Southern Arabian identifiers such as al-Makawi, Ba Zara or al-Zabidi.

The development of Aden, under British occupation, hardly occurred in a random manner. Many "new" Adenis were directly involved in the functioning of the imperial apparatus. One of the fortress garrison's two infantry regiments was always a so-called "native" unit with large numbers of Muslims. More importantly, many of the Settlement's bureaucrats (including such high-ranking officials as Assistant Residents, Registrars and interpreters) and police officers (including "native" ranks like Havildar but also inspectors and sub-inspectors) were Muslims hailing from various enclaves in the Indian Ocean. In addition, starting with the Aden's first Political Agent, S. B. Haines, British authorities purposefully sought to lure merchants and tradesmen from throughout the Red Sea and western Indian Ocean to their new possession in a deliberate effort to create a viable, self-sustaining commercial port at the mouth of the Red Sea. Finally, the new British possession also attracted countless individuals who, while not party to British economic, civil or military designs constituted the inevitable auxiliary population that emerged in any maritime outpost. On the so-called "respectable" end of society this included shopkeepers, skilled artisans, teachers, religious scholars and Sufis. By the same token, dockworkers, porters, carriage drivers, sweepers, incense sorters, coffee-house proprietors, spirit mediums and prostitutes accounted for the equally numerous "disreputable" end of society.[18]

The anthropologist Abdalla Bujra noted that, by the eve of independence in the 1960s not only had the port's population grown exponentially but "Adeni" had emerged as a social, cultural and political category. In a short paper titled "Urban Elites and Colonialism," Bujra stated that while 70 percent of Aden's population could be classified as Arab, this easy categorization belied a more complex historical reality. The category of "Adeni," he wrote, consisted of two broad groups. First, were the descendants of "the small merchant population" found in Aden at the time of the occupation. The second consisted of various immigrants from "the Arab world, Iran and Pakistan," who arrived throughout the nineteenth century.[19] Based on what we find in the colonial archives, Bujra's characterization of who might assimilate into Aden society is overly restrictive.[20] However, he rightly pointed out what ultimately marked someone as an Adeni. "An essential feature of the Adenese group," he noted, was "its ability to absorb other peoples. This process of absorption essentially mean[t] long residence in Aden," along with the adoption of certain "diacritical marks" of Adeni life. These he observed, included, language, dress and religion—particularly Islam.[21]

Given such a diverse community with little in common other than a shared faith, it should come as little surprise that over the course of the period under study, religious ideals and institutions increasingly formed the core of social and communal life for most Adeni Muslims. While reformist-minded discourse such as nascent Salafism (those who subscribed to a strict scripture-based notion of reform) played a role in this, institutions like *waqf* (pious endowments), the Qadi's courts and sacred spaces such as mosques, shrines and cemeteries held even greater importance and became venues for individuals who wished to stake a claim to membership in the community and/or social authority. It was within the arena of Muslim institutions that the act of creating community was carried out.

Such institutions served as important pillars of Adeni identity in varying ways. By endowing mosques or patronizing the tombs of local saints, the wealthy established concrete symbols of their attachment to Aden. Similarly, through participation in communal prayers, annual saints' festivals and spirit-possession rituals both rich and poor literally performed their membership in community. While such institutions were critical in creating a singular sense of community they were equally important in establishing internal boundaries and relations of authority.

The wealthier and politically connected elements of Aden's Muslim community ultimately emerged as a continually shifting set of elites who acquired social capital largely through their association with religious institutions and Imperial authority. It was these individuals, along with a few pre-colonial socio-religious elites, most notably the Aydarus Sayyids, who served as the brokers of power and authority within the Settlement and sought to define the parameters for "belonging" to the community of Aden Muslims. Rather than the mere pawns of their social and political betters, however, the less connected and wealthy frequently contested the boundaries set by their supposed betters. While reform-minded businessmen and *'ulama'* sought to restrict the limits of acceptable religious practice, Sufis and adherents of spirit-possession cults worked to keep such boundaries fluid. As jurists and civil judges wrangled over the nature of Islamic law, lay individuals used their own knowledge of law, practice and custom to retain their flexibility. The actions and agendas of those living in Aden during the colonial period are, of course, central to this study. But equally important were the imperial and religious ideals that continued to inform and shape local society.

An imperial hub in the age of steam and print

Historians have largely reconceptualized the nature of European empire in the Indian Ocean over the last two decades. Using Tony Ballantyne's notion of imperial webs, Thomas Metcalf has convincingly demonstrated the inter-connected nature of Britain's Indian Ocean domain and the central importance of both India and Indians in building it from the mid-1800s onward. Similarly, Lambert and Lester have explored the importance of mobility and the intersection of "personal trajectories" in the creation of space and place. These and other works have amply illustrated the extension of economic, administrative and legal regimes, creating an increasingly interconnected and globalized, if imperial, world. This was not a system created out of whole cloth. Rather, it was the latest iteration of various ongoing economic, social and political processes stretching back to the late first millennium CE, during which time this was a system from which Europeans were largely excluded.[22] Furthermore, even in the nineteenth and twentieth centuries, non-Europeans were as involved in the emergence of such globalized networks as European empire builders.[23] For the social and intellectual lives of Muslims, the most important aspects of these developments were the revolutions in communications and transportation dubbed by James Gelvin and Nile Green "the age of steam and print."[24]

The technological advances of the second half of the nineteenth century were transformative for the personal and spiritual lives of many Muslims. Advances in steamship technology from the 1850s, along with the opening of the Suez Canal in 1869, rapidly increased the mobility of Muslims across the various European oceanic empires. The number of Muslims traveling on the Hajj, for instance, increased exponentially with more believers taking part in the pilgrimage to Mecca than at any other time in the history of the faith.[25] The development of regularized steamship routes also led to the emergence of new networks of commerce and labor as well as religious scholarship.

By the early 1900s, regular steamer connections developed a transportation web that helped expand the circulation of laborers and non-European merchants between the ports of the western Indian Ocean, the Mediterranean and beyond. Regional ports such as Berbera and Mogadishu in Somalia and Mombasa and Zanzibar in (British) East Africa were linked to a wider world via larger Imperial hubs, including not only Aden but Durban in South Africa, Suez in Egypt and Bombay in India. Many of these routes were not new. Movement along them, however, was now faster, more regular and less expensive than ever before, allowing increasing numbers of Muslims to transcend what we may view as their traditional geographic networks.[26]

A number of historians of South and Southeast Asia—including Nile Green as well as Seema Alavi and Michael Laffan—have written about the transformative effect of imperial transportation on the Muslim intellectual networks of India and Island Southeast Asia.[27] Such links, however, were no less important for Muslims scholars in East Africa and Southern Arabia. There are numerous, well-known examples of *'ulama'* from the region who found their way to the cities of the Mediterranean from the late nineteenth century. The famed Comorian scholar Sayyid Ahmad ibn Sumayt Ba-Alawi seems to have initiated this shift when he journeyed to Istanbul in the mid-1880s while the Zanzibari *'alim* Muhammad Barawani published an extensive account of his travels in Egypt and the Levant just before the outbreak of the First World War.[28] Virtually all of this traffic passed through Aden, to the obvious benefit of the local learned classes.

Equally important in Aden were advances in communications technology. The Settlement was first reliably connected to the world at large by submarine telegraphic cable in 1870.[29] Ultimately, this would allow the Muslims of Aden to receive news of events among their co-religionists around the world as well as become active contributors to various ongoing debates in newspapers and periodicals published throughout the Empire and beyond.[30] At the same time, print technology—particularly the invention of the lithographic steam press—revolutionized the accessibility of knowledge among Muslims in Aden and the western Indian Ocean more generally.[31] A great deal of research has focused on the proliferation of Islamic texts that accompanied the development of cheap lithographic printing. Most of this has centered on the impact of print in either the major metropolitan centers of the Arabic-speaking Middle East (mainly Cairo and Beirut) or Persianate South Asia (including Bombay, Delhi and Kolkata).[32] But by the early twentieth century, religious texts printed in Cairo, Bombay and Hyderabad were readily available throughout the wider Indian Ocean littoral, as were reformist newspapers such as Rashid Rida's *al-Manar*. But Muslims in Aden and the western Indian Ocean were not only consumers of print. By the second decade of the twentieth century they were also producing a small but steady stream of religious texts and periodicals of their own.[33]

In his seminal work, *Bombay Islam*, Nile Green has written persuasively about the significance of both transportation and print in the development of innovative religious discourses and their dissemination across the long nineteenth century. Green's work illustrates the dynamism of spiritual discourse and the ways in which steam and print contributed to the emergence of a multitude of religious voices. In particular, he successfully challenges the notion that the mechanisms of "colonial modernity" automatically produced "standardized—'uniform', 'global' or 'national'–forms of Islam." In many cases, he argues, newly emergent movements "were not 'modern', disenchanted, 'Protestant' Islams, but cults that were enchanted, hierarchical and ritualistic."[34] Indeed, as Aden and other cases demonstrate, Sufi Orders and the cult of the saints remained wildly popular among Muslims in the Indian Ocean throughout the period under study.[35]

Furthermore, while many of these began as localized voices, the technological advances of the period contributed to the emergence of an increasingly varied "marketplace" of spiritual ideas with implications that spanned the entirety of the community of believers.[36] By the eve of the First World War, Adeni authors were beginning to produce a small but important oeuvre of texts related to the faith. These ranged from legal primers and saintly hagiographies to reformist poetry and pietistic lectures. Granted, prior to the outbreak of the Second World War printing generally had to take place in foreign centers such as Cairo, Bombay or Hyderabad, but, by the 1930s, this literary production had become a steady and relatively varied stream.

The marketplace of ideas, each with multiple understandings of the faith, was well represented in imperial Aden and is made visible to us via their literary production as well as the imperial archives. Virtually all the individuals who appear in the current study maintained active social, economic or intellectual linkages across the British imperium. The actions and agendas of bureaucrats, religious scholars and anti-colonial activists were shaped by their longstanding connections to the various educational, intellectual and religious networks that traversed (and even transcended) the empire, introducing ideas into the Settlement ranging from post-Enlightenment social theory to scriptural reformism. By the same token, the inhabitants of Aden retained associations with various spiritual (for example, mysticism and spirit-possession cults), economic (labor and commerce) and kin networks that intersected in Aden. It was the confluence of all these that would ultimately create the Muslim community of imperial Aden. The networks of religious discourse and empire were trajectories that bound individuals together and played a critical role in shaping communities, particularly through debates involving "tradition" and acceptable practice. The shape of religious law, the permissibility of saint veneration and spirit possession, for instance, all provided platforms for the delineation of communal boundaries as well as authority. However, by focusing solely on such easily identifiable phenomena, historians may be missing other equally important elements of the Islamic discursive tradition that reveal the role of other, largely "unseen," actors in social processes.

Historicizing ontology

In his brief, but influential work, *The Idea of an Anthropology of Islam,* Talal Asad proposed that Islam should not be approached as a static set of beliefs. Rather, in his estimation, it is more profitably viewed and explored as a malleable and inherently adaptable "discursive tradition."[37] This approach is one that has gained increasing currency among Islamic studies scholars.[38] As Roman Loimier notes in his study of Islamic learning in Zanzibar, "Islam should be visualized as a great pool or corpus of texts, of interpretations of texts, of prescriptions concerning the faith and/or everyday life, of shared rituals, norms and values, as well as teaching traditions," that are "based on a number of basic texts such as the Quran, the Sunna of the Prophet," as well as other legal and theological texts.[39] Rather than constituting a rigid, unchanging body of knowledge, every Muslim community is involved in a process of continuous reinterpretation of this canon that ultimately enables them, in the words of Adeline Masquelier, "to respond to the conditions of a changing world."[40] It is this discursive adaptability and resilience that enables Islam—and indeed any living religion—to retain its relevance as a social and moral guide at any given point in time. The workings of the discursive tradition are certainly evident in colonial Aden, particularly in mediating the challenges presented by scripturalist reform.

Effectively, the discursive tradition created an imagined community of Muslims in the same way as the emergence of print and national vernaculars argued by Benedict Anderson.[41] The Islamic discursive tradition, however, consists of more than the written texts, rituals and mores of the faith. It also includes the very fabric of the cosmos and an ontology of creation. The cosmos evoked by the Qur'an and expounded upon by Muslims over the course of centuries stretches far beyond a simple Manichaean universe characterized by a time-bound mortal world and an eternal afterlife spent in the presence of the Divine. For sure, at the very heart of Islamic cosmology is the idea of *al-Alamayn* or "the two worlds."—this one and "the next." But, for Muslims, the realm of God's creation is a complex multiverse that encompasses far more. In addition to humans there exist rival elemental beings who inhabit their own dimensions. These include the jinn, beings created by God from fire, as well as demons or "afrıt" whose origins are less clear. Time and matter, while linear and static for most, are part of a Platonic conduit of light emanating from the Divine via His Prophet along which the enlightened travel—either spatially or temporally—in the service of God. Significantly, however, rather than a domain limited to esoteric theologians, the ebb and flow of the multiverse is a concern of all believers, impacting many aspects of life. For many Muslims, this realm of the *ghayb* or "unseen" possesses an agency that directly impacts the material world.

With regard to the social salience of the "unseen," historians tend to reflexively take up a rather relativist position, arguing, to quote Jack Hunter:

> The reality of spirits is understood to be socially and culturally determined . . . what is important is whether or not people within a given society believe in spirits. If they do, then spirits are real within that particular cultural framework and it is not the anthropologist's job to question the veracity of such beliefs.[42]

This is essentially the position of important anthropologists such as Evans-Pritchard, and for many historians has become a kind of default setting. As Dipesh Chakrabarty notes, "European political thought and the social sciences," regard "the human [as] ontologically singular, . . . gods and spirits are in the end 'social facts.'" and "the social some how exists," apart from them.[43] We argue that "it doesn't matter whether spirits [or any other aspect of the unseen] are real, what is important is that people believe them to be real."[44] In many cases, such an approach may, indeed, be sufficient. However, it comes with some important pitfalls. First, it creates a kind of hierarchy of ontologies, while "they" may "believe" in a particular natural order, we "know" that it is not "real" because "ours" is the only true reality. As a result, ontologies alternative to our own effectively have an asterisk placed next to them. More critically, such thinking inadvertently limits our ability to interpret and understand the significance of the unseen as we only seek to engage with it through our own ontological lens. For historians, this most often manifests itself in the shape of a kind of "functionalist trap."

When writing about the unseen, historians and anthropologists tend to emphasize its "practical" aspects in relation to human society even when attempting to move beyond simple materialist models. In his essay "Colonizers, Scholars and the Creation of Invisible Histories," Steven Feierman, for instance, calls for thinking about alternative meta-narratives as a way to begin avoiding the traps that the Western academy sets for itself when we seek to naturalize certain categories. Feierman argues that Western-trained academics are frequently unable to unpack the significance of unseen or invisible forces in a given context because of our own intellectual and cultural scotomas or blind spots. Only by confronting and trying to overcome the gaps in our vision, he argues, can we begin to gain insight into other ontologies. However, when examining the importance of public healing mediated by Nyabigini healers among various societies of the Lakes Region of Eastern Africa, Feierman tends to only discuss the significance of the unseen in terms of societal authority and its relationship to power. In several places he talks about the Nyanbingi mediums as manifesting a power that "runs parallel to the king's."[45] For Feierman, the agency—and therefore the social significance—of the unseen is manifest solely if we view such "action as practical," and utilize that lens to "explore the linkage between material conditions of existence and the *symbolic* content of the mediums' actions."[46] This statement is emblematic of the historian's approach to the unseen: agency only occurs within the context of social interactions between human beings. As such, the significance of the unseen is presumed to be entirely material or tangible.

An important theme running through a number of this book's chapters concerns the discursive tradition and the purpose of the unseen in Adeni society. I do not wish to entirely dismiss what Feierman would refer to as the "practical" aspects of this process. Certainly, elements of shrine veneration were aimed at attaining various kinds of tangible redress via the intercession of the saints (such as fertility, the curing of illness, restitution of various kinds of loss—financial, physical, marital and so on). By the same token, becoming the patron of a shrine certainly created a stake in the community and could conceivably serve as a physical manifestation of one's claims to belonging, not to mention entitlement to authority and financial gain. Indeed, as we shall see, the metaphysical could serve as the very basis of one's authority, outweighing scholarly achievement and human recognition.

With that said, however, it is important to recognize that engagement with the unseen may have less to do with the advantage to be gained in this world and more about one's relationship with and understanding of the next. It may entail something as personal as the optimal location for burial while awaiting the day of judgment or as abstract as understanding the cosmic and divine links that connect Aden with the wider Indian Ocean littoral. In the end, it may have little to do with social position or advantage and everything to do with an individual's understanding of their place in relation to the universe. While immensely abstract and often intensely personal, such connections were hardly socially ephemeral. Instead, they provide important insights into how individuals connect across social, economic, linguistic and even theological differences in their efforts to create a community. As Blanes and Espirito Santo suggest in their introduction to the book *The Social Life of Spirits*, in order to understand the significance of these it is important not to simply approach the unseen as "projections of collective representations, imaginaries of resistance and reflections and negotiations of histories and political economies." Rather, is it imperative to also view them through "the lens of the social trajectories they trace in the world."[47] By trying to trace these trajectories in the world, *Imperial Muslims* hopes to suggest ways in which the unseen along with other more commonly considered paths played a role in creating colonial Aden.

Chapters

This book is organized around six thematic chapters, arranged roughly chronologically, that examine various aspects of Aden's history critical to its development as a Muslim community during the colonial period. Chapter 1 provides a succinct overview of Aden's long history as an important hub of Indian Ocean commerce in the centuries before the British occupation that places the colonial history of the port into a deeper, transregional historical context. Its intention, however, is to go beyond recounting a well-worn narrative that positions Aden within the world of pre-modern Indian Ocean commerce. Instead, this chapter illuminates a certain imagined connectivity between South Asia and Arabia dating from the Medieval period that echoes well into the twentieth century. This includes certain Hellenistic understandings of geography that persist from late antiquity into the Medieval period. However, as we shall see, it also includes both Islamic and non-Islamic unseen agency that literally bind Aden and *al-Hind* to each other.

Chapter 2 centers on the development of Aden as an outpost of the British East India Company from the middle of the nineteenth century. It is, however, only marginally concerned with the military operations and diplomatic intrigue that characterize other studies. Instead, it explores the Company's concerns for the security of Indian merchant capital in the region and the localized political instability that warranted such concerns. Circumstances of instability drove the Company to develop a greater and more regular presence in the Gulf of Aden, and at the same time actively work to cultivate Aden as not just a military outpost, but a hub of commerce.

In Chapter 3, we continue the examination of Aden's evolution with a particular focus on the creation and organization of sacred spaces. This most obviously considers the development of physical locations such as mosques, shrines and cemeteries, quintessential Muslim spaces around which belonging could be claimed and performed. This chapter, however, is equally concerned with the emergence of less tangible and more speculative spaces. In particular, as we shall see, the town's most important cemeteries became identified as conduits to unseen metaphysical space that constituted an equally important element in the lives of Aden's Muslims.

Chapter 4 shifts our focus away from physical space to religious law, theology and authority. As a new imperial community, Aden's population had few individuals who could lay claim to being hereditary elites. In addition to the patronage of mosques and tombs, another arena where individuals may exert and create influence was within the realm of religious law and practice. As an imperial possession, Aden was governed by the statutes of the Indian Penal Code. However, as in much of the Empire, family law was generally left to be administered by religious communities and, as such, marriage, divorce and—in some cases—inheritance, were matters left to local Qadis or Islamic court judges. The authority of these judges, however, was increasingly challenged by imperial bureaucrats, the Registrars, who were themselves Muslims and lawyers. This chapter examines the emerging tensions between these two sets of elites and its impact on legal discourse and notions of authority.

While Chapter 4 deals with feuding local elites, Chapter 5 takes up the cause of the "less respectable" elements of society and their struggle to carve out a space for themselves in Adeni society. In particular, we look at the efforts of two spirit-possession cults—Zar and Tambura—to retain their place in the public sphere in the face of growing opposition. As reform-minded businessmen and *'ulama'* sought to restrict the limits of acceptable religious practice in the 1920s adherents of the spirit-possession cults worked to keep such boundaries fluid and ensure their place in society. This chapter suggests, however, that defense of tradition and the unseen were, for some at least, not simply "weapons of the weak" intended to secure their position in opposition to stronger social elements. Rather, rituals were also critical to how individuals engaged with the unseen in ways that impacted their daily lives that also ultimately helped structure the community.

Finally, Chapter 6 explores the dynamics of religious mobilization, reform and discourses of authority among Muslims in Aden. While ideologies such as Salafism—scripture-oriented religious reform—were transregional in nature what we will see here is how, in practice, they were ultimately shaped by local contexts. A critically important element of this was the differing approaches to authority of various constituencies. Both scripturalists and Sufis viewed discursive authority as emanating ultimately from God and His Prophet, Muhammad. For scripturalists, authority lay in particular foundational written texts that they alone could interpret. For Sufis, however, the mantle of spiritual power emanated from a less tangible source: the realm of the divine and the *Nur Muhammadiyya*, literally the Prophetic Light that formed creation.

The various chapters of this study are linked by several themes. All are concerned with the ways in which the various personal and intellectual networks of Indian Ocean Muslims combined in Aden to create a single and distinctive community. In addition, Chapters 1, 4, 5 and 6 actively engage the notion of Islam as a discursive tradition and the ways in which various interpretations of the faith came together in order to structure a community. Chapters 1, 3, 5 and 6 also seek to integrate understandings of the "unseen" as an element of that tradition equal in importance to the more tangible and visible world of texts and rituals. Taken together they illustrate not only how Muslim networks intersect to create a single community, but the multiple layers involved in the process.

1937?

The reader will notice that the time frame for this book ends in 1937, a date that, at first glance, seems odd, if not outright arbitrary. It is, in fact, a date critical for the town's colonial and post-colonial history. Following its occupation in 1839, Aden was administered by the East India Company as part of the Bombay Presidency. This was an arrangement that continued under the Raj, following the Company's dissolution in 1858 in the wake of the Sepoy Rebellion and remained largely unchanged until the end of the First World War. The war and the changing military and political realities that followed into the 1920s caused officials in both Delhi and London to question this organization. Rising nationalism in India and a rapidly evolving post-Ottoman Middle East rendered the administrative and strategic position of Aden precarious. As a result, it was quickly acknowledged that Aden should be removed from the purview of Bombay and placed under the control of the Colonial Office. This, however, was easier mooted than accomplished and over the course of the next two decades, bureaucrats in India and Britain wrangled over how this change should take place. It was not until 1932 that the town was removed from the control of Bombay and made a "Chief Commissioner's Province," controlled directly by the Viceroy in Delhi. Then, in 1937, it was transferred entirely to the Colonial Office where it would remain until independence and the creation of the People's Democratic Republic of Yemen in 1967.

While colonial rule would continue for thirty years, a great deal about Aden changed after 1937. On a bureaucratic level, the records for the town were now collected by the Colonial Office and as such are found in the National Archives in Kew Gardens rather than the India Office Library. But, more importantly, the character of these records begins to change dramatically from the advent of the Second World War. The records of the Aden residency frequently have the character of a local municipal government mediating relationships between town residents. Officials, both European and non-European, demonstrate a great deal of familiarity with the local inhabitants and their dealings with one another but also reveal a deep affection and even loyalty toward those who called the port home. With the move to the Colonial Office, the records betray a shift in this relationship. Files become increasingly terse and bureaucratic and, as a result, less informative. While previously, the Resident and his officers occupied themselves with negotiating conflicts between members of the community, the Governor and his staff devoted themselves increasingly to surveilling and combatting the emerging forces of Arab nationalism. As a result, not only do the archives become less concerned with town life, but Aden was increasingly imagined as a wholly Arab, rather than an Indian Ocean, community. For this reason, while some of the sources used stem from the 1940s and in one or two cases even the 1950s, I have chosen to end the study in 1937 when the era of rule from India came to a close.[48]

Note on sources

The materials for this study are derived from a number of sources. First and foremost are the archives of the India Office Library of the British Library in London. The India Office records for Aden contain a wealth of data stretching from the station's occupation in 1839 through the Second World War. As noted above, after 1937, responsibility for Aden shifted from the India Office to the Colonial Office and, as a result, increasing numbers of records can be found in the National Archives. Yet, records in the India Office Library extend through the mid-1940s. Why this shift did not occur all at once after 1937 is not clear. The series dealing with Aden (primarily R/20/A and R/20/E) are a treasure trove of life in the Settlement. Intelligence and police reports, petitions to the State, court affidavits and numerous other materials paint a vivid picture of the public lives of imperial subjects. Unlike many colonial archives where only official documents and translations of materials from the original language in to English survive, the Aden records are significant because many of these original documents are included in the files. As a result, petitions, *fatwas* (religious scholarly opinions), affidavits and sermons frequently survive, allowing the historian to strip away at least one layer of mediation, allowing us to move one step closer to our interlocutors.

One unfortunate gap in the records occurs for the years 1875 to 1888—a period of time for which numerous files are missing.[49] Such gaps are, of course, not unfamiliar to historians. In many instances lapses in the official record are explained by some sort of calamity, such as a natural disaster or break down in government authority. The cause of Aden's documentary short fall is somewhat more unique: petty larceny. In 1897, it was discovered that two cleaners and a security guard had been systematically pilfering files from the residency records in order to sell them to dealers in waste paper who supplied the local markets with wrapping materials. The investigating officer provided a tantalizing list of records forever beyond our grasp. The missing files range from consular reports from around the Red Sea to intelligence on gunrunning and the activities of freed slaves in the Settlement. At least one missing file referenced the presence of a "Lock Hospital"—for the treatment of prostitutes with venereal disease—in Aden, which is mentioned in a few other records. There are also several missing volumes on Hajj traffic and quarantine reports (1878–84). Perhaps most intriguing, however, is a missing file located in volume no. 986 of 1886, which contained "accounts in connection with the detention of Duleep Singh at Aden." Singh was the last ruler of the Sikh Kingdom of the Punjab (although overthrown by the British as a boy). Raised in Britain as "an English gentleman," in the mid-1880s he attempted to return to India in an ill-conceived effort to liberate his kingdom and regain his throne. The episode has always been clouded in mystery and we can only speculate what light these records might have shone on the affair.

This study, however, is not entirely dependent on the British colonial record. I have also utilized a large number of Arabic language works related to Aden. For the premodern period this includes largely well-known published sources such as the *Mustabsir* of Ibn Mujjawir and the *Tarikh Thaghr Adan* of Abu Makhrama. During the latter part of the colonial period, despite having little in the way of a printing industry, Adenis also began to produce a small but significant stream of material related to their hometown. These include al-Makki's legal handbook, *The Overflowing River*, as well as various religious texts related to the theological debates of the 1930s. Among the most varied and important, however, are likely the writings of the two Luqman brothers, Muhammad Ali and Hamza. Sons of a retired Chief Interpreter of the Residency, and separated by nearly twenty years in age, both siblings emerged as prominent intellectual voices in Aden. Muhammad Ali founded the first newspaper in the Settlement, *Fatat al-Jazeerah*, in 1940. But, he also authored numerous essays, short stories and accounts of his various travels that provide rich fodder for the social history of Aden. A large portion of these were collected and republished in the early 2000s by his son Maher who lives in Jiddah, Saudi Arabia with the assistance of an Adeni academic, Professor Ahmed Ali al-Hamdani. I am deeply indebted to him, as well as his sister Huda Wildy, for making these available to me.

Hamza's efforts do not seem to have been as extensive as those of his brother, and were devoted largely to the town's history. When I first visited Aden in 2005, several of his works, including *Tarikh Adan* (A History of Aden) and *Tarikh qaba'il al-yamaniyya* (A History of the Tribes of Yemen), both published in the late 1950s, were still available in photocopy format for sale in local Adeni bookstores, testimony to their continued relevance.

These and many other Arabic-language materials help provide a more nuanced sense of Aden's history and the importance of Islam in the emergence of community in an imperial context. However, I would caution that it is not the end of the story. Even as I write, newly discovered Arabic works from the period continue to come to light. Furthermore, while most of the local literature on Aden appears in either Arabic or English, as an Indian Ocean port, there exists a considerable amount of material in other languages, most notably Gujarati, Urdu and Hindi. Unfortunately, due to my own limitations, I have been unable to include works from this body of literature and their inclusion must await a more linguistically agile historian.

1

Hanuman's Tunnel: Collapsing the Space between Hind and Arabia in the Arab Imaginary

If you climb to the top of Sira Island in Aden's harbor, thirteenth-century traveler Ibn al-Mujawir tells us, you'll find a well. Only, it's not really a well but the entrance to a tunnel connecting Arabia and India, with its egress in Ujjaini, the capital of the ancient kingdom of Malwa. The passage, we are told, was excavated by the "demon" Hanuman and the tale is a variant of the Rama–Sita story better known as the *Ramayana*. Sita, according to this particular narrative, was abducted by the demon "Hadathar" who hoped to transform her into a jinn. Hanuman, "a demon in the shape of a monkey," overheard their argument and proceeded to dig the passage that would rescue the unfortunate woman. Tunneling through the night, he arrived to find the maiden asleep beneath a thorn tree and, throwing her on his back, returned her safely to Rama.[1]

The millennia-old networks connecting the peoples of the Indian Ocean littoral have been the subject of historical inquiry for more than thirty years. Beginning with the coasting trade that linked Harappa with the Persian Gulf in the second millennium BCE, scholars have increasingly recognized the continuities that span the *longue durée* through the age of European imperialism.[2] Focusing largely on economic and—to a far lesser extent—social connectivity, historians have convincingly demonstrated that such links tend toward resiliency in the face of regime change and political transformations, such as the advent of European colonialism. Far less attention, however, has been paid to cultural continuities that can endure across similar distances and expanses of time.

In addition to its ethnically and confessionally diverse Muslim community, nineteenth-century Aden was home to several Hindu shrines, a Parsi fire temple and towers of silence (for funerary rites). What frequently goes unremarked upon, and thus little explored, is that this very visible connection to India was hardly a new state of affairs in urban coastal Arabia. The Indian demi-god's feat of supernatural engineering is only one example of Aden's imagined cosmological and historical connections to India. From Adam's son Cain and Alexander the Great to a dispossessed Yemeni prince disguised as a "one-eyed Indian" roaming the Tihama, South Asian motifs are scattered across the writings of the Hijaz and Southern Arabia from the Middle Ages through the mid-twentieth century.

The object of this chapter is twofold. First, it provides a succinct overview of Aden's long history as an important hub of Indian Ocean commerce in the centuries before the British occupation. By doing so, it places the colonial history of the port into a deeper, transregional historical context. But my intention is to go beyond simply reiterating a well-worn narrative that positions Aden within the world of premodern Indian Ocean trade. Instead, this chapter also illuminates a certain imagined connectivity between South Asia and Arabia that spans the same period through the examination of a number of texts (ranging from the Middle Ages to the era of British colonial rule) each of which engages with India as part of a larger narrative for an Arabic-speaking/reading audience. Certainly, as in the case of Ibn al-Mujawir's Hanuman, such stories often conjure an "enchanted" India, a strange place full of monkey-demons and ten-headed gods whose connection to Arabia is supernatural. In many other instances, however, we find narratives that, rather than exoticize, normalize the relationship between India and Arabia through intermarriage, genealogy, piety and shared associations. Such accounts demonstrate the existence of a particular Indian Ocean imaginary fashioned by Arabian writers that highlighted the connections between themselves and those living in India predating the colonial era of the nineteenth and twentieth centuries. Both fantastic and mundane, tales of India in Arabia and Arabs in India served to bring the commonalities shared by both into sharp relief. Far from static, it was also an association that evolved over time, accommodating itself to larger changing world views and realities. In some instances, Arabia and India inhabit the same Hellenistic geographic frame as a "Greater Hind." In others, their connection is premised on political, familial and genealogical bonds that cross the frontiers of religion and emerging ideas of the sovereign state. These are linkages that continued to be cited—at least by members of the local Arab literati—well into the twentieth century as part and parcel of Aden's history.

Aden—ancient hub of commerce

The earliest literary reference to Aden is in the first century CE Greek sailor's manual, *The Periplus of the Erythraean Sea,* where it is referred to as *Eudaemon Arabia*.[3] Most likely founded by either the Minaean or Sabaean kingdoms of Southern Arabia during the latter part of the first millennium BCE, by the early Common Era it was the principal port for the trans-shipment of goods between the Indian Ocean and the Mediterranean. In her important work on Medieval Aden, Roxani Margariti notes that Arab traditions counted it among the "fabled pre-Islamic markets of the Arabs (*aswāq al-arab*) prized for its trade in incense."[4]

Aden did not emerge as a major commercial center until the latter part of the first millennium CE. Margariti writes that during the ninth and tenth centuries "the shift of focus of Islamic [political] power from Iraq to Egypt," with the rise of the Isma'ili Fatamid dynasty, precipitated a vast increase in commercial traffic between the Mediterranean and Indian Ocean via the Red Sea. As a result, Aden emerged as the primary trans-shipment point. The Arab geographer al-Muqaddasi signaled the town's importance when he referred to Aden as "the anteroom of China, entrepot of Yemen [and] treasury of the West."[5]

Politically, Aden fell solidly within an Arab sphere of influence during its medieval prime, dominated by either regional powers such as the Ayyubids or more local Yemeni regimes. From 1083 to 1173 it was ruled by the Zurayids—a Yemeni dynasty with close ties to the Fatimids in Egypt. The city was added to the fledgling Ayyubid state of Salah al-Din[6] when it was conquered by his brother, Turanshah, in 1173. Under both sets of rulers, Aden came into Egypt's orbit, which had obvious economic motives for insuring a friendly political environment. In 1228, following the Ayyubid withdrawal, the port came under the control of another local set of rulers, the Rasulids, whose power would last until the mid-fifteenth century. They were succeeded by the Tahirids, who reigned from approximately 1450 until 1517.

The city prospered under all of these. Commerce was brisk, wealthy merchants built lavish homes on the plain fronting the harbor and the city's rulers spent large sums on extensive fortifications, palaces and congregational mosques.[7] The Tahirids, in particular, oversaw a period of enormous civic renewal, building schools and overhauling the city's famous ancient system of aqueducts and reservoirs—the centerpiece of the latter being large tanks for collecting rainwater originally built by the Sabaens high above the city in the surrounding mountains. At its peak Aden may have had as many as 50,000–60,000 inhabitants in the late fifteenth century.[8]

Travel accounts, geographical dictionaries and the voluminous Geniza records privilege the economic and the political. However, careful parsing has shown that we can tease more from the existing documentation. Amitav Ghosh, for instance, through the fragmentary records of the Cairo Geniza, introduced readers to the complicated, transregional professional and family life of the eleventh-century Jewish Tunisian merchant, Bin Yiju and his Indian factotum, Boma.[9] By the same token, the appearance of Ibn al-Mujawir's "demon engineer" in Southern Arabia provides a window on to the imaginative spaces produced by the centuries-long relationship between Arabia and South Asia.

While politically dominated by Arabs, Aden was an unsurprisingly cosmopolitan city due to its commercial importance. Thanks to the more than 400 merchants' letters and other documents found among the texts of the Cairo Geniza we are well acquainted with the port's influential Jewish mercantile community and its connections to Egypt and India.[10] Medieval Arab geographers and travelers all remark on Aden as a destination for South Asian traders. Writing in the early thirteenth century, Yaqut al-Humawi noted in his *Mu'jam al-Buldan* that Aden was a favored destination for Indian merchants. Similarly, Ibn Battuta who spent time in the city in the late 1320s, wrote that, although oppressively hot, Aden was the favored port of "the people of al-Hind, who come in great ships" from as far afield as "Cambay, Calicut, Mangalore and Goa among others."[11] Many of these—along with large numbers of Egyptian merchants who seem to represent the single largest foreign community—were not simply casual or seasonal visitors but permanent residents. So wealthy were some, according to Ibn Battuta, they could afford to embark on large maritime business ventures on their own, chartering entire ships for their cargos, foregoing the traditional precaution of underwriting commercial voyages in partnership with others to defray risk.[12]

The well-heeled businessmen of Aden could also be given to ridiculous displays of conspicuous consumption and venal competition. According to one story recounted by Ibn Battuta, two slaves were sent by their respective masters to purchase a ram. Unfortunately, that day there was only one to be found in the market. The bondsmen entered into a bidding war and the price skyrocketed to an astonishing four hundred dinars. The winner took possession of the sheep, declaring that the money represented his life savings. If his master reimbursed him for the expense, it was all well and good, but if he did not, "I will pay myself, as the victory will be mine and I will have defeated my rival!" When his owner learned what had transpired he gave the successful slave a thousand dinars. The other, who returned empty-handed, was beaten, had his own money confiscated and was driven from his master's house.[13]

Not all of those living in Aden, Ibn Battuta was at pains to point out, were so crassly materialistic. There were many merchants and "people of religion" who were pious and God fearing—individuals who gave to the poor, regularly helped strangers in need and "paid the *zakat* as God demands."[14] It was also a town of upward mobility. Among the most pious was the local qadi, Salim bin Abdullah al-Hindi (the Indian) whose father had been "an enslaved porter." Despite this social handicap, Qadi Salim managed as a youth to study the religious sciences and by the time Ibn Battuta came to be a guest in his house the Moroccan scholar was able to regard his host as among the most superior of judges.[15] Indeed, as other medieval commentators point out, Aden was as much a hub of religious learning and piety as it was commerce. And, as the example of Qadi Salim suggests, South Asians were a visible and active part of this milieu.

The accounts of geographers like al-Humawi and travelers such as Ibn Battuta are brief and general. There exist others, however, who provide far more detailed accounts of the city. Of particular importance are the *Tarikh al-Mustabsir* of Abu Bakr b. Muhammad b. Mas'ud b Ali b. Ahmad al-Baghdadi al-Nisaburi ibn al-Mujawir[16] (d. 1228) and *Tarikh Thaghr Adan* by Abu Muhammad al-Tayyib ibn Abdullah Abu Makhrama (1465–1540). Ibn al-Mujawir was a Persian-speaking merchant originally from Khurasan with a literary bent who visited Aden at the beginning of its medieval prosperity under the Ayyubids.[17] Abu Makhrama, on the other hand, was a local Adeni who wrote of the city in the sixteenth century as Portuguese and Ottoman ambitions began to impinge on its autonomy and fortune. While chronicles of their own times, both works self-consciously fit Aden into broader temporal and geographic frameworks.

The enchanted world of Ibn al-Mujawir

Ibn al-Mujawir's *Tarikh* is a wide-ranging work, framed in large part as a typical *rihla* or travel account of his journey through the Hijaz and Southern Arabia. As such, it provides detailed itineraries of the routes of his travels, along with descriptions of the manners, customs and traditions of those he encountered. Like other narratives of this nature, it often includes meticulous sketches of economic and commercial life particularly in relation to Aden proper where he appears to have spent considerable time. Unlike similar works, however, Ibn al-Mujawir sought to also make a contribution to what he termed "the discipline of historical topography" (*fann al-tarikh*), describing not only the places he visited but also elements of their past—especially their origins. So, for instance, we learn the historical etymology of the name Mecca and the tribal origins of the oasis town of al-Ta'if.[18]

In creating his narrative, the author occasionally resorted to the literary canon.[19] The history of Mecca, for instance, is drawn in large measure from al-Fakhihi's *Tarikh Makka*.[20] While Alexander the Great's excavation of the Red Sea—more on this below—is recounted from Amir Abu al-Tami Jayyash b. Najah's *Kitab al-mufid fi akhbar zabid*.[21] More often, however, Ibn al-Mujawir enjoyed relating stories from the people he encountered on his travels. Thus, for example, we learn from a certain Ali ibn Salih al-Uquli of the four mountain fortresses in Yemen constructed by Solomon's workforce of jinn.[22] By modern standards it can be argued that Ibn al-Mujawir was a suspect historian. He frequently provided incorrect dates and misidentified individuals involved in key events.[23] By the same token, he possessed a predilection for relating the magical, supernatural and the outright bizarre. So, we "learn" that the Red Sea was, in fact, "not a sea in ancient times," but excavated by Dhu al-Qarnayn (aka, Alexander the Great). He introduces the reader to the people of Taran, descendants of a woman named al-Faliqah who "came out of the sea" and had the power to change the course of floodwaters in the local wadi by virtue of "her enormous bulk"[24]; while Socotra, off the Arabian coast, was a land of sorcerers who could make their isle disappear at will. And, according to "the Indians," Aden was once used as a prison by the ten-headed jinn "Das Sir."[25]

Ibn al-Mujawir's utility as an empirical source of history for Aden and its environs is, of course, questionable. However, given his use of locally produced written and oral sources (not to mention the fact that he is frequently thoughtful enough to reveal their identities) the somewhat fantastic stories related by him can provide us with insight into the imagined topography of Aden in relation to the wider Indian Ocean and the importance of the unseen in its construction.

In his discussion of Aden, Arabs and Arabia take center stage only during the port's most recent history beginning with the twelfth-century Zurayids. The more distant past, including its origins, is rooted in legend and places Aden within a much wider geographic frame of reference. One element of this mythological history was based—unsurprisingly—on pre-Islamic events recounted in the Qur'an and its exegetes. Ibn al-Mujawir, however, expands this universe by pulling in stories from other traditions. The effect, on one hand, is to place Aden within a much larger sacred topography. More importantly, the "enchanted" Aden that Ibn al-Mujawir conjures up from both written and oral sources provides insight into the port as an inherently transregional locale within a much larger whole that encompassed India, Africa and Arabia in a single geographic and narrative frame.

Aden, Ibn al-Mujawir tells his readers, was not always a city by the sea. "From Suez to Aden, to beyond the mountain of Socotra, all was once [a single] stretch of land," a desolate, dry valley, in fact. That was, until Alexander the Great suffering from oppressive heat, dug out the southern end, allowing the waters of the sea to rush in as far north as Egypt.[26] The Greek conqueror created the sea not simply to cool-off, but to separate "Abyssnia" and Arabia whose peoples were in constant conflict. "We want to separate the two," he declared, "so that each knows its lord, each takes possession of [only] its own territory and there is an end among the people to domination and hostility."[27] These efforts at terraforming were not entirely successful.

> [Despite the barrier] the Abyssinians would wade across the sea, both on horseback and on foot, to raid the land of the Arabs. One of the Arabs therefore built a fortress on Jabal al-Mandab called Bidd and he extended a chain on the Arabian side opposite Abyssinia. Any ship arriving would pass along side the chain until dues were paid and it would then journey in whichever direction it wished.

The fortress remained in place until the era of the Aksumite invasion of the sixth century when "the Abyssinians, rulers of Zabid, destroyed it and the chain was removed."[28]

Ibn al-Mujawir also linked Aden to the stone-worshipping tyrant Shaddad bin Ad, mentioned in the Qur'an. According to various commentaries, Shaddad ruled much of Arabia from his capital Iram Dhat al-Imad (the Pillars of Iram), a city of idolaters who defied the Arabian prophet Hud and were ultimately wiped out by Alexander's irrigation project. During his reign, Shaddad undertook an inspection tour, traveling "from the land of the Yemen," to Hadramawt. Near present-day Lahej, he spied a mountain known as Jabal al-Urr, "and said to his aids, 'Go and take a look at that mountain and what lies before it.'" Upon returning, the minions informed him that before the mountains lay "a *wadi* [valley] and in its bed are trees with large vipers overlooking a briny sea." This was the spot that would become Aden.

Desolate and without water, Shaddad had a number of wells dug near Lahej. In order to supply the settlement, he ordered two captive demons (*ifritayn min al-jinn*) to excavate a water channel from the mountains to the coast—a task that took seventy years. "When much time had passed, Shaddad bin Ad began sending all those who had to be imprisoned to this place; he would imprison them there and it remained a prison until the latter part of the dynasty of the pharaohs, rulers of Egypt. After their demise, the place fell into ruin."[29] Later, Ibn al-Mujawir offers several potential etymologies for the name, including, "It is said that the first person imprisoned there was a man called Adan, so the place was called after him."[30]

Ibn al-Mujawir points out that the tyrant's behavior was hardly unique. Indeed, great rulers, he noted, commonly used cities distant from the centers of power as places of exile or imprisonment. To demonstrate this tendency, Ibn al-Mujawir lists more than twenty examples. Beginning with Solomon—who used Kashmir to intern his enemies—and Alexander, the majority were well-known Medieval Muslim rulers such as Harun al-Rashid and the Great Saljuq Toghrilbeg. The last entry on the list, however, was neither a Muslim ruler nor even human. Das Sir, the jinn with ten heads, "the Indians have reported," also used Aden as a prison for his enemies.[31] Das Sir lived "on Jabal al-Manzar and took walks on the sands of Huqqat."[32] When he died, Hanuman took up residence in his place.[33] Whether this was before, after or as a result of the latter's rescue of Sita we are not told. Aden, it seems, was popular with South Asian demigods and was only saved from permanent infestation by Solomon who ultimately expelled the "demons."[34] Predictably, among its many names, Ibn al-Mujawir, notes Aden was often referred to as *Habs al-Fir'awn*—Prison of the Pharaohs—and *Muqam al-jinn*—Abode of the jinn.

The section on Aden as prison is followed by the story of Hanuman and Sita that began this chapter. The *Ramayana* is a staple of Sanskritic mythology in which the hero Ramchandra—or simply Rama—rescues his wife Sita from the demon Ravana who kidnapped the latter and held her hostage on the island of Lanka. Rama is aided by Hanuman, a demigod in the shape of a monkey, who aids the hero by building a bridge from the mainland to Lanka so that an army may cross to defeat Ravana.[35] Ibn al-Mujawir's is one of countless versions recorded around the Indian Ocean.[36] As we saw, this version differs significantly from the one with which we are familiar. Hanuman sought to rescue the wife of Ramchandra not from Ravana, the King of Lanka, but the demon "Hadathar."[37] Rather than build a bridge he dug a tunnel. The story is greatly truncated, but the teller makes it quite clear that he is aware of its place in a larger tradition. "This is a long story the telling of which would take too long. But the tunnel remains."[38]

It was not only India, however, to which Ibn al-Mujawir linked Aden. In addition to being occasionally threatened with Aksumite invasion and occupation, it was for a time an Egyptian—as well as a Persian—outpost. But, "when the dynasty of the Pharaohs came to an end, the place fell into ruins as their dynasty disappeared." In their place a group of fisher folk arrived who remained there a "long time, provided with God's sustenance and a livelihood," until they were in turn expelled by a group of Madagascans[39] who appeared by sea in large numbers. While ultimately driven out themselves, they were remembered for their introduction of "reed houses" that became a hallmark of Aden and for their ability to link the Arabian coast with the southern seas through their use of paddle-driven boats.[40]

Ibn al-Mujawir's account, as Smith and others have pointed out, privileges the fantastic and the enchanted.[41] Even so, his story does include glimpses of historically verifiable events. The Ptolemaic Pharaohs, for instance, were active in the southern Red Sea as were the Sassanid Persians. The Aksumite kings of Ethiopia did, indeed, invade Southern Arabia on at least two occasions, most notably in 525CE.[42] And other sources confirm the use of a large sea chain deployed along the Arabian coast to foil the invaders.[43]

More important than antiquarian factoids, his account—taken in the aggregate—allows us to understand Aden as part of wider geography expressed in legendary and sacred, as well as, topographic terms. In the ancient period, Greek writers commonly applied the term "India" to a region stretching from western South Asia to coastal East Africa and the southwestern corner of Arabia. Writing in the sixth century, the Byzantine Christian geographer, Cosmas Indicopeustes, for instance, referred to both the Horn of Africa and Himyar as belonging to "inner India," a term he also applied to Ceylon, which represented the easternmost extent of his travels.[44] Ibn al-Mujawir's narrative locates Aden within the same geographic frame, utilizing not only physical description but sacred and legendary imagery. As such, he ties the city (and Southern Arabia more generally) into a vast Indian Ocean cosmology in which Aden is connected—quite literally, in the case of Hanuman—to India. The Aden of Ibn al-Mujawir was thus not only an integral part of the Indian Ocean economic world, but also belonged to an Indian Ocean imaginary whose geography was quite Hellenic in scope.[45]

That Ibn al-Mujawir's topography was not simply the product of his own vivid imagination, but indicative of a wider cultural vision can be deduced from the sources he cites and indeed synthesizes into a narrative whole. Nowhere is this better observed than in his treatment of Aden as a hub of supernatural activity. Stories of Alexander the Great are ubiquitous in early Islamic writing but Ibn al-Mujawir cited his anecdotes from a local Yemeni chronicle, *Kitab al-Mufid fi Akhbar al-Zabid*.[46] Das Sir's use of Aden as a prison for jinn is reported "by the Indians" while Shaddad bin Ad's use of it for a similar purpose is related on the authority of Muhammad al-Kaysani's Qur'anic commentary or *Tafsir*. The tale of Hanuman was told to him by his father's *mawla* or client, Mubarak al-Sharabi.[47] By doing so, Aden serves to bring a pre-Islamic tyrant, a proto-Muslim superhero and several Indian demi-gods into a single narrative. This is not simply literary window-dressing. Rather, it signals an ontology that conceives India and Arabia as connected not merely through physical space but also via the unseen. The port emerges as a city linked to its wider geographic context by winds and ocean currents but also by feats of superhuman engineering and enchanted alternate dimensions in a reality where humans are not the only agents directing the course of events and where physical space frequently intersects with the metaphysical.[48]

Abu Makhrama's Aden in an age of instability

Ibn al-Mujawir's account of Aden was written at the very beginning of what we can regard as the city's commercial ascendancy under the Egyptian Ayyubid dynasty in the early part of the thirteenth century. This was a trajectory that would continue upward, despite various dynastic changes, over the next several centuries through the rise of the Tahirids in the fifteenth. The principal text available for this latter period situates Aden within a broad imaginative canvas similar to that painted by Ibn al-Mujawir, although the picture is more self-consciously Islamic by this time. *Tarikh thaghr adan* (A History of the Port of Aden) was written by a local Adani, Abu Muhammad al-Tayyib ibn Abdullah Abu Makhrama (1465–1540). The text is part historical narrative drawn from "legends, tales, ancient literary works, poems and other than these," and part biographical dictionary with entries relating to prominent religious scholars, rulers and merchants associated with the city.[49] As a history, Abu Makhrama provides copious descriptions of commercial practice and the critical role of merchants as patrons of the town's religious establishment. Along with a number of other contemporary works, such as the *Tarikh Ba Fakih al-Shiri* and the *Tarikh Shanbal*—R. B. Serjeant's famed "Hadrami Chronicles"—he was one of a number of local writers who related the emerging conflict between the Portuguese and various Muslim powers of the western Indian Ocean.[50] Taken together, these works help us recover the political travails of the city in a period of increasing instability. The geographic context of Abu Makhrama's Aden is very different from that of Ibn al-Mujawir. Rather than the fulcrum upon which the connection between India and Africa hinges, Aden is a place apart, endlessly besieged by hostile interests, from the Arabian hinterland as well as across the sea, who threaten the port's independence. Critically, however, while less concerned with defining Aden as a place, Abu Makhrama's *Tarikh* reveals the continued importance of a wider Indian Ocean—especially South Asian—presence in the Arabian imagination.

Like Ibn al-Mujawir, Abu Makhrama's history places the city within a cosmological topography, albeit one that is far more Islamic. He recounts the excavations of Alexander the Great that created the Red Sea, but omits the tales of captive demons and Hanuman's feat of submarine engineering. Aden's founding, instead, is tied to Abrahamic myth albeit with a South Asian twist. "It is said," Abu Makhrama writes:

Cain, after he killed his brother Abel—in fear of his father—fled from the land of Hind to Aden. He, and his people, settled there on Mount Sira. As he was devastated by the separation from his homeland—and other than that—Iblis appeared to him and [gave him] things of distraction such as flutes and things like it, and [Cain] was the first to learn its use.[51]

While not a demonic prison, Abu Makhrama's Aden had an equally dark origin linked to the supernatural. It becomes the site of exile for the first homicide and introduction of the first wind instrument by Satan, regarded in the Qur'an as a symbol of moral degeneracy—the playing of which is regarded as, at best, inadvisable. Indeed, Aden he related, sat near a gateway to hell:

Imam Abu Muhammad Isa al-Andalusi mentioned in his book, *Ayoun al-akhbar*, there was a man from the people of Khourasan living in Mecca, he was a man of many pious exertions in terms of worship and good acts, and people would often deposit money with him. A man left him with ten thousand dinars and left [Mecca] on a journey. When he returned to Mecca he discovered that the man had died. He asked the man's sons and people about his money and they said, "we have no knowledge of your money." The man then went to a group from among the learned and abstemious of Mecca and complained to them about his affair. They said to him, we will ask about this man among the people of paradise. [They instructed him] that he should sit at the well of Zamzam until half or a third of the night had passed. He should then turn his head towards it and call out in a loud voice, *O'Fulan* [lit. "so and so"], I am *Fulan* owner of the deposit, what have you done with it? The man did thus for three nights with no response. He returned to the group and told them nothing had happened. They then said to him. . .verily we fear that this man is among the people of fire and you must go to Yemen to a *wadi* in Aden called Barhout.

There he would find a well and they instructed that he should put his head in it once again when half of a third of the night had passed; he should then ask about the deposit. When the man did as instructed, this time the deceased replied that the money was buried in his room "in such and such a house" and told the depositor to return to Mecca and ask his son to dig it up. Abu Makhrama concluded ominously, "verily, the souls of the profligate moan in the well of Barhout, and verily it is correct—what al-Andalusi mentioned—that it is in Aden . . . where the people exiled to fire reside until the resurrection."[52]

Despite these rather dark associations, Abu Makhrama depicts his hometown as a vibrant commercial and intellectual hub, attracting merchants and religious scholars from the Central Islamicate lands as well as the Indian Ocean. The *Tarikh* constructs a picture of a prosperous town of numerous warehouses, well-built stone houses and neat palm-thatch huts. In addition to a lookout on Jabal al-Hawqat, the Tahirid ruler Abd al-Wahhab ibn Dawud built a large two-story structure in the center of town that functioned as a public platform for viewing shipping traffic, "providing," in the words of Roxanne Margariti, "a place where the people of Aden could stroll and rejoice in the maritime vistas."[53] The city unsurprisingly was also home to numerous mosques, Sufi *khanqah*s (hostels) and shrines that attracted religious scholars, holy men and pilgrims from across the Central Islamicate lands as well as the wider Indian Ocean.

In addition to being a commercial hub, Abu Makhrama—along with his near contemporary, Abu al-Abbas Ahmad al-Zabidi—was at pains to portray Aden as a center of religious learning and sanctity. A number of sources, including Abu Makhrama, contend that among the city's earliest mosques was one founded by Abban ibn Uthman ibn Affan, son of the third Caliph and that Ahmad ibn Hanbal (eponymous founder of one of the four Sunni law schools) studied *fiqh* under the tutelage of the former's son, al-Hakim.[54] These were only two of the most notable luminaries. Scholars from as far afield as Egypt, Baghdad, Persia and India traveled to Aden in order to "drink" knowledge at the local fonts of wisdom. Aden's most venerated *wali*, or saint, Sayyid Aydarus al-Adani (d. 1506) was, of course, from Hadramaut. However, the town boasted numerous other friends of God who hailed from across the *umma*. There was, for instance, Isma'il ibn Abd-al-Malik al-Baghdadi, who once revealed the *ayt al-kursi* written in the "divine light" across the Aden sky and was a frequent companion of *Khidr*;[55] Rihan ibn Abdullah al-Adani, an Ethiopian slave known as a "master of extraordinary miracles and authentic secrets," whose tomb was the site of a major *ziyara* or festival by the fifteenth century;[56] and Abu Sarrrour Iqbal ibn Abdullah al-Hindi, the slave of a prominent merchant, who was "wise in matters of religion having learned the seven modes of Qur'anic recitation from al-Harazi in Aden."[57] While Aden was certainly a center of commerce, for Abu Makhrama and others, it also reflected the diversity of the community of believers with connections from al-Andalus to Hind.

Aden: between the Ottoman hammer and the Portuguese anvil

Written during the first half of the sixteenth century, the social and political context of Abu Makhrama's Aden was significantly different from that of his thirteenth-century counterpart. The city was still a prosperous commercial port, although its position of dominance was increasingly difficult to maintain. Through the first half of the century, Aden was threatened with Portuguese attack, Ottoman hegemony and an Arabian interior of the period that has been described as politically chaotic. Abu Makhrama's history reflects all these contemporary contexts.

It is easy to imagine the arrival of the Portuguese in the Indian Ocean at the end of the fifteenth century, and their desire to dominate the luxury trade with the East, having a chilling effect on Aden's prosperity. The list of commercial centers either destroyed or captured by the Portuguese *Estado da India* in the sixteenth century is lengthy. Kilwa, Barawe and Mombasa were all prominent ports that felt the brunt of Iberian aggression.[58] Aden was attacked by a Portuguese fleet in 1513.[59] This incursion hardly seemed crippling, however, it signaled the start of a conflict that would see Aden caught in between Portuguese and Ottoman interests for much of the sixteenth century.

Duarte Barbosa, a mid-level functionary of the *Estado* and chronicler of the early Portuguese in the Indian Ocean, tells us that as part of his effort to dominate the spice trade, Afanço d'Albuquerque, the Governor India, led a fleet against Aden in March 1513. Taking the port by surprise, d'Albuquerque managed to capture or destroy a considerable number of vessels lying at anchor in the harbor. Portuguese success, however, ended there. Despite an assault with a sizeable landing force they were unable to invest or occupy the city.[60]

The Portuguese, however, were not the only threat facing the city. In 1517, in a bid to retain their own political relevance, a sizeable fleet belonging to the—soon to be defunct—Egyptian Mamluk Sutlanate attacked Aden as part of a wider incursion into Yemen. The town was ably defended by its Tahirid governor, Murjan ibn Abdullah al-Zafiri, who managed to repulse the invaders with heavy losses on both sides.[61] These failed attacks were hardly mortal blows. However, they signaled the port's vulnerability and were almost certainly one factor in sparking Ottoman interest in Aden's security, along with that of the wider Red Sea. From the first quarter of the sixteenth century through much of the seventeenth, Aden and the Yemen would become critical elements of the Ottoman Empire's Indian Ocean policy.

Beginning in 1525 the Ottomans, who succeeded the Mamluks, took an increasing interest in exerting more direct influence over Yemen and the Red Sea. This was in large part due to the rising presence of the Portuguese of which the attack of 1513 was only one example. The European presence threatened the security of the holy places (Mecca and Medina), on the one hand, as well as imperiling Jiddah and the spice trade from India and points east—all of which fell under their control following their defeat of the Mamluks in 1517.[62]

During the first two and half decades of the sixteenth century the Portuguese had not yet truly entered the Red Sea in force but it was really only a matter of time before they did so. Indeed, in 1525 a Portuguese incursion penetrated deep into the region. In a raid lasting only a few weeks, Portuguese vessels burned or captured twenty-six Muslim merchant ships spreading alarm throughout Ottoman maritime circles.[63]

Making matters even more urgent, the province of Yemen itself was hardly secure. The Ottomans became the technical suzerain over southwestern Arabia following their defeat of the Mamluks in 1517. However, exerting direct and real authority was more problematic. Never an easy place to conquer, in the mid-1520s Yemen was even more fractious than usual. In addition to the Imam in Sana'a and other assorted tribal chiefs, much of the region during this period was under the control of a group of Levantine and Circassian mercenaries—the remnants of a last, failed expedition by the Mamluks to regain control. Furthermore, the Tahirid regime in the south collapsed in 1517, leaving Aden up for grabs.[64] The result, according to the chronicler Qutb al-din al-Makki in his *Akhbar al-yamani*, was that Yemen existed in "a state of incessant anarchy and discord, during which there was nothing but spurted blood, violated hearths, spoiled goods and spilled tears."[65] The Turkish viceroy of Egypt, Ibrahim Pasha, was ultimately convinced by, what Giancarlo Casale refers to as, the Indian Ocean faction, to intervene and pacify Yemen.[66]

In January 1527, a large Turkish force landed at Mukha, which would ultimately become the Ottoman's main base of operations. Over the next several months, the Turks managed to subdue much of coastal Yemen through a judicious use of force and bribery. One of few holdouts was Aden whose rulers, according to what can be garnered from contemporary chronicles, did not necessarily deem themselves in need of rescue from the Portuguese. Rather, the town's elites attempted to navigate a middle course between the rival powers.

Having successfully repulsed Albuquerque's fleet, the town's governor, Murjan ibn Abdullah al-Zafiri, twice provided assistance to Portuguese fleets. First, in 1517 he hosted the fleet commanders to a sumptuous banquet and then provided pilots (possibly under some duress) to assist their run up the Red Sea to Jiddah. Then, in 1520, a large fleet of twenty ships that had run into heavy weather arrived in the harbor following a brief skirmish with an Ottoman force. Murjan again received the Portuguese relatively warmly, provided them with provisions and even ransomed a number of Muslim captives.[67]

Managing to keep the Portuguese at arm's length it is little wonder the rulers of Aden were not overly anxious to submit to what they viewed as a new set of invaders. An unnamed successor of Murjan, according to the *Tarikh al-shihri*, refused to allow Turkish troops to enter the city in 1527 and the town's formidable defenses caused the Ottoman commanders to be wary of undertaking a risky frontal assault. Ultimately, a compromise was reached and the governor agreed to read the Friday sermon in the name of the Sultan, mint coins with his name and turn over a portion of the revenues from the annual Indian commercial fleet to the Porte. In return the Ottomans agreed to withdraw.[68] It was soon after this that the tribal ruler who controlled Aden, Shaykh Amir ibn Da'ud ibn Tahir, committed a grave strategic error.

In an effort to keep the Turks out, Shaykh Amir sought to make a deal with the Portuguese. In 1529, apparently at his invitation, a squadron of Portuguese vessels arrived to open negotiations.[69] In exchange for safe passage for ships traveling between Aden and India, the Shaykh agreed to allow the Portuguese to leave a garrison of about forty men in the city and prevent ships leaving from traveling northward toward Jiddah. According to the *Tarikh al-shihri*, the small contingent sought to very publically demonstrate the might of the Portuguese crown by parading through the streets every Friday fully armed. The scholarly class of Aden reproached Shaykh Amir for allying with the Franj, but he ignored their council. Al-Shihri noted that the ruler's fear of the Turks was understandable but "upon my life, his judgment erred, [and] the measure was a bad one." As a result of his poor judgment he would incur the wrath of God.[70]

The unsound nature of Shaykh Amir's decision was not as readily apparent as al-Shihri makes out. A Portuguese fleet had recently inflicted two serious defeats on Ottoman naval forces in the region and forced them to withdraw from their recently established base on Kamaran Island. In addition, they had also coerced trade concessions from the Sultan of Shihr.[71] Consequently, it is not difficult to imagine that the ruling elite and merchants of Aden saw accommodation with the Portuguese as all but inevitable. Tragically for Shaykh Amir, his calculus could not have been more wrong.

The Turkish setbacks were only temporary. Over the next ten years, Ottoman fleets began to inflict their own damage on the Portuguese, and Turkish diplomatic efforts established the Porte as an important player in the royal courts of western India.[72] Shaykh Amir very quickly realized the error of precipitously siding with the Portuguese as early as 1531. He quickly switched allegiances and jailed the European garrison.[73]

Despite annulling his alliance with the Europeans, Shaykh Amir continued to be wary of Ottoman power. In 1537, a Turkish diplomatic mission headed by Farhat Shubashi arrived in Southern Arabia to secure the loyalty of Sultan Badr of Shihr and Shaykh Amir. Badr wisely accepted the robe of honor presented to him and instructed that the Friday sermon in the main mosque of Mukalla be read in the name of the Ottoman Sultan, Sulayman. Whether out of fear of retribution for his ill-advised alliance with the Portuguese or disdain for Turkish power, Shaykh Amir clumsily avoided the Turkish envoy. When the Turks arrived in Aden they were met by a party of minor functionaries who sought to fob them off with a paltry gift of pepper. Amir ibn Da'ud, for his part, claimed that pressing business in the interior prevented him from welcoming the ambassador. This slight outraged Farhat Shubashi and would be Shaykh Amir's undoing.[74]

The following year, an Ottoman fleet, under the command of Pasha Hadim Suleiman, arrived in Aden en route to India where they would ultimately lay siege—unsuccessfully—to the Portuguese controlled port of Diu.[75] As the strongest fortified position in the western Indian Ocean, Pasha Hadim understood that Aden could not simply be bypassed. However, he also seems to have realized, based on his actions the year before, that Shaykh Amir was hardly a reliable ally. Arriving in Aden, the Pasha invited Shaykh Amir and several of his officers aboard the Turkish flagship for a celebratory feast. Following the festivities, however, the Pasha had the Shaykh and his men seized and executed either by hanging in the ship's rigging or crucified on shore—the accounts differ—and their property looted.[76] Significantly, the Pasha forbade a general looting of the town and, instead, left behind a sizable garrison of 500–600 Janissaries to secure the port for the Sultan.[77]

Aden was now an Ottoman possession and would remain so until 1635. The struggle over the port attests to its continued economic and strategic importance through the sixteenth century. Indeed, according to Ottoman and Portuguese accounts, Aden remained prosperous despite its position on the edge of a war zone. Abu Makhrama was witness to many of these events and reported most of them up to his death in about 1540. One curiosity in his account is despite the fact it was trade with India that gave Aden its strategic importance, Hind receives little mention in Abu Makhrama's narrative of contemporary events. India, however, was not absent.

India as refuge

South Asia receives a number of important mentions in Abu Makhrama's text relative to Aden's more recent and historic—as opposed to legendary—past. Significantly, not only do these draw a close and direct connection between India and Aden or Southern Arabia, in each case they involve tales of political oppression or intrigue. For instance, when recounting the construction of one of the city's most important warehouses, the Dar al-Salah, Abu Makhrama noted that it was built by:

> Salah al-Din ibn Ali al-Ta'i, a merchant of Aden. When tyranny arose during the days of a-Nasr al-Ghasani, the merchants fled from Aden to Jiddah, Hind and Malabar. Salah al-Din ibn Ali fled to Malabar and the state confiscated his property.[78]

While the merchants of Aden might flee the tyranny of an unjust ruler, in some cases the tables could be turned—as in the instance of a certain Ibn Baksh, who, the shaykh tells us, was a merchant who "the Qadi Abd al-Rahman al-Ansi nearly made ruler." Citing a fellow Yemeni chronicler, al-Jundi, Abu Makhrama notes, Ibn Baksh became embroiled in some unnamed scandal in which he deceived the judge. As a result, the former absconded from "Aden and the company of Muslims and lived among the *kuffar* [unbelievers] of Hind and served men from among the kings of *Hind al-Kuffar* until his death."[79]

In what is certainly Abu Makhrama's longest and arguably most interesting anecdote, India emerges as a place of refuge but also plays a direct, if somewhat imaginary and figurative, role in the political intrigue of Southern Arabia. The *Tarikh* relates the story of Abu al-Tami Jayyash ibn Najah, "Master of the Tihama." Jayyash was the brother of Sa'id ibn Najah who ruled the Tihama from the city of Zabid in the late eleventh century. Sa'id was defeated and killed by the Fatamid-backed ruler of Sana'a, Queen Arwa, in 1088 and Jayyash was forced to flee for his life. After a brief stop in Aden, the young prince traveled to India with a small body of retainers, including his close adviser, Khalaf ibn Abi al-Tahir al-Amawy. In Hind, they encountered a fortune teller from Sarandib (Sri Lanka) who told Jayyash that, ultimately, he would not be deprived of his throne. Heartened by prophecy, Jayyash and his *wazir*, Khalaf, plotted their return. Drawing from the prince's own work, *Kitab al-mufid fi akhbar zabid*, Abu Makhrama continues the story:

> I purchased an Indian slave girl who became pregnant by me in Hind. I returned with her to Yemen when she was five months along. When we arrived in Aden I sent the *wazir* ahead of me to Zabid along the coast road and instructed him to seek his own safety and make known that I had died in Hind. Verily, he hid the truth preserving [word] of our arrival . . . [In the mean time] I ascended to Dhu Jibla where I learned of the state of al-Makram ibn Ahmad al-Sulayhi, and that he had become addicted to pleasure [*liza*] and his body had become weak [*adatrab*, lit. "disordered"] leaving the affairs of state to his wife, Sayyida bint Ahmad [Queen Arwa]. Then I went down to Zabid and met with [my] *wazir*, Khalaf ibn Abi al-Tahir, who told me that I continued to have many supporters [among] my cousins and slaves [retainers] and they were in many towns and were ready to rise up. So, I adopted the costume [lit. customs] of Hind and grew my fingernails and hair long and covered my eye with a black patch.

In Zabid, Jayyash took up residence near the governor's residence. One day, "as the people dispersed in the morning [after the dawn prayer] I made a beeline for the *mastaba* of Ali ibn al-Qom the *wazir* of Zabid's governor, Sa'ad ibn Shihab. And out came Husayn ibn Ali ibn al-Qom [son of the *wazir*] who was regarded by the people of Zabid as one of the best chess players [in the city]. And he said to me [Jayyash], *ya'Hindi* do you want to improve your chess playing? Yes, I replied and so we played. [But] I beat him and he lunged at me. He then told his father of this and the latter replied, 'what is this? The only person who could ever beat you was Jayash ibn Najah and he died in Hind.' Then the *wazir* went out to play Jayyash, who was 'was loathe to beat him,' for fear of revealing his identity, 'so the game ended in a draw and he was delighted by this.'"

The prince continued to bide his time, while Khalaf the *wazir* gathered their forces until "5,000 spears" were secreted in and around Zabid awaiting orders. In the mean time, it was revealed to Jayyash in a dream that his opportunity would come on the night that his Indian slave-girl gave birth. Jayyash continued to play chess with the Ali al-Qom and his son, Husayn, becoming a regular presence in their household. During one of these matches, *wazir* Ali said to his son, "if you beat the Indian, I will place you in charge of this year's revenues," a reward that would result in a windfall of several thousand dinars. Jayyash, unsurprisingly, played a "careless game," allowing the wastrel to win. Intoxicated with false-pride, Husayn "uttered foolish words," and snatched the eye patch from Jayyash's face in celebration. The *wazir* Ali upbraided his son for his lack of decorum, but the prince rose and boldly declared, "I am Jayyash!" Rather than have him arrested, *wazir* Ali pledged his loyalty to the prince and installed him in a royal residence along with his Indian concubine who was by this time in labor. That night, a son—Fatek—was born and at a signal from Jayyash, his supporters rose in revolt. The governor was arrested and Jayyash was restored to the throne of the Tihama. When he died in 1104, the story points out, he was succeeded by Fatek, son of the Indian concubine.[80]

The tale of Prince Jayyash is a rousing story of political intrigue. But it also offers insights into the imaginative significance of India among Aden's intellectual and political elite. At its most basic, India represented a safe haven and political refuge for both merchants and political figures. The story also reveals a certain cultural familiarity, if not outright kinship, between Southern Arabia and India. While Jayyash's disguise may resemble the plot of an "*opera buffa*" it speaks to a certain level of cultural awareness, not to say comfort, with the plausibility of individual Indians—with a command of local colloquial Arabic—living and traveling throughout the Tihama.

Equally intriguing is the critical role that India plays in the way events unfold. It is the mysterious "man from Sarandib" who sets Jayyash's plan in motion when he predicts that the prince will reclaim his patrimony. The acquisition of a conveniently fecund Indian slave-girl provides the prospect of an heir and, indeed, it is her birth pangs that signal the start of the revolt. Finally, the ascension of the half-Indian son after Jayyash's death cements political stability after a long period of chaos and uncertainty. The Hellenic world view of Ibn al-Mujawir, in which India and Arabia shared a common geographic frame, seems to have largely receded by the time of Abu Makhrama. But the story of Jayyash reveals the extent to which Adenis—or at least one of them—continued to perceive the world of India as intertwined with their own. While critically important for their economic livelihoods, Hind was also imagined as exerting an influence over Arabian political and social worlds to the extent that it made them who they were.

The history of Aden between the time of Abu Makhrama and the beginning of the British occupation was one of general economic decline and increasing political instability. The Ottomans occupied the port from 1570 to 1635. However, beginning with the late sixteenth century the focus of economic activity in the southern Red Sea quickly shifted away from Aden in favor of the ports of the Tihama along the Red Sea coast. Chief among these was Mukha as well as the smaller ports of al-Hudayda and al-Luhayya.[81] The reasons for this shift appear both economic and political.

First, as part of their colonization effort, the Ottomans heavily promoted the development of coffee production as a way of making Yemen pay for itself. The areas of Southern Arabia most suitable for commercial coffee growing were found in two parts of Yemen—the mountainous region immediately behind the Tihama and the highlands around Sana'a in the far north. As Nancy Um has noted, the coffee-producing areas around Ibb, Ta'iz, al-Udayn and Jabal Rahma were close to the coast and easily accessible. While the areas around Sana'a were further north, and at least a week's travel from the coast, a series of mountain passes made this a relatively easy trip.[82] None of these areas were easily accessible via Aden.

Second, the Turks may have preferred to privilege the ports of the Tihama for reasons of security and bureaucratic convenience. The Ottomans chose to establish their primary naval base and administrative center at Mukha during their initial foray into Yemen and the Indian Ocean in the early sixteenth century. They may have continued to do so even as the Portuguese threat began to recede as the position of these ports within the Bab al-Mandab (the mouth of the Red Sea) enabled them to defend their interests more easily. At the same time, the troublesome nature of the local political and mercantile elites—whose own interests seemed to supersede religious and political solidarity with the Sublime Porte—may have made Aden not worth defending or investing in, from the Turks' point of view. So, while a garrison was maintained there until the Ottoman withdrawal in 1635, the focus of Turkish economic and military investment became the Tihama and the Red Sea proper.

Following the Ottoman withdrawal, Aden's autonomy and economic importance slipped even further as various Southern Arabian polities from the interior sought to control it. By the mid-eighteenth century, the town fell into the orbit of the Abdali Sultans of Lahej, but by then an irreparable economic decline had set in. Trade continued but at a much-reduced level with a small community of "Banian" merchants making yearly trips into the interior. However, by the time of the East India Company's occupation in 1839 the town was a shadow of its former self.

The Luqmans and the continuing legacy of connection

As we will see in the following chapters, the Company's occupation resulted in a rekindling of Aden's economic fortunes, precipitating an influx of new residents from across the western Indian Ocean. Arabs from the Red Sea, Somalis and Ethiopians from the Horn of Africa as well as significant numbers of Indians streamed into the Settlement from the 1840s. Drawn to Aden from across Britain's Indian Ocean Empire by the promise of economic opportunity, over the course of the next century, the town's Muslim residents developed a cohesive community from their disparate parts. It was a community, however, that would remain self-consciously transregional in outlook. In these terms, it was a place neither Ibn al-Mujawir nor Abu Makhrama would have trouble recognizing.

From the time of its occupation in 1839 until its transfer to the Colonial Office in 1937, Aden was administered as part of the Bombay Presidency. As such, the fate of Aden became, if anything, even more entwined with India for much of its time as an imperial outpost. The final section of this chapter examines the continued significance of an Aden–India axis through the intellectual lives of two brothers,

Muhammad Ali and Hamza Luqman. The Luqmans were a prominent family of intellectuals in early twentieth-century Aden with close ties to South Asia. As such, the imaginary they exemplify involved both a deep familial connection as well as the common cause of the colonial subject.

Luqman family traditions portray a historical trajectory reminiscent of Jayyash ibn Najah. Originally from the Yemeni region of Hamdan, the family was forced to flee to India due to their Isma'ili affiliations.[83] They settled for generations in Gujarat among other Bohras as minor merchants. The Luqman partiarch, Ali Ibrahim, arrived in Aden in the 1880s to work as a clerk in a local Bohra merchant house. Entering government service in the 1890s he ultimately rose to the position of head interpreter and built a considerable personal fortune through shrewd investments in real estate. In the 1890s and early twentieth century he married two different Sunni women by whom he had several children, all of whom were raised as Sunni Muslims, including Muhammad Ali (1898–1964) and Hamza (1919–94).

Both brothers emerged as prominent intellectuals in Aden: Muhammad Ali as a journalist and social reformer, Hamza as a teacher and historian. Although self-consciously identifying as "Arab nationalists" both looked to links with India as an important element of both Aden's past and present. This final section looks at how their interactions with and portrayal of South Asia reveal a continued legacy of the trans-cultural imagination. While, as in the case of Muhammad Ali, this relationship suffered certain disruptions when faced with realities of the twentieth century, the interactions of the Luqman brothers (real and imagined) with India reveal an imagined connectivity that harkens back to the pre-colonial era that continued to define Aden's Muslim community.

Muhammad Ali Luqman's fraught relationship with Hind

Muhammad Ali Luqman is regarded by many Adenis as the premier intellectual voice of the late colonial period. Born at the end of the nineteenth century his life spanned both the era of high colonialism and—what was in Aden—a long slow move toward independence. He received the usual basic religious education in the Qur'an with some additional instruction in the religious sciences. However, he was educated mainly at the Marist Brothers Secondary School in Aden. As a young man, Muhammad Ali followed a number of professions, including shop owner, high-school teacher (including in the local Gujarati school), commercial agent and lawyer before finding his true calling as a political activist and newspaper publisher.[84] Luqman's life of activism is treated in Chapter 6. Here we want to briefly use elements of his personal life to uncover the family's continued connections with South Asia.

While his father was from Gujarat, Luqman's mother was the daughter of a local, prominent Arab family.[85] This, however, seems not unusual among young, male Bohra immigrants in Aden. The leader of the local Bohra community, Shaykh Aref, complained repeatedly to the authorities during the early twentieth century about the epidemic of young Isma'ili men associating with Sunni women of purportedly low character.[86] Muhammad Ali's mother, however, had her own India connections. While her mother was a "descendant of Shaikh al-Hakami, a well known Yemeni saint," Luqman's maternal grandfather was Muhammad Yusuf Munshi, Assistant Postmaster of Aden and a Bohra. Muhammad Ali noted that his grandfather "married five Arab wives," in Aden as well as "two Indians in Bombay," by whom he had three sons—one of whom was a medical doctor while the others were prominent civil servants in Bombay and Kathiawar.[87]

On the paternal side, the Luqmans maintained equally close connections to family in Hind. In 1923 Muhammad Ali traveled to India for the first time in order to bring an unamed maternal aunt from Surat to Aden. In Bombay, he and two younger brothers were hosted by a maternal uncle, who was head clerk of the Post Office. During a visit of several months he traveled widely throughout northern India, visiting the Princely state of Junagadh—where another maternal relative was Postmaster —as well as Delhi and Simla among others. While enjoying many of the popular tourist haunts, such as the Bombay Zoo, Muhammad Ali also sought out the leading intellectuals of Indian independence, including Gandhi (who he failed to meet on this visit but subsequently met in Aden in the early 1930s) and Dr. B. R. Ambedkar with whom he discussed the plight of the Harijans, or untouchables.[88]

Muhammad Ali's professional ties to India continued well into the 1930s. He maintained connections with Aligarh Muslim University and in the mid-1930s returned to study law in Bombay.[89] These trips to South Asia convinced him that Indian nationalist activities along with their approach to modernization could serve as a model for his fellow Adenis. This is especially apparent in a short story titled *Kamala Devi*, written in 1947.[90] A lightly fictionalized account of his travels through the sub-continent in 1923 and 1936, the story focuses on the plight of the people of the princely state of Baulapur[91] who lived destitute lives under a despotic prince and corrupt police.

Luqman's protagonist, "Muhammad," arrives in Baulapur by accident when he discovers that he does not have an onward ticket for Simla, the summer capital of the Raj and his final destination. When he alighted from the station, Muhammad found himself engulfed by a sea of beggars—the blind and crippled, impoverished mothers and starving children—all dressed in rags. It was a town of low, mudbrick buildings with neither schools nor hospitals. This was despite, as he soon learned, that Baulapur was a land of agricultural plenty where rich soil bore bountiful crops. Muhammad makes the acquaintance of a fellow Yemeni from Hiraz, who had lived in Baulapur for forty years and ran a small hotel. Abu Ahmad, as he was called, told him the current state of affairs existed because the local—and unnamed—ruler oppressed the people with heavy taxes used solely to finance his own life of luxury and debauchery. Filled with anguish, Muhammad continued on his journey a few days later and tried to put the entire episode behind him.

Luqman tells the reader, his protagonist thought little of Baulapur until more than a decade later when he once again found himself stranded in the town's railway station. This time when he left the terminal, Muhammad found not the run down, poverty-stricken town of his memory, but a modern bustling city of prosperous inhabitants, modern well-constructed buildings, hospitals and schools. The cause of this transformation was due, he soon learned, to the "people's beloved," Kamala Devi ("Flower of the Gods"). A teacher from Jaipur, Kamala Devi came to Baulapur to open a school. Outraged by her impudence, the prince had her brought to court and beaten nearly to death. Rather than breaking her spirit, she continued to upbraid the ruler from her sick bed. Stricken with remorse, the prince resolved to change his ways but not before his chief minister (fearing for his position) attempted to assassinate him. Kamala Devi arrives at the palace just in time to thwart the *wazir*'s plans. Grateful, the prince calls to her in despair, "You have saved my body, [now] save my soul." Although suffering mortal wounds from her earlier beating, the young teacher obliged by taking him into the streets and showing him the poverty caused by his greed. Overcome by her exertions, Kamala Devi collapsed in the street. Seeing that she was dying, the prince repented fully and cried to her, "'What must I do to enable my people regain happiness?' 'Give them freedom,' she said. But, 'what is freedom he asked?'" With her dying breath she said:

> Freedom is education, knowledge of human rights, security, safety, emancipation of women ... freedom of expression and criticism ... observance of the law. The King cried [out,] 'Azad [i-]Zindabad!' [Long live Freedom!][92]

In his introduction, Luqman advised his readers that while taking place in India, the tale should have resonance for the people of Southern Arabia. In their own time, he chided, society was overcome by extravagance, greed and other "nonsense." If the people of Aden were to proceed along the "path of advancement" then it required sacrifice. The story of Kamala Devi, therefore, "perhaps held a moral lesson and perhaps moral advice of which we should take account."[93]

His enthusiasm for India, however, should not be mistaken for a naïve romanticism. As the story of Kamala Devi illustrates, Luqman was very aware of the presence of extreme poverty alongside Imperial plenty and he showed nothing but disdain for the rulers of the princely states. While an admirer of Gandhi, he was ultimately much more circumspect about other Indian nationalists residing in Aden. In his memoir, *Men, Matters and Memories*, Muhammad indicated that many of those who agitated against Imperial rule were unsympathetic to Aden's desire for self-determination, dismissing such ideas as "communal." Luqman was similarly disenchanted with supporters of the Khilafat movement, regarding their "enthusiasm for the Ottoman Caliphate," as credulous.[94]

Indeed, although deeply connected to South Asia, Muhammad Ali Luqman—in print in any case—never represents himself or his family as anything but Arab. While resident in India for generations, he is always quick to point out the "pure" Arab nature of his family. His maternal grandmother, as already noted, was a "descendant of Shaikh [sic] El Hakami, a well known Yemeni Saint." The ancestors of his father were from Hamdan and his own mother was a "Yemeni from the tribe of Dubaa," and he frequently refers to his wider maternal kin resident in India as "Arabs."[95] However, his demonstrated facility in Gujarati, obvious fondness for his Bombay- and Gujarat-dwelling relatives and cultivation of close relationships with numerous Indian intellectuals seems to point to not only a very fluid notion of ethnic identity but also the idea of an organic bond between India and Southern Arabia. Certainly, part of this connectivity was due to the structures of empire and the common cause he found with Indians in their anti-imperial struggles. However, these were relationships the Luqman family had cultivated with ease for generations.[96]

Tellingly, this was a relationship that would be disrupted rather than maintained by colonialism. Luqman wrote that in 1928 he, among others, established the Arab Reform Club in Crater and Shaykh Uthman.[97] A number of prominent Indian Muslim intellectuals, however, declined to join, declaring that such clubs were "communal" and that Muslims should eschew creating such distinctions. Muhammad Ali believed that such a stance ignored the unique nature of Aden, which needed to be protected and "finding that educated men of India and other parts of the world were not sympathetic" to this, "I started propagating Arab Solidarity [sic] and disseminating Arab aspirations."[98] It is, of course, ironic that it was European colonial notions of the ethno-nation state that seem to disrupt the imagined social and cultural bonds between Southern Arabia and India. As Luqman seems to indicate, by the late 1920s the politics of anti-colonialism (which by and large based their ideas of sovereignty and nationhood on the European model) strained the connectivities of his childhood. The morality tale of "Kamala Devi" notwithstanding, from the 1930s, Aden—and Arabia more generally—would turn in an increasingly insular way to the idea of Pan-Araxbism and an Arab-dominated Middle East. India, it seems, would recede increasingly into the background and Indians come to be viewed as colonial interlopers.

Hamza Luqman and distant echoes

Muhammad Ali Luqman's change of heart presaged the growing dominance of Arab nationalist discourse that would ultimately determine Aden's course during the twilight of colonial rule.[99] However, it did not mean a sundering of the connection between the port and South Asia. Following Indian independence, for instance, not only did numerous large and small Indian businessmen remain in South Arabia, so did many Indian civil servants and policemen.[100] Equally important, while the intellectuals of Aden gravitated increasingly to Arab nationalism politically, India—for one individual at least—continued to exert an imaginative pull.

Born in 1919, Hamza Luqman was twenty years his brother's junior, coming of age during the Second World War and as decolonization and Arab nationalist aspirations were being realized. While Muhammad Ali was famed as a publisher, essayist and writer of fiction, Hamza maintained a lower profile. Educated entirely in Aden, he worked for a time as a teacher in local government and private schools and ultimately as the librarian for the British Council.¹⁰¹ But he made his mark as a local historian. From the late 1950s to the mid-1980s, Hamza Luqman wrote a number of works focused on the history of Aden and Southern Arabia more generally.¹⁰² Most relevant here were two works from the earliest period: *Tarikh 'adan wa janub al-jazira al-arabiyya* (A History of Aden and Southern Arabia) published in 1960 and an undated typescript in English, *Stories from the History of Aden and Southern Arabia*, that appears to be from the early 1960s.¹⁰³ Both were intended as straightforward histories of the city, presuming an integral connection to Arabia. However, the constituting role of India can still be discerned in both.

Tarikh 'adan approached Aden's past in a manner that in many ways was a product of a European colonial education and Arab nationalism. It is a largely political narrative history that traces the city from its roots as a Manaen and Sabaen port through the Romans, Persians and finally its medieval and early modern periods through to the British occupation. While there are occasional mentions of Aksumite invasions and Ottoman or Portuguese aggressions, for Luqman, Aden's is a wholly Arabian story. As a result, the main narrative focuses almost exclusively on the rise and fall of various Yemeni dynasties and Aden's place in their various struggles. The legends of Alexander the Great, Cain and Abel not to mention India and the wider Indian Ocean disappear almost entirely. Brief mentions of Hanuman, Cain and the stories surrounding Sira Island do appear in the book but only in abbreviated form in an appendix labeled, "The Sights of Aden," alongside descriptions of the town's physical topography and other points of interest, including historic mosques and its famed ancient water-tanks.¹⁰⁴ Aden's legendary past, along with the wider Indian Ocean is largely relegated to a footnote.

This wider context had not disappeared from Luqman's consciousness entirely. Large elements of his—apparently–slightly later and unpublished *Stories from the History of Aden* appear to be a translation of his *Tarikh*. Significantly, however, many of the legendary features of Aden's past that appear as footnotes in that work were reinstated in the main narrative. Cain, Shaddad bin al-Ad, Solomon and, most importantly, Hanuman, all reappear as foundational stories of Aden.¹⁰⁵ Even the story of Jayyash ibn Najah is recounted in all its detail.¹⁰⁶ The net result is that in this narrative the larger sense of Aden inhabiting a world beyond the shores of Arabia is largely restored. While solidly within the camp of Arab nationalism in a political sense, within the realm of the imagination, however, Aden remained a transregional space.

The legacy of the imaginary

As we shall see in the next chapter, the nineteenth-century revival of Aden was one largely driven from India. The British East India Company's desire for a foothold in Southern Arabia derived in part from their need for a coaling station midway between Bombay and Europe at the dawn of the age of steam. Equally important, from their point of view, was the need for a large forward naval base that could protect the growing interests of Indian capital in the Red Sea and East Africa. From the establishment of the Aden Settlement in 1839, Southern Arabia and India would become increasingly intertwined, economically, politically and socially for more than a hundred years. However, as this chapter has demonstrated, this was only the most recent iteration of an Indian Ocean imaginary that stretched back centuries.

Undoubtedly, the shape of this connection shifted over time, representative of its age. The Hellenic unity of Ibn al-Mujawir that imagined Aden as part of a "greater" Hind—along with East Africa—was replaced in the time of Abu Makhrama by an image of Aden that, while fiercely independent, looked to India as a kind of political hinterland where refuge could be sought and also play a pivotal role in reconstituting one's fortunes. The connections brought by Company rule were qualitatively new with direct rule and integration into the imperial economic and political apparatus. However, as the writings of the Luqmans reveal, elements of an older imaginary persisted. For them, familial links as well as stories of a shared past sustained a deep bond. The brothers were molded by colonial and post-colonial politics, pinning their hopes on Pan-Arabism and the nascent nation state. But the idea of India still loomed large, constituting a part of their joint patrimony that played as much a role in shaping their community as the Imperial state.

2
Aden, the Company and Indian Ocean Interests

The British East India Company's decision to acquire Aden by force in 1839 is generally written about as a strategic decision. One of the few natural deep-water harbors in the western Indian Ocean, Aden was an ideal location for a coaling station, a necessary element of infrastructure needed to support emerging steamship technology. Located just beyond the southern end of the Red Sea, the Company's lines of communication could also be greatly shortened with the development of a mail route via Aden and Suez that cut months off the route around Africa and the Cape of Good Hope.[1] Generally overlooked, however, has been the Company's more regional agenda that sought to protect and expand its own commercial interests. Far from being perceived as simply a distant military outpost, Company officials sought from the outset to develop Aden as an extension of their economic and political power. While military muscle was a critical element in this—as we shall see—equally important was the Company's desire to portray themselves as the protectors and patrons of non-European—but especially South Asian—merchant capital.

Ultimately, Aden's growth was self-perpetuating, as its harbor facilities and status as a free port, not to mention the security offered by imperial military might, attracted laborers and merchants from throughout the Red Sea and western Indian Ocean who sought to improve their economic fortunes. This, however, was not always the case. In 1839, Aden was among the least prosperous anchorages in the region. Mukha, Jiddah and even Mukalla accounted for more trade and were home to far larger communities of affluent merchants. Once the port was secured, it became almost immediately evident to S. B. Haines, the expedition's commander and soon to be Company Political Agent, that Aden was little more than a ruin with few inhabitants and little commercial life. It was readily apparent to him and others that for Aden to become a permanent Company outpost it required a "native" population that was economically and socially self-sustaining.

This chapter is concerned with what we may refer to as the "peopling" of Aden. How did a place that was little more than a large village at the time of occupation transform into a major Imperial port and urban center within the space of a generation? We will begin with an overview of the Company's historic interest in Aden and Southern Arabia as a strategic link in its evolving Imperial network. The heart of the chapter, however, centers on the efforts of Company officials, especially

S. B. Haines, to establish Aden as an attractive place of settlement. This was accomplished, in part, through Haines's conscious efforts to create an environment that was attractive to Indian and Arab merchants. This involved, at its most basic, securing the perimeter of the Settlement against hostile local political forces. However, as we shall see, it also required him to overcome opposition from his own officers and military culture. The latter would ultimately prove his undoing.

The objectives of Haines and the Company were aided by wider political turmoil. Other ports such as Mukha, Jiddah and Massawa (located in modern Eritrea, on the opposite shore of the Red Sea) were far more prosperous than Aden at the time of the occupation. The stability of these enclaves, however, was deceptively fragile and, in fact, on the verge of collapse. Civil war in highland Yemen and the unraveling of the Egyptian Pasha, Muhammad Ali's Red Sea Empire, offered the Company the opportunity to not only permanently secure the Aden harbor and its environs, but to present it as the lone safe, politically stable anchorage at the southern end of the Red Sea. These were circumstances that Haines would ultimately exploit to great effect.

The Company, Napoleon, Muhammad Ali Pasha and the lines of communication

The characterization of the Company's designs on the Red Sea and Aden as driven by strategic concerns is not without basis. Like most European trading companies, the British East India Company maintained a regular presence along the Red Sea coast of Yemen, known as the Tihama, from the mid-seventeenth century. Company agents exported coffee from the port of Mukha until 1767 when prices began to fall and it was deemed uneconomical to maintain a permanent presence.[2] As we shall see, this did not actually mean the end of Company commercial interests since Indian merchants remained an important economic presence throughout the region. It did mean, however, that strategic and political concerns tend to dominate the archival record from this period. Of particular concern, was the Company's ability to maintain and, when possible, shorten their lines of communication between the Directors in London and the Governor-General in India. And it was in this vein that Aden and the Red Sea would figure most prominently in Company thinking.

The shortest route of communication between Europe and South Asia was via either the Red Sea or Persian Gulf. Political realities and the hostility of the Ottoman state in the seventeenth century made the development of such a direct route impractical at best, necessitating the use of the much longer Cape route, pioneered by the Portuguese around the southern tip of Africa. By the late eighteenth century, the Sublime Porte had become more receptive to diplomatic efforts and the Company experienced a measure of success in developing a relatively regular post service between London and India via Suez in the Red Sea and Basra in the Persian Gulf.[3] The vulnerability of these routes, however, was made readily apparent in 1789 with Napoleon Bonaparte's invasion of Egypt. Bonaparte's relatively brief Egyptian adventure was part of an ambitious plan to re-establish French influence in India by exploiting ongoing conflicts between the Company and various Indian rivals.

Far from the hegemony enjoyed by the Raj later in the nineteenth century, the political fortunes of the British East India Company through the early 1800s, while ascendant, were far from unchallenged. Through the last decade of the eighteenth century and the first few years of the nineteenth, the Company's expansionist designs in the sub-continent were threatened by two principal foes: the Maratha Confederacy, a fairly loose collection of "Hindu chiefs" with their political center in Pune and the Sultanate of Mysore ruled by Tipu Sultan. Like most princely rulers since the appearance of the Portuguese in the sixteenth century, both the Maratha chiefs and Tipu Sultan availed themselves of European military expertise in their efforts to develop modern armies to defend against the Company as well as one another.[4] Among these mercenaries were many French officers with Republican, and even Bonapartist, sympathies.[5] Following his occupation of Egypt, Napoleon's intention was to build a fleet at Suez and sail with his army to India. There he would link up with his supporters and join the Tiger of Mysore against the Company army led by Arthur Wellesley, the future Duke of Wellington.[6]

Company agents intercepted copies of the correspondence between Napoleon and Tipu Sultan along with reports of French activity in the old Ottoman shipyard at Suez where a number of older vessels were being refitted apparently as the vanguard of an invasion fleet.[7] The British moved quickly, seeking to bottle-up the French in the Red Sea with a small force being dispatched to occupy the tiny island of Perim in the Bab al-Mandab, at the mouth of the sea.

Perim, it was believed, possessed enormous strategic advantages. It had a "good harbor" and passage on the Africa side was a narrow slot of only about fifteen miles and littered with rocks and shoals that would force any passing ships to sail close to the island. A similar situation, naval officials believed, held true for the Arabian side so no vessel would be out of reach of shore batteries. Based on this information, the Bombay Government authorized the occupation of the island by a small garrison and the installation of shore batteries in an effort to turn the small desert island into a strong point.

In early May 1799 a small force under the command of Lt. Col. J. Murray arrived on Perim only to find that virtually none of the Company's intelligence regarding the island was accurate. In his first report, Murray noted that nothing was as expected. "The island," he wrote, "is perfectly barren," and possessed no fresh water or other supplies, so that the tiny garrison would have to depend on foraging from the nearby African coast. He also dispelled the notion that coastal batteries could command the entrance to the Red Sea. "It is with no less regret that I inform you that no Batteries [sic] erected on the Island [sic] can command the entrance." This may, he allowed, be effected on the eastern or "Arabian" side, but was quite impossible on the western African side that, he informed his superiors, could be held open by a determined enemy with "a squadron of men of war."[8]

Life on Perim was enormously difficult and water, in particular, was a constant problem and in short supply. Murray wrote about a month after landing that "every exertion has been made to procure water on the Island but hitherto without a shadow of success. Wherever we dig we find the soil perfectly salty, and at a small depth coral rock. There is hardly a living insect on the island, not a bird to be seen or is there a plant or shrub that requires fresh water for its growth." The colonel hoped to obtain supplies of water from the coast by employing local "Arab boats" to take shore parties to Mukha but these attempts were frustrated by the refusal of local merchants to extend the Company's servants credit.[9] "The Muhammadan merchants have refused to advance money on the Government's Bills and the Broker [*sic*] can command no more than what is sufficient to water the Fleet.[10] When our cash fails we must instantly depart [Perim] as not one drop of water is to be had or a sheep to be purchased till the money is actually counted." Unless a large sum of cash could be advanced immediately from Bombay, he noted, not only would he have insufficient funds to pay for supplies but he would be unable to meet the payroll of his men.

To make matters worse, it was increasingly clear to the commander that Perim was effectively indefensible. The barren nature of the island made it impossible to erect the necessary defensive works and in his opinion Perim could only be held by "a garrison of twelve to fifteen hundred men if attacked by a European force." Even then, boats could be landed on any part of the island and the harbor, which was ringed by a long ridgeline, was vulnerable to any enemy who may get a few field pieces to the top. Perim, Murray reluctantly determined, could not be held and he requested permission to evacuate his men. He concluded his report by noting that if the Company doubted his assessment, there seemed "no stronger proof of [the island's] inutility than that the commanding officer of His Majesty's Squadron," had established his headquarters and supply depot at Mukha on the coast.[11]

The entire Perim expedition was a fiasco. The lone apparent positive to emerge from the affair was Colonel Murray's serendipitous encounter with the so-called Sultan of Aden, Sultan Ahmad al-Abdali.[12] Unable to obtain sufficient supplies from Mukha, Murray made a reconnaissance trip to Aden sometime in the late summer. Although deemed too far from Perim to provide practical resupply, when the force withdrew from the island in late September it was there that Murray took his men to await evacuation. Unlike the tepid reception they had received in Mukha, the ruler of Aden welcomed Murray and his men with open arms. The Company officer wrote that in contrast to Mukha, "the friendship and attention of the Sultan much exceed my most sanguine expectations, and the good will and behavior of the inhabitants is in every respect equal to their Sovereign's wishes and orders. The soldiers and natives are on as good and friendly a footing as I have ever seen them in any part of India."[13]

The Sultan's hospitality was, not surprisingly, driven by self-interest. It quickly transpired that he hoped to enter into a treaty relationship with the Company in order to insulate himself from the increasingly fractious political climate of Yemen. Murray wrote, "In my conversations with the Sultan he seemed to me to wish to enter into a much more strict connection with the British Government than I was authorized to form. As it was translated to me, he was desirous to hold his country as the Nabob of Arcot holds the Curuahe."[14] The colonel, unsurprisingly, demurred. The Sultan, however, was not so easily put off and wrote to the Governor of Bombay no fewer than three separate letters seeking an alliance. After considering the possibility, Company policy makers decided not to pursue the opportunity for fear that such local entanglements would turn into a quagmire.[15] While the Burra Sahibs of the Company would not turn their gaze back to Aden for more than thirty years, the closing remarks of Murray's report were prescient.

> I have not hoist the colours [but] the place is as much ours as I could wish it to be—and it so by the Sultan's orders. How far this place might be advantageous in point of trade I cannot judge, coffee, and cotton are the principal productions of the country; but from its vicinity to the African coast it might perhaps become a market from when that country might be supplied with Indian commodities . . . With your Honorable Board it will remain to decide whether this place shall be kept; but I make it a most earnest request that the extraordinary marks of friendship shown to the British name might not be overlooked.[16]

Murray's assessment and Calcutta's response is reflective of a longstanding debate that characterized views toward Aden and the Red Sea within the ranks of the East India Company up to and even after the port's occupation. British individuals on the ground generally touted the potential of Red Sea ports for Indian commodities (later observers nearly always noted the presence of thriving Indian merchant communities as well). Company officials in India, on the other hand, invariably pointed to geopolitical and strategic concerns that rendered greater regional engagement inadvisable. Admiral John Blankett, chief naval officer in Bombay, argued in 1800 that there was little to be gained by establishing a permanent station in Southern Arabia. First, he argued—incorrectly—that Aden was "a place of no trade." And, second, its harbor was a poor anchorage "exposed to the Southward and to the winds from the sea." Far better, he held, to rely on the proven superiority of naval patrols to defend Company interests. Lord Wellesley, the Governor-General, concurred, adding that such a presence would undoubtedly lead to unwelcome entanglements with local polities that would involve the Company "in disputes and even hostilities with the neighbors of the Sultan of Aden."[17]

Although the Calcutta bureaucrats were reluctant to commit too many resources or become enmeshed in onerous treaty relationships, they were not blind to the region's economic significance. Following Murray's withdrawal, the Company did, in fact, acknowledge the importance of Indian commerce in the Red Sea and Arabia. The traveler Henry Salt, later British Consul in Egypt, noted on a brief visit there in 1809 that while the town itself was a "wretched heap of ruins," it was still "of some consequence" as a place of commerce. Trade was primarily in natural goods, including various kinds of gums, incense and some coffee, sufficient to warrant a permanent community of "Banians." Salt noted, in particular, that coffee of the best quality could be procured in considerable quantities, although not as expeditiously as in Mukha.[18] Indeed, the commercial possibilities of the Red Sea appear to have revived sufficiently not only for the Company to reappoint an agent at Mukha—still the most important port on the Arabian shore of the Red Sea[19]—as early as 1802, but to appoint a Mr. Benzoni to the post in 1808 largely because of his knowledge of the region, especially Aden.[20]

The historian R. J. Gavin notes that it was from this point forward that the Company began to take an increasing interest in the commercial security of the Red Sea and Gulf of Aden. In addition to stationing a commercial agent at Mukha after 1802, the Company navy began to provide escorts for Indian merchant vessels, establishing a more regular naval presence in the area. In the same year, they signed a treaty with the Imam in Sana'a in order to lower duties charged at Mukha along with better treatment for Indian merchants who enjoyed Company protection. They also secured a commercial agreement with the Abdali Sultan who controlled Aden. Finally, beginning in 1800 Company naval vessels were charged with the systematic survey and charting of the Red Sea and the Gulf of Aden in their effort to identify and exploit new commercial opportunities.[21] These moves set a precedent. Through the first decades of the nineteenth century, the Company became more involved in the region and not less.

The Company's revived presence in the western Indian Ocean was driven largely by two military threats to their interests. First, as a result of Britain's protracted conflict with Republican and then Napoleonic France, British flagged shipping—European and Indian—found themselves increasingly at the mercy of French privateers operating out of island bases such as Mauritius. The fear of French raiders was pervasive enough, for example, that when Henry Salt and his companions spied an unidentified ship enter Aden harbour they quickly raised the alarm. The vessel turned out to be an American merchantman, but Salt noted that a French vessel had watered there earlier in the year and that it would be in the Company's interests to provide the Abdali sultan with a small number of coastal guns to defend the bay to protect British commerce.[22]

Following the defeat of Napoleon in 1815, the French effectively ceased to be a threat to British flagged shipping. In the mean time, however, an additional menace emerged in the shape of a growing fleet of Arab marauders allied with the rulers of the first Saudi Kingdom. These ranged widely around the Persian Gulf and the Gulf of Aden into the Red Sea, regularly preying on shipping bound for the Hijaz, disrupting commercial as well as pilgrimage traffic.[23] The result was, on the one hand, a state of insecurity but also a steady desertion of the British standard for safer flags of convenience such as that of the Sultanate of Oman and Musqat robbing the Company of valuable revenue not to mention prestige.[24] This Arab threat was countered in part by increased British naval activity.[25] More critical, however, was the timely intervention of the new Egyptian ruler, Mehmet Ali Pasha.

Mehmet Ali Pasha and the Company

The Rise of Mehmet Ali Pasha's Egypt is a critical, if often times underrated, factor in the history of Arabia and the Red Sea in the first half of the nineteenth century. The son of an Albanian merchant, Mehmet Ali first gained notoriety when he managed to ascend to the Pashalik of Egypt in the years following the expulsion of Napoleon's invasion force. Rising from second in command of the Albanian contingent through a combination of ability and guile, by 1805 he had forced the Ottoman Porte to recognize him as ruler of Egypt with what would become growing amounts of autonomy during his more than forty-year rule. Earlier generations of historians regarded him as the "founder" of the modern Egyptian nation through his efforts aimed at modernizing (read Westernizing) the economy, education and especially the military. While certainly true, these innovations were largely in the service of creating a regional empire that ultimately encompassed, for a time at least, Sudan, Syria, part of Anatolia and strategic points along both Red Sea coasts.[26] It is the Pasha's Red Sea conquests that are of greatest interest here.

While seeking to expand his own territorial domain, Mehmet Ali remained for much of his career a loyal Ottoman functionary. In keeping with that, in 1807 the Pasha was instructed to mount an expedition to reclaim the Hijaz and the holy cities of Mecca and Medina recently captured by the forces of Amir Abdullah al-Saud, sometimes referred to rather erroneously as the "Wahhabis" and more accurately as the first Saudi Kingdom. He was unable to launch an expedition until 1811 but over the course of a seven-year campaign managed to not only to expel the Saudis from the holy places but invade the tribe's home region of Nejd in 1818, capturing their capital al-Dir'iyya as well as most of the ruling family.[27] Most important, for our purposes, Mehmet Ali was able to use the Hijaz campaign as an opportunity to extend his influence throughout the Red Sea. Over the next several years, and generally in the name of the Sultan, the Pasha seized control of virtually every strategic commercial node along both coasts, including Suakin and Massawa on the African side and; Jiddah and Mukha on the Arabian, effectively annexing them to his Egyptian province.[28]

For the British Company, Mehmet Ali's expansion was simultaneously fortuitous and a potential threat. On the positive side, the Egyptian Pasha's efforts played a critical role in securing the waters of the Red Sea and Persian Gulf by removing the Saudi danger. Similarly, while he had also used it as an opportunity to grab extremely lucrative commercial real estate he was careful to acknowledge the interests of the Company. He not only guaranteed the safety of Company mail through his territories he also extended the use of Egyptian-controlled facilities to expedite their transmission. This included the establishment of coaling stations as steam power became more important.[29]

On the other hand, the Egyptian Pasha's imperial ambitions were well known. While restoring the Sultan's authority in Arabia and sending his army to fight rebels in Greece, Mehmet Ali also sought to expand the territory under his control to the point of nearly supplanting his Turkish masters. In 1831, he successfully invaded the neighboring province of al-Sham, which included Palestine and Syria, ultimately striking deep into the heart of Anatolia. His forces delivered a number of crushing defeats to the Ottoman army along the way, threatening to upset the balance of power throughout the region.[30] Closer to home, for the Company-*wallahs*, in 1833 the Pasha effected an occupation of the entire Tihama coast, pushing into the Yemeni highlands over the next four years.[31] It was within this context that the Company began to gradually consider the establishment of a more tangible presence in Arabia and the Red Sea.

Of steam and shipwrecks—the occupation of Aden

Historians have posited a variety of explanations aimed at explaining the Company's decision to occupy Aden. The pre-eminent historian of British Aden R. J. Gavin argued that the Company's interests were largely strategic. As the network of their interests grew beyond South Asia, stretching from the Red Sea and East Africa to China, there arose a pressing need to construct a secure network of communication across which men, material and information could move rapidly and unimpeded. Steam power emerged as a practical technology from the 1830s and with this came the need to secure coal depots across the Indian Ocean for the purpose of regular, reliable refueling.[32] As Gavin rightly points out, coal depots did not necessarily have to be located in ports directly controlled by the Company or the British Crown. There were, in fact, numerous examples of anchorages that were not Company territory such as Suez and—ultimately—Zanzibar, where ships regularly replenished their bunkers. Aden proved an exception, Gavin argues, for two interrelated reasons. First, the distance between Bombay and Suez was too great for steamers of the period to make the trip in one leap without refueling. Second, and even more importantly, as the regime of Mehmet Ali seemed to enjoy one victory after another—both in the Red Sea and Syria—Company officials feared that he would eventually occupy all the ports in the Red Sea and Southern Arabia, an act that would leave their carefully constructed communications and transportation network vulnerable to disruption.[33]

There is, certainly, merit in Gavin's argument substantiated with a wealth of empirical evidence. In particular, he demonstrates that the Governor of Bombay during this period, Sir Robert Grant, was particularly keen to not only expand Company holdings but shore-up its growing communications network through direct acquisition—via purchase or seizure—of key points.[34] Strategic considerations were undoubtedly upper-most in the minds of policy makers when it came to the decision to establish an outpost in the region of the Red Sea directly controlled by the Company. These, however, were not their only concern. Also present in their calculations were economic and political considerations that revolved not around grand global networks but regional actors critical to the Company, namely, Indian merchants. There is no better illustration of this than events surrounding the wreck of the *Daria Dawlat*.

The voyage and wreck of the *Daria Dawlat*

During the wee hours of February 20, 1837 the barque *Daria Dawlat*, eight weeks out of Calcutta bound for Jiddah, ran aground just outside of Aden's harbor on an otherwise clear night. The vessel, laden with cargo and pilgrims, was the property of the Nawab of Madras' mother, Ahmad ul-Nisa', and by all accounts was deliberately wrecked as part of a complex conspiracy between the ship's own master, the supercargo and the Abdali Sultan of Lahej. Most histories of colonial Aden cite the wreck as the incident that directly precipitated its seizure by the East India Company. These same sources, however, are equally quick to dismiss this as a thinly veiled pretext that served to cover their true motive, namely the acquisition of Aden as a coaling station that would shorten lines of communication with England.[35]

Aden certainly figured prominently in the imperial designs of the East India Company. Its suitability as a fuel depot, however, was only one element of the Company's calculus. Equally important were the Company's commercial and political interests represented by the numerous Indian merchants, pilgrims and ships that made their way into the Gulf of Aden and Red Sea each year. The events surrounding the *Daria Dawlat*'s loss and the actions of Company officers in the years following Aden's occupation, reveal even more pressing reasons to establish a firm, permanent presence in the region: economic interest in the shape of Indian capital and growing political instability within the region that threatened it. To fully appreciate the reasons for the port's seizure and the rapid development of a sizeable, mostly Muslim, community it is critical to also understand the regional political and economic contexts. On the one hand, these circumstances provided the motivation for British officialdom to create a military and commercial foothold in the Arabian Peninsula. But, equally importantly, they provided Arab and Indian merchants with the incentive to place themselves under Company protection. The accounts given by the survivors of the *Daria Dawlat* provide a view of maritime life in the Indian Ocean that is Conradian in scope. It is a story of malfeasance, dereliction of duty and greed. It is also a tale of perseverance, bravery and compassion. The occupation of Aden was a direct consequence of its deliberate grounding. The details of the ill-fated voyage and its aftermath provide texture and context for the actions of S. B. Haines and the Company and, indeed, help explain the shape that the Settlement was ultimately to take.

Inauspicious beginnings

The last voyage of the *Daria Dawlat* and what came after, is preserved in a series of depositions recorded in Bombay by three survivors following their repatriation from Jiddah: Sayyid Nur al-Dın bin Jumal a native of Colombo and agent of the ship's owner, Begum Ahmad ul-Nisa', mother of the Nawab of Madras; Sayyid Tipu bin Al-Doonebee, a Singaporean merchant traveling on the *Daria Dawlat* with his family on the pilgrimage to Mecca; and Pir Muhammad Mistry, the ship's carpenter.[36] The statements of the survivors are remarkably in accord with one another and provide not only an account of their ordeal but a compelling description of maritime commercial life at mid-century.

Sayyid Nur al-Dın was an experienced seaman and merchant who had previously worked the Bengal–Malaya route as a *Nakhoda*[37] for a European concern. He was returning to sea after a lengthy illness and had secured a berth on the 220-ton *Daria Dawlat*. Sayyid Nur al-Dın took charge of the ship on December 10, 1836 (coincidentally the first day of Ramadan) in Calcutta where it had just arrived from Madras under the supervision of the Begum's agent, Luchmee Pursad. The ship was chartered to an Arab merchant from Mukha, Firuz Edoor, to carry a cargo of rice, sugar and piece goods, along with a small number of pilgrims, to Jiddah. The Sayyid noted in his deposition that—in retrospect—signs of the troubled voyage to come began almost as soon as the ship docked in Calcutta.

Upon arrival, the crew began the process of loading the ship's cargo, a procedure that took ten days. Once completed, the *Mallam* (navigator and first officer) came to Sayyid Nur al-Dın and reported that although the ship was loaded to capacity, Firuz Edoor had asked that even more cargo be brought on board. Luchmee Pursad, as the Begum's agent, intervened and sent the *Mallam* to Firuz to inform him that his request was not possible. Firuz's response was to fire the unfortunate messenger. In his place, he appointed Abdullah Musqati as first officer along with a certain Ahmad BuKhidr as supercargo. With two new officers, and a crew under the supervision of a *serang* (the deck boss), a *tindal* (boatswain's mate) and a seacunny or quartermaster, the ship left port on December 26. It was not to be a smooth voyage.

Sayyid Nur al-Dın noted that the ship's new officers demonstrated peculiar, not to mention less than competent, behavior from the outset. Shortly after disembarking their coastal pilot at Sangur, for instance, the *Mallam* and supercargo produced a letter written in Arabic and apparently signed by Luchmee Pursad and Firuz Edoor that announced the Sayyid's demotion. According to his statement in Bombay, the letter indicated that "the ship was to be commanded and navigated by the chief officer, Abdulla, under the immediate order of the Supercargo, and that I [Sayyid Nur al-Din] had no authority in the command or navigation of the vessel, but that my duty was merely to see that the vessel and her stores were not injured."[38] Rather than create trouble, Sayyid Nur al-Dın relinquished command, at which point the peculiar behavior of the officers quickened its pace.

After ceding control, Sayyid Nur al-Dın noticed that the ship changed course. Rather than heading toward Ceylon to cut through the Palk Strait off the southern tip of India, the vessel headed eastward toward the Andaman Islands. Not a man given to hasty assumptions, he waited four days. When their course did not seem to change, he asked the second officer where they were headed and the latter confirmed their easterly direction. He confronted the *Mallam* and the supercargo and the former declared that they were headed toward the Andamans in order to "avoid a dangerous current which sets from the eastward through the straits."[39]

Sayyid Nur al-Din declared that there was no search current and that a direct approach to the strait was completely safe. After he agreed to bear any responsibility for loss or damage to the ship and its cargo, al-Musqati and buKhidr agreed to change course. After nine days sailing toward Ceylon, Sayyid Nur al-Dın asked his friend, the second officer, when they would sight land. The latter replied the next morning. "Early the following morning the second officer called me on the poop, gave me a spy glass and requested me to look in the direction he pointed. I looked thro' the glass and distinctly saw land." Al-Musqati, the *Mallam*, however, disagreed. "Abdulla was present and said it was not land but merely a cloud and that we should not see land for two days more." Within an hour, however, the Sayyid noted that land was clearly visible with the naked eye. He reported the *Mallam*'s pronouncements to the supercargo, noting that if it had been night they would have run ashore.

The actions of the *Mallam* up to this point appeared merely incompetent as opposed to criminal. And, as such, the Sayyid kept his own counsel. The *Daria Dawlat* sailed on to the Malabari port, Alleppey,[40] where they took on additional cargo and seventeen new passengers, including the Singaporean merchant Sayyid Tipu and his family. Tensions worsened. Now dangerously overloaded, the ship put in at Cochin, its last stop before heading across the Arabian Sea bound for Jiddah. Here the supercargo, BuKhidr, ordered various ship's stores, cable and other necessities thrown overboard to make room for even more freight. When Sayyid Nur al-Dın protested, he was told he had "nothing to do with [the running of] the ship and that they would do as they liked."[41]

Shipwreck!

Full of foreboding, they sailed for Jiddah after two days in port. At noon on February 7, 1837 the second officer had just finished taking his solar readings and the Sayyid asked him when they would make landfall. The former replied that they should be abreast of Aden by about midnight. In what by now would have been comically predictable, had it not been so dangerous, al-Musqati contradicted his subordinate and said that they would not be anywhere near Aden that night. At about midnight, Sayyid Nur al-Dın and Sayyid Tipu sat on the deck chatting with the second officer. The *Mallam*, al-Musqati, approached them and asked the ship's officer why they had changed course, to which he replied that to do otherwise would run the vessel aground. The *Mallam* declared that it was now his watch, ordered the second officer from the deck and summarily changed the ship's heading. Within hours, disaster struck.

At about two in the morning, the *serang* reported to al-Musqati that the water was white (a sign of being too close to shore) and requested permission to "heave to." *Mallam* al-Musqati cursed him and ordered him to hold his course. Alarmed, Sayyid Nur al-Dın, who had remained on deck too worried to sleep, informed the supercargo, Ahmad BuKhidr, of his misgivings but was told that it was none of his concern. Soon after this, the quartermaster manning the helm worriedly remarked that he could hear the breakers on shore. At 3 a.m., the entire hull shuddered as the *Daria Dawlat* struck a reef.

Knocked from his berth by the force of the impact, Sayyid Tipu rushed on deck where he and Sayyid Nur al-Dın called for the anchor to be let go and the sails furled in an effort to keep the ship from dashing itself to bits against the rocks. The former begged the officers to jettison some of the more easily accessible cargo in an effort to float the stricken vessel from the rocks. Al-Musqati and BuKhidr barked at the two men that the management of the ship was none of their affair and refused to take any action for three long hours until 6 a.m. But, by then, of course, it was too late.

Up to this point, both Sayyid Nur al-Dın and Sayyid Tipu (men with considerable experience at sea) seemed to believe that their ship's officers were simply incompetent. With their refusal to take any action to save the barque from sinking, it quickly dawned on them that the ship's officers were engaged in active sabotage and criminal intent. Miraculously, the ship's hull was still in tact, and the pumps were able to keep the hold from taking on water. Ahmad BuKhidr, the supercargo, finally ordered the anchor let go. He then directed that the jolly boat be lowered over the side and, along with four lascars, set out for Aden, which the shipwrecked survivors could see in the distance. By 10 a.m., the pumps, choked with sand, ceased working and the ship began to take on water again. Al-Musqati now ordered the ship's longboat lowered into the water. As the passengers crowded around the rail near the small boat in hopes of embarking, the *Mallam* cut the rope and ordered the crew to row for shore. When the boat neared shore, it capsized in the surf, drowning most of those on board, including al-Musqati and the luckless second officer. The pilgrims and merchants of the *Daria Dawlat* were now truly alone.

Hope briefly revived late in the afternoon when the passengers spied two small local craft emerge from Aden's harbor and make their way toward the stricken vessel. When the boats came alongside, however, rather than bringing relief the crews boarded the vessel and began off-loading the cargo and robbing those still on board of their personal belongings. Sayyid Tipu managed to bribe the men on one of the boats to take his wife, daughter and mother-in-law to safety. The remaining passengers were again abandoned and faced the prospect of another night on the wreck.

As evening approached, an elderly female pilgrim was swept overboard as the rising tide began to wash over the deck. Waterlogged and desperate, Sayyids Nur al-Dın and Tipu—now the de facto leaders of the bedraggled party—directed the remaining score of passengers to take refuge in the rigging as the surging tide and surf made staying on deck impossible. As dawn broke, the two realized that they needed to take a hand in their own fate and so rallied the remaining survivors to construct a raft in an attempt to reach shore. Unable to construct a craft big enough for everyone, the pair struck out for shore with three others (a servant and two unidentified women from Sayyid Tipu's party) with the idea of going to Aden for help.

The safety of shore?

The small party managed to navigate the dangerous surf but as they reached shore they were met by a group of men who set upon the disheveled survivors. The men were shoved into the surf and their heads held under water. All the castaways were then stripped naked and robbed of their valuables. The men were beaten and the women raped.[42] Stunned and bleeding they were left naked and traumatized on the beach. The small party was soon discovered by a horse and rider who turned out to be the representative of Sayyid Zayn bin Alawi al-Aydarus, the *mansab* of the town's most important shrine and likely the most influential figure in Aden. The rider gave the survivors cloth to cover themselves and escorted them to Sayyid Zayn's house.

For a brief moment, the lot of the survivors seemed to be improving. The remaining passengers were plucked from the wreckage by a boat sent by Sayyid Zayn once Sayyid Tipu's wife reached Aden (minus her own jewelry and valuables) and informed him of their plight. A number of the crew who had arrived on shore via one of the ship's two boats also found their way to the Aydarus compound. Sayyid Zayn provided all with clothing and shelter for two weeks while they recovered from their ordeal. Unsurprisingly, Sayyids Nur al-Dın and Tipu now emerged as leaders of the ragged band. They made arrangements for the group to travel by boat to Mukha, where there was a Company agent, and began to collect information regarding what had happened on shore following the disaster. The ship's cargo was quickly discovered in the bazaar and customs house. The Indian merchants learned from various sources that the supercargo, Ahmad BuKhidr, had conspired with the town's governor to dispose of the recovered freight. The supercargo was to take one-third of the profits while the governor of Aden and the Abdali Sultan would take the remainder. In the interim, it seems, BuKhidr managed to abscond and, ultimately, made his way to Jiddah. After fifteen days as the guests of the Aydarus family, the small company made their way to Tawahi where a boat was engaged to take them to Mukha. But the group's trials were only beginning.

Miserable Mukha

It is easy to imagine that as they left Aden the survivors of the *Daria Dawlat* believed that the worst of their ordeal was behind them. It was an undemanding two-day sail to Mukha in largely protected coastal waters. Although the Red Sea was known for its many reefs and hidden rocks, this would be no trouble for an experienced, local crew. Mukha was the largest and most active port south of Jiddah. An East India Company agent was permanently posted there, while Company merchantmen and warships regularly dropped anchor in its roadstead.[43] As the survivors of a ship that both belonged to an important Indian princely family and flew British colors, the party had every reason to believe that their troubles were over. They were sadly mistaken.

Upon landing in Mukha, the small company immediately sought out the Company agent, whom the survivors called by the Arabic *wakil*, and referred to in the records variously as Shaykh Syed or Shaykh Tyeb.[44] Rather than being greeted with sympathy and assistance, the survivors were met with suspicion and extortionate demands. The agent met the party on his veranda and after hearing their story demanded "one thousand dollars to manage their business properly." *Sayyid* Nur al-Din replied that they were destitute and had no money to offer as a retainer and that he did not feel comfortable agreeing to a promissory note that would put his employers on the hook for the money. The agent responded by ordering the group to vacate his property. The party returned to the beach where they spent the night without food, water or shelter.

Over the next several days the agent doled out a pittance to the group that was neither enough to feed or shelter them. Indeed, according to *Sayyid* Nur al-Dın and *Sayyid* Tipu, he seemed to want to intentionally victimize them. While still living on the beach, according to the affidavit of *Sayyid* Tipu, a message arrived from the *wakil* requesting to see his wife. *Sayyid* Tipu sent her to the agent's house along with two female companions and before long the women returned in tears. The agent, they claimed, had propositioned the *Sayyid*'s wife, declaring that "your husband is now poor, he has nothing for you to eat," so "you had better come and live in my house with me."[45]

After yet another failed entreaty to the *wakil* about a week later in which he drove the group from his veranda and had his peons assault Nur al-Din, the party was saved only through the charity of a Hindu merchant they met by chance on the road. The merchant, referred to as Dwarka, took the entire group into his own home and sheltered them for more than three weeks. After continued wrangling with the *wakil* and a fruitless trip to Jiddah to try to contact a Company ship, Nur al-Dın returned to Mukha to find two Company vessels at anchor in the roadstead: the sloop-of-war Coote and the Palinurus. The latter, it so happened, was commanded by a man who would become pivotal in Aden's colonial history: Stafford Betteworth Haines.

Haines listened to the stories of Nur al-Dın and Tipu with undisguised horror. He had both men swear out initial statements and then transported them and other members of the party to Bombay where they could be formally deposed. This set in motion the events that would lead to Aden's ultimate seizure.

The immediate reaction of officials in Bombay and Calcutta was predictable. The *Daria Dawlat*'s officers were denounced as despicable, the agent in Mukha was placed under investigation and the actions of the Sultan of Lahej were declared those of "a barbarous robber." Unsurprisingly, the Chief Secretary of the Bombay Government pronounced "in consequence of the very serious outrage committed against the people and passengers," of a ship "belonging . . . to the Nawab of the Carnatic [Madras] and sailing under British colours, by the Sooltan of Aden, it will probably be requisite for this government to take strong measures for exacting reparations."[46]

Indeed, Haines was soon dispatched to demand compensation form the Abdali Sultan for the ship's loss, a mission that would ultimately end with the port's seizure. However, for the Company, the *Daria Dawlat* incident represented more than just an affront to its pride. It highlighted dangerous shortcomings in their ability to protect their interests in the region with potentially serious economic and political consequences. Most obviously, although the Company maintained a consistent naval presence in the region not only was it incapable of preventing such incidents but their ships were not necessarily able to offer timely assistance to survivors. The dependence on local agents, intended to make up for such a light presence, proved similarly unreliable. This it turned out had less to do with the individual agent's own avarice, a subsequent investigation revealed, than the fact that the Mukha station was financed on a shoestring and the agent had recently had his own salary reduced, resulting in what one Company official referred to as "pecuniary difficulties."

From an economic perspective, Company officials seem to have realized that incidents like the *Daria Dawlat* would ultimately shake the confidence of South Asian merchants who ostensibly enjoyed their protection. This might result in Indian traders searching out other arrangements for their security and effectively cutting their ties with the Company. The crisis surrounding the incident also had a grave political side. The *Daria Dawlat* was not just any Indian-owned merchantman. First, it belonged to a member of an important princely family—the rulers of Madras also known as the Carnatic. The Princely States of South Asia were not nearly as subordinate to the Company as they were to become under the Raj in the wake of the 1857 Rebellion. By August 1837 the Nawab, Azim Jah Bahadur, had sent a letter to Calcutta politely asking what had become of his relative's ship and cargo. And Company officialdom was concerned to maintain good diplomatic relations with them. Furthermore, the ship was carrying a considerable number of pilgrims, among them "respectable females" in the words of Commander Haines.[47] For Company officials the perceived inability to protect Indian Muslims on route to the Hajj would at the very least result in the loss of prestige among their Muslim subjects. At worst, it could be construed as a sign of weakness. Either was, of course, unacceptable.

As we have seen, the Chief Secretary in Bombay had already deemed that strong action would need to be taken. In December 1837 Haines was dispatched from Bombay with orders to seek compensation for the plundering of the *Daria Dawlat*. The Chief Secretary was unequivocal in his belief that due to the "insults . . . offered to the British flag by the Sultan of Aden," the port should be seized for use as a coaling station and to insure security in the region. Lord Auckland, the Governor-General of India in Calcutta, was rather more cautious, indicating that outright seizure was to be a last resort. Instead, Haines should first seek "some amicable arrangement . . . for the occupation of this port as a depot for coals and harbour for shelter," as adequate compensation for the outrage committed against the Nawab's ship. If this could not be achieved, then "further measures may be considered."[48]

Imperial historians such as Gordon Waterfield and R. J. Gavin examine the protracted negotiations that followed between Haines and Sultan Muhsin bin Fadhil al-Abdali of Lahij in great detail. In sum, when the former arrived in Aden aboard the sloop-of-war Coote in early 1838, he very quickly seemed to arrive at an agreement with the Abdali Sultan that would allow for dual control of the port. Sultan Muhsin wished, in essence, to enter into a treaty arrangement with the British along the line of various Indian "Native Princes." In exchange for an offensive and defensive treaty and an annual subsidy, he offered to allow the Company to establish a factory and to garrison British troops in the port. Haines countered with an offer that ceded control of the port to the Company in exchange for an annual subsidy, terms to which the Sultan appeared to agree in late January.[49] Unfortunately, from this point forward the negotiations spiraled into what Gavin refers to as "a morass of intrigue and counter-intrigue," that would last through the year. Both sides consistently acted with suspicion and in bad faith. By December the exasperated government in Bombay authorized taking Aden by force.[50] Haines used the naval and land forces sent to him by Bombay to take the port by storm, expelling those of the Abdali sultan on January 19, 1839.

Military outpost or commercial emporium?

While the East India Company now controlled one of the best harbor's in western Arabia, they also found themselves in possession of a town that was little more than a ruin. The area fronting the harbor during its medieval and early modern hay day was a prosperous port of well-built merchant houses and bazaars, fine mosques, Sufi hostels and tombs. Now it was little more than a rubble-strewn debris field.[51]

The town was home to only 800 to 1,200 inhabitants many of whom—Indian merchants and Somali sailors and stock handlers in particular—were mostly seasonal residents. The better-off merchants, members of the Aydarus family and wealthier elements of the Jewish community lived in well-built, if somewhat dilapidated, stone houses on one end of the plain while the less well-off lived in "kutcha" houses made of reed mats.[52] In the area known as Hawqat Bay there was also a small settlement of fisherfolk. At the time of occupation, there still existed three large mosques. The Aydarus shrine, the Masjid al-Suq (the Market Mosque) and the Masjid al-Jama'a (Friday communal mosque). According to European observers, however, only the first two were in regular use.[53]

In addition to the town's Muslim majority, Aden was also home to a significant Jewish community along with a population of non-Muslim Indian merchants known generically as Banians. Both groups also maintained their own places of worship. J. R. Wellsted, an officer from the survey ship *Palinurus*, who visited the port in 1835, noted that within the Jewish quarter there was "a small synagogue and two schools, in which their children are instructed in reading, writing and a knowledge of the Hebrew language."[54] The Hindu merchants maintained a shrine a short distance from the main town in the Khusaf valley. Dedicated to the goddess Huiglaj,[55] the shrine's precincts consisted of a sacred well along with a small alter beneath a rock outcrop where a "representation of the deity" was painted with "two patches of red paint with a few spots to denote the eyes, nose and mouth, laid on the rock itself." The icon, according to the American merchant John Studdy Leigh, who visited Aden literally within days of the start of the occupation, was "protected by a gallery, accessible by a trapdoor, secured with a padlock."[56]

On the whole, the local community did not appear displeased with the change in regime. While there is little record of how the majority of Aden's inhabitants reacted to the Company's arrival, the town's small, diverse group of elites wasted little time in seeking to accommodate themselves to the new political and economic realities. Sayyid Zayn b. Alawi, the head of the Aydarus family and effective leader of Aden's Muslim community, for instance, quickly made his peace with the Company. In early February, he sent a letter on behalf of himself and his sons to Bombay, declaring the family's loyalty and desire to be afforded protection under the British flag. Not coincidentally, he also took the opportunity to remind the Company of certain traditional privileges the family enjoyed with regard to the port's customs revenue and hoped that these would continue to be honored.[57] In April, when Haines returned to Bombay briefly for medical leave, six prominent Banian merchants wrote to the Governor of Bombay praising the Political Agent and the Company's ability to "install tranquility to the town," and praying for the former's safe return[58]—while members of the Ben Moshe family, a leading element of the Jewish community, seem to have wasted no time in entering Company service.[59]

The Company's intention to develop Aden as a commercial entrepôt became evident soon after the start of the occupation. In a letter dated March 6, 1839, the Bombay Government noted that the site chosen by Major Baillie, the garrison commander, for the barracks and officers' quarters seemed "to occupy the most convenient space for commercial purposes ... A most important consideration with regard to Aden being its commercial advantages, these must have primary consideration in management of the town and the public buildings and Captain Haines should be instructed to be careful that in lining out the town and choosing the sites for publich [sic] buildings this [commercial activity] be kept distinctly in view and strictly attended to."[60] Aden, however as we have seen, while having an excellent harbor was a commercial center of at best minor significance. As a result, it was incumbent on the newly appointed Political Agent[61] to attract new merchants willing to set up shop in the British Settlement. This was unfortunately a task that was more easily imagined than accomplished. There existed, in fact, two major impediments to attracting new settlers to Aden. One was the question of the Settlement's very security in the face of continuing hostility on the part of local Arab tribes. The other centered on the role of the army and what can only be described as their increasingly fractious relationship with the merchants of the bazaar.

Defending the perimeter: Aden under assault

Although the forces of Sultan Muhsin withdrew quickly following the British assault in January, this did not mean the end of hostilities between the Company and the Abdali ruler. During the first eighteen months of occupation, the British settlement was subjected to major attacks on three separate occasions (November 11, 1839; May 21, 1840; and July 5,1840).[62] Each of these were night-time raids that employed several thousand tribesmen armed primarily with matchlocks.[63] As the various military reports indicate, these were well planned and skillfully executed attacks. Rather than immediate frontal assaults, the Abdali forces, along with allies drawn from the powerful Fadhli tribe, deftly outflanked the Company sepoys by advancing along the exposed and lightly defended beachfront. The attackers only engaged the main fortification known as "the Turkish wall" once their comrades had managed to work their way behind the defending lines, pouring shot into them from the hills behind. During the May 1840 attack, the Sultan's troops even managed to break through the British defenses and into the officer's lines. A large number of tents were burned and officers' baggage was pillaged. The raiders were only dislodged when gun lascars swiveled their artillery pieces around and laid down a withering barrage of grape and shot into their own compound.[64]

The Abdali attacks were all repelled through the Company's superior firepower. These large-scale raids, however, were only part of a larger campaign designed to sow unease—and paranoia—throughout the Settlement. Sepoys and officers who ventured outside the defenses were commonly subjected to sniper fire from the nearby hills. Groups and individuals traveling to and from Aden by land were frequently plundered, while the Abdali Sultan initiated an irregular and capricious blockade of the town from the interior.[65] To add to the unease, on several occasions Abdali confederates were caught attempting to smuggle men and weapons into the Settlement perimeter with supply caravans (when they were getting through) in an apparent attempt to spread chaos within the town during the major assaults. In one instance, men posing as caravaneers attempted to rush the main gate in broad daylight in the hope of catching the defenders by surprise.[66]

Such a climate, needless to say, fostered a feeling of unease among the civilian population of Aden. In the run-up to the first attack in 1839, Haines noted that "within the last few days every merchant and labourer in the place have buried their property and the women their ornaments." So great was the state of anxiety that "few among them close their eyes at night," and many among the town's denizens had begun sleeping in the precincts of the Aydarus Mosque, returning to their homes and shops only in the mornings when fear of an imminent attack had lessened.[67]

Haines and the Company countered the Abdali threat by strengthening Aden's outer defenses and reinforcing the garrison with additional troops from Bombay.[68] However, while men of the 10th Bombay Native Infantry and the European Regiment secured Aden against outside attack, they were also a source of tension among the civil population.

The men of the 10th and 24th Bombay Native Infantry, who first garrisoned Aden were a rough and largely unlettered lot. Thus, it is of little surprise that they soon ruffled the religious sensibilities of the population. In the earliest days following the occupation, the 24th billeted some of its men, unthinkingly, in the precincts of the disused Masjid al-Jama'a or Friday mosque. This was bad enough, however, according to the American sailor John Leigh, some of the regiment's Hindu sepoys looted wood from tombs in an adjacent mosque for their cooking fires.[69] The men of the garrison, however, did not limit themselves to offending the religious sensibilities of Muslims.

One morning in late March 1840, two Gujarati merchants, along with a local priest, were performing a ritual at the shrine of Huiglaj Devi described above. As they were completing their prayers two soldiers from the 10th NI arrived with a goat, which they began to prepare for sacrifice. The priest hastily interrupted his ritual to explain to the men that blood sacrifices were not appropriate within Huiglaj Devi's sanctuary. The soldiers acknowledged this, thanked the priest and proceeded to go outside and sacrifice the goat next to the shrine's well. The entire Gujarati merchant community was outraged by what they viewed as a sacrilege and threatened to leave the Settlement if the offenders were not punished.[70]

The new garrison commander, Lt. Col. Capon,[71] responded to the complaint by convening an inquiry made up of senior "native" officers, including the Subhedar-Major, the highest-ranking non-European officer in the contingent. The court found that the men had acted incorrectly but without malice. As such, they should not be punished, although orders were issued to the regiments that a sepoy of low caste should not approach "a temple or sacred place nearer than 5 paces."[72] From the standpoint of military bureaucracy this may have seemed satisfactory; to the Banian community it was not. While they did not follow through on their threat to leave Aden it contributed to a continuing sense of animosity toward the soldiers of the garrison.

Bazaar troubles

Tensions between Aden's civilian population and the garrison, however, were not caused solely by the inadvisable actions of a few soldiers. Problems were also precipitated from the very top of the garrison's command structure: Lt. Col. Capon the expedition's commanding officer.

With the establishment of a large garrison, Aden's commercial community experienced a retail boom. A bazaar quickly sprang up near the military cantonment with small shops vying for the custom of the Company's soldiers and camp followers. The market, as it emerged, was a ramshackle affair of temporary buildings made of reed and mat connected by "an intricate passage covered overhead with mats." The result was a dark maze "wide enough for only two persons to walk abreast."[73] Despite its rather humble appearance, Haines noted, soon one could find all the goods of India and Arabia for sale there.[74] Of course, one could also find the less wholesome pleasures of soldiers and camp-followers everywhere: illicit alcohol, bang and opium, gambling dens and *nautch* girls.

Capon was an officer of thirty years' experience in India who took command of the garrison from Baillie in the autumn of 1839.[75] As such, he was no stranger to the institution of the cantonment bazaar that was a common feature of camp life in the Indian army.[76] This was not, in and of itself, a problem. However, when he relieved Baillie he found a state of barely controlled licentiousness in which the bazaar was only lightly patrolled by a single sepoy acting as a *chowkidar* (essentially a watchman). Soldiers and camp followers came and went as they pleased, and more troubling, public intoxication among the men of the garrison was a growing problem. Men had even been found drunk while on duty at the outer defenses.[77] Such a state of affairs was clearly unacceptable. However, since it was the only commercial district in the Settlement it was impractical to place it off limits to the members of the garrison. Instead, Capon argued that the "mean looking, confused heap of huts called the Basar [*sic*]" should be placed under military jurisdiction and "put into an orderly shape."[78]

In order to exert greater control, the colonel appointed a Bazaar Master from among the regimental officers, along with a Bazaar Guard (consisting of a havildar, a rank equivalent to serjeant, and six sepoys). The Guard began to regularly patrol the alleyways of the market along with the new civil police in an effort to crack down on the open gambling common in the many coffee houses and other shops. Soon, however, following reports of continued drinking among on-duty soldiers, Capon ordered the Bazaar Master to execute a series of raids on various establishments purported to be operating unlicensed stills and selling illegal liquor.[79] The searches found little, other than a small quantity of legal liquor in a Parsi's shop.[80] What Capon's actions did turn up was a legion of complaints from angry and offended merchants.

Following another series of surprise sweeps in February 1840, Haines received a volley of protests from the Bazaar. Umar Saleh, an elderly coffee-house proprietor, swore out a complaint before the Qadi stating, "Captain Stiles [the Bazaar Master], the Chowkidar, red coated sepoys and Arab peons came forcibly into my place and examined everywhere. They went into my Muksom [*sic*] where I sleep and turned over everything to look for liquor and then went into the coffeeshop and [did] the same." Saleh ben Usbac charged, "Stiles Sahib and Ali Chowdry [the *chowkidar*] with soldiers came and entered my coffee shop. Captain Stiles waited in the shop, but Shaikh Ali entered my house among my wife and others and searched among them." For both men, the searches were not just violations of their privacy but moral affronts to their honor as Muslims. Umar Saleh declared that he was both "an old and respectable man," who had "never known liquor," or sold it. Spirits, he and Aden's Qadi reminded the authorities, were forbidden to Muslims and "whoever drinks it, sells it [or] touches it is bad." Saleh ben Usbac similarly declared, "I am an Arab, I neither drink or sell it nor do our women." For good measure, he added, "They had no shame, but went among my women and found nothing."[81] The heavy-handed methods of the Bazaar Guard also spilled over into the streets as Gorleb bin Mawger bin Hamed complained directly to the Political Agent that "while in the Bazzar [sic] and standing and talking by Ibrahim the Jew's shop on the evening of [February] the 15th, a sepoy came with his musket and struck me with his fist and when turning around to speak [to him] he lifted up his musket," apparently intending to menace the bystander.[82]

Capon's overzealousness can be attributed, in large part, to an ongoing power struggle with Haines over the administration of the possession. Capon argued that the entire Settlement constituted a single military cantonment and, as such, was under his authority. The searches in the Bazaar were a futile and ill-advised attempt to exert that authority and undermine the civil power represented by Haines. In the end, the government in Bombay supported the Political Agent's contention that all of the commercial life of Aden fell under civil administration and censured Capon for his heavy-handed overreach.[83] However, such blunders by the military did little to reassure an already nervous population of a future in Aden.

The Tihama's misfortunes are Aden's gain

Despite these problems, Aden continued to grow, attracting merchants, laborers and others who would become part of a prosperous commercial economy. Within nine months of the British occupation, the port's population more than doubled to nearly 3,000 people exclusive of the garrison.[84] The primary reason for this was that the inconveniences of life in Aden—night-time raids by Arab tribesmen, harassment by the military authorities—were relatively minor compared to elsewhere in the region, where life could be a good deal more precarious.

South Asian merchants were to be found throughout the western Indian Ocean. Most tended to cluster around the busiest ports such as Massawa on the African coast of the Red Sea, Jiddah in the Hijaz, the various Tihama anchorages such as Mukha and Hodeida as well as Mukalla and Shihr on the southern end of the peninsula. However, Indian traders were ubiquitous. During his tour surveying Aden's various feeder ports in 1845, Haines' assistant, Lt. Charles J. Cruttendon noted that when he sailed over two miles up a creek along the southern coast of the Arabian Peninsula to a remote port known as Bunder Khor, he was met by a large crowd of Arabs as well as "the never failing Banian."[85] The goods traded tended to run the gamut from bulk commodities to luxury goods. The *Daria Dawlat*, for instance, was laden primarily with rice, sugar and piece goods as well as more valuable ginger, pepper and coconut oil bound for the Hijaz. The agent, Sayyid Nur al-Dın, also shipped a box of high-end piece goods along with a box of attar of Roses worth a stunning 1,500 Rs. Sayyid Tipu, for his part, listed Chinese satins and porcelain, copper ware, bottles of lavender, jewelry and several jars of preserved ginger worth more than 3,000 M.T. Thallers as goods lost on the voyage.[86]

While Indian commerce was clearly lucrative, it was fraught with risk. The apparent conspiracy and malfeasance involved in the case of the *Daria Dawlat* seems exceptional. Merchants in the region, however, regularly faced other threats and types of insecurity. Piracy, shipwreck, or plunder by Bedouin tribesmen were among the accepted risks of trading in the Red Sea. In addition, the capricious demands of local rulers and representatives of various political authorities—that at times seem to border on extortion—were by and large viewed as the cost of doing business. There was a point, however, at which growing political instability and violence in the major ports of the Red Sea and Southern Arabia emerged as decisive issues that drew many to the comparative safety and predictability of Aden.

On the eve of the Company's occupation of Aden, the region's major commercial hubs—Jiddah, Mukha, Hodeida and Massawa—were controlled by the Egyptian ruler Mehmet Ali. The Pasha's Red Sea Empire, however, was on the verge of unraveling. Facing setbacks due to European opposition in the Mediterranean, Egypt was forced to abandon the territories it had gained at Ottoman expense in Syria and Anatolia. This retrenchment also meant withdrawal from its bases on both shores of the Red Sea. Jiddah and Massawa fell back under Ottoman control.[87] Mukha, along with Hodeida, however, became pawns in an emerging civil war in Yemen between the Zaydi Imam, al-Hadi Muhammad[88] and Sharif Husayn ibn Ali Haydar a sayyid of the Abu Arish, traditional rivals of the Imams in northern Yemen.[89]

British-protected merchants experienced all manner of irregularities at the hands of Ottoman officials in Massawa and Jiddah. These generally took the shape of predatory customs practices and forced loans (referred to locally as *sulfa* or *qurdah*—both Arabic terms for cash loans) to meet the financial obligations of the Turkish administration. In 1842, for instance, an Indian merchant at Jiddah, Sayyid Abdullah bin Hashim, was subjected to a surprise customs inspection and in the process a certain amount of his "private" goods were confiscated. While the Company ship's report on this matter is vague, it was implied that in order to have his goods returned, he was forced to pay a bribe to the governor in addition to the customs duty. In Massawa, the same year, a grieving son was forced to pay a "capitulation tax" in the amount of 350 M.T. Thallers in order to retrieve his deceased father's trade goods from the customs house. In both places, merchants frequently paid nearly 20 percent duty on goods that should have been charged three. In a meeting between Lt. Christopher of the Company ship *Constance* and the Ottoman Pasha the latter explained that this was due to the fact that the holy cities of Mecca and Medina were supported by the customs dues of Jiddah and Massawa was its subsidiary.[90] "The Pasha," Christopher wrote, "dwelt on these subjects and appealed to several affluent Mohammadan merchants, natives of India, who happened to be in the *diwan*, who one and all declared they . . . were willing to assist the Pasha according to the ancient customs." However, Christopher also noted that "these very men privately were earnest in their complaint to me of the Pasha's extortions and the distress of trade."[91]

Ottoman demands appear to have been an annoyance for Indian merchants rather than a threat to their livelihoods. Christopher noted that most believed the presence of Company vessels along with the occasional "firm but friendly remonstrance," would be sufficient to keep Ottoman demands at an acceptable level.[92] The situation in the Tihama, however, ultimately proved to be perilous not only to their capital but also to life and limb. It was this instability that would be Aden's windfall.

In March 1840, the Egyptian governor of Mukha received a communication from Ibrahim Pasha, son of Mehmet Ali and commander of Egyptian forces in Yemen, instructing him to seize enough local commercial vessels to accommodate an immediate withdrawal of his men from Mukha; by May the Egyptians were gone.[93] The sudden Egyptian evacuation from the Tihama left Yemen's Red Sea coast in a power vacuum. For reasons that are not entirely clear, the Egyptians transferred control of the Tihama ports (Mukha as well as Hodeida and al-Luhayya) to Sharif Husayn bin Ali Haydar, former secretary to Muhammad Amin Bey late Governor of Mukha.[94] Sharif Husayn's kin, the Abu Arish sayyids, and the Imams of Sana'a had been political rivals since the early nineteenth century. As a result, successive ruling Imams unsurprisingly viewed this as an attempt to check their own re-emerging power in the wake of the Egyptian withdrawal. The effect was nearly a decade of warfare between Sharif Husayn, the Imams and a continuously shifting set of alliances.[95]

Initially, although hostile to the Company presence in Aden and Mukha,[96] Sharif Husayn appeared content to allow Indian merchants to continue trading in his territory. Although the Sharif engaged in many of the same fiscal practices of his Ottoman contemporaries (particularly, the extraction of cash advances from merchants that would be repaid in theory through future deductions from customs duties) many Indian merchants seemed happy to continue to base their commercial operations out of Mukha. As a result, Mukha continued to function as a prosperous port through most of the 1840s.[97] This changed precipitously in 1848 when the Imam in Sana'a (al-Mutawakil Muhammad bin Yahya, 1845–9) managed to dislodge the Sharif from most of his coastal possessions. Imprisoned briefly by the Imam, Sharif Husayn managed to ransom himself and raise a force that he used to besiege Mukha and threaten Hodeida.[98] It is not clear why this particular round of fighting was perceived as any worse than any of the others that had characterized life in the Tihama during the 1840s. However, as Haines noted when visiting the ports in April 1848, the Sharif's offensive created a "sudden panic."[99] Upon his arrival he discovered that a group of Indian Muslim merchants had placed the majority of their goods "afloat" off shore using "native boats" and recently arrived dhows as a security against any potential looting if the town were taken. Haines soon learned that merchants in Hodeida had taken the same precautions despite the fact that traders in both places protested that they would weather the storm. Others were less optimistic, and the three largest Banian firms in Mukha petitioned Haines to evacuate them and their property to Aden.[100]

The professed optimism of the Indian Muslim traders notwithstanding, it was the Banian merchants who proved prescient. As Haines related, by May the bulk of Mukha's population decided to vote with their feet. "Mukha," he wrote, "is now a deserted town with empty houses, the only articles within the wall being commissariat supplies of rice, dates ghee, etc., for the garrison." Indeed, he noted, "all trade is at an end, the poor of the town have retreated to Namaan about 8 miles south of Mukha and the families are living on the beach under whatever shelter from the sun they can temporarily erect. While the monied and influential men have proceeded to Judde [*sic*] or reached Aden with their goods and chattel."[101]

The storm did, in fact, pass. The Mukha garrison held on until relieved and Hodeida was never attacked. However, this moment seems to have been a watershed. While the crisis was resolved and the Imam retained control of Mukha with Ottoman support, Aden now emerged as the preferred port of Indian merchant houses. With the Settlement secured from attack, and a steady influx of people from the surrounding region, Aden's future was assured. It was from this point that we see Muslims from across the western Indian Ocean put down roots and begin to coalesce into a community.

3
Claims to Community: Mosques, Cemeteries and the Universe

By the late 1840s the outside threats to Aden had receded and the Red Sea itself was increasingly secure. For the Company this meant a booming economy and a growing port of trade. For Muslims, too, it meant economic prosperity but also a burgeoning community where individuals were no longer mainly seasonal inhabitants but permanent residents. The remainder of this book is devoted to how individuals drawn together from across Britain's Indian Ocean Empire used Muslim institutions and the discursive tradition to solidify a sense of community. Subsequent chapters look at law, theology and spirit possession as avenues that individuals utilized to lay claim to belonging within the community.[1] The present chapter continues the discussion of Aden's development through the early twentieth century, but with a particular focus on the organization of Muslim sacred space. At the heart of this lay very visible physical spaces, most notably mosques and tombs. Equally important, however, were attachments to these as conduits to unseen metaphysical space that constituted an equally important element in the construction of belonging.

The town grew quickly with the advent of British occupation. Plots were purchased, houses, go-downs and coal bunkers were built. By the 1880s the Settlement constituted four main districts. Crater continued to be Aden's heart—home to the Residency, the courts, the two main bazaars, as well as the wealthier non-European residents. It was also home to the *Chukla* and *Tawilah*, the official and unofficial red-light districts, respectively, as well as a fisherman's village that fronted the bay. In addition, the previously autonomous villages of Ma'alla and Tawahi, home to those who toiled in the port, were quickly incorporated into the Settlement. As Aden became increasingly crowded, the outlying village of Shaykh Uthman was purchased from the Sultan of Lahij in 1881 to serve as a planned suburb but also because there were a large number of wells located there that could supply the main town with water.[2]

Despite the great influx of people, the development of neighborhoods with permanent dwellings was slow. According to a Company surgeon, this was because the "most respectable merchants" hesitated to invest too heavily in property fearing the Company's commitment to Aden was only temporary.[3] Ultimately, these "more respectable" inhabitants built new stone houses in places such as the Aydarus Valley or refurbished older ones in the original town center. These ranged from relatively substantial homes among the wealthiest to more modest affairs constructed by the moderately successful, consisting of two or three rooms and an open courtyard.[4]

Conversely, many among the "laboring classes" hoped to remain in Aden only long enough to save money for a particular purpose back home, such as marriage or increasing their herds. As such, they sought to live as cheaply as possible. The majority of the population—when living under cover at all—inhabited reed and sedge huts that were both well adapted to the climate and cheap.[5] Frequently, laborers would club together, eight or ten men to a dwelling, in order to rent one of these *kutcha* houses, taking their meals in one of the numerous eating houses or *mukhbaza*s (Ar. Lit. bakery).[6] Indeed, many laborers through the nineteenth century do not seem to have enjoyed fixed abodes at all. It was not uncommon, according to multiple accounts, for those of the most modest means to sleep either on the beaches near the port or to doss down at night in one of the numerous tea or coffee houses.[7] As the American traveler Joseph Osgood noted, many Somali laborers at the end of the day simply dug holes on the beach, covering themselves with sand until only their heads were exposed with "but a blanket of atmosphere" for a cover.[8]

While permanent domestic residences may have been slow to develop in Aden, other manifestations of Adeni civil society emerged more rapidly: mosques, tombs and cemeteries. As noted in the previous chapter, at the time of the occupation, Aden had only two functioning mosques and while there was a vast cemetery it was largely derelict and unused. This seemingly moribund sacred landscape is one that would change rapidly over the first decades of settlement.

Tombs, mosques and manifestations of belonging

As the Sepoys, led by Major T. Bailie, moved to secure Aden and raise the flag over the Sultan's residence on the morning of January 19, 1839, they noticed a "flag of truce" appear over the tomb of Sayyid Abu Bakr Aydarus. The Major and a squad of men hurried to the complex where they were met by a small delegation led by Sayyid Zayn bin Alawi al-Aydarus—the tomb's guardian—who offered Aden's formal surrender. In his report, Bailie wrote that "all the inhabitants," of the port had sought refuge in the mosque compound. This included not just the town's Muslim non-combatants but also the large Jewish community and the fifty or so Hindu merchants present when the assault began.[9]

The refuge of Aden's population in the town's most important shrine is glossed over—or even ignored—in most accounts.[10] However, it is a snapshot that reveals two central facts. First, it demonstrates the rather diverse nature of Aden even during a period in which it was at its lowest ebb. Second, it highlights the centrality of Muslim religious institutions (in this case a mosque-tomb complex) in the public life of Aden. Tensions had been rising between the Company representative, S. B. Haines, and the Abdali Sultan for weeks, so when the attack came it was hardly a surprise. When the bombardment began, however, the people of Aden did not seek refuge around the house of the Abdali governor who, in fact, had already decamped rather unceremoniously, nor did they try to flee the city for the inhospitable interior. Instead, Muslim, Jew and Hindu sought out a Friend of God—Abu Bakr al-Aydarus—and his descendants to protect them from the deluge. Thus, it should come as little surprise that Muslim sacred spaces quickly emerged as important sites for the Muslim community in colonial Aden.

Saint veneration—a growth industry

Sufism, and what is often referred to as the "cult of the saints,"[11] was an important element in the public spiritual sphere of Aden from before the beginning of the British occupation. Arabic sources such as Ibn al-Mujawir's *Tarikh al-mustabsir* and Abu Makhrama's *Tarikh thaghr adan* sketch an image of Medieval and Early Modern Aden as not only a bustling commercial entrepôt, but a city of numerous mosques, madrasas and tombs of venerated saints (Ar. sing. *wali*, pl. *awliya'*; literally "Friend of God"). The more recent Adeni historian, Hamza Luqman—drawing mostly on Abu Makhrama—lists fourteen prominent mosques in historical Aden with attendant madrasas, or at least informal lesson circles, supported by copious *waqf* properties (pious endowments), at least some of which had associated tombs dating to the Medieval period.[12]

By the time of the British occupation, there was little left of this grand medieval port and center of Islamic learning. European travelers during the first half of the nineteenth century reported that the town consisted of fewer than 100 stone houses and virtually all of the mosques and tombs described by Abu Makhrama lay in ruins. There were, in fact, only two functioning mosques in Aden proper, the Aydarus and what was known as the Market Mosque.[13] However, it was still a community where the Faith remained important enough for residents to complain when occupying forces pulled down part of one derelict mosque to make way for a field hospital and use another as a temporary barracks,[14] and important enough for S. B. Haines to allow the *ziyara* (Ar. pl. *ziyarat*, visitation, but literally a festival celebrating the death anniversary of saint) of Sayyid Aydarus to be held as usual only a month or so after the start of the occupation. According to Company documentation, despite the political uncertainty the event drew thousands of faithful from the surrounding districts.[15]

As the town flourished through the nineteenth century saint veneration and Sufism constituted the primary expression of popular spirituality and communal solidarity. In 1839, Haines and others reported that there were only two formal *ziyara*s in or around the Settlement: Sayyid Aydarus, mentioned above, and the Shaykh Uthman Urs,[16] whose shrine was located in the village of the same name on the mainland near what would ultimately become the border with the Sultanate of Lahij. But as the population of Aden began to rapidly expand there was a proliferation of tombs and accompanying festivals. By 1877 F. M. Hunter recorded the existence of fourteen annual *ziyarat* within the boundaries of the Aden Settlement.[17]

Many of these were efforts to revive memories of sometimes forgotten, or at least neglected, local holy men. So, for instance, Ismail Habib—a wealthy Memon[18] merchant from Bombay—spent a lakh[19] of rupees to rebuild the Abu Bakr Aydarus Mosque in 1859. Then, fifteen years later, he spent a similar amount to re-establish the mosque of Shaykh al-Hakam ibn Abban, grandson of the third caliph, Uthman ibn Affan, and revive the *wali*'s long-defunct *ziyara* held during the Muslim month of Shabaan.[20] In 1871, Muhammad Kuvar another, apparently, South Asian resident erected a mosque devoted to the memory of Shaykh Salim ibn Muhammad al-Iraqi (d. 1236) sponsoring a *ziyara* for him annually during the month of Rajab. While in 1863, Hunter tells us, the Indian Memon community as a whole rebuilt the mosque and tomb of Jawhar ibn Abdullah (d. 1228) who, according to both Abu Makhrama and Zabidi, was a former slave and successful cloth merchant renowned for his piety and uprightness.[21]

Others were new imports. So, Muhammad Hasan al-Misri, who may well have been one of the many Egyptians who gravitated to Aden as Muhammad Ali's Red Sea Empire began to contract, constructed a new mosque named for Shaykh Ahmad ibn Alwan—who was actually buried near Ta'iz—in 1847 and began sponsoring a *ziyara* each year during Shaaban (although his actual *urs* near Ta'iz was celebrated in Rabi'a al-Awal).[22] New arrivals from Mukha brought with them the *ziyara* of a certain Shykh al-Haradee, celebrated during Rajab.[23] Both these shaykhs were part of a particular category of saint festival, namely *ziyarat* that emerged independent of a particular tomb or mosque but that, again, were aimed at celebrating the memory of a distinguished Muslim *'alim*. Others in this group included Shaykh Alawi bin Muhammad Aydarus, Abdul Latif al-Iraqi and Ali bin Muhammad al-Iraqi.[24]

The proliferation of mosque and tomb building, as well as the subsidizing of *ziyarat* themselves, were certainly pious acts undertaken out of a sense of religious zeal. But, at the same time, the veritable explosion of saints' festivals in Aden during this period appears to represent one way relatively recent arrivals in Aden may lay spiritual claim to their new home. On the one hand, those with the means to endow the renovation of a mosque/tomb or subsidize a festival provided "new Adenis" (to coin a phrase) with a very physical manifestation of their connection. However, such events also provided those of lesser means the opportunity to act as part of a wider community and construct their own personal connections to the local spiritual sphere.

For many, in the nineteenth century, the demonstration of such connections could be quite modest. Some may offer prayers and leave flowers at a tomb while others—and Hunter is at pains to note that this included both men and women—would gather and perform *dhikr* late into the night.[25] For the more casually pious there was, of course, the rather carnival-like atmosphere surrounding each tomb's *ziyara* where you might find vendors selling coffee, sweetmeats and toys as well as various groups of dancers whose performances ranged from the sacred to the profane.[26] While we can find evidence of the importance of saint veneration among new Adenis in the nineteenth century the descriptions are often extremely brief and, as a result, we learn a great deal less about *ziyarat* as lived experience. Fortunately, the data for the twentieth century becomes much more rich and textured and we are able to begin to see how the festivals fit into the fabric of local society.

While the daily life of tombs might be overseen by members of the *'ulama'*, by at least 1900, they were administered by committees of well-to-do individuals who oversaw the upkeep and maintenance of shrines and mosques but most importantly organized events surrounding the annual *ziyarat*. Festivals themselves generally attracted a large cross-section of Aden's Muslim community. A few, such as the *ziyarat* of Shaykh Rihan and Shaykh Ishaq, had particularly narrow constituencies (local fisherman and Somali residents respectively). Most, however, were events with much broader appeal. The *ziyara* of Sayyid Abu Bakr Aydarus was certainly the city's most important local annual religious event. In addition to involving most of the town's inhabitants, the festival attracted hundreds of people from the near and distant Yemeni interior as well as large numbers of pilgrims from the nearby Somali and Eritrean coasts of East Africa. However, other saints were the focus of at least equally broad-based veneration. The *ziyara* of Shaykh Abban, whose tomb was administered by Indian Memon Muslims, was organized and financed by some of the Settlement's leading Arab families. Similarly, adherents of Shaykh Ahmad al-Iraqi frequently referred to his tomb using the South Asian Persianate word *dargah* rather than the more usual Arabic *qabr*, suggesting a serious Indian following.[27]

The ceremonies surrounding *ziyara*s from the start of the twentieth century, included special prayers, recitations from the Qur'an and stories detailing the pious deeds of the venerated, culminating in a formal procession to the tomb for the installation of a new *kiswa* (an embroidered shroud used to cover the tomb). Individuals might seek the intercession of the saint via *tawassul*, but often also sought advice and spiritual guidance from the deceased *wali*'s caretakers and descendants during the festivities. Muhammad Ali Luqman's fictional hero Sa'id from the novella of the same name published in the late 1930s, in fact, undertook a pilgrimage precisely for this kind of spiritual edification as he was about to leave Aden to fight for the Ottomans in the Balkans.

> Sa'id visited the garden of Hasan Ali then [went] to the *ziyara* at the tomb of Sayyid Hashim al-Bahr calling upon him for beneficence and favor. The followers of the saint saw him and asked him to drink coffee [with them]. After that, Sa'id and the followers went to [visit] the Sharifa Aliya, sister of Sayyid Hashim, who had known him since his fingernails were soft [that is, since he was an infant] . . . she was a pure pearl . . . And Sa'id was in awe of this pious *waliya*. She gave Sa'id advice [regarding his travels] and he took her hand and asked from her [blessing].[28]

In addition to these religious observances, however, most festivals were accompanied by a carnival-like atmosphere with numerous diversions for the pious, ranging from the innocent to the risqué. At a typical *ziyara* of the 1920s one would find innocuous entertainments, such as rides, puppet shows, street magicians and games of skill and chance, such as ring toss, the lucky dip and shooting galleries. In addition to such wholesome amusements one could also pay to dance with Akhdam[29] girls wearing "semi-transparent clothes . . . and making indecent gestures," watch

Sufis perform *"majdhib"* (from the Arabic *jadhaba* meaning entranced) in which practitioners would cut themselves with daggers while twirling in a trance, or search out illicit alcohol and gambling.[30]

The popularity of *ziyarat* continued through the nineteenth century and into the twentieth. By the 1920s Aden boasted more than a dozen annual saints' festivals centered on tombs dotted throughout the settlement. Curiously, it should be noted, these were not the same dozen or so *ziyarat* recorded by Hunter forty years earlier. In fact, only about half of the saints' festivals regularly held in Aden from 1910 to 1930 bear names that can be traced to those on Hunter's list. So, for instance the *ziyarat* of Aydarus and Alawi Aydarus, Shaykhs Uthman, Jawhar, Abban and Ahmad al-Iraqi were still not only being held but were massive events on the sacred/social calendar. But the festivals venerating the likes of Salim Muhammad al-Iraqi, Husayn bin Siddiq, al-Haradee and others seem to disappear. The additions to the local calendar of saints were those with particular resonance with the contemporary community. The fisherman of Holkat held a brief one-day remembrance of Shaykh Rihan ibn Abdullah, a saintly former slave of Ethiopian origin whose *ziyara* can be dated originally to the sixteenth century,[31] while particular Somali clans held an annual *ziyara* to commemorate their eponymous clan founder Shaykh Ishaaq. However, we also see the emergence of local holy men during this period with broad appeal and who sprung directly from the contemporary community. The most prominent of these was Hashim al-Bahr—mentioned above—whose image was very much at odds with the erudite objects of veneration elsewhere in the city.

Hashim al-Bahr (d. 1894) was a resident of Crater who earned his livelihood as a porter in the employ of one of the Settlement's wealthiest merchants. The Lebanese-American traveler Amin Rihani provides the only known detailed account of the *wali*. The image he painted of Hashim al-Bahr was something less than a sober religious scholar. When not carrying loads around the Crater, Rihani wrote, al-Bahr spent his mornings napping in the doorway of his employer and his afternoons chewing qat.[32] He was, however, hardly a lay about. Scrupulous in his daily prayers, the *wali* would disappear for long stretches into the surrounding hills where he lived a life of prayer and fasting. As his reputation for asceticism grew, he was increasingly sought out, especially by women, who "unveiled their hearts" to the Shaykh for "council and consolation."[33] With the help of his employer he eventually bought a plot of land in Shaykh Uthman upon which he constructed a mosque that would also, ultimately, house his tomb. When he died in 1894, the shrine quickly became the site of Aden's newest *ziyara* held each year during the month of dhu al-hijja.[34]

The story of Hashim al-Bahr is important because it portrays holy men and saint veneration as part of a living tradition. Not only did the site of his grave quickly become an object of popular veneration, but association with the *wali* while he was alive could be turned in to social, as well as spiritual, capital. Amin Rihani recounts an interview with Hashim al-Bahr's former employer, the merchant who helped him purchase the land for the mosque (who Rihani, unfortunately does not name). He told Rihani proudly that the Shaykh "spoke to me about a mosque in Sheikh Othman which he ... wanted to build. Of a certainty, I said in my heart, he is crazy. But he continued to talk about the mosque even in his hours of sanity. And one morning, I swear, billahi! Hashim-Bahr came to me with a bag of money, paper, silver and gold and asked me to purchase the plot."[35] For the merchant, this was more than brokering a small real-estate deal for a minor employee, it was about his own brush with sanctity.

This method of financing both tomb construction and maintenance in Aden was hardly unusual. While some tombs may be associated with particular Sufi orders others were maintained by local followers with only loose affiliations to any particular path. Similarly, festivals were organized by either the various Sufi orders or adherents of a particular saint, and they were frequently financed by large associations of merchants, landlords and other prominent citizens. These individuals gained the admiration of the community for their charity, but also made a great deal of money from the thousands of pilgrims who came to venerate and honor the deceased.[36] So, for example, while the tomb of Shaykh Abban was still administered by Indian Memon community in the early twentieth century, the saint's annual *ziyara* was organized and financed by some of the Settlement's leading Arab families.[37]

The British administration considered local festivals important enough to provide minor subsidies to the most popular of these civic events each year and occasionally even participate in them, thus conveying de facto official government sanction on them. Through the 1930s, the Office of the Resident provided grants ranging from ten to fifty rupees for unspecified expenses associated with several of the most popular festivals, while government offices were routinely closed in neighborhoods where ceremonies were taking place. So, for instance, a note dated May 24, 1928 states that the Treasury Office would be closed "on account of the Fair of Syed Hashem al-Baher." The official reasoning was that the crush of crowds in neighborhoods surrounding the shrines made work impossible.[38] On a number of occasions in the 1930s the British Resident, Bernard Reilly, became an active participant by joining processions to lay the new *kiswa* over the tomb at several of the more prominent pilgrimages.[39]

Ziyarat and the cult of the saints clearly constituted an important element of the public sphere among Aden's Muslim community. We should note, however, that not all attempts to establish sacred sites of veneration were successful. Some, such as the *ziyara* of the Mukha shaykh, al-Haradee, seem to have fallen by the wayside, perhaps once the original followers or their descendants had become assimilated into the local Adeni community. By the same token, while the appearance of new tombs and the addition of festivals to the sacred calendar were hardly uncommon, as in the case of Hashim al-Bahr, not all such attempts succeeded. Instructive is the case of "Sayyid" Abdu Muhammad.

In November 1922, Fatima bint Ahmad approached the authorities for permission to hold a brief *ziyara* in her son Abdu's honor. She held that Abdu was indeed a *wali*, although not unduly holy during his own lifetime.[40] His grandfather was a *wali*, his father was a *wali*, she declared, so by dint of reason, he too must be a

Friend of God. But Fatima recognized that lineage was not necessarily adequate proof of one's sanctity. Evidence of his holiness she averred lay in the circumstances of his grave. A resident of Aden, "Sayyid" Abdu had been caught in Lahij at the outbreak of war in 1914 and was thus stranded on the wrong side of the Turkish lines. When he died suddenly, he was buried in Bir Ahmad rather than in his hometown. Days later, however, Abdu appeared to his mother in a dream and told her that he so pined for his natal home that he had miraculously transferred his final resting place to a tomb near the Ma'alla police station and to honor this blessed occurrence she should hold a *ziyara* at the tomb immediately following the annual festival of Sayyid Aydarus.[41]

Bint Ahmad's account of her son's sanctity followed many of the themes common to Islamic sainthood. Claims to saintly progenitors, communication of one's wishes via dreams and the commission of miraculous acts (such as moving one's corporeal remains) from beyond the grave are textbook tropes found in almost any Muslim hagiography.[42] The only problem was that no one seemed to find Fatima or her story terribly credible. The police noted that the tomb in question was already occupied by a certain *Wali* Shatri (or Shahri). They knew this because the constables of the Ma'alla station were its caretakers. Furthermore, Fatima had previously been jailed for six months for defrauding prostitutes of their property.[43] As a result, her reputation among both the authorities and the population at large was less than sterling. Needless to say, the *ziyara* for '*wali*' Abdu never got off the ground.

Tomb visitation, saint veneration and the multiverse

The prominence of Sufism and tomb visitation in Aden was part of a larger pattern found throughout the Indian Ocean in the nineteenth century and early twentieth. From Island Southeast Asia to coastal East Africa, Sufi *tariqas* (Lit. path or way) and tomb veneration were fixtures of Muslim life.[44] The majority of recent scholarship on Indian Ocean Sufism has sought to understand the significance of mysticism from a variety of perspectives. Anne Bang and Engseng Ho, for instance, have demonstrated the central role of Sufism in creating and preserving social networks between Southern Arabia and the wider region across both space and time. Nile Green—as well as my own work on Somalia—explored the social importance of shrines and Sufi *tariqas* among local communities seeking to traverse the challenges presented by encroaching European colonialism and scripturalist reformist trends of the age.[45] One thing all of this research has in common is that, while not entirely ignoring the esoteric significance of mysticism for practitioners, there has been a tendency to prioritize what may be referred to as the "practical" significance of saint veneration. In particular, much of this work has a tendency to only discuss the importance of the unseen in terms of societal authority and its relationship to power.[46] To be sure, a relationship with the saints, and the unseen more broadly, held tangible benefits for the Muslims of Aden. However, an examination of Aden's sacred landscape suggests that residents may have also sought more intangible rewards through their connection to the unseen that also connected them to the city and their fellow Muslims.

One thing that is striking about Aden is the sheer extent of the tendency to revive old tombs (or import ones from the nearby coast or hinterland) as opposed to the establishment of entirely new shrines and mosques. This trend may provide insight into an alternative notion of their significance. The majority of these revivals were sponsored by the wealthier elements of the immigrant Muslim population—especially those from South Asia—who rebuilt or refurbished the largest and most important tombs. It is tempting to interpret this activity solely in terms of new residents of the port, seeking to lay claim to legitimate standing by becoming the patrons of religious institutions. Certainly, there is something to this. But if this were solely the case, why the emphasis on reviving ancient tombs with frequently esoteric pedigrees? Why not simply build new mosques? Import saints or create new ones around whom shrines could be built? To be fair, in the cases of Shaykh al-Haradee and Shaykh Hashim al-Bahr, this did occur, but they appear as exceptions rather than the rule.

Aspects of shrine veneration were certainly aimed at attaining various kinds of concrete redress via the intercession of the *awliya'* (such as fertility, the cure of illness and recompense of various kinds of loss—financial, physical, marital).[47] By the same token, becoming the patron of a shrine certainly created a stake in the community and could serve as a physical manifestation of one's claims to belonging—not to mention assertions of authority and financial gain. But it seems that the penchant for revived tombs may reveal something else that has far more to do with how individuals—and the community collectively—understood cosmology and the metaphysical structure of the universe (or multiverse, as the case may be).

The efficacy of shrines in Islamic cosmology is premised on certain—largely neo-Platonic—ideas about the fabric of the universe. The physical universe is created through the "essence" of God, which is mediated through the Prophet, the first created being. This manifests itself in the form of a "green light" that emanates from God literally through the Prophet across time and space in a continuous stream known as the *Nur Muhammadiyya* (the Muhammadan Light). It is this light that creates all matter (animal, vegetable and mineral) as well as time.[48] More importantly, those of sufficiently elevated spiritual status can begin to perceive the elemental nature of this light and ultimately use it to gain entry to the presence of the Divine. The ability to perceive this light was also critical in the ability to perform *karamat*, or miracles, like teleportation, finding lost objects, feeding the multitudes and so on.[49] Because of their ability to access the *Nur Muhammadiyya* the *awliya'* by and large came to be regarded as conduits to these other planes of existence even after physical death. One important rationale behind tomb visitation is that proximity to the *wali* facilitates the transmission of the faithful's supplications from one realm to the next. As such, the tomb becomes a fixed node or point that permits access to the realm of the unseen and the Divine.

In the Indian Ocean of the nineteenth century, this was deemed by many to be a quite literal connection. A common motif in *manaqib* (hagiographies) of the period was the *wali* as a visible conduit of the *Nur Muhammadiyya*. If one entered into the presence of the Somali saint Abd al-Rahman Zayla'i, for instance, it was said that the "light of the Prophet" could be seen emanating from his finger tips.[50] Sufis of the period in the western Indian Ocean frequently cited the early eighteenth-century Moroccan text *al-Ibriz fi kalam Sayyidi Abd al-Aziz* that states, "Some among the pious [the *awliya'*] saw this light . . . that extended and branched out in threads, every thread persisting with grace into [every aspect] of humanity, *even the bread.*"[51] Not only was the *Nur Muhammadiyya* real, but it permeated even the most mundane elements of life.

The Muslims of colonial Aden were, unsurprisingly, closely tied to the Sufi networks of the western Indian Ocean in the same way that the port had been during its Medieval and Early Modern prosperity. This was in part due to the community's geographic and ethnic diversity, but also to its position as a major imperial transportation hub. Countless *'ulama'* passed through Aden's gates over the course of the nineteenth and twentieth centuries either outward bound from their homes either on the Hajj or to centers of learning such as Cairo or homeward, returning after years of study or religious devotion.[52] As such, the Muslims of Aden could be expected to reside well within the main currents of Islamic religious thought of the region.

There is little in the descriptions of *ziyara* ritual that serve to illuminate the precise cosmological beliefs of local practitioners. There are, however, at least two literary sources produced and used by mystics in Aden during this period that help shed light on the topic, both associated with the tomb of Sharif Aydarus. The first is *Risala fi tariqa al-Naqshbandiyya* by Sharif Abd al-Rahman al-Aydarus, surviving in a manuscript copy compiled in 1863. The second, *al-Jiz al-latif fi al-tahkim al-sharif*, was a treatise composed by Sayyid Abu Bakr al-Aydarus in the fifteenth century or early sixteenth and reproduced by adherents in printed form twice in the first half of the twentieth century.[53]

The *Risala* is a set of two letters relating the litanies and ideas that developed among the Naqshbandiyya as it emerged as a *tariqa* separate from other orders as well as enumerating the individuals responsible for transmitting this path in Southern Arabia.[54] The text notes that its purpose is to provide an introduction to "each correct path that is open and the lights of guidance to direct students to understanding."[55] Among the most significant revelations contained in the text—for our purposes, at least—is the understanding that the universe was divided into two realms: the natural (*al-khalq*) and that of "power" (*'amar*). The latter is of the most interest to the author, which he indicates contains five levels or parts: *al-qalb* (the heart), *al-ruh* (the soul), *al-sirr* (the secret or inner-most heart), *al-khafi* (the unseen) and *al-akhfi* (the hidden). These elements, according to some, he writes, are identified by a spectrum of lights (*anwar l'l-ta'if*). The smaller heart (*al-qalb al-sughar*) and the *ruh* are red; the inner heart (*al-sirr*) is white; the unseen (*al-khafi*) is black; and, most importantly, the hidden (*al-akhfi*) is green.[56]

The *Jiz al-latif*, published in its second edition for the Aden market in 1936, is a treatise by Abu Bakr al-Aydarus al-Adani dealing with spiritual authority.[57] The

1936 edition contained far more than al-Adani's original work that, as we will see in Chapter 6, represented a Sufi literary response to scripturalist reformers. Here, what is most important is the Shaykh's discussion of the "noble cloak" (*al-khirqa al-sharifa*) of the Prophet Muhammad that serves as a symbol of spiritual authority whose power was inherently manifest in the unseen. Al-Adani related on the authority of Ali bin Abu Talib:

> The Prophet said: when I went up to the seventh heaven, Jibril took me by the hand and ushered me into paradise. And there I saw a castle of red walls, in it I saw a box made of light with a latch also made of light. I said: O'my beloved, Jibril what's in this box? He replied: in it is your honor and the honor of your *umma* after you, until the Day of Judgement, here is the cloak of the ragged [*khirqa al-faqir*]. Then he opened the box took out the cloak and draped me in it. And he said: ya'Muhammad, The Truth [God] has ordered me to bestow this upon you, do not entrust it to anyone who is not worthy.[58]

Al-Adani related how the "lineage of the cloak" was conveyed from the Prophet to successive pious luminaries primarily through Ali bin Abu Talib and his son Husayn to Hasan al-Basri and many others down to his own time.[59] More pointedly, the "lights" of the "cloak of noble mysticism, with its great, sacred lineage," spreads its "*baraka* to the *two worlds with its reality*[60]. . ., [along with] whiffs of sanctity from the essences of the created. . ." This "noble cloak"—that of the Prophet—he concluded, brings "a general benefit to all Muslims."[61]

Much of the *Jiz al-latif* is primarily about spiritual authority in a very temporal, concrete sense as al-Adani describes how the mandate of "the cloak" was passed from "hand to hand" from shaykh to disciple—the authority of the former literally "draped" (*ilbas*) over the latter.[62] However, the authority and power of "the cloak" was not manifest merely symbolically. The *khirqa* intersects the *'alamayn*, the two worlds—this one and the next—as al-Adani and many others note, evoking the immanent nature of the divine reality (*al-haqiqa*) and humanity's everyday contact with it.

Location, location, location: burial in Aden

The idea that the boundary between our world and the realm of the divine was more of a permeable membrane than a solid wall was not a concept limited to the esoteric ruminations of sixteenth–century saints. Rather, it was a notion that could be found widely within colonial Aden's Muslim community. In addition to the practice of tomb veneration and numerous *ziyaras*, we find a number of instances in the colonial record where the concept that the divine realm was close and, indeed, accessible is evident among many of the town's residents.

In late 1910, Sharifa Aliyya bint Ali, the sister of Hashim al-Bahr and memorialized by Muhammad Luqman as a pious and saintly woman in her own right, was gravely ill and at death's door. Looking to the not too distant future, Umar bin Abdullah Sharaf, the Qadi of Shaykh Uthman, and "other notables of Aden," petitioned the state for permission to bury her next to her brother within the same shrine. Their reasoning for this was twofold. First, Sharifa Aliyya was recognized as having a saintly status as elevated as that of her brother. But, extensive tombs were not cheap and they hoped to avoid the expense of building a second dome. More importantly, Aliyya was a "pious and sacred woman" the petitioners stated, and "we cherish the hope of deriving the benefit of her blessing," from the grave.[63]

It was not only the living who hoped to benefit from close proximity to the saints. The Residency files contain a steady stream of petitions from individuals who wished to see their deceased relatives buried in one of the two cemeteries in close proximity to the tomb of Abu Bakr Aydarus. For countless among the faithful, association with the tombs of the saints extended beyond regular visits and the yearly *ziyara*. Many, in fact, hoped to spend the period between departing this life and the day-of-judgment in the company of the saints, especially Sayyid Abu Bakr Aydarus.

Following the British occupation two main cemeteries emerged within the Settlement both near the Aydarus Mosque. The first became known as the Aydarus burial ground used primarily by the saint's descendants, their retainers and friends. The second became known as the Kati cemetery that grew up adjacent to the Aydarus cemetery and became the primary burial ground for Aden's less well connected Muslim residents. In 1866, the Resident ordered burials at these two sites cease due to concerns for public health—largely fears over the spread of cholera. In its place a new cemetery was established outside the Main Pass Gate, which itself was closed in 1875 and replaced by another new burial groud near Ma'alla.[64]

Despite this official closure, individuals continued to seek exceptions to have either themselves or their loved ones interred near the tomb of Aydarus al-Adani. In some cases, these were prominent local notables such as Muhammad Umar a former Qadi or Sayed Rustom Ali, a retired judge of small causes in the Residency.[65] In many others we find people like Fatima bint Ali Ba Hada, Muhammad Wazir and his wife Manoo who as "old citizens and respectable resident of Aden," wished their final resting place to be near the tomb of al-Adani.[66]

One easy explanation for the continued demand for burials near the venerated saint is, of course, social capital. Burial in the Crater cemeteries was certainly a sign of prestige and social connection. The majority of those buried in the Kati and Aydarus cemeteries were either important local notables (such as sayyids, wealthy merchants and even foreign dignitaries)[67] or people with at least minor connections to the administration. As such, it was far easier for Salma bint Ahmad, whose son was a clerk in the registry office, to be interred in the Kati cemetery than it was for Fatima bint Mawadth, the mother of Muhammad Mahjub, "mosquito hunter."[68] But at the same time, for Adenis, burial in Crater near the tomb of Sayyid Aydarus carried with it more than mere social prestige. It served as both a symbol of belonging, of being Adeni, but it was also a very potent reminder of the tangible importance of sanctity in people's everyday lives.

Aside from a close association with the Aydarus family or being a sayyid, long residency of one's family in Aden was the most common rationale used to petition the British authorities for burial permission in the otherwise closed cemeteries. From the turn of the twentieth century, an increasing number of petitions were lodged with the Residency for permission to be buried in the cemeteries of Crater. Through the early 1930s—when restrictions on burials were lifted[69]—nearly thirty requests for exemptions were recorded in the Residency files, most of which were granted. Nearly all of these cited long residency and being from "respectable" families as sufficient grounds for exception.[70]

In 1915, for example, Sayyid Abdullah Aydarus,[71] the family's head, solicited the state for permission to bury the terminally ill Sayyid Taha bin Alawi al-Safi. Sayyid Aydarus petitioned not on the grounds that al-Safi was a descendent of the Prophet but because he was "a very respectable merchant of long standing and an old resident of Aden." Sayyid Umar Hasan declared in a petition made on behalf of his brother, that their family had been resident in the port for more than two hundred years and were a "well known, respectable family."[72] When Ali Murshid requested permission to inter his dying mother in the Aydarus Cemetery this was based not on his employment as a clerk in the Residency, but the fact that his family were "old and respectable residents of Aden, possessing landed property in the Settlement."[73] Such claims were often made irrespective of the ethnic origins of one's family. While in many cases it is impossible to determine the ethnicity of the families requesting burial in the vicinity of the righteous saint, several—Sayyid Rustom Ali; Inayat Shah Mohamed; "the wife of Ali Chaudhuri"; and Kulsom bint Nanabhoy, "an old resident of Aden and landlady"[74]—are identifiable as South Asian Muslims of long residence in Aden and thus worthy of being granted exceptions.

The social capital that could accrue to the families of the deceased almost certainly represented one motivation for seeking to have one's kin buried in the vicinity of the town's most important holy figure. As such, this could be viewed as the kind of "practical" outcome of unseen agency: by winning the right to be near the saint, your position as an "old" family was tacitly recognized by the state. While such material considerations were undoubtedly important, we should be careful not to eliminate other motivations that, while more esoteric, may also provide insight into the emergence of Muslim community in Aden.

Such petitions also hint at the singular importance of an Islamic cosmology within individual lives. Particularly relevant is belief in the concept of "awareness within the grave." From the earliest centuries of the faith, Muslim theologians argued that the soul remained self-aware in the grave after death. Specifically, following earthly death, the soul inhabited the region of *al-barzakh* (literally, "the bow-length"), a dimension of Islamic space–time that lay between the "two worlds": this one (*al-dunya*) and the afterlife (*al-akhira*) until the day of resurrection (*al-yawm al-qiyama*). During the interstices between death and resurrection the individual soul experiences either torment or bliss determined largely by the good or bad deeds committed during life.[75] It was widely believed, however, that the deceased could benefit from the *baraka* of the *awliya'* while in the grave. From the Middle Ages, believers were frequently enjoined to "bury the dead close to persons whose righteousness and grace is assured and as far from the graves of the sinful as possible."[76]

In his book, *In the Vicinity of the Righteous: Ziyara and the Veneration of Muslim Saints in Late Medieval Egypt*, Christopher Taylor provides numerous examples of individuals in Medieval Cairo who expressly wished to be buried near the tombs of particular saints in order to benefit from their *baraka*.[77] The pious of Aden were, indeed, no different. We should note that given the ritual restrictions surrounding death in Islam—namely, that the body of the deceased be interred before sunset on the day of death if at all possible—the petitions lodged with the Residency were more likely the last wishes of the dying than the desires of their survivors. In other words, these were requests made by those less concerned with the petty affairs of this world and more with the prospects for their immortal souls in the next.

For individual believers, the light that emanated from the tombs of the saints tied them to both physical place and the cosmos simultaneously. Cosmic and physical planes were thus intertwined, and, as such, Adenis could use the *Nur Muhammadiyya* to substantiate their claims to place. But we should be careful not to rule out the likelihood that for many this was simply a by-product and not the central goal. Rather, the desire for proximity to the Light of the Prophet was not driven simply by the venal desire of one's kin to secure position, but the need of the deceased to find succor near God.

Tombs and a sense of belonging

For Muslim residents of Aden, the development of sacred space was a priority that frequently took precedence over domestic and even commercial construction. In this sense, spiritual well-being seems to have been more important to many than creature comforts. But what does this tell us about the nature of Muslim community and belonging in the imperial context? At its most basic, the construction of mosques and revival of tombs certainly signaled one's commitment to remaining in Aden long-term. Such undertakings required the investment of considerable amounts of capital from individuals and even entire communities—for example, the Indian Memons—that certainly expressed a sense of permanence. Similarly, evocation of "long residency" as supporting the right of the deceased to burial near the tomb of al-Adani, can be read as an act by the living to cement the permanent nature of their connection to Aden. Even the notion of the *Nur Muhammadiyya* and the revival of particular tombs had an impact on the emergence of local political hierarchies, as patrons became local power brokers between the Imperial state and the Muslim populace. By the same token, it may also represent challenges to that authority as certain spirit-possession groups—detailed in Chapter 5—claimed to be able to channel the souls of the *awliya'*. But the social trajectory of the *Muhammadan Light* can be traced more broadly as people sought to connect themselves to Aden.

The revival of tombs, establishment of festivals and burial of kin in the most prestigious spots were not simply symbolic claims to space that had the "practical" impact of substantiating individual or group claims to residency—although this was certainly partly the case. If we allow ourselves to consider the cosmological beliefs current among Muslims during this period, other explanations for this engagement with the unseen begin to suggest themselves. For a large proportion of the pious, God's universe did not consist of a single earthly reality with a distant and somewhat imaginary divine realm inaccessible to the believer. It was, instead, a complex multiverse with various dimensions; in addition to "this world" and *al-akhira*, the jinn—another of God's created beings, for example—inhabit their own dimension that similarly intersects with the world of humans. Rather than separated by insurmountable barriers, the divine realm, or at least portions of it, were accessible to the pious. Some, such as the saints, could transcend this while alive by virtue of their own enlightenment. But even the ordinary Muslim could access the divine realm after death through the permeable membrane of the *barzakh* if buried in the vicinity of the *awliya'* where it was at its most porous.

By reviving tombs with linkages that date not only to the earliest period of the port, but indeed to the founding generations of the faith (for example, the grandson of the third Caliph), Muslim residents of Aden inserted themselves directly into the discursive traditions of Islam in a way that connected them not only to a relatively ephemeral recent past, or one dominated by the theological discourse of books. Rather, by reviving already established spiritual nodes, residents of Aden gained access to a sort of cosmic discursive tradition that linked them to earlier generations not simply metaphorically but literally across time via the neo-Platonic *Nur Muhammadiyya*. Burial in its proximity enabled even the most oridinary believer to plug into the Divine realm directly. From this perspective, the tomb tradition represents an engagement with the unseen that was not simply about claims to puerile, temporal authority, but power in a much larger cosmic sense. It represents a certain understanding of the cosmos and an attempt to engage with it in a meaningful way—sometimes for material benefit, but often times simply for the benefit of one's soul. The Islam of books and dogma was not irrelevant, as we shall see in subsequent chapters. However, the neo-Platonic understanding of the cosmos, represented by the tombs, provided a template for comprehending the faith that also served as a not uncontested field for defining and asserting membership in the community. We shall return to this theme in Chapters 5 and 6. But here let us turn to the faith of books as we look at the importance of the law.

4
"The Qadi is not a Judge": The Qadi's Courts, Community and Authority

"The Qadi," declared Saleh Muhammad al-Makkawi, Assistant Registrar of Aden, "is not a judge or [one] invested by Government with judicial powers. He is [merely a] Registrar of Marriages and Divorces."[1] Writing several years earlier, but no less pointedly, the Qadi Umar ibn Abdullah remarked in a letter to al-Makkawi's boss, the Registrar Sayyid Rustom Ali, that, "it is not legal for [even] a learned man—who is not proven to be well versed and proficient in the law—to question marriages [ruled lawful by the Qadi] and give an opinion on them. Whoever does so, pretends to have a character that he really does not possess."[2]

Exchanges between Aden's Qadis and the Registrars (lower civil court judges) were, more often than not, pervaded by a tone of petty bickering that included attacks on one another's competence in the law, honesty and, indeed, personal character. As such, aside from a certain perverse entertainment value, what is to be gained from examining the vain and seemingly small-minded squabbles of minor "native" officials in a sweltering outpost like Aden?

While certainly self-important and petty, the combative relationship between these officials may help illuminate certain questions about the evolution of individual Muslim communities under imperial rule within the context of wider, translocal forces. On the one hand, these cutting remarks highlight a long-running and contentious question among Aden's civil and religious elite: who had the right to interpret and administer Islamic law? To some this may seem a matter of only local interest. The shape and content of these debates, however, were infused with ideas emanating from British imperial policies concerning Islamic law as well as pan-Islamic ideologies of religious reform. As such, these local conflicts can help us understand how individuals sought to translate such abstract ideas from theory into practice using them to shape not only the local application of the law but also using them to underwrite claims to communal authority.

As a colonial possession from the mid-nineteenth century, the British administration of the Aden Settlement can be described as eclectic at best. While a select few Europeans always occupied the upper-echelons of power, it was mainly non-Europeans—mostly Indians and Arabs—who staffed the station's bureaucracy. Many of the daily affairs of the Settlement were overseen by Gazetted and non-Gazetted officers of the Civil Service whose importance ranged from sanitation inspectors and patrolmen on the beat, to Inspectors of Police and lower civil court judges—the Registrars. However, the British administration also depended on the local religious elite, along with other "respectable" citizens, to oversee various bureaucratic and social needs of the community. Qadis, for instance, oversaw the registration of marriages and divorces while the leading member of the Aydarus family of Sharifs was charged with mediating minor civil disputes and, as we saw in the last chapter, supervision of the Settlement's numerous cemeteries.

As such, by the early twentieth century, there existed two distinct—although intertwined—sets of "elite" Muslims in the Settlement. One consisted of formal members of the Imperial bureaucracy, such as Sayyid Rustom Ali and Saleh Muhammad, the aforementioned Registrars or "judges of small causes," who were largely secular in education. The other was made up of "traditionally" educated religious scholars and notables whose connection to the state and authority was far more tenuous. Not surprisingly, the presence of two sets of social elites created tensions within the Settlement. Both saw themselves as the natural leaders of the Muslim community in Aden and both sought to defend what they considered their "turf."

Such disputes were in part about local authority and who had the right to wield it. However, they were also about differing visions of the faith. Among the disputing parties some, such as Qadi Umar, were adherents of what we may term—for lack of a better descriptor—a "traditional" approach to *fiqh*, or jurisprudence, that valued mediated solutions to the complex issues surrounding marriage as opposed to enforcing hard-and-fast rules. Such an approach ran directly counter to the Registrars who viewed *shari'a* through the prism of Anglo-Muhammadan Law, which they hoped to use to codify and rationalize the faith, creating a forward thinking and "enlightened" society that mirrored an idealized version of the one propounded by their colonial masters.[3] Still others, such as the Qadi Da'ud al-Battah (who we shall meet a bit later), subscribed to ideas promoted by scripturalist reformers (subsequently known as Salafism) and opposed the easy accommodation that some *'ulama'* maintained with local custom but also expressed a certain reticence toward the codifying tendencies of Muslim bureaucrats. These latter two categories have been explored in detail by historians and scholars of religious studies.[4] However, the impact of the first on the emergence of Muslim communities under British imperial rule has been much less studied. Indeed, virtually no work has sought to examine how all three of these threads coalesce within a single community.[5]

It would be deceptive to conceive of what emerges in Aden as a simple rivalry between "Western secularists" and "religious diehards." Certainly, and unsurprisingly, rivalries and competition appear aimed at gaining influence both with the state and the Muslim community at large. At the same time, however, we see cooperation, alliances and even admiration for individuals across ideological lines. This chapter explores the negotiation of communal authority across these ideological boundaries along with how understandings of religious law and theology and their application were transformed as a result.

Imperial administration and legal pluralism

The occupation of Aden in 1839 is often portrayed in imperial histories as driven primarily by the British East India Company's need for a coaling station and communications hub mid-way between Britain and its South Asian possessions. While this is certainly true in part, as we saw in Chapter 2, both the Company and the first Political Agent,[6] S. B. Haines, actively campaigned to develop Aden as a mercantile hub in the western Indian Ocean, expanding British economic interests in the region by providing protection to the large numbers of South Asian merchants operating in the increasingly unstable theater of the Red Sea and Gulf of Aden.[7] Largely as a result of Haines' recruitment efforts throughout the ports of the Red Sea, Aden's population exploded as the town's long-flagging commercial fortunes began to revive.[8]

From the beginning the administration of Aden was something of an ad hoc affair premised as much on the cooperation of local elites as military force. Haines was assisted by a small staff of no more than five, an Assistant Agent, an interpreter and three clerks. In addition, there was a separate military staff responsible for the garrison.[9] During these early years, the top priority of Haines and his small staff was the development of a self-sustaining merchant population large enough to make the Settlement a going concern. On the one hand, this meant establishing Aden as a viable sanctuary from the increasingly violent political upheavals of Yemen and the wider Red Sea that afflicted the region through the 1840s—a largely military task for which the Company's officers were well suited. But, it also meant creating a sense of law and order within the Settlement by overseeing the civil and criminal disputes that are part and parcel of any community. This was, not surprisingly, a job for which army and naval officers felt themselves far less well prepared.

The system of legal administration that emerged in Aden—lasting well into the twentieth century—was one of legal pluralism. The laws of the East India Company, and later the Raj, had their place. However, within the course of their daily lives the non-European residents of Aden had recourse to a number of legal avenues for the redress of civil and criminal wrongs. As Lauren Benton has demonstrated, regimes of legal pluralism figured as common features of European imperial regimes from the Early Modern period. She notes that "wherever a group imposed law on newly acquired territories and subordinate people, strategic decisions were made about the extent and nature of legal control." In some cases, imperial powers sought to impose their own legal systems wholesale. "More common," Benton writes, was a deliberate tendency to "retain elements of existing institutions and limit legal change as a way of sustaining social order."[10]

Haines and his staff were, theoretically, empowered to "exercise civil and criminal authority";[11] in Aden, however, they were ill equipped to do so. To begin with, although a dependency of the British East India Company, Haines was instructed that the laws and regulations of the Indian Government were "not to be enforced" in the Settlement but should merely serve as "guidelines."[12] Furthermore, the only member of Haines' staff fluent in Arabic was his "Native Resident" and interpreter

Mulla Jafar. However, his duties centered primarily on negotiating the tenuous relationship between the Company and the surrounding Sultanates leaving no time to adjudicate civil and criminal disputes even if he were qualified.[13] By the middle of 1840 a small force of Muslim and Hindu constables—recruited from villages near Bombay—were charged with maintaining law and order within the Settlement perimeter. While keeping criminal activity in check, this force was neither equipped nor empowered to prosecute criminal or civil offenses.[14]

The solution arrived at by Haines, and followed by his successors until the latter part of the century, was to allow the non-European communities to police and settle most civil, and even some criminal, matters themselves. It would be inaccurate to say that he and other Company officers simply permitted pre-existing legal regimes (Islamic or otherwise) to function under Company rule. Rather, they allowed non-European residents to avail themselves of a number of legal avenues that required only indirect European involvement. Some, such as *Panchayyat* (binding arbitration) were Company creations based on largely specious notions of "native tradition."[15] Others, namely the Qadi's court, had a basis in local Muslim legal and social tradition, but were subject to imperial modification and oversight. Under the guise of legal pluralism, both institutions allowed British officials to maintain a thin veneer of official distance from the legal dealings of their subjects in Aden. In fact, the sanctioning of such legal remedies had a dramatic impact on emerging Adeni Muslim society. By requiring official recognition of both Qadis and those adjudicating *Panchayyat*, imperial functionaries played a direct role in creating social hierarchies and solidifying claims to authority within Aden's emerging community. By the same token, British imperial machinations affected the tenor of legal Islamic discourse in Aden by bringing about the intersection of various individual and ideological trajectories that shaped the practice of *shari'a* in the Settlement and served as the basis for various individual claims to communal, as well as legal, authority.

Judges and arbitrators

It should come as little surprise that the overstretched administration of Haines should opt to leave in place the system of justice found in the town at the time of occupation with some modifications. Under the Abdali sultans, who ruled Aden before the British, civil and criminal justice was overseen by a Qadi who held jurisdiction over virtually all matters of a civil, criminal or moral nature. In a report to Bombay, Haines noted that the Abdali Qadi oversaw the prosecution of criminal matters such as theft and murder; the resolution of civil affairs, including marriage, divorce, estates and debt; and the policing of public morality, most notably public drunkenness. Based on this it was determined that the most efficient course of action was to leave well enough alone. Haines was told that, for the time being, Islamic law and custom among the Muslim inhabitants was to be respected and he and his staff were not to involve themselves in minor disputes. Instead, the Qadi, who had been in office at the time of the occupation, was to be retained as a servant of the Company at 30 Rs a month.[16]

We know relatively little about the activities of this judge under the nascent British administration. Referred to in records simply as Qadi Abd al-Razzaq, Haines seems to have taken an instant dislike to him, accusing the judge of colluding with enemies outside the Settlement and sowing dissention within.[17] The Political Agent dismissed Abd al-Razzaq in 1840 and the office continued but—in theory at least—no longer responsible for civil cases that were decided by a committee made up of representatives of the plaintiff and defendant under the leadership of the Assistant Political Agent.[18]

The office of Qadi re-emerged as a central element of the Aden bureaucracy more as a result of administrative desperation than design. The post was re-established as a government office in 1854 "for the purpose of adjusting, at the police office, cases connected with Mahomedan [sic] rites and ceremonials as well as disputes and claims for debts under the orders and supervision of the Assistant to the Political Resident."[19] However, in 1860 the First Assistant Resident, R. L. Playfair (by now the Resident had three official assistants), found himself awash in paperwork when both the Resident (W. C. Coghlan) as well as the Second Assistant were seconded to different posts outside of Aden for more than a year. Finding himself performing the work of three administrators, the enterprising Playfair expanded the responsibilities and authority of the serving Qadi in an effort to relieve the bureaucratic pressure. Playfair's appointee was Shaykh Ahmad Ali (serving from 1859 to 1873) who, as it turned out, would be the most powerful Qadi of the colonial period. In addition to recording marriages and divorces and mediating local disputes, Shaykh Ahmad was empowered to hear civil cases involving property up to 200 Rs in value. For a time, he was also authorized to commit "defaulters" (presumably both debtors and those who had cases decided against them but who failed to pay the settlement) to either Civil or Criminal jail. Likewise, he was, in the words of one official, "authorized to send persons to Chowkey," for disobeying his directives.[20]

Panchayyat

The revival and expansion of the Qadi's powers were not the only consequence of Playfair's administrative fatigue. It was under his watch that we see official recourse to another legal avenue for settling disputes among Aden's "native" population, namely the *Panchayyat* or Committee of Arbitration. The *Panchayyat* as a Company legal tool dates to seventeenth-century Bombay where the Governor Gerald Aungier (1670–7) granted judicial power to leading individuals to decide "cases amongst persons of their own castes who agreed to submit the controversies to their arbitration."[21] *Panchayyat* emerged as a particularly important tool of administration in the regions of the Deccan that fell under the Bombay Presidency in the 1820s where Company officials hoped it would serve as "an efficient, accessible, and inexpensive form of justice."[22] Curiously, this initiative lasted only a few years and was declared a failure in the Deccan by the end of the same decade and had fallen almost entirely from use in Bombay by the middle of the century.[23] But, in Aden, it was precisely at this moment of decline that it appears in the residency records.

It is not clear when British administrators began turning to *Panchayyat* as a method of settling largely minor civil disputes. However, in the mid-1850s a number of cases appear in the Residency files in which the Assistant Political Resident granted permission to individuals to settle various civil suits through arbitration.[24] These ranged from the determination of an individual's assets in relation to his ability to repay certain debts to disputes over commercial goods. So, for instance, Dhumraj Hemsay, Lutif Ghumee and Ali Bhayee were asked by the creditors of Navalram Marwaree to make an inquiry into the latter's ability to pay his debts while Ali Daruti and Abdullah bin Salim agreed to abide by the decision of a three-person panel of their peers regarding a dispute over the transfer of a consignment of wood (presumably construction materials).[25]

At a glance, the use of the *Panchayyat* seemed designed to relieve the Residency of the need to adjudicate minor civil disputes and was in accord with the earlier directive of the Company to allow the inhabitants of Aden to observe their "native" customs in most legal matters. In fact, however, the arbitration committees—at least tacitly—played a role in solidifying (if not creating) local social hierarchies. The *Panchayyat* recorded in the Residency files are uniformly vague and mundane. All concern matters related to business dealings gone awry and the disputants all appear to come from the better-heeled class of merchants.[26] We learn very little else from their cases. Far more instructive, however, is a committee convened without official sanction and involving some of the community's less desirable members.

Dhandie and Nathia, two laborers in the Settlement's Engineer Department, went out drinking one night in early 1860. After making the rounds of the many illegal stills found in the bazaar, an alcohol-fueled argument erupted between the two and Nathia ended the dispute by picking up an iron pestle and bashing his friend over the head with it. Nathia was eventually convicted of assault by the magistrate and sentenced to six months of hard labor. On this night, however, instead of going to the police, Dhandie took the matter to Bhissao a "pettywalla"[27] in the Camp Lines who referred the dispute to Bhaw Bhasker "a Brahmin Karkoan in the Engineer Department possessed of considerable influence."[28] Bhaw called together several leading men of the Camp Lines, including Sayyid Isma'il—another pettywalla—and several *muqadams* or supervisors from the Engineer Department to meet as a *Panchayyat* to settle the matter. After lengthy discussions, the parties agreed that Nathia should pay Dhandie 10 Rs by way of compensation for the latter's injuries. Not having the money on him, Nathia agreed to leave his ring with Dhandie as surety against payment until he returned and paid his debt the following day.

According to Lt. Arthurs of the Settlement Police, who wrote the incident report, the resolution of this dispute as a "private" matter would have been acceptable were it not for what transpired next. As the meeting broke up, Nathia was accosted by one of the arbiters, Sayyid Isma'il, who asked him to come by his house later that night in order to discuss an important matter. When Nathia arrived, Sayyid Isma'il informed him that he needed to pay an additional 10 Rs to himself and presumably Bhaw if the matter was not to reach the ears of the Magistrate. What followed is worth detailing at length from Arthurs' report.

Nathia, an ignorant, untutored countryman, rather addicted to spirits, hardly remembered what happened, in his drunken frenzy, to Dhandie; but seeing Dhandie's head . . . and being persuaded that Dhandie had been seriously wounded, pictures to himself Dhandie's death and the consequences to himself. The effects of his debauch had not yet passed away, confused and distracted he fancies in his ignorance that the opportunity generously afforded to him by these petty Lords, of extricating himself from the unpleasant position his dissipation has placed him in—should not the case [be set] aside; and he therefore eagerly assents to the unreasonable demands imposed on him . . . On the following morning Nathia was seen in the Camp Lines on his errand of fancied safety . . . It was early, shortly after the gunfire, an unusual time—when he arrived at Bhaw's; he called Bhaw who was asleep; Mumia Sowar whose apartment is separated from Bhaw by merely a straw mat screen answered, a light was burning in the Sowar's house and Dhakoo was there smoking a hooka[29]; Nathia, without preface placed 10 Rupees into Dhakoo's hand for Bhaw saying that it was on account of "yesterday's business."[30]

The entire episode came to the attention of the magistrate as the result of a chance encounter between Nathia and a certain Fukeer Muhammad.[31] After leaving Bhaw's home, Nathia went on his way to Isma'il's house "with the view of purchasing his silence." However, "not far from his destination he met Fukeer Mahomed [*sic*] who surprised at meeting him there at that unusual time naturally interrogated him. Nathia thereupon unbosomed [*sic*] himself and displayed the money intended for Syed Ismail [*sic*]." Fukeer Muhammad reported this conversation to the authorities and the subsequent investigation uncovered a number of other witnesses and the tale related above.

Arthurs', and by extension the European magistrate's, objections to the affair were only partly based on what they regarded as Sayyid Isma'il's attempt to extort hush money from the hapless Nathia. More troubling was that, in their view, Bhaw, Sayyid Isma'il and the others had failed to properly perform their duties as overseers in the Camp Lines and—even more troubling—had begun to lay claims to authority among their fellow workers. Once again, the police report is revealing:

> We cannot, of course, question Nathia's right to compromise the matter with Dhandie as the latter was quite at liberty to demand privately [underline in original] compensation for his injury in the shape of money. But I conceive we can legally and consistently question the right of a number of very subordinate officials to enquire into and decide the case on the brief authority they possess among their fellow workmen.

Arthurs conceded that the demands for compensation exacted on Nathia by Bhaw and Sayyid Isma'il were "not strictly unlawful." However,

> Bhaw, Dhakoo, Ismail, Bhissoo, Babajee, and Madhew are all subordinate officials in the Engineer Department possessing authority or influence to a greater or lesser extent, to these Dhandie's case was communicated and by these concealed for some consideration . . ., if therefore the exactions of money in the manner and for the purpose already described is not strictly unlawful; their conduct in concealing a serious breach of the

peace wherein a fellow subordinate had sustained injury and from the effects of which it is supposed he subsequently died, in my opinion decidedly unlawful. It was clearly the duty of one and all of them to have communicated the circumstances of the case to Captain Fuller [their European superior].

But, again, their failure to report a crime up the chain-of-command was only part of the problem. In the eyes of the state, Bhaw, Bhissoo, Sayyid Isma'il and the others, were men of poor character, unworthy of authority.

The trouble these men have given in this case and that of the assault on Dhandie, and their equivocal behavior throughout the proceedings leave no doubt in my mind that they form a clique whose intrigues are neither advantageous to the state or the workmen generally of the Engineer Department. Bhaw, Dhakoo, Mahdew, Babjee all live together and are all employed in the office . . . Bhissoo who has recently been degraded [demoted] by Captain Fuller is a man of dissolate habits and Syed Ismail is a man of notoriously bad character.[32]

For the authorities in Aden, legal pluralism and the following of "native" custom through, for example, *Panchayyat*, were clearly not for all. The adjudication of local civil disputes, at least based on the available evidence, was reserved for those deemed by the authorities as responsible and respectable members of society.[33] Merchants and religious leaders cleared this bar; clerks and common laborers did not. The difficulty, however as Arthurs' report attests, was how could the state ensure that only those deemed worthy were permitted to arbitrate local disputes. The simple answer was they could not.

As Arthurs' report makes clear, there was no easy way to limit who could and who could not oversee a communal arbitration. While the British intended that only those presumed to hold appropriate moral authority should oversee disputes, it was beyond their power to effectively enforce. It should come as little surprise, then, that *Panchayyat* soon disappeared from the state's repertoire of recognized avenues of legal redress. Minor disputes continued to be settled outside the formal confines of the courts. However, they fell increasingly under the purview of the Qadi, at least in cases involving Muslims.[34]

The growth and curtailment of the Qadi's office

The use of officially sanctioned *Panchayyat*s appear to have waned by the end of the 1850s.[35] The position of Qadi, on the other hand, continued to play an important role within Adeni Muslim society through the nineteenth century and into the twentieth. Indeed, the office expanded in the 1890s with the addition of a new judge's position in the suburb of Shaykh Uthman.[36] However, their role and functions became increasingly contested over the course of the century from various directions.

From even before the death of Shaykh Ahmad in 1873 the legal jurisdiction of the Qadi was increasingly circumscribed. In 1872, the judge was ordered to send all persons he imprisoned for debt to the Court of the Resident. Following his death, his successor's salary was cut in half and the position stripped of many of its judicial functions.[37] The impetus for this appears to have emanated not so much from within the Settlement administration as from the desire of the Bombay bureaucracy to exert greater control and integrate Aden more fully into the imperial system. This was the result of two unrelated developments: the commission of what were viewed as administrative irregularities by Commander Haines and the consequences of the 1857 rebellion in India.

During his lengthy tenure, Haines had run Aden as his own fiefdom. In 1854, his rather cavalier methods of administration caught up with him when he was charged with embezzlement and prosecuted for malfeasance. Although acquitted of these charges he was cashiered from Company service and spent the remainder of his life in debtor's prison. The main consequence of the Commander's demise was tighter central control that culminated in 1864 with the passage of the Aden Act that fully extended the laws of British India to the Settlement.[38] The rebellion of 1857 had no immediate effect on Aden as the Indian element of the Settlement's garrison and police had remained loyal. However, as Scott Kugle has noted, in the aftermath of the uprising the newly installed administration that replaced Company rule took the opportunity to speed through various acts and reforms that completed the process of turning Islamic law within the Empire into a purely personal code of law and stripped Qadis and other Muslim jurisprudents of what little authority they retained until then.[39] Taken together, these measures served not only to ultimately restrict the official role of the Qadi in Aden but also introduce a new legal counterpart cum competitor in the shape of the Registrar.

The Aden Act also created the Court of the Resident and vested in it the administration of both criminal and civil justice. Apparently in recognition of his long service, Shaykh Ahmad's court was allowed to continue hearing civil cases. With his death, the Qadi's jurisdiction over such cases was revoked and placed instead in the hands of a newly created Registrar who acted as a small claims judge within the Resident's court.[40] Despite such restrictions, the Qadis of Aden retained a number of functions that made them important figures in the lives of most Adeni Muslims.

In a series of memos written in 1893, the First Assistant Resident (FAR), E. V. Stace, outlined the areas of responsibility that remained open to Aden's judges. This highlighted their position as functionaries of the state but also recognized their continued social relevance. "Kadhis [sic]", he noted "are judicial officers and under the orders of the First Assistant Resident . . . their functions are to perform marriage and divorce ceremonies," as well as "settle religious affairs of their community." The latter included the announcement of the beginning and end of the Ramadan fast but also the mediation of local disputes that did not require action in the Courts. In two subsequent memos Stace endorsed the right of judges to issue certificates of sale, mortgage or property transfers of property not exceeding 99 Rs in value as well as adjudicate inheritance cases.[41] The continued ability of Qadis to exercise judicial authority over civil matters when they had long since been stripped from Islamic legal practitioners in India proper was, again, most likely a matter of expediency. Although the Residency staff had expanded exponentially by the 1890s,[42] the administration continued to be perennially short-handed due to secondments, medical leaves and the increasingly heavy demands of administering the busiest British port in the western Indian Ocean.

The office of Qadi was also expanded numerically during this period. By the late nineteenth century, the Aden Settlement was bursting at the seams. In addition to the central quarter known to Europeans as the Crater,[43] neighborhoods near the coaling station known by locals as Tawahi (Steamer Point) and Ma'alla, continued to grow while an entirely new one sprang up near the barracks at Khor Makasar. In 1881/2, the Settlement further expanded when the village of Shaykh Uthman was purchased from the Sultan of Lahij. Important originally because of a number of wells, the British saw the area as a solution to overcrowding in the Settlement. Laying five miles inland on the edge of British territory, Shaykh Uthman was seen as a possible outlet for the crowded neighborhoods of Tawahi, Ma'alla and Crater (the areas closest to the harbor). In the hopes of encouraging new arrivals to move there rather than the crowded harbor area, the British set out to remake Shaykh Uthman as a "modern town," building 150 houses, a school and a dispensary along a pre-planned grid of streets.[44] Tawahi, Ma'alla and Khor Maksar were deemed close enough to Crater to fall under the jurisdiction of the Settlement's original Qadi. Shaykh Uthman, however, was viewed as too distant to be covered efficiently by a single official, so an additional judge was appointed to serve the new suburb.

During this period, the position of Qadi in both Aden (with authority over Crater, Tawahi, Ma'alla and Khor Maksar) and Shaykh Uthman were family affairs. For a time, the al-Hazmis, a family of Sayyids, controlled both positions. Sayyid Yahya bin Muhammad al-Hazmi was Qadi of Aden from 1881 until his death in 1901, while Sayyid Muhammad bin Hasan (referred to as Sayyid Yahya's son, although the name discrepancy is not explained) served as Qadi of Shaykh Uthman from 1897 until he took over his father's post in Crater upon the former's death. He served in that post until his own death in 1918. From 1901 until at least 1940 members of the Sharaf family dominated the Qadi's post in Shaykh Uthman. In that year, Umar bin Abdullah Sharaf (whose father had been a port officer) was appointed to succeed Muhammad al-Hazmi. He served until about 1911 when his son Muhammad bin Umar succeeded him until 1918. Unique among Aden's twentieth-century Qadis we know very little about Muhammad bin Umar's tenure or the circumstances under which he left office. It is unclear if he left to take up another post, retired or died. This is largely—it would seem—because his tenure proved very unproblematic for the authorities, although the fact that for at least part of this time Shaykh Uthman was occupied by the Turks during the First World War may also be a factor. In any event, in 1918, Awad bin Abdullah Sharaf, brother of Umar bin Abdullah, took office serving until his retirement in 1928 at the age of fifty-six (he had apparently held other posts before this time, although again the record is unclear as to what these were). Qadi Awad was succeeded by his nephew Abdullah bin Umar at the rather tender age of twenty-five. His tenure continued—again, apparently—until his removal in 1940 for his part in a public disturbance.[45]

By the time that the last two Sharafs and Da'ud al-Battah took up their offices, the Qadis had been stripped of all of their official functions except for the registration of marriages and divorces. Writing in terse, bureaucratic language, Sayyid Rustom Ali, Registrar of Aden's Court of Small Causes, summed up his legal opinion of the place of Islamic judges in the functioning of Aden's legal system:

> The legitimate duties of the Kadies [sic] are, the performance of marriage and divorce among parties; settlement of religious affairs of their community; and the rendering of assistance to the Court in granting or writing certain papers regarding inheritance. They should not interfere or take any action in matters of testamentary and interstate succession, administration of the estates of deceased persons [or] minors as those are the matters that should be disposed of by the Court according to the procedure prescribed by several Acts of Legislature. Of course their duty in this respect is simply to advise the Court to take administration where there seems to be no fit individual to take charge and manage the estate of a deceased person or a minor. But they are not supposed to interpose and deal with estates, a right which absolutely rests in Court.[46]

As Saleh Muhammad, Sayyid Rustom Ali's assistant, would write a few years later, the Qadi of Aden is not "a Judge or [one] invested by Government with judicial powers. He is [merely a] Registrar of Marriages and Divorces."[47]

The registrars

The position of Court Registrar was created in 1873 largely as part of the drive to regularize the administration of the Settlement and bring it more fully under the umbrella of British–Indian law. The official duty of the Registrar was the adjudication of any civil cases involving property under 500 Rs in value. However, they were also informally charged with overseeing the running of the Qadi's courts in Crater and Shaykh Uthman. In the twentieth century, the Settlement's Registrars emerged as not so much the greatest opponents of the Qadis and "traditional" religious authority, but more as their greatest competitors for that authority.

Of the four occupants of this office between its founding and 1930 all were of South Asian origins (at least ethnically), the first two were Parsis while the latter pair Muslim and two held law degrees (L. L. B.) from Bombay. All were career bureaucrats. The first and longest serving Registrar was Mancherji Rustom Dohlu, a Parsi, who joined the Aden administration in 1866 as Head Clerk of the arsenal. In 1871, he was appointed to the post of Settlement Accountant—a position he continued to hold through his first two years (1873–5) as Registrar. He occupied the position of Registrar until his retirement in 1903. His replacement was Nusservanji Koyaji, another

Parsi from Bombay, who held a law degree. His was to be the shortest tenure of the four, serving as Settlement Registrar for just a little over a year and a half from April 1904 until December 1905.[48] Koyaji was followed by Sayyid Rustom Ali. Born in Aden to an Indian family of Sayyids in 1863, Rustomji[49] entered the administration in 1877 at the age of fourteen, serving the Residency in what is simply described as a "non-gazetted appointment." From his knowledge of English, as well as his early appointment to government service, we can surmise—in the absence of any other evidence—that Sayyid Rustom was educated in what was known as the Residency School. More importantly, he appears to have been something of an autodidact, especially with regard to the law. He owned an extensive personal library (estimated to be worth 300 Rs), containing numerous works of Western and Islamic law that formed the basis for his comments on problematic cases involving the local Qadis.[50]

Sayyid Rustomji retired from Government service in late 1919 and was replaced by M. Yasin Khan. Like Nusservan Koyaji, Yasin Khan was a Bombay-trained lawyer originally from Meerut in the United Provinces. He was posted to Aden in 1918 as a temporary Extra Assistant Resident until appointed as Acting Registrar upon Sayyid Rustom Ali's retirement and confirmed in the position in 1920. Yasin Khan remained Registrar until at least 1935, performing other prestigious temporary duties during his tenure, including serving as the Pilgrimage Officer at Jiddah on three different occasions in the mid-1920s (1923, 1924 and 1925). Following the Second World War he was elevated to Aden's newly created High Court.[51]

Shaykhs and lawyers

There seems to be no record of Muncherji Rustom's relationship with the Settlement Qadis while the relationship between Koyaji and the judges appears to have been relatively free of tension. In a report on the jurisdiction of the Qadis over estates of the deceased, the latter noted that while the Court of the Resident could technically exercise control over all such estates regardless of size, in cases where all of the heirs were in agreement, the Qadi might be consulted. In instances where the estate was particularly paltry, he stated, the Qadi performed a valuable service by seeing that the funeral expenses and various small claims "such as rent and servant's wages" were paid from the deceased's estate and the remainder transferred to the state. This he seems to regard as saving the Resident's Court a great deal of time and a practice that should be encouraged.[52]

It seems likely that, as non-Muslims, Muncherji Rustom and K. N. Koyaji were reluctant to interfere in legal matters with a religious dimension—and inheritance in an Islamic context was by definition a "religious matter." Their successors, however, showed no such reticence. Both Rustom Ali and Yasin Khan made it a habit to weigh in on matters of a religious nature and frequently challenged the competence of their legal colleagues, the Qadis. This occurred partly within the context of the Settlement's legal system but could—as we shall see in the case of Yasin Khan— also involve matters reaching beyond the courts.

The relationship between Aden's Qadis and the Registrars in the twentieth century was complex. The contentious nature of their interactions appears rooted in fundamentally different approaches to Islamic jurisprudence and the role of the law in society. For the Qadis of Aden, decision-making was primarily about arbitration and reconciliation. Rather than seeking to determine a winner or a loser in legal disputes, Islamic court judges were interested in arriving at amicable solutions that at least partly satisfied all parties—an approach that had a lengthy tradition in Islamic jurisprudence.[53] The Registrars, on the other hand, were staunch advocates of what has become known as Anglo-Muhammadan law. Developed over the course of the nineteenth century, Anglo-Muhammadan law was an attempt by Company and later imperial officials to codify and—in their minds—"rationalize" Muslim *fiqh* into a system that more closely resembled their ideas of "natural law."[54] Within this framework, rules (as laid out in ossified texts) and precedent were meant to outweigh individual circumstance or social contexts.[55] Such differing views of the social function of law not surprisingly placed Qadis and Registrars at odds, as we shall see presently. At the same time, the interests of both parties in maintaining what they viewed as a just and pious community, in certain instances made them—if not exactly allies—partners in social authority.

When is a divorce not a divorce?

Sayyid Rustom Ali was an advocate of restricting the local Qadis to only the most mundane clerical roles (that is, registering marriages and divorces). In 1907, he convinced the First Assistant Resident to withdraw the Qadis' authority to oversee inheritance cases and write certificates of deed or mortgage.[56] From this point the Registrar took an increasingly active role in cases involving the limited authority left to the Qadis, namely marriage and divorce.

From 1906 to 1916 Rustom intervened in a succession of cases involving divorce, disputed dowries, allegedly under-aged brides and confessional boundaries. While certainly doing so as an imperial official, what becomes apparent within the documents was a growing tendency of the Registrar to draw his own conclusions and enforce what he viewed as the proper execution of Islamic law. In the first instance on July 4, 1906, Fatma bint Hasan complained to E. O'Brien—the First Assistant Resident—that her ex-husband, Muhammad Dunhji, divorced her, but with the connivance of Qadi Umar bin Abdullah Sharaf, bilked her of her *mahr* (commonly glossed in the records as "dower") of twenty-five Maria Theresa Thallers.

In a complaint filed through one of her male relatives, Sayyid Isma'il bin Ali, Fatma held that on June 15, 1906 she and Muhammad Dunhji, accompanied by two witnesses, went to the Qadi of Shaykh Uthman to be married. Qadi Umar was not present so another individual, named Qadi Awadth Jama, who was acting in Umar's place, solemnized the contract. Awadth Jama wrote out the contract stipulating a dower of $25. What followed was a confusing series of events in which the unhappy couple were divorced, "undivorced" and, divorced again, with charges of fraud thrown in to the mix. According to Qadi Umar Abdullah:

> On the 24th June, 1906 at 10am Mahomed Dhanji [sic] came to my office along with his brother-in-law Mohamed Hizam. He said that Mahomed Hizam insisted [that he] divorce his wife Fatima. After a short conversation with Mohamed Hizam, Mohamed Dhanji told me *iktab la-ha warqa wa ana bi-irja'* ("write her a card and I will return")[57] An hour after Mohamed Dhanji returned to my office. I told him that I have written one divorce in the register. He said that he had not intended any divorce. On his taking [an] oath that he never intended to divorce her, I expunged the writing from my register.
>
> On the 29th June 1906, before noon, Mahomed Dhanji came to my office [again] and [demanded a] divorce. I asked him about the wife's dower and he said it was fixed at $15. I gave him a divorce certificate and he went away. Subsequently, on asking Awadth Jama who performed the marriage ceremony and on looking at the register I found that the dower was $25. Shortly afterwards Sayed Isma'il came to me and asked if Mohamed Dhanji paid me a visit. I replied in the affirmative and told him that he had pronounced one divorce as payment of $15 as the dower of the woman. He said the dower was fixed at $25. I told him that after I have given the certificate I found that the dower was $25.[58]

Ultimately, the actual amount of the *mahr* was determined by an examination of the Qadi's register where $25 Thallers was indeed recorded. Muhammad Dunhji was forced to pay the remaining $10, although he continued to insist that he had never agreed to this.

Curious in this matter was the official response of the Registrar. In wrapping up the matter, the FAR O'Brien concerned himself exclusively with what appeared to be the carelessness of Qadi Umar. "It will be seen that the Kazi [sic] has not kept up his register of Marriages and Divorces," he noted, "and that lately he committed a very careless mistake with reference to a divorce. The Kazi has also been in the habit of going into Aden without leave and appointing a substitute to act for him during his absence. He has been ordered to obtain leave from the Superintendent of Sheikh Othman [sic] whenever he wishes to go to Aden or elsewhere."[59] Registrar Rustom Ali in his own report was far less concerned with this aspect of the case. Instead, his own remarks focused almost exclusively on the validity of the divorce.

> The statements of Mahomed Dhanji [sic] and the Kadi [sic] of Sheikh Othman [sic] taken by me in connection with the application of Sayed Ismail are herewith forwarded. *The question is whether there was a valid divorce on the 24th June, 1906 or not.*[60]
>
> It appears that Mohamed Dhanji used certain words to the Kadi in connection with his wife Fatima. The Kadi took these words [as] one of revocable divorce and made an entry to that effect in his rough register. Subsequently, on the oath of Mohamed Dhanji he expunged the writing from the register as he found out that Mahomed Dhanji by using these words to the Kadi had no intention to repudiate the marriage by one divorce.
>
> With what intention then did Mohamed Dhanji use these words to the Kadi?

The intention can be gathered from the circumstances of the case. Mohamed Dhanji distinctly stated in his statement that his brother-in-law declined to send back his former wife unless Fatima was divorced. He then took her back and used the words "write to her a card or letter." These words seem to me to clearly convey an idea of repudiation of marriage by one implied revocable divorce, notwithstanding no express word of divorce was used.

Before entering in his register, the Kadi ought to have satisfied himself more fully by questioning Mahomed Dhanji as to what he meant by these words and not to have entered in the register as "one divorce" and then to exchange them on the ground that Mohamed Dhanji had no intention to repudiate the marriage by one divorce.

The Kadi should be more careful in future in matters of this kind.[61]

Sayyid Rustom Ali seemed far more concerned with determining, to his own satisfaction, the correctness of the Qadi's actions under Islamic law than with uncovering the presence or absence of fraud or even taking the Qadi to task for his poor clerical habits. This, indeed, seemed to be the thin edge of the wedge for Sayyid Rustom, who began to make a habit of critiquing the legal validity of actions taken by the judges within his own reading of *shari'a*. Over the course of the next year the Registrar increasingly weighed in on the legal decisions of the Qadis of Aden and Shaykh Uthman concerning marriage, decrying their incompetence and calling for them to either take more care in their administration of religious law or be removed from office. In the interests of space, we will limit ourselves to one further case: Zamla bint Ayd.

The case of Zamla appears as a family squabble that turned into a Settlement political issue as the result of the rivalry between the Qadis of Aden and Shaykh Uthman. According to the husband, Abd al-Ghaffur bin Sulayman, at the end of July 1904 a local marriage broker, Hajja Safiyya, came to his father's house and told him that his sons were of an age to marry and that she had just the girls for them. Two Jabali or "country" girls had just arrived in Shaykh Uthman and were living with their uncle and brother. If he liked, she could arrange a meeting. At the end of August, instead of going to school, Abd al-Ghaffur's father took him to Hajja Safiyya's house where they met with the girl's relatives, a brother and two uncles, Sa'id Husayn and Abd al-Rub Husayn al-Nahmi. The latter was acting as Zamla's guardian. They spent much of the day at Hajja Safiyya's home negotiating the marriage. At 4 p.m., according to Abd al-Ghaffur's statement, he, his father and the girl's relatives proceeded to the Qadi's residence. In front of witnesses, the Qadi asked her uncles if she were "an adult," questioning, in this case, whether she had reached puberty. They indicated she had and he registered the marriage.

Two years later, in the summer of 1906, Zamla left the house of her in-laws. According to them, she left of her own accord. By her account, her mother-in-law threw her out, saying "her son was now grown-up and did not want letter" her. In any case, it was as a result of Zamla's brother's efforts to somehow resolve the situation that the case came to the attention of the Residency.

In August, Qadi Umar in Shaykh Uthman sent a note to his counterpart, Muhammad bin Hasan al-Hazmi in Aden, saying that Zamla's brother had turned up at his residence claiming the girl's husband had driven her from his home "for no reason." Since the family lived in Crater, could Qadi Muhammad look into the matter and take the appropriate action? Rather than oblige his colleague, the Crater Qadi opted to make political hay out of the case that occurred just weeks after the Fatma-Muhammad Dhanji incident.[62] Qadi Muhammad sent a letter to the Resident accusing Qadi Umar of contracting an illegal union. He claimed that the Shaykh Uthman judge contracted the marriage between Zamla and Abd al-Ghaffur despite two glaring irregularities. First, the girl claimed that she was underage at the time and had informed the judge of her wish not to marry.[63] Second, her uncle, Abd al-Rub Husayn, was not "a proper guardian" authorized to marry the girl if she had not reached puberty. Al-Hazmi argued that his Shaykh Uthman counterpart should be investigated for this and other irregularities (and presumably removed from office, although he did not say this explicitly). Qadi Umar, he held, was completely ignorant of the law of al-Shafi'i and, if allowed to continue unchecked, would go on encouraging people to transgress the law.[64]

Sayyid Rustom concurred with the Aden judge, and reported that Qadi Umar had clearly acted "contrary to the Shafa'i [sic] school of law. According to the Shafia [sic] doctrine no other person except a father or a grandfather of the girl can contract her marriage." In this case, her agent was an uncle, which, he concluded, made the marriage invalid. Citing an earlier decision by his predecessor Muncherji, Sayyid Rustom declared that, because of these irregularities, the marriage was invalid and the "husband" must pay the girl half of her dower and "break off the matrimonial tie."[65]

This was not a rebuke that Qadi Umar was willing to take lying down. The Shaykh Uthman judge responded to the charges quickly and forthrightly, utilizing the legal concept of *ikhtilaf* or "legal differences" between law schools.[66] Yes, he had performed the marriage and it had been done in accordance with the law, the dower was agreed, witnesses were present and he had certified the girl's majority through the testimony of her kin. Furthermore, he wrote back rather sharply, "her uncle" *was* one of her guardians and even "if he was not empowered to marry her [explicitly]" he was fully entitled to do so "if he knew that [it] was a necessity," to avoid hardship on the part of the girl. There followed several extracts from a *Shafi'i* legal text, *al-Bughayt al-mustar shidin fatawa Sayyid Abd al-Rahman Mashhur*, supporting and explaining this point in detail. First, if, at the time of the marriage, the woman/girl and/or her kin attested that she had reached maturity a post facto declaration that she had really been underage was not sufficient to nullify the marriage. Second, while within the Shafi'i tradition the uncle may not be recognized as a lawful agent, under the Hanafi School he could be. Quoting the *Bughayt* he states, "The learned men Ibn Ugayl and Isma'il al-Hadrami, as well as his son, said that it is lawful to follow the doctrine of Abi Hanifa who permits every guardian or judge to marry a girl [who is] underage." Furthermore, "other learned men [such as]

Humad empower an [individual who would not normally be qualified as an agent] to marry [off] an underage girl on the grounds that they do so owing to the hardship that would be caused to the girl if she were not married."[67] Qadi Umar then took seemingly direct aim at the Registrar. "On the whole, it is not legal for a learned man—*who is not proved to be well versed and proficient in the law* to question such marriages and to give an opinion on them. Whoever does so, pretends to have a character that he really does not possess."[68]

He concluded by noting that statements by a husband or wife regarding her minority after the fact of a wedding (especially when it comes as much as two years after the fact!) could not be tolerated and would result in social and legal chaos. If such a thing were allowed, any husband who wished to avoid repaying the dower in the event of divorce, or wife who was simply dissatisfied, could have a union nullified through such a ruse. In short, the Registrar should stick to his own line of expertise lest social chaos ensue.

Sayyid Rustom was undeterred. Not even bothering to acknowledge the Qadi's argument, in November he relayed his decision to Umar. "As the marriage of Zamla bint Ayed with Aboul Ghafoor Suleman [*sic*] performed by you through her uncle without ascertaining her age was inconsistent with Mohomedan [*sic*] Law" the union was void. Furthermore, "the Resident considers this is the second irregularity which has come to notice recently and . . . any further delinquency on your part will probably entail your removal from office."[69]

Even though the competence of both Qadis Umar and Muhammad continued to be questioned over the next several years, neither was ever dismissed from their post. However, neither did Sayyid Rustom desist from commenting on religious law. He involved himself in a number of other marriage cases over the next year and in 1916 became embroiled in a dispute with the Bohra Isma'ili community, arguing that within the precincts of the Settlement *Sunni* law should trump Shi'i where there was a conflict.[70]

It might be argued that Sayyid Rustom was simply an arrogant, pompous bureaucrat who thought he knew more than his troublesome (and to his mind, ill-educated) colleagues. No doubt, this may be partly true. However, he was not an anomaly. Sayyid Rustom was not a rogue mid-level administrator, rather, he represented a new kind of Muslim elite—in Aden at any rate—who believed that his Western connections and education entitled him to both a position of leadership within the community and a right to adjudicate ritual and social behavior, establishing mores within the Muslim community. His understanding of Muslim *fiqh*, however, appears derived almost entirely the rigid perspective of Anglo-Muhammadan law.

The tenor of the relationship between the Registrars in Aden and the wider *'ulama'* can certainly be described, in general, as oppositional. However, it can hardly be described as one of unremitting conflict. In certain instances, we see a great deal of nuance in the way that both parties deal with each other, either through reaching out to those with opposing ideals or, in at least one important case, creating a de facto alliance in an effort to achieve certain social/political ends.

The Overflowing River

The earliest example we have of one side seemingly reaching out to the other occurs in the shape of a curious *fiqh* text that appeared in 1899 entitled *The Overflowing River of the Science of Inheritance and Patrimony, together with an exposition of The Rights of Women and the Laws of Matrimony*, composed by an otherwise little known local legal scholar, Abd al-Qadir bin Muhammad al-Makki. The work itself is a legal primer that provides an overview of various issues revolving around marriage and inheritance from both the Shafa'i and Hanafi traditions.[71] As such, it is a good example of a common genre known as *al-kutub al-ikhtilaf* or "books of differences" that lay out the distinctions between two or more Muslim legal schools regarding specific questions of law. While belonging to a well-established form and with his fellow Adeni believers in mind, it was a work that—at least in its 1899 edition—was produced as a self-consciously imperial text published with larger political and religious discourses in mind. In particular, the Shaykh seemed to, at least tacitly, wish to engage the codifying tendencies of Anglo-Muhammadan law with the hope of re-introducing some of the flexibility and nuance that characterized traditional Islamic jurisprudence.

By the start of the twentieth century, Anglo-Muhammadan law had emerged within the British Empire as an imperfect and generally impractical system that bore little resemblance to traditional *fiqh* in either theory or practice. As noted earlier, by the 1870s the government of the Raj had successfully transformed Islamic law into a kind of Muslim personal law restricted to matters of a largely domestic nature, such as marriage, divorce and inheritance. More critical was the fact that their efforts to do so were premised on the creation of a codified Islamic law based on what were believed to be certain authoritative legal texts such as the twelfth-century Hanafi legal handbook, *al-Hidaya* (literally *The Guide*), compiled by Burhan al-Din Ali al-Marghinani (d. 1196). Such works were wrongly believed to constitute the core of Muslim jurisprudence when really what they had done was, in the words of Scott Kugle, mistake "a limited portion of the juridical resources of each [Muslim] community to be the entire, immutable code. And then through practice, they forged this mistake into a reality."[72] From an administrative standpoint, the purpose of this streamlining was to create a code that could provide quick, clear-cut direction to magistrates and judges when deciding civil issues among Muslims, an intent clearly evident in Rustom Ali's legal reasoning. At the same time, it stripped the law of important nuances, such as the advisory versus prescriptive nature of the *shari'a* or the legal commonplace of consulting multiple schools of law in an effort to arrive at an equitable decision that best fit a given situation.[73]

Al-Makki's work appears as a deliberate attempt to reinsert the nuance of traditionally practiced *fiqh* into the imperial system. In its 1899 edition, *The Overflowing River* is a bi-lingual, Arabic–English, facing-page translation.[74] This, according to al-Makki, was in order to make the text useful to "those officers who are employed in the Court of Justice at Aden," but also in order to "impart to them a good knowledge of Arabic, and enable officers to understand parties before them without the aid of an interpreter."[75]

At the same time, the book sought to address various important questions relating to marriage and inheritance based on the doctrines of "the most approved authorities of the two schools [Ar. madhhabs] of Abu Hanifa and Ash-Sha'afee [sic]." The first of these, he informs the reader, "predominates in India, Afghanistan, and it is the creed of the Ottoman Government and all Turks" as well as many people in the Hijaz and Egypt. The latter, "is followed by the people of the Yemen, Hadramout [sic], Somaliland, Dankaliland, Harar, Ceylon, Java, the Malay Peninsula and Egypt."[76] Makki sought to compose a text that would be relevant across the British Empire and provide guidance to both members of the 'ulama' and imperial officers of the court. More importantly, his decision to compose a work that placed Hanafi and Shafi'i jurisprudence in dialogue with each other signals a clear attempt to promote a certain legal flexibility that the British imperial framework sought to eliminate.

Written in the question-and-answer style typical of *fiqh* manuals, *The Overflowing River* covers a wide array of issues surrounding inheritance and the laws of marriage—all of which were of great relevance to both Islamic and British Imperial courts. Within the realm of inheritance, for instance, al-Makki took up the incredibly complex questions of who had the right to inherit and in what amounts. So, not only was there a basic section on "The Rights to which the Deceased's Estate is Subject," but also chapters regarding the rights of "Distant or Uterine Kindred," as well as those of missing persons and hermaphrodites. There is a chapter regarding "The Rules for Calculating the Division" of inherited property, but also separate ones covering the rules governing the increase or decrease of shares based on the number and kind of lawful claimants to an estate. Part II of the work on "The Rights of Women" provided guidance on issues of marriage and divorce, guardianship, dower, *'Iddat* (the required waiting period between a woman's divorce and remarriage) and the custody of children.[77]

In al-Makki's lengthy treatment of *walayya* or "Guadianship" it should come as little surprise that his understanding of the laws of marriage and betrothal echo those of his contemporary, Qadi Umar. In answer to the question, "Who is the guardian according to the doctrine of Abu Hanifah [sic]?" al-Makki provides a lengthy response describing a hierarchy of guardianship that includes both paternal and uterine kin as well as distant and near relatives ending with the Qadi and government authorities who, in the absence of all others, may act as a woman's guardian in matrimonial matters.[78] Several pages later, he gives the same treatment to Shafi'i, who as the local authorities above noted, privileged a much narrower group of almost exclusively paternal kin along with the state when other sources failed.[79]

Taking the text as a whole, it seems clear that al-Makki hoped, as he states, to provide guidance to aspiring Muslim legal scholars while at the same time bringing greater nuance to Islamic law as it was adjudicated by the imperial courts in places like Aden. Indeed, the book appeared well received. The serving Qadi at the time of its publication, Yahya bin Muhammad al-Hazmi,[80] wrote a review of the text declaring it "clear and lucid" and a book that was "excellent in every respect," that spoke "to the excellence of its author and bears witness to his wonderful talent."[81] Another reviewer, Ahmad bin Ali bin Muhsin, asserted, "Its fountain [of knowledge] will be frequented by comers and goers, and townsmen and villagers will speak highly of its great excellence."[82] It is therefore curious that, although widely available in Aden (and, indeed, remained in print until the late 1950s), *The Overflowing River* seems to have had no visible impact on the legal debates of the early twentieth century. Neither the Qadis nor the Registrars cite al-Makki in any of their correspondence or decisions. And it certainly does not seem to have contributed any greater understanding of *fiqh* to the officers of the Residency, as he had hoped. The reason for this may lie in the book's structure.

The Qadis most likely failed to cite the book because as a primer it held a relatively low status.[83] Instead, as we saw above, they preferred to draw on what they considered more prestigious works to support their opinions. For Rustom Ali's part, as a known bibliophile and autodidact, it seems probable that *The Overflowing River* resided in his considerable legal library. Unfortunately for us there is no hand-list of its contents. However, the structure of the work would, in all likelihood, have done little to challenge the judge's ideas about Islamic law. As an *ikhtilaf* text, al-Makki faithfully expounded on the positions of both the Hanafi and Shafi'i schools with regard to various legal questions. What the text did not do, however, was place the two *madhhab*s in dialogue with each other. Instead, the Shaykh simply laid out the opinions of both schools in series. So, for instance, there is a five-page discourse on the Hanafi position regarding guardianship followed by a further three relating the Shafi'i view.[84] Furthermore, at no point in the book does al-Makki indicate that a competent authority may choose between the differing positions based on, in the words of Umar Sharaf, "need." From al-Makki's point of view—as well as any other religious scholar with even a basic education—such direction would have seemed unnecessary as the flexibility of legal decision making was second nature. For the Registrars, however, the structure of the book offered little that may nuance their ways of thinking. Instead, it merely reinforced the codifying prejudices of Anglo-Muhammadan law: there was a position in Hanifi and a position in Shafi'i and never the twain should meet.

Despite the failure of al-Makki's book to influence imperial juridical circles the existence of the work is instructive. Al-Makki's foreword, in particular, reveals an understanding—among at least some *'ulama'*—that the imperial courts' conception of Islamic law was very different from their own. As such, it represents a conscious attempt to reach out and influence them. Although ineffective, the existence of *The Overflowing River* reveals that rather than simply regarding colonial officials, such as the Registrars, as parvenus encroaching on their traditional territory, there was recognition of a need for engagement. Scholars such as al-Makki understood that they could not sit back and allow British officials (European or otherwise) to define Muslim legal practice. Not all attempts at engagement between religious authorities and Muslim imperial bureaucrats were failures, however. The relationship between Sayyid Rustom's successor—Yasin Khan—and the new Qadi of Aden, Da'ud al-Battah, was a long and fruitful one, if at times fractious.

Registrar Khan and Da'ud al-Battah

Sayyid Rustom was not the only Muslim bureaucrat to take a hand in what could be described as largely religious matters. If anything, his successor M. Yasin Khan involved himself even more deeply in the religious affairs of his fellow believers. A native of Meerut in India, Yasin Khan arrived in Aden in 1918 as a fresh Bombay law graduate to serve as a "Temporary Extraordinary Assistant Resident." In 1919, he was named Acting Registrar, an appointment made permanent in 1920. He served for at least fifteen years in this position in addition to a number of secondments as Hajj officer in the mid-1920s.[85] Registrar Khan did not involve himself in the matrimonial affairs of Aden's Muslims that seemed to preoccupy his predecessor. As Mitra Sharafi has pointed out, however, for many, engagement with the law offered "special opportunities for social mobility," and the opportunity to act as important intellectual and cultural brokers between one's community and the state.[86] Registrar Kahn was certainly an exemplar of this kind of ambitious culture brokering, and, as such, he took an even greater interest in the religious concerns of the Settlement's Muslim community. The result was a long-standing and complex association with the new Qadi of Crater, Da'ud al-Battah. Over the course of more than a decade, their association in some ways mirrored the confrontational relationship of their predecessors but was in others far more mutually beneficial.

Unlike Rustom Ali, Yasin Khan's relations with the religious establishment of Aden began on a relatively promising note. Early in his tenure a group of notables led by the *Shams al-'Ulama'*, Sayyid Abdullah Aydarus, with the support of the Aden Qadi, Da'ud al-Battah, petitioned the Resident for official recognition of a Wakf Committee to oversee the administration of local properties designated as "*waqf*"or "pious endowments,", dedicated to the support of various mosques and shrines. In a letter to the Resident in February 1921, the notables stated that while there were numerous *waqf* properties[87] in the Settlement, the agents charged with overseeing them frequently embezzled the rents. As a result, the mosques, whose upkeep was supposed to be paid for through them, as well as the properties themselves, were in a disgraceful state of repair. If steps were not taken, they wrote, the mosques of Aden would soon "become a danger to the public and the public health."[88] In an effort to remedy the situation, they wrote, "A number of leading citizens of Aden have met in [the] *Shams al-'Ulama*"s house and appointed a committee of 6 persons[89] . . . with [the] *Shams al-ulema* [*sic*] as chairman to take delivery of these houses, to recover the rents [and] spend the same in the interests of the mosques and generally to look after (preserve) the mosques and their interests."[90] The British administration declined to formally recognize the Committee but acknowledged that the formation of such a group would undoubtedly improve the state of sacred sites within the Settlement. As such, they permitted Registrar Khan to act, in "his private capacity," as an advisor to the group. In its first year of operation, the Wakf Committee encountered a number of problems in which Khan played a pivotal role, becoming an ardent partisan of the so-called traditional elite or, as we shall see, at least some of them.

Not surprisingly, a number of individuals serving as *waqf* administrators were not pleased with the formation of the Committee or its self-appointed charge. Soon after its creation, *waqf* property administrators were served notice that the Committee would, henceforth, collect all rents. At least two of these agents refused to cooperate and raised formal objections. In April, the *waqf* agent Ahmad bin Abdullah Khayyat protested the actions of the self-appointed committee to the First Assistant Resident. Khayyat stated that he had been "superintendent and collector of the incomes of certain wakfs [sic] in Aden," for a great many years. He carried out his duties, "with all honesty and energy to the entire satisfaction of the judges and the last Kazi [sic] Sayyid Muhammad bin Hasan al-Hazmi," who appointed him, and the usurpation of his duties by the Committee was both egregious and illegal. The Committee Chairman, Sayyid Abdullah al-Aydarus, had told him that "I must hand over my charge to him and he has instigated the tenants not to pay the rents to me as customary." This, he argued was "contrary to all usage for I have not been guilty of any breach of trust or misconduct in [my administration] of the Wakfs [sic]."[91] A similar petition was lodged by Ali bin Ghalib bin Noman who also sought legal action for trespass against members of the Committee when they began collecting rents from tenants of *waqf* properties administered by his father, Ghalib bin Noman.[92]

Whether encouraged to do so by the Residency or on his own initiative, Yasin Khan stepped in as negotiator for, and advisor to, the Wakf Committee, assuring acceptance of their authority in principle over the Settlement's *waqf* property. In a note to the First Assistant Resident, Bernard Reilly,[93] dated September 20, 1921, Khan reported that he and the Committee had overcome Khayyat and Noman's objections by agreeing to add them to the group. "All persons concerned," he wrote, "agree that the *Wakf* property should be placed in charge of the Wakf Committee and that Ahmad Abdulla Khayyat and Ghalib Noman should also be members of that Committee." Furthermore, "past accounts, so far as possible, will not be considered and that any dispute relating to the management of the *Wakf* property will be decided amicably by the members and that if any dispute arises it will be referred to the undersigned [M. Y. Khan] for [adjudication] in his private capacity. The matter is considered settled and everyone promises that he shall abide by it and make no further petitions."[94]

The importance of Khan's role in this matter was twofold. First, from the point of view of the Administration, his participation (in his "private capacity," of course) established the legitimacy of the Committee and secured their right to collect rents from endowed property. Writing to the parties involved a few days later, FAR Reilly endorsed not only the supremacy of the Committee over *waqf* property but also Mr. Khan's place as arbiter of any and all disputes:

> With reference to the correspondence ending with your letter dated 8th August 1921, we write to inform you that Mr. Yasin Khan, Registrar Court of the Resident, has informed us that the question regarding the management of *wakf* property in Aden has been amicably settled and that all persons concerned agree.

1. That *wakf* property should be placed in charge of the *Wakf* Committee.
2. That Ahmed Abdulla Khayat [*sic*] and Galib [*sic*] Noman should also be members of the Committee.
3. That past accounts will not, so far as possible, be considered.
4. That any dispute relating to the management of the *wakf* property will be decided amicably by the members
5. That if any dispute arises, it will be referred to the Registrar, Court of the Resident, for opinion in his private capacity.
6. That the matter is considered settled and every one promises that he will abide by it and make no further petition.

We are glad to hear of this and we trust that the wakf property will prosper under the management of the Wakf Committee as now constituted.[95]

In addition to securing the Committee's legitimacy, Reilly's statement effectively recognized Khan as the Wakf Committee's most influential, if informal, member as well as making him (in the words of Qadi al-Battah) a "leading Mohamedan" of the Settlement. From the state's point of view, Khan was an individual competent to comment upon and decide matters related to Islamic law.[96] For Aden's elite Muslims he was a man who could present their views to the Residency and more than likely insure a favorable outcome.

Despite obvious conflicts of interest, Khan was allowed to rule on petitions concerning the Committee that, needless to say, had a chilling affect on complaints. Still not satisfied with the result of mediation, for instance, Ali Ghalib Noman once again sought to bring a case against the Committee, on behalf of his father, for the return of their seized *waqf* properties in October 1921. Khan dismissed the case summarily, noting that the suit had already been decided against Noman and that while he was sure to appeal, "no action [was] necessary on petitions that don't come under any rule of law." FAR Reilly anxiously agreed, writing on the following page, "as suggested by the Registrar no action need be taken in the matter."[97] It can hardly be seen as coincidental that no further cases were brought against the Committee before the Registrar for more than ten years.

The aim of those who founded the Wakf Committee was certainly to exert influence over an important local social institution that could serve to establish their own claims to authority and right to speak for the community as a whole. As we will see below, by taking control of the Settlement's sacred endowments at least some of the Committee's members hoped to extend this authority to include most other sacred spaces in Aden (notably mosques and tombs) with the goal of making themselves arbitrators of acceptable religious behavior that could be used to define the community. The enthusiastic inclusion of Khan provided the Committee with the bureaucratic weight to give their claims to real power. At the same time, Khan's official sanction to take an active role on the committee provided him with his own social capital and the ability to influence his adopted community.

While successful in gaining control over the Settlement's religious endowments, all was not well within the ranks of the Committee. In April 1922 Sayyid Abdullah al-Aydarus composed an impassioned letter to the First Assistant Resident denouncing the very committee that he had helped form. He accused certain members of attempting to expand their authority beyond the simple administration of the religious endowments to encompass virtually every aspect of public religious life. The Sayyid noted that he had initially given his support to the Committee because many of the city's *waqf* properties had come under the control of "unsuitable persons who did not properly maintain their trusts."[98] The Committee was formed at a meeting held in his own home and given a charge of one year. Unfortunately:

> After the aforesaid agreed upon period had expired, Muhammad Abd al-Qadir Makawi [*sic*] made 27 clauses, like a Law, which I did not consider to be suitable for the Mahomedan minds of Aden because it detracted [from] the respect [given to the Sufi Orders] and gave all the power of authority in the Mosques and their employees and repairs of the Mosques and their *Wakf*s to his Uncle's son Saleh Abdulla Khalifa so that everything connected with reading prayers for the dead, or addresses in the mosques could not take place except by permission of Saleh Abdulla Khalifa.[99]

Sayyid Abdullah's complaint was not entirely disinterested as the letter was accompanied by three separate petitions calling for the Resident to recognize him as "*Mansab*" /(leader) of the Muslims and "chief" of all mosques and *waqf* property.[100]

Ultimately, Da'ud al-Battah was identified as the leader of this effort to take control of the town's public religious spaces along with a number of confederates, and the incident reads as an attempt to establish uncontested control over the city's sacred spaces as part of what Aydarus implied was their own ideological agenda. Following the Sayyid's own pre-emptive complaint to the Residency, al-Battah and his supporters were forced to abandon their plans and instead found themselves defending the Committee they now largely controlled against charges of being a disruptive influence. Khan, who had already proved effective in assuring the ascendancy of the Wakf Committee over endowed properties, was quickly—and one could say cynically—pressed into service.

The Registrar composed a letter regarding the legal position of the Committee under both Islamic and British law, supporting the actions of al-Battah and his supporters. Unfortunately, the text of that letter appears lost and is merely referred to by Qadi al-Battah in his denunciation of Sayyid Abdullah. From the text of the Qadi's missive, however, it is evident that Khan, rather than being a mere pawn, exerted his own influence over the ideas and rhetoric employed by the Wakf Committee dissenters. The Qadi wrote:

> With all due respect we beg to state that we are British Subjects and have, according to Mohamedan law as well as the laws of the British Government certain rights which nobody can deprive us of (so long as we are under the protection of the British Government) by such threats as the occurrence of a breach of the peace. If this were possible nobody's rights would be safe and no court of justice can pressure them for him. The

Mahomedan law and the British laws, the last of which is the Wakf Act of 1920 provide the necessary facilities for every Mahomedan to ask for an account and for all other particulars relating to wakfs from any trustee and to ask for his removal and the appointment of another trustee if necessary. Can Sayed Abdulla deprive any Mahomedan of this right by saying that a breach of the peace will take place if an account is demanded from him or if he is not allowed to preside over the Wakf Committee?[101]

In the end, neither side won a clear victory in this encounter. Al-Battah and his allies did not gain control over the mosques but Sayyid al-Aydarus found himself quietly forced off the Committee. However, the real importance of this incident lies in the correspondence and Khan's apparent success in shifting the scope of the legal boundaries used to define the community. Unlike most correspondence from the local *'ulama'* prior to this, the Qadi's letter did not invoke custom and *shari'a* was mentioned only as a vague principal and only in concert with "British Law." Instead, the letter focused on the Committee's right to exist under the Wakf Act of 1920 and emphasized "the rights" under the law due to all British subjects.[102]

Al-Battah's adoption of such rhetoric was almost certainly opportunistic and should not be seen as a sudden, heartfelt recognition of the equality of British civil law and the holy *shari'a*. His letter does, however, indicate Khan's success in shifting an important communal boundary in which the law of the Empire was now accepted as an important tool that could be brought to bear on the public religious lives of the community. The constitution of the Wakf Committee was not Khan's only encounter with religious authority during his tenure. In 1925 Registrar Khan was embroiled in another religious controversy. This time, however, he found himself at odds with his ally, Da'ud al-Battah.

The incident on Kamaran Island

Like Rustom Ali before him, Yasin Khan believed that his own ability to interpret Islamic law was superior to that of the traditionally trained scholars in Aden. The incident that brought this to the fore occurred not in the Settlement but on the British administered island of Kamaran in the Red Sea. The dispute focused on a proposed extension to the local congregational mosque and highlighted the gulf between bureaucrats and *'ulama'* when it came to understanding religious law.

Kamaran was an Ottoman possession until the end of the First World War, and its primary importance was as a quarantine station for pilgrims on their way to the Hajj—a use continued under the British. Due to its seasonal importance, the island maintained a colonial presence much greater than its small population would have otherwise warranted, including a full-time European "Civil Administrator," a sizeable police contingent, hospital and large administrative support staff.[103]

In July 1924, a wealthy local merchant on the island, Sayyid Muhy al-Din Nur Ahmad, applied to the Civil Administrator (CA) for permission to extend the Friday mosque. The CA consulted with the local Qadi who indicated that as long as the people of the community did not object there was no obstacle to the plan. In order to cover his decision, the Qadi also sent a letter to a certain Sayyid Abd al-Aziz of Hodeidah seeking a *fatwa* or legal opinion on the matter that was returned in the affirmative. The mosque extension could go forward.

In mid-August, however, another wealthy merchant, Taher Rajab, returned to Kamaran from the mainland and demanded that work cease. He carried with him three *fatwa*s from *'ulama'* in Hodeidah, declaring the work unlawful according to the *shari'a*. According to the CA, before moving to the mainland, Taher Rajab had served as the island's *'nazir'* (essentially leader or spokesperson) and his family retained business interests on Kamaran. His opposition to the mosque extension was seen by locals as an effort to undercut the influence of Sayyid Muhy al-Din who was perceived as an up-and-coming rival. Work ground to a halt and a meeting of the "leading inhabitants" was called by the CA to resolve the matter but without a satisfactory result. The administrator then decided to embark on a rather peculiar exercise in direct democracy. "I then suggested that a secret vote be taken by myself as to what was the true wish of the people, which I did yesterday, both parties agreeing to abide by the result. The question was: 'Do you wish the extension of the mosque on the Northern [*sic*] side [?]' The responses were, 43 'yes', 107 'no' and 18 'as the *shari'a* orders.'" He further noted that "many did not express an opinion, and I think belong to the third class." The work halted and, apparently going no where, the Civil Administrator wrote to the First Assistant Resident of Aden to ask if they could inquire among the learned of Aden "by whom should the expenses incurred by Sayyid Muhy al-Din [for the work already done] be borne."[104]

By now, the Residency viewed Yasin Khan as a noted expert on Islamic jurisprudence. As such, the FAR, Bernard Reilly, sent the request to the Registrar for his opinion. Khan, in turn, forwarded the case to Qadi Da'ud for the learned man's view. The judge responded by noting that the authorities were, in fact, asking the wrong question. The notion of whether or not Sayyid Muhy al-Din should be reimbursed—as far as he was concerned—was beside the point. The real question, from the perspective of religious law, was whether or not the extension of the mosque itself was lawful. He stated uncategorically that those who opposed the extension—and claimed to provide a legal basis for their opposition—were in error. His opinion is worth quoting at length.

> On the subject of the permissibility of enlarging the Mosque [*sic*] situated at Kamaran about which there is a dispute among the Mohammedan [*sic*] inhabitants there, I inform you that . . . the two written opinions contradict one another. One of them supports the permissibility and the other precludes it, hence the difference in its legality and illegality . . .
>
> I have already received the contents of both opinions from Kamaran through one of the merchants of Aden, named Muhammad Awadth Moharez, and I have made my endorsement . . . I quote from the *Fatwa*s of the learned Ibn Hajjar—
>
> He was asked "Whether it is permissible to pull down and enlarge a Mosque [*sic*]?" He replied saying, "Ibn Igal Al-Yamani permitted it, but the Asbaha disallowed it." Some

commentators in the book "al-Wasit" [declared] that it was permissible provided there is a need for it and the Imam or his representatives supervises it. Such work has been done on the Mosques of Mecca and Medina on several occasions . . . and no one objected to such work.

As long as the intention of the person undertaking the work was to please God and to serve the interests of the people, and the *mihrab* or *minbar*[105] were not pulled out of their proper alignments, there could be no objection to such a project. He concluded, "I concur with the learned men who gave permission for this [work] and I am of the opinion that it should not be prevented. No attention is to be paid to the majority of voters when there are no grounds for it."[106]

In his own response, Khan began by dismissing the Qadi's opinion. He remarked to Reilly that he had asked the judge for his opinion on the matter, but that his reply was "irrelevant." The matter, as far as he was concerned, had "already been decided by votes against Muhy al-Din. He was building the mosque for his own spiritual benefit and must bear the costs. A mosque is the property of God in the eye of the law and any money that is spent in extending or repairing it is an act of charity, and is not recoverable. If Muhy al-Din had held the position of a trustee and spent money out of the trust funds in his hand, the position might have been different, but I presume this was not the case."[107]

In a striking fit of evenhandedness, Reilly forwarded both responses to Kamaran as well as a third joint opinion written by the Qadi and Sayyid Abdullah al-Aydarus that reiterated the former's original points. The dispute over the mosque continued on Kamaran for several months and, in the end, the expansion project was abandoned and Sayyid Muhy al-Din was never reimbursed. In the local wrangling that followed, the opinions of both the Qadi and the Registrar were largely ignored.

The exchange, however, sheds light on the complex relationship between Muslim bureaucrats and traditional religious elites in colonial Aden. As the case of the Wakf Committee demonstrates, secularly educated bureaucrats such as Khan and more traditional *'ulama'* could work together in order to push a social agenda that both found mutually agreeable. At the same time, this was not a relationship without its cleavages. Yasin Khan believed that his education and position entitled him to weigh in authoritatively on religious matters and even critique the views of the traditional scholarly class. At the same time, as we see in the Kamaran mosque dispute, the *'ulama'* did not view this as a one-sided partnership. Friction between members of the *'ulama'* and high-level bureaucrats, like the Registrars, occurred throughout the period in question.[108] Conflict, however, was not necessarily axiomatic. While frequently at loggerheads, local notables and scholars may also find common cause with their bureaucratic co-religionists as the case of the Wakf Committee demonstrates. The result was an almost continuous renegotiation of the boundaries of authority among Aden's Muslims that were, of course, key to defining the community's moral limits. Such struggles invariably centered on Muslim ideals and institutions, with the various participants drawing on the broader intellectual networks to which they belonged. At the same time, those involved also inevitably drew on the imperial context that formed the other important backdrop of their lives that ensured that their paths ultimately intersected.

Personal trajectories, community boundaries

When thinking about the development of community and authority within Britain's colonial context, the significance of the Imperial state can never be discounted. As we have seen throughout this chapter, even when the state claimed disinterest in how its subjects adjudicated certain domestic and civil matters their specter was never far away. The British Imperial apparatus was always present in the legal lives of the colonized. Ideologically, the state's presence was felt via spurious constructions of "native" custom, such as *Panchayyat* or experiments in codifying and reinventing Islamic law. Administratively, the imprint of empire was manifest through the state's ability to determine who had authority within the community to oversee the adjudication of law and custom. What must be remembered is that, within this framework, Muslim rather than European functionaries carried out much of the day-to-day implementation of legal practice. As a result, certain Muslim elites retained a significant hand in shaping not only legal procedure, but also the moral and social boundaries of their community.

Doreen Massey suggests that the construction of place can best be understood as the confluence of the trajectories of individuals.[109] Examining the intersection of individuals such as Qadi Umar Abdullah and Rustom Ali as well as Yasin Khan and Da'ud al-Battah helps construct not only a history of place by way of the physical and ideological trajectories that brought them together, but also how such trajectories helped shape the ideals that these people ultimately held in common (or contested). Place is not a free-for-all as both Massey and Lambert and Lester are at pains to point out. "Trajectories," Lambert and Lester write, "impose constraints on the material practices that humans adopt in a place and condition the imagination of place."[110] Hence, it should come as little surprise that not only would Aden's public sphere be defined as inherently Islamic but that any Muslim seeking to shape the community would have to do so through that rubric. The diversity of personal trajectories among the Settlement's Muslims, however, meant that the boundaries delineating what it meant to be a member in good standing of that community would be subject to regular contestation.

The public careers of these figures provide an instructive window on to how the intersection of individual trajectories—and the intellectual networks they inhabited—could shape a local social context. It may be tempting to dismiss the Registrars as stooges of an Imperial bureaucracy determined to strip local authorities of their power. However, as we have seen, it was frequently the Registrars who took the initiative to intervene in local religious matters and made the loudest (and most persistent calls) for restriction and state intervention. It was Sayyid Rustom Ali who argued most vociferously for curbing the authority of the Qadis in adjudicating inheritance cases in the face of European officials who were in favor of their maintaining such authority. By the same token, it was Yasin Khan who inserted himself into the activities of the Wakf Committee, creating a space for himself as one the Settlement's "Leading Mohamedans." Although sanctioned—and probably welcomed—by the state, they did not dictate his actions. In short, while certainly agents of the government, the Registrars—by dint of their position and education—also saw themselves as influential members of their community who were entitled to an active role in shaping it.

By the same token, the emergence of the Registrars (as well as other Muslim civil servants) as community leaders was not necessarily resisted by the so-called "traditional" elites. Certainly, when it came to matters of religious law, the Qadis and other members of the *'ulama'* did not easily tolerate incursions into what was viewed as their domain. But, as al-Makki's *Overflowing River*, as well as the forceful and learned arguments of individuals such as Umar Abdullah Sharaf, demonstrate, rather than simply dismiss them—initially, at least—traditionally trained scholars were open to engaging with their counterparts in spirited debate. Furthermore, in cases involving wider community politics, local bureaucrats could also serve as useful allies. While seemingly paradoxical, the complex relationship between Aden's "traditional" elites and the imperial bureaucratic elite reveals the importance of not only the translocal flows created by empire, but the continued importance of Muslim intellectual trends in constructing the social milieu of colonial Aden.

The introduction of Muslim bureaucrats to Aden was bound to have a transformative affect on the power dynamics within the community of believers. As virtually all educated Muslim elites of the period, bureaucrats such as Rustom Ali and Khan were reform-minded individuals. Unlike various other "new" elites in Aden such as the scripturalist reformers[111]—among whom al-Battah could be numbered—these civil servants were reformists who subscribed to European imperial ideology. Transformation of the faith and betterment of society, to their minds, could only be accomplished through the implementation of a European rationalist filter. Only by applying "superior" Western notions of law and logic as embodied in Anglo-Muhammadan law could one hope to re-invigorate the faithful and retrieve society from the depths of ignorance and barbarism.[112] As persons with power, it seems inevitable that their interpretations of the faith would have broad social implications for the Muslims of Aden. By placing individuals in positions of power over other Muslims, the imperial bureaucracy played a role in not only the spread of reformist ideology but facilitated transformations in notions of authority and who had the right to wield it.

While Rustom Ali and Yasin Khan represented an ideological translocal flow emanating from the intellectual heart of empire that often ran counter to other intellectual trajectories this was not always the case. Aden during this period was also home to a growing number of scripturalist reformers who believed that Muslim society could only prosper and revive its fortunes by cleansing itself of unlawful innovation (*bid'a*) and local custom. Among these was Qadi Da'ud al-Battah who, as we shall see in the next chapter, devoted a great deal of energy during the 1920s to stamping out what he viewed as illicit and immoral customs such as local forms of spirit possession (that is, Zar and Tambura). While al-Battah was averse to his contemporary's attempted foray into religious law, he regarded Khan as an ally on the Wakf Committee. This seems in large part because both maintained ideological trajectories with a common goal: the revival of Muslim society by purifying it of backward and superstitious practices and corruption. The personal trajectories of Khan and al-Battah pointed both men in what can be viewed as divergent, although not wholly incompatible, directions. Khan was an urbane, dedicated civil servant who ultimately saw Westernizing trends as the savior of the faith. Al-Battah was a traditionally trained religious scholar from a far more provincial background who, not surprisingly, found the scripturalist school of reform more appealing. When the networks of imperial service caused their paths to cross, ripples and shifts resulted within the framework of public religiosity in Aden. Theirs were not the only trajectories among the Muslims of the Settlement, however. The following chapters examine the influence of others whose paths similarly sought to define the boundaries of community in Aden. In the end, the imperial record preserved an image of these currents that allows us, to paraphrase Frederick Cooper, to see at least part of the lives built within the communal "crevices" created by the colonial moment.[113]

5
"An Innocent Amusement": Marginality, Spirit Possession and the Moral Community

It was the Muslim month of Safar and the usual rumors were once again beginning to circulate, Lt. Mosse of the Aden Police noted in his official report. The Jabartis (the "African sweeper class") steal children. They eat them. They sell them to the Free Masons who render the bodies to extract gold from their blood . . . but only during the month of Safar. But on this April morning in 1906 things had really started to get out of hand. An Arab child had been reported missing the night before and several Jabartis were severely beaten as a result. In retaliation, a mob of some seventy to eighty Jabarti men swept into the Tawahi bazaar the next morning bent on pay back. Following a tense stand-off, Lt. Mosse, with the assistance of a Somali Havildar,[1] managed to get the crowd to disperse with only limited causalities. Curiously, despite the violence, the authorities chose not to pursue the matter. No charges were brought against the garbage men and no arrests were ever made. The primary reason for this, according to the lieutenant, was that had legal action been pursued the sweepers would very likely have gone on strike, precipitating a public sanitation and health crisis in the Settlement.[2]

Since the publication of K. N. Chaudhuri's *Trade and Civilization in the Indian Ocean* thirty years ago, a vast library of scholarship has been dedicated to the social and cultural history of one of the earliest and longest-lived examples of a transregional arena, the western Indian Ocean. For most, however, this has been a world dominated by elites. Long-distance merchants, ocean-going religious scholars and European colonial officials—along with the networks and webs woven by each over the course of hundreds of years—constitute the bulk of this scholarship.[3] Largely absent from this picture are tens of thousands of individuals like the "Jabarti" whose lives were no less cosmopolitan and mobile but because of the low social status ascribed to them by wider society tend to be less visible in the historical record. One place where they frequently become more observable, however, are along the often-contested moral boundaries utilized to delineate membership in the community.

As we have witnessed in previous chapters, Aden's majority, non-European population was an ethnically diverse community whose members were drawn from across Britain's Indian Ocean imperium with little in common other than a shared faith. As a result, over the course of the nineteenth century and early twentieth religious ideals and institutions increasingly formed the center of social and communal life for most Adeni Muslims. Institutions like *waqf*, the Qadi's courts and sacred spaces, such as mosques, shrines and cemeteries, and, later, reformist organizations, became venues for individuals who wished to stake a claim to either membership in the community and/or social authority. It was within the arena of Muslim institutions that the act of creating community was carried out.

The wealthier and politically connected elements ultimately emerged as a continually shifting set of elites who acquired social capital largely through their association with religious institutions and imperial authority. It was these individuals, along with a few pre-colonial socio-religious elites, most notably the Aydarus Sayyids, who served as the brokers of power and authority within the Settlement and sought to define the parameters for "belonging" to the community of Aden Muslims. The town's wealthy merchants, civil servants and religious scholars, along with others that imperial authority recognized as "respectable" citizens were the people who led public committees, founded reformist organizations and administered shrines and mosques. As such, they emerged as the chief arbiters of who did and—more importantly—who did not belong within the bounds of moral, upright society.

The authority and assertions of these elites, however, rarely went uncontested. Rather than mere pawns of their social and political betters, the less connected and wealthy frequently contested the boundaries set by their supposed superiors. While reform-minded businessmen and *'ulama'* sought to restrict the limits of acceptable religious practice, Sufis and adherents of spirit-possession cults worked to keep such boundaries fluid and ensure their place in society.[4]

Like all urban centers, Aden was home to numerous individuals who inhabited what may be referred to as the social and moral margins. Some, like the Jabarti, constituted corporate groups whose marginality was rooted in some perceived genealogical or occupational stain that placed them beyond the pale of acceptable society. The marginality of others may be the result of some unfortunate circumstance, such as poverty or employment in an occupation considered morally suspect by "respectable" society, such as incense or coffee sorting—both regarded as covers for prostitution. Using the imperial archives, this chapter begins by outlining the lives of certain marginal groups in Aden generally ignored by the historical record. Its focus then narrows to the efforts of certain so-called peripheral elements to claim and maintain their membership in the community. Specifically, it looks at two groups who created a place within local society via what may be termed the "spiritual economy" and the realm of spirit possession: the Jabarti—the much-maligned "sweepers" mentioned above—who were practitioners of Tambura, a spirit-possession cult from the Sudan, closely associated with various local saints' tombs and their annual festivals or *ziyarat* and a more loosely affiliated group of low-status Ethiopian and Somali women who presided over the local practice of the well-known Zar cult found throughout eastern Africa and littoral Arabia.

Both traditions maintained a long-standing presence in Aden. However, by the 1920s they were under attack by early scripturalist reformers (commonly referred to today as Salafis) who viewed their rituals as licentious performances that ate away at the moral core of society. Curiously, even though their spiritual practices were similar and both sought remedies via the same channels, the two groups experienced very different outcomes. The women who practiced Zar were entirely unsuccessful in their efforts and were ultimately forced outside the Settlement or underground. The Jabarti practitioners of Tambura, however, succeeded in avoiding an outright ban, although certain restrictions were placed on their activities.[5] Here we consider the place of Tambura and Zar as part of the religious public sphere and the ways in which their socially disadvantaged practitioners sought to protect their position in the face of nascent scripturalist reform and the shifting boundaries of acceptable morality during the 1920s. At the same time, it suggests that defense of tradition and the unseen were, for some at least, not simply "weapons of the weak" intended to secure their position in society in opposition to stronger social elements. Rather, rituals were also critical to how individuals engaged with the unseen in ways that impacted their daily lives.

Cosmopolitan imperial society—"servile" groups and "marginal" people in Aden

As we saw in earlier chapters, Aden, from its founding as early as the first century BCE, served as a cross-cultural epicenter for virtually all of the trading civilizations of the Indian Ocean and Mediterranean worlds. This cosmopolitan character only increased under British rule as the port attracted individuals from throughout the Red Sea and western Indian Ocean in search of economic opportunity. The social and economic profile of the Settlement's Muslim residents encompassed an increasingly broad spectrum. On the upper end of the scale, those British authority dubbed the Settlement's 'respectable citizens,' were wealthy merchants, shop owners, religious leaders, doctors, lawyers, clerks and policemen. As Aden grew, these individuals were drawn from across Britain's Indian Ocean domain and included Arabs, Indians and Somalis among others. On the other end lay the vast majority of the population who scraped together an existence as porters, stevedores, carriage drivers, bum-boatmen, day laborers, mosquito hunters, incense and coffee sorters (largely a female profession), domestic servants, prostitutes and, lowest of all, the sweepers or garbage men. The members of this end of society were no less—and possibly even more—diverse than their elite counterparts. While a significant number of Aden's laboring class were drawn from the near Yemeni interior, many others hailed from the East African and Red Sea coasts as well as India.

Many of these may simply be classified as members of "the urban poor," whose arrival in Aden was driven by multiple factors. Some came to settle and start new, more prosperous lives. These included "Jabali" villagers from the Yemen highlands or Hadramis from the southern Wadi Hadramaut, seeking to escape the more precarious life of small-hold farming and herding for what they saw as the greater security of wage labor or petty commerce in the city. Indian Memon and Bohra Muslims from western India sought to parlay skills such as tin-smithing or bricklaying into some semblance of prosperity. And, indeed, there are many stories of modest successes, such as the illiterate Sayyid from Hadramaut who became a successful butcher or his contemporary, a poor fish monger, who came to dominate the town's trade in seafood, both of whom became prominent and "respectable" citizens.[6]

Others came for what they anticipated would be shorter stays, hoping to earn enough money to achieve some short-term goal. Pilgrims returning from the Hajj trying to earn enough for the passage home or young Somali men working on gangs "bunkering" coal in the harbor or ferrying ship passengers to and from shore in small boats, hoping to save enough cash to buy the livestock needed for contracting a good marriage back home.[7] As such, there were few theoretical limitations on the social or economic mobility of most of these individuals.[8] There were others in Aden whose place in society was much more circumscribed. These included the Sidis, the Akhdam and Jabartis, frequently referred to in the colonial literature as "outcaste groups" who society viewed as distinct communities and whose status was the result of perceived genealogical impurities nearly impossible to shed.

The Akhdam and Jabarti

The Sidis were former slaves, and their descendants, captured by the British antislavery squadron and liberated in Aden during the second half of the nineteenth century. The majority of liberated Africans did not remain long in Aden but were either repatriated to the continent or transported onward to India where they usually came under European Christian mission tutelage for at least a short time. As a result, the community was never large and we know little about those who remained in Aden.[9] The Akhdam and the Jabarti, on the other hand, were more prominent and permanent fixtures in Settlement society.

The Akhdam (Ar. lit servants, sing. Khadim) were a community native to southern Arabia but distinguished by their physical appearance. While Arabic speaking, the Akhdam were characterized by their "African"—specifically Ethiopian—features. Rather than the scions of slaves, they were popularly believed to be the descendants of soldiers and colonists left behind after the end of the ancient Aksumite Kingdom's occupation of Himyar in the sixth century CE. According to one legend recorded in the mid-nineteenth century, "when the Arabs succeeded in shaking off the Abyssinian yoke (which they did with the assistance of the Persians), a number of Ethiopian families were scattered over the country. The Arabs, in order to perpetuate the remembrance of their victory, condemned them to the condition of serfs."[10] Commonly referred to as *Mukhallafat Abraha* (Abraha's leftovers)[11] the Akhdam were forbidden from engaging in important social rituals with "noble" Arab families, including sharing food and intermarriage, for fear of ritual pollution. They were also prohibited from living in close proximity to "Arab" families, in structures more than a single story in height or in properties with an enclosed fence.[12] Not surprisingly, they were relegated to the most menial jobs, including haircutting and garbage collection. Many Akhdam were drawn to British Aden seemingly by economic opportunity. However, in doing so they escaped few of the restrictions or humiliations experienced in the highlands. They occupied their own neighborhoods both in Crater and Shaykh Uthman, working primarily as musicians "in the low coffee-shops," sweepers and incense sorters—not to mention maintaining a reputation for engaging in prostitution.[13]

The Jabarti, as a group, are much harder to pin down. In the Aden residency records, they are simply referred to as "the African sweeper class." Although identified collectively by the British as "a community," living mostly in the Settlement "sweeper lines," the Jabarti do not appear to have been a single group linked by blood or common ancestry. F. M. Hunter, who makes one of the few references to them in the colonial literature, referred to them simply as "low born Somalis and negroes," who "do scavengers' work."[14] Records from the early twentieth century indicate that the community's core was made up of non-Arab Sudanese as well as riverine Somalis and even some Ethiopians, whose names appear on various petitions and reports.[15] Regardless of their ethnic make-up, the Jabarti were charged with the collection of garbage as well as "night soil," throughout the Settlement. While technically municipal servants, they also often maintained private arrangements, cleaning the cesspits and latrines of well-to-do households throughout the port.[16] In the close-quarters and fetid climate that characterized life in Aden, while roundly despised for their contact with human waste, the Jabarti performed a civil function whose importance cannot be overemphasized.

The term "Jabarti" and how it came to refer to the sweepers of Aden remains unclear. The word appears frequently in the European travel literature of the Horn of Africa but is rarely explained in detail. J. Spencer Trimingham, writing in the 1960s, noted that the earliest identified use of the term in an Arabic text was al-Maqrizi in the mid-fifteenth century who used it to refer to the region around Zayla. Trimingham held that the name came to refer to Muslims from any of the southern Ethiopian kingdoms and was ultimately generalized to all Ethiopian Muslims. Indeed, it was—and to a certain extent still is—a regional word for some Amhara- and Tigrinian-speaking Muslims of the high Ethiopian Plateau who claim the "Abyssinian Hijra" of the early seventh century as the date of their arrival.[17] The word itself, at least in popular etymology, derives "from *gabr* (plur. *Abert*) servant (of God)." Trimingham is at pains to point out that while used as a general word for Muslims, "it must be clearly understood that in no sense" is it "the ethnic name of a people."[18]

This was certainly the case in colonial Aden. Based on the names recorded in the residency records, the Jabarti appear as a diverse collection of low-status individuals from the Red Sea and Gulf of Aden, hailing from as far south as the Benaadir coastal region in Somalia to as far north as the Sudan. Thus, among those recorded we find the common *nisba* 'Sudani' along with individuals whose names were distinctly Somali such as Hasan Robleh and Yusuf Abdi.[19] Although the records do not explicitly say as much, those categorized as "Jabarti" appear to have been recruited by the imperial state from the African coast for the express purpose of employment as sweepers in the Settlement. This notion seems supported by the provision of government housing for them within the civil lines.[20] Trimingham notes that, in Ethiopia, the phrase could occasionally carry a derogatory meaning, but how it came to identify those recruited to collect the Settlement's refuse and human waste remains unclear.

On the margins of public spirituality—Zar and Tambura

While the Akhdam and Jabartis occupied a reviled, although crucial, place in the Settlement as refuse and "night soil" collectors they also maintained a similar space in the town's spiritual arena. The public spiritual sphere in Aden from the beginning of the colonial occupation through the early decades of the twentieth century was dominated by two not unrelated phenomena: the Sufi "cult of the saints" and spirit-possession groups (that is, Zar and Tambura). In addition to keeping the streets of Aden free of trash, the Akhdam and the Jabarti played important, if sometimes indirect, roles in both of these activities.

Sufism and the "cult of the saints,"[21] as we have already seen, was a prominent element of the public sphere of Aden from the beginning of the British occupation through the early decades of the twentieth century. As the town grew through the nineteenth century saint veneration and Sufism continued to emerge as an important expression of popular spirituality and communal belonging. By the 1920s Aden boasted more than a dozen annual saints' festivals centered on tombs dotted throughout the settlement. Some of these were associated with particular Sufi orders or *tariqa*s; others were maintained by local followers with only loose affiliations to any particular order. Newcomers seeking, at least in part, to establish their connection to the Settlement, founded virtually all of these.

Central to most festivals was a carnival-like atmosphere with numerous diversions for the pious, ranging from the innocent to the risqué. At a typical *ziyara* of the 1920s one would find innocuous entertainments such as rides, puppet shows, street magicians and games of skill and chance such as ring toss, lucky dip and the odd shooting gallery. In addition to such "wholesome" amusements one could also see groups of Akhdam musicians and dancing girls, wearing "semi-transparent clothes" and Jabarti 'Akils' leading *Tambura* ceremonies.[22] While festivals were organized by either the various Sufi orders or adherents of a particular saint, they were financed by large associations of merchants, landlords and other prominent citizens. These individuals gained the admiration of the community for their charity, but also made a great deal of money from the thousands of pilgrims who came to venerate and honor the deceased.[23] For their part, the Akhdam and Jabarti gained valuable connections that served their mutual economic and spiritual benefit and may well have helped them retain their spot in the public sphere. As we shall see, such connections could be parlayed into important social capital, a resource the disciples of Zar conspicuously lacked.

Spirit possession in Aden

Tambura was only one of two spirit-possession cults popular in Aden through the 1920s. The other was the more widely known cult, Zar.[24] Both Zar and Tambura were concerned primarily with curing individuals of illness caused by largely malevolent spirits. The few anthropological studies that focus on both cults hold that while likely related to each other they were distinct phenomena. Both were believed to have roots in the Horn of Africa and share close affinities with the Bori cult of the Western Sudan. However, while Zar is believed to have originated in what is today Ethiopia, Tambura seems to have separate origins as part of an ancestor cult among the tribes of southern Sudan, most notably the Zande.[25] In addition, Zar tended to be dominated by female practitioners and in Aden at least, never seems to have been associated with the *ziyarat*[26] while Tambura was dominated by men who maintained close ties to the "cult of the saints."[27] As two recent researchers have noted, while there appear to be overlaps between the two traditions in terms of the conceptualization of spirits and illness, "similarities in ritual process" as well as amicable relationships between the two groups, the practitioners "themselves stress the differences rather than the similarities between the cults. The distinction between 'we' and 'they' is emphasized and. . .expressed in terms like the 'bori (Zar)' people and the 'Tambura people.'"[28] To better understand their individual trajectories within the context of Aden, it is helpful to examine the known history of each.

Zar

Zar is—historically speaking—a widely spread phenomenon found throughout Northeast and coastal East Africa, the Red Sea and Persian Gulf coasts of Arabia, Egypt, Sudan and even southern Iran. As a ritual found across a large geographic area, as Richard Natvig has pointed out, the "ceremonial and cosmological differences," sociosexual make up of its participants as well as the social and cultural "consequences of participation" vary considerably across time and space.[29] Two constants, however, tend to stand out. First, the purpose of the practice is invariably "the curing of illnesses or misfortunes caused by possession by a species of spirit called 'Zar.'"[30] Second, and more important, while affliction strikes women from across the social spectrum, its practitioners are unfailingly either women of slave origin or ascribed low social status.

The origins of Zar are, unsurprisingly, somewhat murky. References to a "Zar" spirit have been found on Ethiopian protective amulets excavated at Aksum that can be dated to the sixteenth century. The earliest mention of a Zar ritual—in European sources, at least—dates only to the first half of the nineteenth century. In 1839, two evangelists of the Church Mission Society, John Lewis Krapf and Charles William Isenberg, witnessed a possession ceremony held in a home in highland Ethiopia. Their account is strikingly similar to modern descriptions of Zar ritual:

> The Gallas[31] and all of the people of Guragueand Shoa, believe that there are eighty-eight spirits, which they call Sarotsh—in the singular Sar. These spirits are said to walk about and inflict men with sickness; and hence, when such persons feel sick, they take

their refuge in superstitious means. By smoking and singing, moving their body, and particularly by offering a hen to the Sar, they imagine that they can frighten away the bad spirit and secure themselves against being sick. The Sartosh are divided into two parties, each having its Alaca or head ... When persons perform such a ceremony, they speak in another language. Thus, for instance, they call a hen, "Tshari"—in the Amharic, a hen is called Doro. The hen is afterward slaughtered and eaten by the assistants, except the brains which are only eaten by the person who has performed the most part.[32]

While Natvig refers to this as "proto-Zar ... at an early stage of development," as opposed to "the fully developed Zar cult," the ceremony described bears many of the hallmarks of rituals recounted by later observers. These include the use of tobacco, smoke or incense, dancing, speaking in "tongues," gift giving to placate the spirit and sacrifice.[33] Over the course of the nineteenth century through the middle of the twentieth, there are numerous accounts, written mostly by Europeans, of Zar rituals around the western Indian Ocean. Although ranging over a wide geographic area, all describe strikingly similar ceremonies and cosmologies, as well as attributing the cult's origins to a single source: Ethiopian slaves.[34] C. B. Klunzinger, a quarantine doctor on Egypt's Red Sea coast, Salma bint Said (also known as Emily Ruete, the errant Zanzibari Princess) and Snoucke Hurgronje, the noted Dutch Orientalist, all link the practice explicitly to "Abyssinian" slave women who introduced the ritual to the households of their masters if not the very notion of jinn and possession.[35] The descriptions provided by Salma bint Said and Hurgronje of ceremonies in Zanzibar and Mecca, respectively, are of particular significance. Both offer a level of detail found in few historical sources, but more importantly each affords insight into the broader appeal and social context of the cult.

Hurgronje was an Orientalist and sometime adviser to the Dutch colonial state, who penned what is probably the earliest detailed ethnography of daily life in Mecca based on his sojourn in the Hijaz from 1884 to 1885. His observations on Zar are of interest as much for his ability to perceive their wider social significance as for their detail. Zar, he noted, was a fact of everyday life in nineteenth-century Meccan society.

> From youth upwards the women hear so many tales told of the Zar that when they are attacked by the diseases mentioned, those diseases generally take in their view the form of the dominion of the Zar over the will of the individual. In some cases this dominion shows itself in the woman being thrown at certain times to the ground and lying there for hours in convulsions; sometimes she appears to be suffering from some known disease, which however now and then passes away suddenly leaving only the pale colour and the wide-strained, open eyes. Sometimes the patient is during the attacks as though wild and raging. Learned men, doctors and in general most of the men are always inclined to employ either medicine or else orthodox religious exorcism of the Satanic powers; the female friends and relations on the other hand advise unconditionally the calling in of an old woman who is versed in dealings with the Zar [Hurgronje contends the word Zar had no plural] (a Sheikhat ez-Zar[36]) and they in the end overcome all resistance.

> The Sheikhah does not put questions to the sick woman herself, but to the Zar who is lodged in her body; sometimes the dialogue is in common language and so can be understood by the bystanders, but often the speakers use the Zar language, which can be understood by no one without the interpretation of the Sheikhah. Essentially there is little difference to be observed in the results of such conversations. At the repeated request of the Sheikhah the Zar declares himself willing to depart, on a certain day on the performance of the customary ceremonies, but stipulates certain conditions. He demands a beautiful new dress, gold or silver ornaments, or the like. As he himself, however, escapes human perception, his wish can only be gratified by the articles mentioned bestowed upon the sick body which he inhabits. It is touching also to see how the evil spirits consider the age, taste or needs of the possessed person. On the day on which the departure of the spirit is to take place, the invited female friends of the sick woman come to her in the afternoon or evening and are regaled with coffee, tea, pipes and also often with food; the Sheikhah and her slave girls, who must attend these functions with beat of drum and with a species of song, partake of the refreshments and prepare for their work.[37]

Hurgronje's detailed description of Zar ritual reflects his training as an Orientalist and early ethnologist. However, what sets him apart from other contemporary observers is his ability to perceive the wide social appeal and function of the possession cult. Zar, he tells us, was not a limited phenomenon. Traditions of spirit possession, he wrote, could be found "among all the nations that are represented in Mekka" and while they might have various appellations for it "they soon here take on the local name, which is derived from the Ethiopian and shows that the superstition was introduced by Abyssinian slaves." Rather than a single, homogenous tradition, there existed, at least in theory, various methods for driving out spirits. There were "for instance, a Maghrebin (North-West African), a Sudanese, an Abyssinian and a Turkish method."[38] However, in the end, most of the afflicted ultimately called on the services of the Ethiopian "Sheikhah," the acknowledged expert.

In addition to recognizing its widespread presence in Meccan society, Hurgronje also noted its importance particularly for women. "The struggle with the Zar," he wrote, "exemplifies the saddest and gayest sides of the lives of the Mekkan women." While women were undoubtedly tormented by possession it also represented a social and material opportunity for them.

> It is easy to perceive that this work very rarely means the expulsion of real Zar; fine clothes and nice parties are what the Mekkan women love above all things, and they are shrewd enough to act at the same time the part of the Zar and the possessed ones: this disease-comedy has however actually become an endemic sickness. It would be necessary to keep a woman away from all intercourse with other women in order to preserve her from this infection: just as it may be said: "I must go tomorrow to the wedding of such a one", so another day it is said: "I am going to such a one this evening she has a Zar" (the word is used for the company that attends the exorcism as well as for the evil spirit itself). Nay, some too even give away the show and say to their husbands: "It is high time for me to give a Zar for I have been to so many at my friends". "What is the use of all his objections and how can he use his legal right to prevent his wife from leaving

the house when he knows that she upon his refusal will behave like a madwoman until he gives way or divorces her? And what is the use of a divorce when he cannot do otherwise than marry another who similarly after a short time commences her Zar? The Zar in fact is just as much a necessity of life to most women as tobacco or gold or the gilded embroidery of their trousers.[39]

Salma bint Said similarly recorded the broad appeal of the cult in East Africa. Although dominated by female 'Abyssinian' practitioners, possession, she noted, could afflict anyone and all segments of Arab society in Zanzibar participated. Even recently arrived, and largely skeptical, Omanis were not immune. "The Omanites," she writes, "reject such nonsensical practices as I have been describing." Indeed, "when they come to Africa, they at first think us barbarians, and would like to return immediately; however, they soon become receptive to the very notions they denounced, and adopt the most absurd. I was acquainted with an Arabian of that sort, who believed herself possessed by an evil spirit which made her ill; she was convinced that it could be propitiated if she held festivities in its honour."[40]

Zar, as practiced in Aden, closely mirrored the descriptions of Hurgronje and Bint Said. The Settlement was home to a number of independent possession circles each led by a priestess or '*Alaka.*'[41] Groups were primarily composed of Somali and Ethiopian women from low-status social groups who filled various functions either assisting the *Alaka*, singing musical accompaniment or helping the possessed. While led and dominated by women, the groups' musicians—mainly drummers—were mostly men.[42] Although the practitioners were almost universally drawn from socially marginal groups, their clients—as in other places—came from across Adeni society. These included women of limited means but also individuals from some of the wealthiest and most respectable households in the Settlement as well as a few men. Ceremonies were, on some occasions, semipublic affairs held on bits of open common ground in neighborhoods like Shaykh Uthman. At other times, they might be held in the women's quarters or courtyards of private homes.[43] Presumably, the latter was the privilege of Aden's wealthier women who could afford to pay for such privacy.

The premise of the cult, as elsewhere, was rooted in the belief that women frequently came under the thrall of certain malevolent spirits or jinn becoming ill as a result.[44] Once possessed it was believed virtually impossible to rid one's self of the intruder. The task of the *Alaka* and her coterie was thus not to expel the jinn, but to negotiate with and placate it through ritual as well as expensive presents such as perfumes and jewelry. Descriptions of Zar rituals in Aden vary and none are as detailed as Hurgronje's or Bint Said's.[45] However, all include drumming, clapping and chanting along with some sort of ritual sacrifice (a sheep, goat or chicken, depending on the client's means) as well as feasting.[46] Performance of cult ceremonies was undoubtedly a noisy, boisterous affair. Even when performed in a private home, as a number of testimonies are at pains to point out, it could hardly go unnoticed by the neighbors.[47]

Finally, a few words must be said regarding the cult's links to broader religiosity. Later twentieth-century examinations of Zar—particularly in Sudan—highlight the lengths to which practitioners go in order to link their beliefs with Muslim cosmologies and the Islamic calendar. Writing in the late 1940s, the anthropologist Sophie Zenkovsky noted that at the conclusion of an "ordinary Zar," the "shaikha invokes Shaikh Abd el Gadir el Gilani and Shaikh Mohammed, and they [the gathered participants] all bow as in the performance of a Zikr [sic]."[48] In addition to invoking the saints, the Zar *shaikhas* also tied their beliefs to the Islamic calendar, Zenkovsky writes:

> During the month of Ramadan all the "good" Islamic spirits have great powers and all the *afarit, shayatin* and *riyah*[49] are hidden under the earth. Nobody can or will attempt to *darab al-Zar*; all the implements of the *shaikha* are collected on a table and covered with a cloth. On the 15th day of Ramadan the *shaikha* burns incense in front of the table and may uncover them.[50]

In her seminal work on possession in the contemporary Sudan, Janice Boddy notes similar conscious parallels with *tariqa* Sufism and adherence to the Muslim calendar.[51] In the urban Omdurman of the 1970s a Zar Shaykha "commands honor from adepts much as a *tarıga* [sic] shaykh does from his following." Furthermore, "public *zar* ceremonies periodically organized by individual shaykhat greatly resemble in their format the public *zikrs* [sic] of the *tarıgat* [sic]; both use a common set of ceremonial props including flags, and both direct prayers to Allah and the Prophet."[52]

What stands out about Zar in Aden is the near complete absence of such imagery. Boddy has amply demonstrated that, in the Sudan, Zar circles consciously coopted the imagery and even the terminology of *tariqa* Sufism. Significantly, this does not appear to have been the case in Aden where no such references occur. As we shall see below, the *Alakas* of Aden portray Zar—much like the depictions of Hurgonje and other early writers—as a practice that existed parallel to Islamic custom rather than within it. This was a characterization that would ultimately work to their disadvantage.

Tambura

While depictions of Zar organization and ritual must be pieced together from fragments in the colonial record, descriptions of Tambura ritual in Aden are even more scant. As a result, we need to turn to the colonial literature on the Sudan to develop a fuller picture. As described by observers and participants in the 1930s, Tambura in the Sudan was a complex, horizontally organized association whose membership consisted primarily of men from low-status or slave backgrounds. Unlike Zar, officiates of Tambura were generally those who were previously possessed by spirits and cured by the ritual. As G. P. Makris notes, "affliction," was "a precondition for becoming a cult group leader."[53] Also distinct from Zar, where each group was autonomous, a number of groups—"tanabir" (pl. of Tambura)—recognized the authority of a senior practitioner known as the *dalil* or guide who determined the timing and frequency of ceremonies. In the Sudan, the leader of an individual group held the title of *Sanjak*, an Ottoman military rank, while in Aden such individuals were known as *Akils*.[54] The principle distinctions between Zar and Tambura ceremonies, however, appeared to be the choice of musical instrument and, as we shall see in Aden at least, a curious and overt relationship to Sufism.

Zar traditionally relied primarily on drumming for its ceremonies. While drums were certainly used, at the center of Tambura ritual was a six-stringed *rababa*[55] that appeared to serve as the principle medium of communication between the group and the offending spirits. Each *rababa* received a name from the *Akil/Sanjak* that also served as the group's name.[56] So in Aden Mansur Ba Yasin was "the keeper of the tombora Salah"; Said Banda was the keeper of "tombora Nasra"; Khamis Barut was that of "tombora Jaria";[57] and Muhammad Sa'ad was keeper of "tombora Jamala."[58] In addition, male participants wore a leather girdle or belt decorated with cowries, sheep bones and goat hooves.[59] Probably the most curious distinction between Tambura and its Ethiopian cousin as the latter was practiced in Aden was its close connection with Islamic mysticism.

Tambura in Aden was performed by the sweepers on a weekly basis, most usually on Thursdays and Saturdays. However, it was also a prominent feature of almost every major *ziyara* in the Settlement.[60] Performances of Tambura might be viewed as an anomalous entertainment particularly since these were located not in the vicinity of the tombs but further away among the dice games, puppet shows and shooting galleries of the wider festival. Indeed, both imperial authorities and Tambura practitioners stressed—for reasons to be discussed below—that theirs was a simple pastime, "a sing-song ... among people of slave origin" in the words of one *Akil*, with no religious significance.[61] Other evidence, however, suggests that this was a carefully constructed picture meant to deliberately obscure the connections between Tambura and *tariqa* Sufism.

While it could hardly be argued that Tambura was simply an idiosyncratic form of Islamic mysticism, descriptions and testimonies from Sudan in the 1930s and 1940s reveal the use of a great deal of Sufi imagery within its ritual as well as self-conscious ties to the Islamic calendar. According to one observer, every Tambura group possessed two banners, "one is red with the words *Abd el-Gadir* [Jilani] with a star and a crescent moon written on it in white lettering, the other is white with *Saidi Billali*[62] and the star and the same moon in red. On the top of the banner staffs are rattles ending one with a crescent moon and a star; the other with a crescent moon and something like the head of a spear."[63] The resemblance of such banners to ones used for processions by nineteenth- and twentieth-century Sufi *turuq* is striking. The similarities did not, however, end there. During the ceremony known as *al-Kursi* (the throne) the banners were "hennaed" and then on Friday a procession was undertaken to visit each saint's tomb in the vicinity whereupon "dates and sweets are thrown at each site." In a separate ceremony seven pigeons were sacrificed "in the name of Abd al-Qadir Jilani, who is thought of as the 'king' of the *Tambura* spirits."[64] The banners were again taken out during the principal feasts of the Muslim calendar, Id al-Fitr marking the end of Ramadan and Id al-Adha (the feast of sacrifice) that marks the Hajj and during every local *mawlid* or saint's festival.

While ritual processions resembled those of their Sufi counterparts, other ceremonies also bore at least a passing similarity to local Muslim custom—in particular, the rituals surrounding *mawlid* or celebrations of the Prophet Muhammad's birthday. Writing in the 1940s, Zenkovsky noted that at the time of the *mawlid*:

> The floor is strewn with mats: the *rababa* with her singer is in the centre near the wall facing east, and on her left is the bearer of the big staff who is an old woman. The small staff reclines on the wall near her. In front of the *rababa* is a big incense burner with female attendant. Near the right hand wall are two drums with their attendants and the belt; near them are more burners. Near the entrance of the veranda are seated the women and children with big rattles in their hands.
>
> The singer tinkles the stings, the big drum gives one or two beats, the audience shake the rattles: it is the prelude. Then the singer being his [sic] chant by a sentence ordered by the *rababa*, the choir takes it up; the drum catches the cadence and the rattle shake in rhythm. The ceremony has began [sic].[65]

To anyone familiar with the performance of Maulidi along the East African coast, which is also used to celebrate the birth of the Prophet, this description will sound strikingly similar. However, this was not the only connection of the cult to the Islamic ritual calendar. As one informant noted, as with Sudanese Zar, Tambura ceremonies were not held during the holy month of Ramadan. Instead, at the start of the month the strings of the *rababa* were "plaited across with date palm leaves [rendering it unplayable] and the whole instrument is clothed and shut in its room." It remained so until the fourteenth day of the month when it was taken out and the strings unplaited, the instrument would be incensed and then returned to its cupboard until the Id at the end of the month.[66]

Like Zar, the descriptions of Tambura ritual in Aden are scant and there is no firm evidence that the Sufi-like rituals observed by Zenkovsky in Khartoum carried over to Aden. Other evidence exists, however, that does indicate a close association between the Tambura adherents and local tombs. As we will see below, by the mid-1920s Tambura practitioners in Aden sought to distance their rituals from what may be regarded as unseemly religiosity. For many, however, the ceremony certainly held spiritual significance connected directly to the Settlement's many tombs and shrines. In a 1932 petition to the Chief Commissioner, a group of *Akils* stated that Tambura was a ritual "created from our ancient days, [the] time of our grand-fathers," if "our saints [go] without worship . . . our relations [will] fall . . . sick . . . one after [another]."[67] In a similar petition from a few years earlier the *Akils* Mahi Ibrahim and Yusuf Abdi requested permission to hold a Tambura ceremony during the *ziyara* of Shaykh Ahmad in Tawahi as "We got a Vow [sic] to complete as we solemnly promised To [sic] God to complete ... on the day of the fair."[68] Finally, one police report noted, in 1931, that the practitioners of Tambura sought to become possessed by the spirit of whichever saint's *ziyara* they happened to be at.[69] For some at least, the practice of Tambura remained closely intertwined with the cult of the saints and the public performance of spirituality even while they distanced themselves from it within the official narrative. Unique among spirit cults in the region, Tambura practitioners seem to have engaged in what may be called a "positive" form of possession, where, rather than an affliction, the spirit was called upon in an effort to do good. Although this is quite speculative, it could be argued that the practitioners of Tambura viewed the saints, as well as the Prophet, as benevolent ancestors whose spirits could still assist the living in ridding them of less beneficent specters.[70]

Zar and Tambura, if the claims of their adherents are to be believed, held a secure spot within public spiritual space from the earliest days of the British occupation if not before.[71] By the 1920s, however, elements of Aden's more "respectable" Muslim population found both of these groups to be at best a public nuisance and at worst serious moral dangers. The campaigns against them stemmed directly from the growing religious reformism that suffused most public Muslim discourse from the late nineteenth century.

Religious reformers and the campaigns against Zar and Tambura

> The undersigned inhabitants of Aden-Arabs, Somalis and Indians beg most respectfully to approach your honor on a subject of the utmost importance to the whole Moslem community in Aden ... The subject that we bring forward for consideration is the great nuisance caused to us by an irreligious performance usually held in Aden among women, which is call "ZAR". It has been formerly tolerated because it used to be on [a] smaller scale very rarely [performed], but now it has turned out to be most unbearable.[72]

The late nineteenth century and early twentieth has been referred to as the era of the imperial petition, an instrument employed by colonial subjects across Britain's Empire in their efforts to gain the attention and favor of the state for various economic, social, religious or political purposes.[73] Such appeals might be intensely personal and individual (for example, an application from an Indian clerk asking to hold a Zar ceremony in order to honor a personal vow).[74] Others, such as the one above, could purport to represent much larger groups demanding action by the imperial state on some matter of grave public concern—in this case, the spirit-possession cult Zar.

Beginning in 1923, Aden's spiritual status quo began to come under pressure from a certain influential segment of Aden's male Muslim population that began to agitate against various practices deemed "un-Islamic" and a danger to the moral hygiene of the local Community of Believers. Their efforts, of course, were inspired by the growing discourses of Islamic religious reform that flowed across the British Empire from Cairo to Kuala Lumpur in the early twentieth century. Reformists in Aden varied greatly along socio-economic, ethnic and ideological lines. They were united, however, in the perceived need to eliminate (or at the very least "purify") particular local spiritual practices deemed morally suspect. These included spirit possession in any form, certain Sufi practices and various long-established religious rituals regarded as *bid'a* or "unlawful innovations." Reformists used a variety of old and new media forms to accomplish their goals. In addition to petitioning the state, reformers also utilized relatively new forms of social media to spread their message and attract adherents, including pamphlets and the formation of social clubs (for example, the Arab Literary Club) whose members regularly led discussions of current events and delivered lectures to the unlettered on pressing social, moral and political matters.[75] At the same time, we should note, reformists continued to avail themselves of more traditional Muslim social media in the form of mosque sermons, *fatwas* (religious opinions) from respected local religious scholars and religious poems intended to galvanize public support.[76]

The earliest and, in some ways, easiest targets of reformist efforts were the local spirit-possession groups.[77] Whether as a result of incipient reformist influence or fears over the cult's sudden growth in popularity, Zar was targeted first when, in December 1923, a group led by the Qadi of Aden, Da'ud al-Battah, initiated a petition seeking to have it banned.[78] The *'alim* and his fellow petitioners argued that the custom should be proscribed partly because it was *haram* but more importantly because the practitioners preyed on women of "rank and honor," duping them out of their savings and "introducing bad moral behavior into the entire community."[79] Backed by the signatures of many of Aden's "respectable citizens" as well as *fatwas* from three notable religious officials, including the representative of the Imam in Sana'a, the Residency and Superintendent of Police, quickly outlawed the practice.[80]

The reformers, however, were not the only ones to exploit the imperial medium of the petition. The practitioners of Zar and Tambura resisted the efforts to put them out of business by taking their case to the state. Both utilized formal petitions in an effort to convince the Resident to overturn their respective bans while the adherents of Zar even ultimately resorted to the British colonial courts. Curiously, even though their spiritual practices were similar and both sought remedies via the same channels, the two groups experienced very different results. The followers of Tambura succeeded in avoiding an outright ban, although certain restrictions were placed on their activities.[81] The women who practiced Zar, however, were entirely unsuccessful in their efforts and were ultimately forced underground or outside the Settlement entirely.

Zar priestesses versus The Powers That Be

Following their prohibition, the four Zar priestesses of Aden wasted no time in organizing their own petition. On the same day—January 18, 1924—that the Resident issued his final pronouncement regarding the cult's prohibition, the women filed their own petition seeking to have it overturned. The January appeal was the first of many that the *Alakas* of Aden submitted to the state from 1924 to 1932. In their initial salvo, the women addressed the charges brought against them by, on the one hand, disputing the moral and religious validity of the accusations, but also by challenging the very authority of those who made the allegations.

> We the undersigned prefer our complaint against those who complained to cancel the existence of Zar (i.e. a sort of females play [added by the translator])
>
> 1. We inform your honour, Sahib, that it is unlawful to prevent the existence of Zar because it is being practiced in this country as well as in the other countries throughout the East and West. In this country, the Zar has been practiced since the last hundred years when Aden was an Abdali territory and not of late and at that time neither the complainants nor their fathers or fore-fathers were there and we can prove this by original residents of Aden.
> 2. We inform your honour, oh Sahib, that the complainants are not originally Aden people but are foreigners some of whom are from Hadramaut, some from Syria and some from Yemen and other places.
> 3. Oh Sahib, we have heard that the above complaints against the Zar have obtained the signature of Sayed Mahomed Dawood Battah the Kadi of Aden for the discontinuance of the Zar and on that account we inform you, oh Sahib, that the aforesaid Kadi knows nothing about the locality, for it is [only] three or four years since you have appointed him as kadi. He belongs to Zabid and the Zar which he has declared in writing to be unlawful is being practiced in Zabid, Hodeida and the other countries in that direction. If the practice of Zar was unlawful, the people of Zabid and other countries would have stopped it because there were many Kadis and learned men who know better than him.
> 4. Oh Sahib, if the practice of Zar was not lawful and should not have been practiced in the town the original people of Aden would have stopped it, such as the Mansab of the country Sayed Abdulla Aydaroos and the former Kadi of Aden Kadi Sheikh Ahmed, Kadi Sayed Yehia, Kadi Sayed Hasan and his sons Mahomed and Hamood bin Hasan, the Kadi of Sheikh Othman, Kadi Abdul Rehman Nijm, Kadi Omer Abdullah Sharaf, his son Mahomed Omer Sharaf and his present brother Kadi Awad Abdulla Omer Sharaf. The above persons being the Kadis of Aden and Sheikh Othman and its Mansab would have stopped the performance of Zar if they could find any harm or corruption in its practice because they are more conversant than any one else with the principles of the Islamic faith.
> 5. We inform your honour, oh Sahib, that there are several immoral acts strictly forbidden from a religious point of view being practiced in this country such as the Toombara in which both male and female play... Such playing are openly made in the fairs [saints' festivals] and other places. There are people drinking liquor, committing adultery and Sodomy, practicing usury and gambling and do[ing] other objectionable acts which God has forbidden in the Koran. Why the complainants and the Kadi who complained against the Zar have not raised objection to the existence of these immoral acts which are forbidden by both God and His Apostle? We further say that the acts pointed out by us are not permissible by God nor His Apostle or the Islamic religion. The Zar is not an objectionable act, on the contrary some good is derived out

of it. The complainants against the Zar are wrong in their action and have no right to stop it, as it is not one of the objectionable acts but they have done that out of jealousy on their part. Oh Sahib, we are widows and have no any other means of livelihood except the performance of Zar and whatever we gain from the blessings of God and the Zar. You have now suspended the practice of Zar and said that you have done so until you go through this case. We obeyed your orders but this Zar is now being practiced by people at Sheikh Othman both in day and night time. It is unfair, oh Sahib, to stop us as we are widows. We now request God and you kindly to grant us permission to continue the Zar. Oh Sahib, when any one (female) of Aden people intend to perform Zar he (she) firstly pay us a visit at our home and we then go to his (her) place and perform the Zar under purdah. The people who perform the Zar are respectable (females) of Aden but we do not do as those who act against the Commandments of God.

Meanwhile, oh Sahib, the complainants have fabricated lies against us but God forbid that from a just point of view you would listen to the tale of liars and thus we become the victim of wrong while you are in 3existence. We invoke blessings for you as we are helpless widows.[82]

The women argued, first, that their practices in no way violated the legal precepts or moral community of the Faith, a contention that they sought to support by calling upon both local tradition as well as the wider regional context. Zar, the women held, had been a part of Aden's spiritual landscape since before the arrival of the British in the middle of the nineteenth century, when the port belonged to the Abdali Sultan. The ritual, they argued, was practiced throughout Yemen from Zabid in the mountains to Hodeida on the Tihama coast. And, finally, not only was Zar a longstanding tradition, but it was one tolerated by religious authority and they provide a lengthy list of *'ulama'*, past and present, who had never objected to the ritual.

This list invoked the names of virtually every prominent Adeni Qadi since the late nineteenth century as well as Sayyid Abdullah Aydarus who, as a descendant of the town's patron saint Abu Bakr Aydarus (d. 1506) and caretaker of his tomb complex, was recognized as one of the most learned and influential Muslims in the Settlement. Indeed, for a brief spell the Sayyid defended the women before the Resident as the practitioners of an innocent pastime. When interviewed by the First Assistant Resident regarding the ritual's permissibility under Islam, the Sayyid noted, "The Zar is not in accordance with the Sharia, but is a long standing tradition in Aden, after all there are many things—such as photography—which are not in accordance with the Sharia."[83]

Those who objected to Zar, on the other hand, the women charged were "not originally from Aden . . . but . . . foreigners some of whom are from Hadramaut . . . Syria . . . Yamen [*sic*] and other places." This included Qadi al-Battah who, they pointed out, as a native of Zabid should have known better. "If the practice of Zar was unlawful," they noted, "the people of Zabid and other countries would have stopped it because there were many Kadis [*sic*] and learned men [living there] who know better than him."[84]

Finally, they argued, while the town's so-called respectable citizens were busy persecuting a group of poor widows, other, flagrantly immoral activities, that *were* "strictly forbidden from a religious point of view," were allowed to continue uninterrupted. Tambura, for instance, was far worse than Zar where men and women mixed openly, getting up to God only knew what. The annual *ziyarat* associated with various tombs in the city hosted festivals where people drank liquor, "committed adultery and sodomy," and practiced "usury and gambling," all of which were "objectionable acts which God has forbidden in the Koran [*sic*]." How could Zar—a widely followed and wholesome practice—be banned when these immoral acts were not?

By invoking the Faith, correct practice and belief (not to mention scholarly authority) the *Alakas* initially sought to place Zar within the acceptable moral boundaries of the Muslim community using arguments that were not unlike those of their opponents. Curiously, neither side in this dispute attempted to bring to bear any specific theological or legal arguments frequently found in reformist debates of the period.[85] Instead, both employed much more vague protestations revolving around ideas of morality and what Islam would and would not allow as determined by agreed-upon-practice or a perceived "common sense" notion of the boundaries of the public sphere. Unfortunately, for the priestesses it was the Qadi's view of morality, along with the signatures of more than 100 townsmen that the British accepted. In response to the women's petition, the Residency replied, "Respectable citizens of Aden and Sheikh Othman [*sic*] are against the custom of Zar. This question has already been fully considered and orders issued to the police to refuse permission to hold the Zar in Aden and Sheikh Othman in future."[86]

For reformists, the matter was settled successfully in their favor and they, for the most part, moved on to other issues (most immediately their campaign to ban the town's other spirit-possession cult, Tambura). The four *Alakas*, however, did not concede defeat quite so easily as they continued to petition the state to lift the injunction over the next eight years. Continuing to utilize the medium of the formal petition, the women quickly abandoned the notion that Zar fit easily within the realm of acceptable Islamic practice. However, they continued to argue that the cult's practices were consistent with the community's broader moral economy.

Starting with petitions sent in March and April 1924, the women began to recast the matter. They argued, first in an application on March 31, that their services hardly represented a strain on the pocketbooks of women, stating that such ceremonies—at their most expensive—cost an individual a mere 15 Rs (if she were a woman of means) and only 4 Rs if she were poor.[87] The women held that this was no more than was often paid to someone performing a wedding and, as such, did not represent an unreasonable expense. The amount spent on Zar, they averred, did not in any way amount to "prodigality." Indeed, the opposite was true. As poor widows, they argued in an April 16 statement, they had no other major source of income and as a result the ban on Zar imposed an undue burden on their ability to earn a livelihood.[88] The prohibition, they argued, created rather than alleviated economic hardship.

With this, the *Alakas* started to shift their arguments away from those who sought a place within the Muslim moral sphere and began appealing to British moral authority. Specifically, they appeared to deliberately appeal to the British conceit that they were the enlightened champions of colonized womanhood. Rather than a religious ceremony, they sought to re-characterize Zar as a "harmless meeting" held by "Muhammedan womenfolk" since "times immemorial." These were, they argued, "simply a sort of social meeting where women meet together to pass a few hours listening to small drums being played and sing songs."[89] Gatherings were held "according to strict *purdah*," and men never allowed to attend.[90] Such gatherings they held were among the very few forms of entertainment that women in seclusion could enjoy "being for . . . most . . . of their lives cooped up."[91] By permitting the resumption of Zar, the Resident would in fact be taking a stand in favor of the rights of women.

> Your lordship knows that even in such an enlightened country as England, there are many people who hold it to be a grievous sin to even dance, smile or go to any theatre . . .
>
> As it is, the enjoyment of Zuhr [*sic*] has nothing obnoxious about it, and no harm has ever been caused to anyone and it is therefore [we] humbly hope that your Lordship will mercifully be pleased to allow the Zuhr to be played as before and thus all the *purdah* . . . ladies who used to attend . . . *will look upon and remember your Lordship as their Champion*.[92]

In subsequent petitions, the *Alakas* refer to their craft as "Zar theatre" and emphasized the hardship that the ban had placed on them, precipitating grave misfortune. "Your humble petitioners are insolvent old females who have no other source of income to maintain ourselves and our large family . . . We have been living in a terrible condition and crisis and are likely to perish with hunger having none on whose protection to rely except God and your Lordship." They went on to declare that "your humble petitioners have every confidence . . . that your Lordship will . . . confer your protection on poor females like us who deserve pity."[93]

Through these and other petitions, the *Alakas'* appear to try to enlist the Resident as a new moral arbiter—one who protected women from religious overzealousness and physical deprivation. When this, unsurprisingly, failed, they sought out one last desperate remedy: the courts. On August 2, 1932 the Chief Commissioner received a letter from I. J. Sopher, Barrister-at-Law, who pled the women's case before the Magistrate's Court.

> On behalf of my clients Mariam bint Mohamed, Zainab bint Omer, Amina bint Ali, Fatoom bint Awad and Amoon bint Hasan [Ibrahim], I have the honour to state that two of these persons are Zar women and along with the rest form a company of singers who are frequently engaged by the local people to sing at their private residence. The singing is accompanied by the playing of drums. The hours of singing vary, sometimes during

the day and at nights their engagements do not exceed the limit of 11pm, within which period they cannot be styled as a nuisance to the public.

It appears that a few years ago the Police were instructed not to issue any permits to the Zar women as this was being restricted under Section 48 of the Bombay District Police Act. For your information, I may point out that in Jammada Bhukhandas I. L.R. 19 Bom. 737 it has been held that the words of Sec 48 of the District Police Act does not empower the D.S.P. or the A.S.P. to stop music in private houses.

My clients have now and again been illegally meeting with opposition from the Police in view of the department orders. In view of the authority quoted above as also in absence of any legislation on this point, I have to request you to vacate the order refusing permits to Zar women to perform in private houses.[94]

The lawyer's main point was that rather than any kind of religious ceremony, Zar gatherings were in fact musical performances held in private residences. As a result, based on the Bombay Police Act, the authorities could not move to disrupt them as long as they did not violate long-standing customary rules regarding public nuisances. The Aden District Magistrate was reluctantly forced to agree, noting, "Sopher's point must, I fear, be conceded."[95] and the *Alaka*s were informed via their lawyer that they may once again practice their craft.[96]

Their victory, however, was short lived. By early September another petition from the "respectable citizens" was lodged with the Residency and by late October the state moved once again to ban Zar's practice.[97] And this would, in fact, be the death knell of Zar within the Settlement. A new rule was added to the Settlement Regulations (260A to be exact) that specifically defined Zar as a public nuisance and forbade its practice.

Following this defeat, it seems that the four *Alaka*s knew when they were beaten and ceased petitioning the state. Instead, they appear to have packed up and moved beyond the Settlement limits in the Sultanate of Lahej, at least temporarily, where they continued to exorcise spirits unmolested.

Emboldened by their seemingly easy victory over Zar, the reformists turned their attention to Tambura. Curiously, while the campaigners succeeded in winning what were largely nominal restrictions on Tambura and other activities associated with the *ziyarat*, unlike Zar, none of these were ever completely barred.

Gender, as we shall see, certainly played its role in this discrepancy. Zar practitioners were uniformly poor foreign women with little to protect them from patriarchal elites well connected with the imperial state. Reformist attempts to outlaw both Tambura as well as more risqué elements surrounding the *ziyaras*, however, were no less aggressive than those mobilized against Zar. Ultimately, however, they bore far less fruit. The question we must ask, of course, is why. Rather than a case of simple misogyny, the different outcomes for Zar and Tambura may also be tied up in a number of other issues, including spiritual patronage, "respectability," and the reinforcement of accepted social hierarchies. The practitioners of Tambura, as well as the Akhdam musicians and dancers, appear to have survived through a fortuitous

Tambura survives

Beginning in the early months of 1925, Qadi al-Battah and others submitted a number of letters and petitions calling for similar measures against the Tambura cult as well as what were viewed as the more salacious activities surrounding the various *ziyarat*. In this case, their rationale was not the ill affect it had on the moral fiber and pocketbooks of upstanding women, but that Tambura and other activities (drinking, gambling and dancing with the women of the Akhdam) promoted a general air of licentiousness throughout the settlement and frequently led to drunken fights and a general disturbance of the peace.[98]

The Deputy Superintendent of Police concurred, noting that "whenever this instrument is played, loafers, such as Arabs, half-breed Jaberti [sic] boys and women of ill-fame and loose character join in a dance around the instrument . . . As the 'Zar' was [banned] around a year ago I have the honor to request that the playing of this instrument be similarly prohibited."[99] Curiously, however, while the campaigners succeeded in winning what were largely nominal restrictions on Tambura and festival activities, unlike Zar, a complete banned never emerged.

Following a flurry of memos within the Residency it was decided that Tambura should only be excluded from the celebrations surrounding saints' festivals. Adherents were allowed, however, to continue holding ceremonies on a weekly basis (usually Saturday evenings) at various locations throughout the Settlement after each group obtained a permit.[100] The dances of the Akhdam, by the same token, were deemed harmless and its practitioners left undisturbed. The survival of both appear due in no small part to their close association with the tombs of the saints. The *Akils* of Tambura, in particular, seemed able to achieve a relatively favorable outcome through two strategies. First, unlike the women of Zar, they managed to successfully cast themselves as a benign entertainment. Second, and more importantly, the leaders of Tambura activated their own network of patrons within the Settlement who were willing to support them.

When the same reformists who led the outlawing of Zar turned their attention to Tambura, its practitioners reacted quickly. While the Residency debated whether or not to ban the custom in response to reformist petitions, several Tambura leaders submitted their own plea to the First Assistant Resident who was responsible for issues surrounding public order. The *Akils* wrote:

> Sir, Being aggrieved by the order prohibiting us from playing the Tambuura [sic] a native string instrument, we most humbly appeal to your Honor to set aside this order, for the following reasons.
> 1. That this playing and dancing with the Tamboora [sic] is an ancient custom used only by persons like us who are of Negro origin and no religious meaning attaches to it.

2. That the playing of Tambuura [*sic*] is merely a Negro method of having a sing-song of passing a couple of hours in enjoyment of an innocent amusement.
3. That ever since the British government entered Aden no trouble whatsoever has been caused by the playing of the Tamburra [*sic*] and we have always been allowed to play it and thus peacefully enjoy ourselves as can be verified by inquiry and it has no connection with Zar. Therefore, we humbly venture to hope that your kind and merciful Honor who is well known to be the protector of the poor and helpless will mercifully allow us to play Tamburra as before in understanding to keep the peace as before. And we, your humble petitioners, shall be forever grateful [and] pray for your honor's long life and advancement.[101]

The most detailed of a number of requests sent to the Residency, this petition lays out certain key elements of the *Akils'* strategy for preventing an official ban. Unlike their Zar counterparts, whose first instinct was to try to defend their practice as lying within the bounds of acceptable Islamic morality, the Tambura men quickly denied the presence of any religious or spiritual meaning in their practices. Instead, it was merely an "innocent amusement," meant to pass "a couple of hours in enjoyment." In addition, they explicitly and vehemently denied any connection to Zar, noting that no public trouble had ever been caused by their performances unlike the disreputable practice that had just been banned.

The *Akils* need not have worried, as the authorities had already decided against a complete ban, instead prohibiting the practice only at the local *ziyaras*.[102] Over the next several years Tambura groups continued their weekly rituals with few interruptions. However, they also periodically challenged their exclusion from the local saints' festivals. Petitions appear in the residency records about every two years with different groups requesting permission to perform their rituals at the *ziyaras* (either that of Abu Bakr Aydarus in Crater or Shaykh Ahmad of Tawahi). In addition to their petitions, they also called upon the good offices of Sayyid Abdullah al-Aydarus, the guardian of the Aydarus shrine, who the British recognized as the *mansab* or titular head of Aden's Muslim community. On at least two occasions, Sayyid Aydarus supported the requests of Tambura *Akils* to perform their ceremonies at important *ziyaras*.

In the first case, in 1925, Sayyid Abdullah personally petitioned the Residency for special permission to allow a Tambura ceremony at the Aydarus *ziyara*:

I most humbly and respectfully beg to request your honor to grant permission to the Tumbra [*sic*] players (drummers) to play this evening from 4 o'clock to 1pm [*sic*] because they were suspended by the Police Inspector to hold it as usual although they have not made any riot or quarrel to make them deserve suspension by the police authority. I hope your honor will be kind enough to grant them the above request as a special case for the occasion of the Aidroos fair.[103]

Several years later, in November 1930, when petitioners sought permission to perform at the *ziyara* of Shaykh Ahmad in Tawahi, they noted, "People have [an]

Marginality, Spirit Possession and the Moral Community 131

endowment and they desire to fulfill it ... if they do not do so it is very bad for them." And in case the authorities were not convinced of the spiritual urgency of the matter he requested that they "forward our petition to Shams-ul-Ulama Syed [*sic*] Abdullah Aidroos [*sic*] for his opinion on the subject."

In neither case was an exception granted. However, the fact that the Tambura *Akils* viewed the *Shams al-Ulama* as someone who understood and supported their cause certainly indicates that on some level the practitioners of Tambura enjoyed an amicable relationship with the local Sufi religious establishment.[104]

An additional, if more general, show of support for both the Akhdam and the Jarbarti Tambura adherents arose from the entrenched economic interests of their social betters. In a number of counter petitions merchants and tomb functionaries implored the government to leave the festivals as they were. They held that apart from the spiritual aspect, the activities surrounding the *ziyara*s were an important source of income for small traders and entertainers throughout the year. Any disruption, they argued, would cause serious hardship.

In 1931, for instance, the committees of two shrines in the suburb of Shaykh Uthman (Hashim al-Bahr and Uthman Damreel) wrote to the Resident begging that the carnival activities surrounding the saints' days should be left alone for economic as well as religious reasons. They noted that the majority of the Settlement's inhabitants were "much pleased with the Fairs as well as the Homage to the saints," and it was only the conniving of meddling, puritanical reformists who wished to put an end to them. In addition to their spiritual benefits, they opined, the annual *ziyaras* were important as a major source of income generation. Visitors to the *ziyara*, they noted, came from all around and could number 20,000 or more. If each person spent 5 Rs, as they estimated, this accounted for the major portion of the yearly income of local small merchants and traders. To limit the "entertainments" of the fairs would invite economic disaster.[105] The Residency was apparently convinced by this logic and quickly declared that the carnivals—including "mixed dancing"—could continue, although those responsible for overseeing the festivities should make every effort to curb the worst excesses.

The petition does not explicitly endorse the participation of Tambura. However, the expressed desire of the committees to leave the festivals unregulated certainly suggests a tolerance, if not outright support, for the cult. Indeed, at least some groups may have skirted the ban on performing at festivals by holding their ceremonies not in close proximity to the tomb but within the sweeper lines.[106]

The lives of the socially circumscribed, the public spiritual sphere and the importance of the unseen

The official records of the *ziyaras* end in the mid-1930s and so does our information on Tambura, Zar and, for the most part, references to the "servile classes." We know from other sources that the practitioners of Zar survived first by moving their ceremonies beyond the Settlement boundary, although this seems to have been a temporary exile. Indeed, by the 1960s, R. B. Serjeant, the distinguished historian of Southern Arabia, noted that although formally outlawed, Zar continued to "flourish" within the Settlement.[107] Although there is no record indicating whether or not they were ever able to again hold their rituals openly at the local saints' festivals, Tambura continued and Serjeant again mentioned its continued practice in the 1960s.[108] By the same token, while moved to the margins of the celebrations, the Akhdam were permitted to continue what was regarded as their traditional entertainment. Unfortunately, however, following this glimpse in the official records the Akhdam, the Jabarti, the Zar priestesses and all forms of public spirit possession recede into the social background.

At first glance, it is all too easy to accept the characterization of European observers and officials that so-called "serviles" held little importance in society beyond the menial tasks they performed. While occupations such as garbage and night soil removal were critical in a port such as Aden their place in society could be viewed as largely marginal. The evidence presented here, however, suggests otherwise. Certainly, the Akhdam, the Jabarti and the women who led Zar lived existences viewed as peripheral by both European and wider Muslim society. They all worked at menial jobs and were frequently associated with the outer edges of morality (such as drinking, gambling and prostitution). However, the evidence suggests a need for closer examination of not only the role of such people in the religious public arena, but their ability—or inability—to protect that space when under threat. It may also leave us room to interrogate what these rituals meant to the actors in a broader sense. Was it only about the power to belong or was there more at stake?

At the start of the 1920s, all of these practices were integral components of public spirituality in Aden and, as such, they became targets of early scripturalist reformers. Tambura and Zar each sought to safeguard their place through the same state channels and by self-consciously distancing themselves from any connection to what could be defined as religious practice. Instead, both tried to recast themselves as "mere entertainments." Yet, neither ever shed their connection to the unseen in practice. For both sides—pro and con—the conflict over spirit possession was not solely over the authority to define public space. It was also about differing visions of the universe. Reformists subscribed to a post-enlightenment view of rationality in which other realms (such as the divine and the jinn), although they existed, were largely inaccessible to the world of humans. Proponents of spirit possession, however, maintained a different view. Not only could the realms of human, jinn and the divine intersect with one another but these alternate dimensions regularly influenced the world of people. As such, in order to understand the conflict more fully, we need to see it as one grounded not only in questions of authority but also differing understandings of the universe and humanity's place in it.

Spiritual hucksterism or communing with other realms?

The practitioners of Zar were all low-status women with little in the way of social protection. Many of the participants in Zar rituals, however, were women of means who may spend relatively lavish amounts on ceremonies. In other periods and contexts—nineteenth-century Zanzibar or Mecca, for instance—this was viewed as a comparatively harmless aspect of elite female life; however, in twentieth-century Aden it was deemed socially disruptive and morally corrupting. At issue was not just perceived impiety—although this played its role. The original petitioners charged that Zar targeted women of "rank and honor," preying on their religious ignorance and superstition. But they also averred that Zar ceremonies constituted an unhealthy drain on the income of respectable Muslim households. Writing more than ten years after the initial ban, Ahmad al-Asnag—an Adeni essayist and supporter of scripturalist reform—noted that "women believe that Zar is a beneficial remedy to chronic maladies and they hold celebrations upon which they expend great wealth."[109] Women, however, were not solely culpable. Al-Asnag held that "many husbands lend a hand in this," paying for the ceremonies and sacrifices needed to placate the jinn and "cause the pain of his wife to abate." As a result, "the people's wealth flows to these tiresome women [that is, the practitioners] and their souls are bound to Zar."[110] Zar threatened not only the piety of respectable Muslims, but also the economic security of the domestic realm. This, Asnag was at pains to point out, was as much the fault of the men of the house as the women. Zar was not the only danger to respectable Muslim domesticity in his view. Just as bad were the "swindlers and deceivers who wear white turbans and carry long strings of prayer beads, [who] deceive people by leading them to believe they are from among the learned *'ulama'*." These "fraudsters," he wrote, convince people that all illnesses are the work of the devil and possession; they promise to cure the "naïve" with folk remedies and "fleece the ignorant of their wealth."[111]

Piety and scripturalist notions of orthopraxy were central to the campaign against Zar. Equally important, however, was an additional current running through Adeni society of the 1920s, the notion of "respectability." Both Asnag and Muhammad Ali Luqman wrote with concern of a growing materialism and profligacy that afflicted Aden's Muslims. Luqman wrote in the introduction to his novel *Sa'id*, that while women "believe in silly practices like Zar, charms and amulets, vows [or votive offerings, *nadhur*], pilgrimages and tomb visitations," of equal concern was the profligate behavior of young men and the conspicuous consumption found in many households.[112] Liquor, drugs[113] and lewd public behavior among young men of respectable homes were at the top of their lists. Families waste their wealth on "costly automobiles and gasoline; electricity and ice; the cinema, *mila*,[114] and clothes; none lasts but a few days then it becomes an old fashion."[115]

Curiously, Asnag believed that the people who sought the services of Zar priestesses and the hucksters in "white turbans," suffered from genuine illnesses. Resorting to such remedies, he argued, was misguided and naïve at best and a great waste of resources. The money of Aden's inhabitants, he argued, would be much better invested in women's education, the founding of hospitals and the training of female doctors who could treat the needs of women in either clinics or the home.[116]

For many, Zar and Tambura were lewd superstitions that drained family resources, precipitated moral delinquency and threatened respectability. For others, the rituals remained an important conduit to the unseen and the divine—the performance of which were critical to their physical health and well-being. As we have already seen, *Akils* in the early 1930s argued that if they were not allowed to perform at the tombs the saints would "go without worship" and their relatives would "fall . . . sick . . . one after [another]."[117] In a similar petition, the *Akils* Mahi Ibrahim and Yusuf Abdi requested permission to hold a Tambura ceremony during the *ziyara* of Shaykh Ahmad in Tawahi, as "We got a Vow [sic] to complete as we solemnly promised To [sic] God to complete . . . on the day of the fair."[118] As one police report noted, these were not metaphorical rituals. The practitioners of Tambura, as noted earlier, also sought to become possessed by the spirit of whichever saint's *ziyara* they happened to be at, becoming physical agents for the intersection of different realms.[119] Even while they distanced themselves from the notion publicly, for these *Akils*, at least, the practice of Tambura remained closely intertwined with the unseen.

But it was not only the practitioners of Tambura who saw interactions with the jinn as a necessary part of life, particularly in times of crisis. In June 1931, for instance, Hasan Khan Mirza—a typist for the Anglo-Persian Oil Company—filed a petition with the Residency. He stated that in 1929 he was struck with an unspecified "serious illness" from which he did not expect to recover. Faced with the end, he wrote, "I made a vow to perform a 'Zar' ceremony after 2½ years, should I regain my health." Hasan miraculously recovered and now he asked for permission to hold a ceremony "as a special case."[120] Another petitioner, Husayn Fazoo, appealed to the authorities to host an "Indian Zar" in his home. He argued that "Indian Zar is not a public nuisance," like that practiced by the Arabs "who used large drums, etc." Instead, "it is simply a lady's party called Gamat," held in the name of the Sufi saint Abdul Qadir Jaylani.[121]

Like the revival of specific tombs and the desire of individuals to be interred near particular sanctified spots, the "positive" form of possession evinced by the Tambura adherents and the performance of Zar as a method of vow fulfillment can be read as active engagement with the unseen rather than simply as attempts on the part of the disadvantaged to assert political power. Certainly, they represent efforts by individuals to convince the state to reverse their position on ritual practice or at least make temporary exceptions. But, in these cases, we see not just social and political maneuvering aimed at securing space within the community. Rather, they illustrate the perceived importance of unseen forces in daily lives. Rituals must be held in order to prevent the physical illness of loved ones; vows kept to remunerate the divine realm for services rendered, whether this might be God, the *awliya'* or spirits. Indeed, in these instances questions of social space and political power were relatively moot. The Tambura *Akils* were not banned from their rituals merely from certain locations, while those petitioning for exceptions to the sanctions against Zar were otherwise "respectable" citizens with little stake in the woes of the cult's practitioners. However, their relationship with forces of the unseen was deemed important enough for them to continue to defy elite society and the imperial state. This was not because they hoped to derive some social benefit, but because the maintenance of such relations was deemed critical to their own well-being and that of their families.

Explaining the different outcomes

Finally, we must turn to the question of why these two cults, so similar in nature, achieved such different outcomes. The campaign against Zar was certainly, to a large extent, about women in the domestic sphere and control over definitions of proper piety during a period when such notions were in a state of flux. Also at issue, however, were concerns about social class, economics and "respectability" that not only resonated with Adenis across the social spectrum but insured that Zar had no public champions. Tambura and the Akhdam dancers were more fortunate. The relative success of the latter and failure of the former to defend their place in the public sphere, however, hinged little on their ability to navigate the currents and eddies of the colonial petition regime. Rather, success in the end seemed contingent on their perceived impact on the moral, political and economic interests of what the British would refer to as "respectable" society.

On the face of it, Tambura and the Akhdam shared many of the same disadvantages as Zar. The followers of Tambura were similarly drawn from a reviled low-status group, the Jabarti; the Akhdam dancers belonged to what was likely the most despised community in the Settlement. Both were associated with activities (public debauchery, mixed dancing, alcohol consumption and spirit possession) widely associated with moral turpitude if not outright heterodoxy. In addition, their pursuits were, if anything, more public than those of Zar, taking place in the streets, coffeehouses and shrines of Aden's various neighborhoods. Yet circumstances and interests appear to have enabled them to emerge relatively unscathed.

Tambura was more successful, it can be argued, not because its leaders managed to navigate and manipulate the new world of petitions and bureaucracy any more successfully than the *Alakas* of the Zar, nor simply because the state and society tended to favor men in the public sphere over women. They, and the Akhdam, survived because each managed in large measure to retain support from certain "respectable" elements of society despite their ribald reputations. The persistence of both practices was due in part to their economic importance but also the fact that their presence helped to reaffirm rather than subvert certain social and spiritual hierarchies.

Within the context of the Sudan, both Tambura and Zar communities maintained a close connection with the Islamic spiritual calendar as well as with shrine

Sufism.[122] In Aden, however, it was only the practitioners of Tambura who appear to have such associations. While proclaiming in some petitions that their dances had no religious or spiritual connections, in others the Tambura *Akils* betrayed the continued importance of the saints in their ceremonies. Their reputed ability to channel the spirits of deceased saints could be read as attempts to subvert local hierarchies by claiming power equal to that of their spiritual and social betters. However, the continued support of the head of the most important shrine in Aden—on more than one occasion—suggests that the *Akils'* ceremonies were interpreted as a sign of their love for the Friends of God and a reinforcement of the spiritual status quo rather than a challenge.

Similarly, important elements of the local merchant community who subsidized the festivals surrounding each *ziyara* were willing to go on record—tacitly, at least—in support of Tambura as well as the Akhdam entertainers. Like Zar, many denounced these practices as beyond respectability. However, they were central elements of the lucrative carnivals that popped up around all of the major *ziyara*s. It was one thing for them to intervene to supposedly protect respectable women from exploitation. But large merchants and shrine caretakers seemed less willing to police the moral probity of the rural bumpkins and urban riff-raff who constituted the bulk of fair goers and, thus, the principal source of profits at the annual festivals. As such, they rushed to the Akhdam's defense along with all the other members of the "carnival economy" when faced with opposition from religious reformers.[123]

While it is difficult to draw definitive conclusions from the available evidence, one thing is certainly clear. The public spiritual space of British imperial Aden was broad and even those considered to be on the fringes of respectable society had their place. More importantly, these were spaces that, once acquired, they were loathe to give up easily. In the end, however, the ability to navigate the bureaucratic alleyways of the Aden Residency was insufficient to insure survival. The *Alaka*s of Zar proved themselves to be quite adept at using the medium of the petition to set out their claims and even re-inventing themselves in terms that they hoped would appeal to the imperial state. But the interests of Muslim elite society proved decisive. Both Tambura and Zar were subjected to the prevailing winds of scripturalist morality sweeping "respectable" society. Zar's close association with the domestic sphere of Aden—whose moral and fiscal probity were central concerns of reformers—appears to have left the priestesses irrevocably exposed. With the virtue of respectable women and the fiscal security of the home at stake, none could be seen to be championing their cause. Conversely, and somewhat ironically, Tambura's identification exclusively with the "lower" elements of society worked to shield it from complete prohibition. While Zar's perceived profligacy impinged on respectable domesticity, the imagined licentiousness and borderline heterodoxy of Tambura and the Akhdam, by contrast, directly impacted only those already considered on society's fringe. Indeed, it could be argued, they even reinforced certain elite interests. As a result, "respectable" merchants and those associated with the shrines could rise to their defense with British authorities with fewer fears of consequences. By the same token, those who defended Tambura were driven by more than crass economic self-interest. The scripturalist movement's campaign against spirit possession foreshadowed a broader effort to define the acceptable spiritual parameters of the community as they began to take aim at a new target of alleged impiety: Sufism and the cult of the saints.

6
Scripturalism, Sufism and the Limits of Defining Public Religiosity

On a February evening in 1932 Shaykh Muhammad Rashidi, the head of the Ahmadiyya Sufi order in Aden, was relaxing after breaking his fast when two visitors arrived. As it was the holy month of Ramadan there was nothing unusual in this except, after the exchange of pleasantries, the two men began to question the *'alim* about his beliefs and practices in a hostile manner. As they got up to leave, they suggested that he may want to cease holding Sufi rituals in public or "problems" could arise.[1] The aggressive activism of scripturalist reform in Aden had shifted its sights from spirit possession to Sufism. But it was not to go unchallenged. Rather than a narrative that relates the strong-arm victory of reformist ideology over local practice, this chapter looks at the ways in which promoters of Salafism—proponents of conservative scripturalist reform—were ultimately forced to accommodate local institutions and notions of piety in order to become meaningful social actors. This last chapter continues to explore the dynamics of religious mobilization, reform and the discourses of authority in early twentieth-century Aden. While ideologies such as Salafism were transregional in nature what we will see here is how, in practice, they were ultimately shaped by local contexts. A critical element of this was the differing approach to authority of various constituencies. Both scripturalists and Sufis viewed discursive authority as emanating ultimately from God and His Prophet, Muhammad. Scripturalist authority lay in certain foundational written texts that they alone could interpret properly. For Sufis, the mantle of spiritual power emanated from a less tangible source: the realm of the divine and the *Nur Muhammadiyya*.

Salafism is the term most commonly used to describe the scripturalist reform movement that arose across the Islamic world from the middle of the nineteenth century. Proponents of this ideological school called upon Muslims to return to the practices and beliefs of their "pious ancestors" (*al-salaf al-salih*) as the only way to purify and revive what was perceived as a flagging faith. The Salafi definition of "the pious ancestors" most often included the Prophet Muhammad. his followers and the two or three generations of Muslims following them.[2] As such, only the earliest scriptural texts (primarily the Qur'an and the Hadith) were accepted as sources of belief and practice. As numerous authors have pointed out, a primary aim of Salafi thinkers was the elimination of the sectarian boundaries that many believed had crippled the community of believers over the centuries and made them vulnerable to European domination. As such, they advocated sweeping away, what was viewed as, the divisiveness of the four law schools and the revival of *ijtihad*, allowing believers to directly consult the above-mentioned foundational texts of the faith as a guide for their own lives. Return to the foundational sources, as one recent author has noted, would recreate "the utopian era of the *salaf*," resulting in "greater unity within Muslim communities, political strength and intellectual vitality," and ultimately enable the *umma* to throw off the yoke of European domination.[3] This revitalization, however, also included the eradication of what Salafi proponents regarded as centuries of unlawful innovations (*bid'a*) that included, among other things, tomb visitation and saint veneration, supplements to established prayer rituals and any local customs deemed out of step with "orthodox" practice.[4] The term "Salafi" is a notoriously slippery one. As Henri Lauzière has argued, it was not in general use among reformers before the 1930s.[5] Reformists in Aden, before the Second World War, only rarely use it to self-identify. However, their beliefs do coincide with its general outlines. As such, I have chosen to use it interchangeably with the term, "scripturalist reformers," or simply "scripturalists."

Scripturalist ideology first appeared in Aden in the early 1920s and its adherents mirrored the diverse character of the town's wider Muslim community. Proponents ranged from aspiring Arab notables and intellectuals, Indian policemen and civil servants, to Somali street hawkers and qat sellers. The movement was bankrolled by the deep pockets of a newly arrived Gujarati merchant and received its intellectual energy from a well-traveled scholar from Ibb—in the Yemeni interior—who had lived and studied extensively in Persia, India and Afghanistan. This broad, cosmopolitan group typified the rise of transnational Salafism in the early twentieth-century Indian Ocean. As we saw in the last chapter, their popularity was marked by a number of early victories in the realm of public piety, including the banning of Zar (spirit-possession rituals) and curbing some of the worst excesses (for example, mixed dancing and public drunkenness) associated with the annual festivals centered on the tombs of local saints.

When activists began to specifically target local Sufis, the latter responded with their own tactics of disruption, holding *dhikr* in Salafi-controlled mosques and engaging in street scuffles with local pro-Salafi toughs. And it was the reformists who backed down. A series of mediation efforts resolved the immediate conflict and the reciprocal baiting carried out by both sides ceased.

The reactions of local Salafi intellectuals and their sympathizers were mixed. Some continued to denounce what they viewed as "unlawful innovations," although in a somewhat less militant manner. Others adopted a significantly different approach, and rather than the elimination of such abominations, they began to call simply for the "pious" observance of local traditions. Through poems, essays and even short stories dating from the mid-1930s, certain scripturalist partisans initiated a more literary engagement with the broader Muslim community, seeking to influence rather than eliminate the local practices they found abhorrent. Without provoking their religious counterparts, these reformist thinkers advocated versions of *dhikr*, *ziyarat* and saint veneration that conformed to their own notions of piety while at the same time trying to find some sort of common ground. Their efforts were mirrored by partisans of Sufism who engaged in their own literary production intended to blunt scripturalist influence.

In this chapter, we look at how a transregionally informed reformist discourse could be vulnerable to local interpretation and begin to unpack the transformation of Salafi activism from a broad, doctrinaire and, above all, foreign ideology to an integral part of local religious discourse in Aden. It approaches reform as part of an evolving Islamic discursive tradition that in part developed as a result of its own theological logic but was equally shaped by historically contingent local institutions, social practices and power structures. As such, it explores Salafism as a dynamic tradition that could be adapted by local intellectuals to engage the problems inherent in their own communities.

Changing views of "Salafism"

The historiography of modern Islamic reform has been one of growing complexity. Until recently, the dominant trend in scholarship followed the narrative laid out by Albert Hourani in which contemporary reformist discourse emerged from the singular root of "modernism" promoted by Jamal al-Din al-Afghani and Muhammad Abduh, ultimately giving rise to the version of Salafism espoused by Rashid Rida in the 1920s and 1930s.[6] The accepted narrative held that Salafi ideology sought a return to the "pure" spiritual practices of the "religious and political way of the [pious] forefathers." This renewed path would eschew sectarian divisions and eliminate centuries of "unlawful innovations," represented most visibly by traditions associated with "popular" Sufism such as saint veneration and tomb visitation. While not disputing this as a particular strain of scripturalist thought, more recent scholarship has begun to increasingly complicate this picture.

Oliver Scharbrodt, for instance, has demonstrated the heretofore underestimated importance of Sufi thought in the early work of Muhammad Abduh.[7] More importantly, David Commins and Itzchak Weismann have established the existence of a significant group of early Salafis centered on Abd al-Qadir al-Jaza'ri in Damascus in the 1880s who were reluctant to condemn mystical beliefs.[8] The anti-Sufi trend in Salafi thought, Weismann argues, is in reality a reflection of the dominance of Rida in the 1920s and 1930s and his belief that "latter-day tradition, both scholarly and mystic ... was the cause of the decline of Muslim civilization and ... an impediment to the adoption of useful Western innovations."[9]

However, probably the single most important recent work on Salafi-scripturalist reform is Samira Haj's *Reconfiguring Islamic Tradition*, that examines the work of the Egyptian scholar Muhammad Abduh (1849–1905) widely regarded as one of the founders of modern Salafism. Haj's study approaches Abduh's reformist thought as part of a dynamic tradition that drew upon a "corpus of Islamic knowledge," in order to respond to contemporary challenges. This corpus included not just written texts but positions, institutions and social roles. Drawing on the ideas of Talal Asad and Alasdair MacIntyre regarding the nature of "tradition," Haj argues that while Salafism looked to an ideal of the Islamic past for inspiration "tradition is not simply the recapitulation of previous beliefs and practices. Instead, each successive generation" employs it to "confront its particular problems via an engagement with a set of ongoing arguments [or problems]"[10] in a process that results in almost constant reinvention. She argues persuasively that, far from being anachronistic, the Salafism of Muhammad Abduh and others was a dynamic framework of inquiry that sought to continually reinterpret Islam in light of changing circumstances while at the same time remaining faithful to the spirit of the faith's teachings.

The significance of Haj's work and others is that Salafism begins to appear as less of a movement with a single, linear origin, than a dynamic intellectual milieu that evolved from a number of centers from the late nineteenth century. While adherents looked to the scriptural sources, the Qur'an and Hadith, as the primary fonts of guidance, it was an ideology always shaped by a unique combination of local contexts and the vast repertoire of Islamic tradition.[11]

While important, most of the scholarship that has engaged the dissemination of reformist discourse within the broader context of the nineteenth and twentieth centuries has tended to focus on the movement of ideas through print culture and to privilege the highest levels of debate.[12] Far less attention has been paid to the impact of these ideas on particular communities.[13] Unsurprisingly, a great chasm frequently separates ideologies in the abstract and their application on the level of the local amidst the far more concrete realities of day-to-day living.[14]

The Arab Islamic Reform Club and the arbitration of public morality

Sufism and the "cult of the saints"[15] dominated the public sphere of Aden from the beginning of the British occupation through the early decades of the twentieth century. Religious reformers first began to challenge the dominance of the popular spiritual status quo, as we saw in the last chapter, in the early 1920s when a group led by the Qadi of Aden, Da'ud al-Battah, initiated a campaign against the performance of Zar within the Settlement limits.[16] The anti-Zar movement, although seemingly tinged with Salafi ideas, did not coalesce into a formal association calling for broad social and religious reform. Qadi Da'ud's interest in issues of reform seems to have taken him in a different direction. Most notably he was instrumental in the creation and running of the local Wakf Committee discussed in Chapter 4 and played little role in later events. The campaign against Zar, however, introduced a number of individuals to the public spotlight who sought to continue cleaning up Aden's immoral streets. These became the founders of the Nadi al-Islah al-Arabi al-Islami (The Arab Islamic Reform Club).

The Nadi al-Islah[17] was established in 1928 or 1929 by a varied group of individuals, all of whom were involved in the anti-Zar campaign and whose stated common goal was to undertake various "reforms in society."[18] The organization's founders were individuals from various stations in Aden society. The group was financed by Zakariya Muhammad al-Hindi, a Gujarati merchant long resident in Aden and Sayyid Ali Isma'il, a self-made man originally from the Hadramaut, who owned a large slaughtering business in the Settlement.[19] The intellectual impetus for the group was provided by two younger men with largely secular educations, Muhammad Ali Luqman and Ahmad Muhammad al-Asnag. Luqman, as we have seen, was the eldest son of the Settlement's Chief Interpreter and had been educated first in the Residency school and then by Marist Fathers.[20] Al-Asnag was the son of an entrepreneur of humble origins who by the 1920s dominated much of the local fish trade. Like his son, he was also prominent in the anti-Zar movement.[21]

The scripturalist orientation of the Nadi al-Islah and its leadership was inherent from its inception. Muhammad Ali Luqman noted in his autobiography that he was inspired to establish the society by Abd al-Aziz al-Thaalibi, the Tunisian founder of the Destour Party and a Salafi proponent, whom he met in Aden while the latter was on his way to India.[22] Al-Thaalibi, Luqman recounted, was astonished by the lethargy of the Muslims of Aden and encouraged him to establish an association or club to promote self-improvement.[23] Initially, the club served as a kind of salon where members gathered to read various Arabic-language newspapers from Egypt and Lebanon, discuss current events and listen to inspirational political and religious lectures.[24] At the same time, they engaged in charity work, raising money for Libyan refugees in Egypt and assisting with quarantine efforts during a smallpox outbreak in 1929.[25] In 1930, the membership decided to open a school to provide religious instruction for the children of members as well as any Muslim child who sought instruction. To run the school, the Club recruited an *'alim* resident in nearby Lahej, Shaykh Ahmad bin Muhammad bin Awad al-Abbadi.

Shaykh al-Abbadi was, according to his biographer Muhammad bin Salim al-Bayhani, a highly trained religious scholar, a dedicated Salafi and an individual who did not shrink from controversy or confrontation when it came to his beliefs. Al-Abbadi had family ties to the Hadramaut, but was born and raised near the town of Ibb in about 1882.[26] In the manner of traditional scholars he studied the Qur'an and the religious sciences under his father. At seventeen, he decided to leave home "in order to seek knowledge and study religion."[27] He traveled first to Afghanistan where he studied *tafsir* (Qur'anic exegesis), *fiqh* (jurisprudence) and other religious sciences under Muhammad Taqi al-Din al-Afghani for nine years.[28] The shaykh then moved to Bombay, studying in the al-Qasab (or al-Qasba) mosque for a year and a half.[29] It was this foreign part of his training that would seem to be the most formative.

Following this decade of semi-itinerant study, al-Abbadi settled into a life of teaching as well as Salafi activism, first in Oman and then briefly in Ibb.[30] The Shaykh's commitment to a life of activism rather than quietist scholarship is revealed by the choices he made after completing his Central and South Asian sojourn. Upon leaving Bombay, al-Abbadi settled in the Omani port of Sur, securing a position as the Imam of a Sunni mosque. According to al-Bayhani, he spent most of his twelve years there engaged in literary skirmishing with scholars of the Ibadhi community, seeking to convince them of the error of their ways. While on the Hajj near the end of First World War, he received word of his father's death and determined that it was time to return to the town of his birth. His time in Ibb, however, was brief, as he almost immediately became involved in a number of unspecified theological disputes on various matters with the local Zaydi *'ulama'* that were vociferous if not outright violent.[31] Whether or not his departure was somehow linked to these quarrels is not known, but in 1920 the Sultan of Lahej, Abd al-Karim Fadhl, asked him to take over a charitable school.[32] It was from there that the Reform Club invited him to open a school in the Shaykh Uthman suburb of Aden in 1930.[33]

Al-Abbadi's arrival in Aden was significant because it coincided with the Club's movement from a literary and occasional social-service organization toward a stance that emphasized proselytizing and activism. It is impossible to determine, based on the available evidence, whether or not al-Abbadi's appearance was directly responsible for the Reform Club's more visible public profile in the early 1930s, however the evidence is suggestive.[34]

Salafis on the offensive

Henri Lauzière has argued that the term "Salafism" did not begin to come into wide usage until the 1920s. As it did so the label was accompanied by a great deal of ambiguity, encompassing individuals from a broad spectrum of thought, ranging from scriptural literalists to "modernists"—all of whom looked to the *salaf al-salih* as role models.[35] The leadership of the Nadi al-Islah was reflective of this trend. Al-Abbadi and al-Bayhani were scripturally oriented scholars who believed that Muslims needed to rigorously cleanse the faith of erroneous doctrinal beliefs and practices (unlawful innovations) returning Islam to the purity of its earliest generations.[36] Luqman and al-Asnag, as we shall see below, were concerned less with doctrinal purity than individual intent and personal action.[37] All, however, were concerned with the moral fiber of the community and it was this central problem that held them together under the auspices of the Club.[38]

In the spring of 1931 the Nadi al-Islah began to take a broad interest in the public spiritual sphere. A number of mosques throughout the city were controlled by either members of the Club or individuals sympathetic to them. In Shaykh Uthman, Zakariya al–Hindi, with backing from his father-in-law, founded what became known as the Masjid Zakoo (the Zakariya Mosque) in 1929 and installed al-Abbadi as Imam. During the same period Sayyid Ali Isma'il successfully took control of the Masjid Ahl al-Khair, formerly known as the Qadi's mosque, in the same neighborhood. And the main mosque in Tawahi allowed Club members to deliver the Friday *khutba*, or sermon, on a number of occasions.[39]

In these mosques, according to British Residency and Police records, Salafi-inspired sermons became a regular feature of Friday noon prayers. In May and June

1931 prominent Club members, including Muhammad Ali Luqman and Ahmad al-Asnag, delivered sermons in the neighborhoods of Shaykh Uthman and Tawahi that were typical of reformist rhetoric. One address delivered on May 8 chided the community for tolerating "drunkenness, sodomy, adultery and scandal," in their midst and upbraided them for "scoffing at the religion of [their] Prophet" and casting aside the precepts of religious law. Calling on them to "forsake habits of laziness and carelessness," it urged the believers of Aden to reawaken society through "the exercise of piety which is the main guide to good deeds and protection from sin."[40]

While the orations at Friday prayers sought to inspire greater moral behavior via words, pro-Salafi activists in the Club took more direct action in order to root out sin and irreligious behavior. Sayyid Ali Isma'il and others, for instance, began to circulate petitions calling on the Residency to crack down on immoral behavior, most notably drinking, gambling and mixed dancing, at the local *ziyarat*.[41] At the same time, Sayyid Ali and Zakariya al-Hindi prohibited the performance of *dhikr* in the mosques they controlled and banned a long-standing custom in Aden's mosques, the recitation of certain verses from the Qur'an between the call to prayer and the start of communal prayers, arguing that both were un-Islamic and dangerous innovations.[42]

Resistance against the reformist campaign was swift. Supporters of one of the most important festivals, Sayyid Hashim al-Bahr, quickly sent their own letter to the Residency denouncing the Club's actions, arguing that the activities surrounding the *ziyara* represented a financial boon to the community. They claimed that more than 20,000 people attended the festival of Sayyid Hashim annually and each one spent a minimum of 5 Rs. Money earned at the festival, they argued, enabled many of the poorest of Aden to make it through the year. Any curtailing of activities, they stated, would cause untold hardship.[43]

In other cases, reactions were not simply quick but aggressive as well. The response to Club members' attempts to end *dhikr* in the early months of 1932 was particularly fast and unambiguous. Several nights after the incident recounted at the beginning of this chapter, on February 24, a large contingent of Shaykh Rashidi's followers gathered for the night prayer at the Salafi-controlled Zakoo Mosque at about nine in the evening. After completing their prayers, the group stood and began to rock back and forth rhythmically reciting "*Allah hayy*," the beginning of a *dhikr*. Horrified, the mosque's caretaker jumped up and tried to stop the swaying men, telling them that the mosque's *mansab*, Zakariya al-Hindi, forbid such things. According to one report, several of the Sufis produced staves from beneath their robes and duly informed the caretaker that they would finish their ritual. The caretaker went around dousing all of the lights, hoping to break up the meeting, but not needing light to worship God, the mystics continued their remembrance.[44]

In a similar show of resolve several months later, local worshippers displayed their disdain for Salafi attempts to modify another local ritual, the recitation of a verse from the *surat al-Ahzab* (The Confederates) immediately following the call to prayer.[45] Shaykh al-Abbadi, Zakariya al-Hindi and others banned this practice from mosques under their influence on the grounds that it constituted *bid'a* or unlawful innovation. This move resulted in a number of confrontational responses. Among the most belligerent was an incident in the Ahl al-Khair Mosque in January 1933. The presiding Imam had just begun the evening prayer, when another group of worshippers arrived on the mosque's verandah and began to start the prayer anew. A near riot erupted between the rival parties and violence was only averted by the efforts of a quick-thinking, plain-clothed policeman who defused the situation. When asked why he had sought to restart the prayer, the leader of the late arrivals stated that since the verse from the *Ahzab* was not recited following the *adhan*, prayer could not possibly have started yet.[46]

The seriousness of these incidents steadily escalated from the beginning of 1932 and by January 1933 the British authorities were determined to put an end to matters. Those identified as responsible for the disturbances on both sides were brought before the Resident. Zakariya al-Hindi, Muhammad Ali Luqman, Ahmad al-Asnag and Shaykh al-Abbadi, from the Reform Club, and the Qadis Awad and Abdullah Sharaf, proponents of the opposition, were warned that if the groups did not manage to resolve their differences the Government would intervene. Jail and deportation from the Settlement were suggested as possible consequences for the parties identified as leaders.[47] As a result, both sides finally engaged in a serious attempt at mediation in mid-January 1933 and the incidents ceased.

British officialdom in Aden tended to view all of these disputes as essentially personal squabbles among elites that spilled over into the public sphere. Police reports and notes from the Residency were unanimous in their conclusion that public disruptions caused by these disputes were a result of the machinations of elites intent on serving their own venal ends. Certainly, a strong odor of personal dislike permeated these quarrels. Muhammad Ali Luqman, for instance, attacked the character of the ex-Qadi Awadh Abdullah in a piece in the Egyptian newspaper *al-Shura*. At the same time, Zakaria al-Hindi in an affidavit to the Residency accused the former Qadi of embezzling mosque funds and Sayyid Ali Isma'il formally requested that charges be brought against the judge for slandering his good name.[48] Those on the other side acted no better. The ex-Qadi referred to Luqman as a boy meddling in the affairs of men while Zakaria al-Hindi was viewed disdainfully as "that foreigner" who thought he could simply buy his way into the leadership of the Muslim community. The worst slurs were reserved for al-Abbadi who was vilified as a "Wahhabi" bent on forcefully imposing his teachings on the faithful.[49]

If we move beyond the petty name calling, however, we can see that these disputes were about very real issues of authority, ritual and practice that were of concern to all Muslims in Aden. Pro-scripturalists, such as al-Hindi and Sayyid Ali, believed that their financial support of mosques in Shaykh Uthman gave them the right to determine what was said and done within their precincts.[50] Others, including the Qadis of Shaykh Uthman and the Ahmadi and Shadhili Sufis, disagreed. From their perspective, an individual could not simply buy their way into a position of spiritual authority. This is surely their greatest complaint against the likes of Muhammad Ali Luqman who, they held, felt that his right to preach to the community was guaranteed by the fact that his father had become a "great landlord" in the Settlement.[51] Communal leadership was not something for sale. Neither could it be obtained through mere learning.[52] Authority, they would have argued, meant not only being able to talk knowledgeably about religious matters, but, more importantly, it meant representing the needs and respecting the beliefs of the wider community. To them, the likes of Zakaria al-Hindi, Sayyid Ali, Ahmad al-Abbadi and the rest were crass parvenus, interested not in protecting the beliefs and views of the community but in imposing their own ideas from above.

The question of whose authority was more "authentic" or representative of the community becomes moot when it is realized that both parties obviously had widespread support. What is of interest, however, is the nature of that backing that frequently defies easy characterization. Many of those expressing support for the pro-Salafi line are hardly surprising. Zakaria al-Hindi, Muhammad Ali Luqman and Ahmad al-Abbadi were all well-educated and well-traveled individuals who were clearly in touch with the wider currents of Islamic religious and political discourses of their age.[53] Likewise, it should come as little surprise to find Muslims employed in the colonial civil service (including the Head Clerk of the Port Health Office, the Senior Boat Fare Clerk, the Head Postal Clerk and the unnamed Indian Police Inspector of Crater) among the exponents of the pro-Salafi camp.[54]

The scripturalists, however, also drew support from quarters that at a glance would seem to be less than natural allies. These included individuals who are listed on various petitions as shopkeepers, butchers, artisans and even laborers. Most striking of all is the presence of a number of Sayyids. Most prominent among these, of course, was Sayyid Ali Isma'il, a self-described illiterate butcher whose social standing as a Yemeni descendant of the Prophet—one may have reasonably assumed—would have given him more in common with the Sufis and adherents to the cult of the saints than the *Salafi*s with whom he allied himself.[55]

Those who opposed the scripturalists were no less diverse. While including the "usual suspects," such as many of the local *'ulama'* and the Sufi community, the anti-Salafi camp also included at least two employees of the Anglo-Persian Oil Company and a Havildar of the Mounted Police. The first two were South Asian clerks listed as petitioners for the re-establishment of Tambura as part of local *ziyarat*. The Havildar, Ali Husayn Murkashee, whose ethnicity is unclear, took it upon himself to write a note to the Resident warning that Ahmad al-Abbadi was spreading dissension among the Muslims of Aden by "provoking the people who refused to obey his orders through sermons which consist [of] a prayer to God to ruin those who do not follow his doctrine."[56]

Print and the fluidity of reform

With both sides dug in, the physical confrontations and mutual baiting of the previous two years abruptly fell off. One reason for this was almost certainly the government threat of deportation aimed at the supposed leaders backed up by an increased police presence in the streets during periods when tensions may be heightened.[57] But those identified by the administration as the most visible reformist voices were not silenced. Rather, they shifted from proselytizing in person to a new medium in Aden—print.

The emergence of print was a relatively recent phenomenon in Aden, but one that was part of a much larger trend. As such, it is helpful to review some of its relevant aspects as they pertained to Muslims and the wider empire. Aden's incorporation into Britain's empire coincided with the beginning of a transportation and communications revolution that would have a decisive impact on the Muslims of Aden—what James Gelvin and Nile Green have termed the "Age of steam and print."[58] The first of these, of course, was an integral component of Aden's growth and imperial importance. Advances in steamship technology from the 1850s, along with the opening of the Suez Canal in 1869, rapidly increased the mobility of Muslims across the various European oceanic empires. The number of Muslims traveling on the Hajj during the second half of the century, for instance, increased exponentially with more believers taking part in the pilgrimage to Mecca than at any other time in the history of the faith.[59] The development of regularized steamship routes also fostered new networks of scholarly exchange. Scholars of East Africa and Southern Arabia who traditionally looked to the religious centers of the Hadramaut or Hijaz for advanced learning now also gravitated to cities like Cairo, Istanbul or Beirut.[60] Aden quickly emerged as an important hub within these networks and imperial transportation directly and very visibly facilitated the emergence of scripturalist reform there.

Advances in print technology—particularly the invention of the lithographic steam press—revolutionized the accessibility of knowledge among Muslims.[61] A great deal of research has focused on the proliferation of Islamic texts that accompanied the development of cheap lithographic printing. Most of this has centered on the impact of print in either the Arabic-speaking lands of the Middle East or Persianate South Asia.[62] Religious texts printed in Cairo, Bombay and Hyderabad as well as reformist newspapers, such as Rashid Rida's *al-Manar*, were readily available throughout the Indian Ocean by the start of the twentieth century.

By the second decade of the century, Muslim scholars in the western Indian Ocean were also producing a small but steady stream of religious texts and periodicals of their own. These works ranged from popular newspapers like Shaykh al-Amin al-Mazrui's *al-Islah* (*Reform*) published in Mombasa to dense theological works such as *al-Majmu'a al-Mubaraka* by the Somali scholar Abdullahi al-Qutbi to popular—and easy to read—collections of poetry and hagiographies aimed at extolling the virtues of the *awliya'*. Such works were concerned with matters from language politics and local practice to broader reformist issues such as the application of *shari'a* and *kafa'a* (the Islamic legal notion that a woman may only marry one who is of the same—or superior—social, genealogical or moral rank) or more prosaically, the shape of the cosmos.[63]

From one perspective, such works represent engagement with the intellectual, especially, reformist trends of the period on the part of those we may describe as regional scholars. As such, these materials demonstrate a dynamic, multidirectional flow of knowledge[64] and the emergence of a more horizontally integrated and intellectually engaged global community of Muslims. Thus, not only are the ideas of what we have come to regard as the "big guns" of reformist thought—such as Muhammad Abduh and Rashid Rida—disseminated to a large audience, but we begin to see local scholars actively engaging with those ideas, seeking to become part of a broad globalizing discourse.

However, this newly emergent discourse was not driven by a few stray copies of *al-Manar*, but by sustained interactions made possible by a combination of new imperial networks of transportation and print. By the early 1900s, regular steamer connections developed a transportation web that helped expand circulation between the ports of the western Indian Ocean and the Mediterranean. Aden, of course, served as an important imperial center, linking regional ports such as Berbera and Mogadishu in Somalia, Mombasa and Zanzibar in British East Africa with Egypt via Suez and India via Bombay. Zakaria al-Hindi's business interests, Ahmad al-Abbadi's education and Muhammad Ali Luqman's encounters with Thaalabi were all made possible by the development of regular steamer routes. Print was slower to arrive at the mouth of the Red Sea. However, it also ultimately had an important influence on reformist discourse in Aden.

Although well connected to the Empire via steamship and telegraphic cable, Aden did not enjoy a well-developed print industry akin to those found in other imperial centers before the Second World War. A government press was operated by the Settlement jail and produced mostly official circulars, almost exclusively in English. The Settlement did not have its own newspaper until 1940 when Muhammad Ali Luqman finally received permission to publish *Fatat al-Jezirah*, which emerged as the port's Arabic paper of record, lasting through the 1960s.[65] From the mid-1940s, Luqman's newspaper presses began to print other material by local authors.[66] Before then, those who wished to see their words—or, more often, the words of their mentors—in print were forced to look further afield; most often they turned to the bustling publishing houses of Cairo.

Cairo was regarded as a capital of Arabic printing and book production by the start of the twentieth century. Low production costs led to the rapid development of a lively print culture in urban Egypt from the latter half of the 1800s. Literally dozens of small firms, mainly in Cairo and Alexandria, produced an eclectic array of books, pamphlets, and newspapers for the consumption of a growing reading public.[67] Concentrated in the area of "old" Cairo around the Khan al-Khalili and al-Azhar University, a few of these, such as the Maktaba al-Salafiyya—literally, the Salafist Press—established in 1909, were founded to serve a particular ideological agenda, in their case scripturalist reform.[68] Most, however, were small shoestring affairs that subsisted largely by printing what they judged the public wished to read and producing works on commission or for a flat fee.

The area around al-Azhar in the early twentieth century was surrounded by these small "boutique" publishing firms that specialized in running up quick, cheap editions of works brought to them by the growing international community of students and scholars resident at the university. These may include scholarly commentaries, collections of sermons, mystical poetry or hagiographies of local saints among many other texts. One of the most prominent of these was the firm Mustafa al-Halabi & Sons. Founded in about 1859, al-Halabi & Sons was a commercial publisher that, like most, operated on a flat-fee basis. By the 1920s, it was a firm with a growing reputation for publishing a wide variety of Sufi-related texts and other works that were often implicitly, if not explicitly, opposed to the growing trends of literally minded scripturalist reform. During this time, al-Halabi & Sons appear to have become the publisher of choice for pro-Sufi, anti-scripturalist elements from East Africa and Aden to Southeast Asia. Works under their imprint varying from Shadhili and Qadiri hagiographies, anti-scripturalist theological texts to collections of Sufi poetry were produced for audiences across the Indian Ocean.[69]

After the acrimonious scuffles of the early 1930s, scripturalist reformists and Sufis alike continued to espouse their causes. But they did so through the printing press rather than the pulpit. Over the course of the decade both sides published works through presses in Cairo that appeared most sympathetic to their side.

Scripturalists were most active in this vein. Shaykh al-Abbadi composed a collection of Salafi religious verse edited and published by his disciple Muhammad al-Bayhani as *Hidayat al-murid ila sabil al-haq wa tawhid*.[70] Ahmad al-Asnag published *Nasib 'Adan*, a series of essays aimed primarily at "the youth" of Aden. And Muhammad Ali Luqman produced what is widely regarded as the first serious work of fiction by a modern Adeni author, the novella *Sa'id*. Each of these addressed the issue of religious reform at least indirectly. Adherents of the saints, however, were not silent and in 1936 devotees of Sayyid Abu Bakr Aydarus al-Adani published *al-Jiz al-latif*, a collection of the great shaykh's poetry and miracles but also a spirited defense of saintly authority.

Given the erratic nature of publishing data, it is difficult to discern precisely in what order the works in Aden appeared and, as a result, it is nearly impossible to tell if authors were responding directly to one another or simply putting forth their ideological positions on saint veneration.[71] So, we will begin with the scripturalist critique of Sufism by Shaykh al-Abbadi. Although this work appeared in print after *al-Jiz al-latif*, as a collection gathered by his protégé al-Bayhani, we can argue that his poems were in circulation much earlier. As such, I will lay out the scripturalist argument first, followed by the Sufi defense and ending the chapter with what appears to be an attempt by intellectuals such as Luqman and al-Asnag to find a middle ground. Although it was the scripturalists who seem to have initiated the confrontations of the 1920s and 1930s with the followers of the *turuq*, it was by and large the former who ultimately sought accommodation with the latter.

Al-Abbadi and *Hidayat al-murid*

As a "response to the charlatans and their following,"[72] Ahmad al-Abbadi composed a set of poems in the simple and accessible *rajaz* meter meant not only to smite "the willful oppressors," but to "spread good among the Muslims." These were collected by the Shaykh's student Muhammad al-Bayhani and published by al-Matbaah al-Salafiyah wa-Maktabatuha in Cairo in about 1938 while the latter was studying at al-Azhar.[73] Al-Bayhani contributed a biographical introduction of the poems' author as well as critical commentary included in footnotes.[74] A close reading reveals the *Hidayat al-murid* to be a strict interpretation of the faith dedicated to stemming the tide of *bid'a* and ending "reprehensible customs" common among the believers of Aden.[75] The collection is replete with scathing attacks on practices such as *dhikr* and *ziyarat* as well as condemnations of various local customs. But both the composer and his editor attempted to tread a careful line that sought to condemn certain practices without directly alienating the Muslims of Aden.

The poems in the *Hidayat al-murid* address various broad topics with clear simple titles such as "On the Boundary between Learning and Ignorance," "On Doctrine," "On Faith," "On Idolatry and its Types," "On the Tariqa and the Shari'a" and "The Verdict on Tomb Visitation." Contained within both the poems and al-Bayhani's voluminous footnotes there is much that one would expect from a strict Salafi text.

Al-Abbadi's views on much of Sufism and tomb visitation are unmistakable and in accordance with what could be regarded as the mainstream scripturalist reform of his day. In his poem, "On the Tariqa and the Shari'a" the Shaykh condemns most mystical practices and beliefs as at best theater and at worst debauchery. *Dhikr*, as practiced locally, is clearly at variance with God's law, an occasion for depravity rather than remembering God:

> Know! That His Path
>   Is the Path of the Law and His truth
>   As God willed in His Book
>
> . . .
>
> And what is proper in the *shari'a*—that is pleasing to Him
>   Is what God sent through His Prophet
> As for dancing, "listening" [*sama'*] then wailing
>   And the revelry and yelling of trance
> It is as if they are drunk without drinking
>   [drunk] with dancing and "listening" but not with Remembrance
> They resemble the branch of the willow tree
>   They sink to the ground in a state of passion
> They claim to be impassioned for God
>   But the heart is unaware or absent.[76]

The visiting of tombs, not surprisingly, comes in for equally harsh criticism. In "On Idolatry," al-Abbadi declares:

Whomever calls upon the dead or unseen
And looks to it with reverence and desire
In repelling harm or attaining benefit
That is unbelief among the people of the *shari'a*[77]

And in "The Verdict on Tomb Visitation," the faithful are warned unreservedly:

> Cursed is any who approach a dome or mosque
>   That is an unrestricted tomb or shrine
>   And all who light the lamps
>   In tombs, are warned of the abyss
>
> . . .
>
> The Messenger, the Chosen, forbids it
>   And one is disgraced by his curse, it is known

And finally:

> No Muslim can visit a tomb
>   Without committing some vile, forbidden act.[78]

Al-Abbadi and his editor al-Bayhani were equally quick to condemn local custom. In detailed footnotes al-Bayhani provided the reader with a number of examples of unlawful behavior common among the believers. Some were customs that had evolved from the already suspicious activities surrounding tomb visitation while others were simply heretical practices akin to sorcery. "Some go to the local tombs," Bayhani writes,

> And make a vow to his master that he be favored with a child, male or female . . . even though such a request is impermissible to any other than God. And they say '*ya'shaykh Fulan*,[79] with your favor and station with God, I petition you . . .' and when the child reaches seven years of age he goes with his father, *the idolater*,[80] to the grave of the one to whom the pledge was made and shaves a circle in his head, deeming his hair to be a very good thing, and buries it next to the tomb. He then butchers a ram just to be sure. If it is a girl-child, he makes half a payment to the pious shaykh at the time of her marriage to support the performance of festivals and the lighting of his tomb. There is no power of strength save in God![81]

Bayhani relates other heinous practices that tempt the believer, including "a woman in Shaykh Uthman,"

> Who goes by the *kunya* Um Aqil [Mother of Reason] upon whom they break eggs and present to her other kinds of sacrifices, and she stops dead many of the brethren and they fear her gaze. God gives them their reward! And there are many horrible things like this.[82]

The remedy to these ills was, in part, the elimination of customs that were viewed as un-Islamic, a stricter observance of the law, as they interpreted it, and a more rigid reading of doctrine. At the same time, the approach of al-Abbadi and al-Bayhani was not without its accommodations. For instance, while many of the poems condemn various practices others in the collection were concerned with elements of belief that were far less controversial. Several of the earliest poems deal with topics such as "doctrine," "faith" and "The Boundary between Learning and Ignorance," all of which focus on issues with which few believers could disagree. "Between Learning and Ignorance," is concerned almost solely with the idea of the oneness and indivisibility of God.[83] In one of several poems dealing with *tawhid* or the "unity of God," al-Abbadi condemns those who are guilty of unbelief but the statements are so vague that they point to no one in particular. For example:

> Whoever says that he believes firmly in the forbidden
> > That it benefits you [to know] that he commits unbelief with his message
> The people of idolatry, oppose them
> > They are the worshippers of the forbidden, do not believe them
> They follow a path other than the Truth
> > Because of that they become wicked beings[84]

In general, those who are "wicked" are left largely unidentified as simply "certain shaykhs." In cases where specific examples of heterodoxy are given, the perpetrators are not only vague but far removed from the precincts of Aden. In "Idolatry and Its Types," al-Abbadi decries the common practice of seeking the intercession of the saints, declaiming:

> Whomever attributes sovereignty to [any being] other than God
> > He is an idolater
> Whomever calls upon the dead or the unseen
> > And looks to him with desire and reverence
> In repelling harm or attaining benefit
> > That is unbelief among the people of the *shari'a*[85]

This was certainly a strong statement condemning the idea of saintly intercession or *tawassul* with God on behalf of the believer. However, it was one with which few mystics would disagree, as common Sufi belief of the period teaches that the *awliya'* perform miracles only through God and not as a result of their own powers. As if recognizing this as the case in Aden the poem is quickly followed by a footnote added by al-Bayhani that reassured the reader that while such things go on, no one in Aden would ever make such a claim. Instead, he noted, while such "odious and malicious" beliefs exist, he had never heard them in Aden. Rather, "I heard such in 1351 [1932] in Djibouti when a person in a mosque said "Wallahi! The saints can cause harm and good without God,' God protect us from such words!"[86]

Certainly, al-Abbadi and al-Bayhani were dedicated reformists who saw it as their duty to bring the beliefs and customs of their brethren into line with "proper" Salafi teachings. Following the controversies of the early 1930s, however, both demonstrated a desire to affect change without direct confrontation (or at least limiting it as much as possible). As a result, al-Abbadi's collection sought to create at least some common ground by highlighting elements of belief that all could agree upon. In places where criticism was unavoidable it was kept relatively general and in places outright vague. Exemplars of poor behavior are women, foreigners or most generically "those people," individuals who could safely be identified as suspect. The so-called "people of the tombs," however, did not allow such insults to go unchallenged.

Al-Jiz al-latif *and the Prophet's cloak*

The *Jiz al-latif*, as we noted in Chapter 4, was a sixteenth-century text of Abu Bakr Aydarus al-Adani's writings collected posthumously by his student Abd al-Latif ibn Abd al-Rahman BaWazir. It had at least one other print edition before the one produced in the 1930s: a lithograph published in Hyderabad in the early twentieth century. The 1936 edition was a reset typescript published without additional commentary by the Cairo firm, Mustafa al-Halabi & Sons. While this print edition makes no reference to the ongoing disputes in Aden over the permissibility of saint veneration, the timing of its production seems hardly coincidental. In addition to the timing, the great Shaykh's writings on mystical and scholarly authority as well as the reports of his miraculous deeds included in the text, serve as a rebuke to those who would impugn saintly authority.

Al-Jiz al-latif is a book on mysticism. However, it is primarily a work about authority: who wields it, how it is bestowed and why the believer should follow those invested with it. As we have already seen, al-Adani discusses the "noble cloak" of the Muhammad, its investiture upon the Messenger of God by the archangel Gabriel and its bestowal on subsequent generations of spiritual notables. The cloak (*khirqa*), of course, was a symbol of spiritual authority and al-Adani's text lays out in great detail its transmission or investiture from person to person as well as various acceptable channels of transmission (most importantly through the Ahl al-Bayt but also via various Sufi notables, such as Suhrawardi, Abi al-Hasan al-Shadhili, al-Rifa'i and Abd al-Qadir Jilani).[87] The saint, however, also emphasized the necessity of seeking guidance only from those who recognize and lay within those networks. "It was said of Abu Yazid that he said: the one who does not have a teacher, his teacher is the devil and all of his knowledge—*batin* [internal] and *zahir* [external]—is invalid, he who does not have a teacher in these two [forms of knowledge] his Imam is the devil." Furthermore, according to Shaykh al-Suhrawardi, "A tree that sprouts by itself without being planted, it has leaves but not fruit and its results are weak, like the fruit of trees that grow in ravines and on mountains, not like the fruits that grow in gardens."[88]

The source of al-Adani's authority was certainly esoteric. But his hagiographer, Abd al-Latif BaWazir, was quick to point out that the Shaykh was a scholar among scholars who emphasized the importance of the exoteric alongside so-called "hidden knowledge." BaWazir begins his own section of the text by quoting the Qur'anic verse "it is the learned worshippers who fear God," and that according to the Prophet, "the *'ulama'* are the heirs of the prophets."[89] Al-Adani, he continued, "taught the people of his age the *sunna* as they sat around him . . . I saw *'ulama'* of hadith and of the roots [*usul*] and branches [*faru'a*] . . . [of the law] and other than them gather around him taking down all of his expertise until they understood what they heard . . . he would cite 'so and so' said 'such and such' in this book and 'so and so, such and such, in this book' it was as if he had all of the books of hadith and law—and their intricacies—on the tip of his tongue."[90]

To be sure, *al-Jiz al-latif* is a mystical text. In the hagiographies that preface al-Adani's *diwan*, the *wali* rescues people at sea, encounters *Khidr*, cures the sick and engages in the kinds of miraculous activities one expects of a Muslim saint. His poems are similarly typical for their age when he enjoins his readers to seek intercession through the guidance of the prophets, the *'ulama'*, the saints and all the pious.[91] Its publication in the 1930s, apparently for the Aden market, can be viewed as a strong rebuttal to the scripturalist reformers of Crater and Shaykh Uthman who impugned the reputation of the saints. Rather than "charlatans," the proponents of Sufism use their text to argue that the authority of the saints comes directly from the Prophet and, indeed, the divine realm itself via Jibril. Furthermore, al-Adani's hagiographer declares that, far from being at variance with the *shari'a*, the saint was in fact a master of *fiqh* recognized and praised by the *'ulama'* of his age. To be sure, the *Jiz al-latif* does not address all of the charges laid out by al-Abbadi and his followers, particularly with regard to what the reformers viewed as unlawful custom and superstition. Rather than a point-by-point rebuttal, al-Adani's collection appears intended to substantiate the validity of the Sufi approach to the faith based on their own conceptualization of Islamic tradition—a position that at least some reformers were ultimately willing to acknowledge.

Luqman and al-Asnag

Al-Abbadi and al-Bayhani did not tailor their message of reform so much as soften its presentation in an apparent effort to gain greater influence over the spiritual topography of Aden. Two other prominent members of the Reform Club, however, took a very different approach in their continued efforts toward transforming the faith, focusing less on ritual and the finer points of theology and more on notions of individual moral conduct. The goal, it seems, was to meet devotees of tomb veneration and mysticism somewhere in the middle.

Muhammad Ali Luqman and Ahmad al-Asnag were, in many ways, enormously different from al-Abbadi and al-Bayhani. The latter were *'ulama'* schooled exclusively in the world of the religious sciences, while the former were educated primarily in secular schools with a Westernized curriculum.⁹² More importantly, Luqman and al-Asnag were both natives of Aden whose fathers had risen from relatively humble origins to positions of prominence. Al-Abbadi and al-Bayhani, although from scholarly families and ultimately well traveled, were from rural backgrounds in the interior of Yemen; they were not *of* Aden. As a result, it is probably more than coincidence that in the writings of both Luqman and al-Asnag we see a concerted effort to reconcile the needs of reform with local ritual, custom and belief.

Ahmad Muhammad al-Asnag (d. 1972) was a person of growing importance in the early 1930s. A founding member of the Reform Club, he was also a confidant of the Sultan of Mukalla (a British dependency and part of the so-called East Aden Protectorate) and a growing intellectual presence in Aden. While much of his education was secular he studied the religious sciences under the tutelage of Shaykh al-Abbadi in the early 1930s. Al-Asnag's professional career is difficult to piece together. He appears to have earned his living first as a petition writer and then as a teacher in local secondary schools (as well as dabbling in business) but he was most notable as an essayist and local lecturer.⁹³

Muhammad Ali Luqman (1896–1966) was also a principal force behind the Arab Reform Club. In the mid-1930s, his activism took a slightly different turn. After working for a period with Antonin Besse Company, one of the wealthiest trading houses in Aden, he attended law school in Bombay in 1936, becoming Aden's first native born lawyer. In 1940, he founded *Fatat al-Jezirah*, the first of a number of newspapers culminating in a virtual media empire by the 1950s that he used to push a variety of social agendas.⁹⁴

In 1934 al-Asnag published a set of essays called *Nasib 'Adan min al-haraka al-fikriyya al-haditha* (Aden's Part in the Modern Intellectual Movement).⁹⁵ A few years later, in 1939, Luqman published a novella titled *Sa'id,* the story of Sa'id ibn Salman and his family as they navigated the struggles of life in colonial Aden, widely regarded as the first work of modern fiction written by an Adeni.⁹⁶ Like al-Abbadi, al-Asnag and Luqman were concerned with the spiritual health of the community around them. Their anxieties, however, were couched in far broader social terms. In *Nasib 'Adan*, al-Asnag critiqued the dangers facing Adeni Muslims and the perceived moral turpitude and social malaise evident most obviously among "the youth." "Dazzled by charm" and ignorant, he wrote, they had fallen into "a chasm of depravity . . . like a fly into squalor."⁹⁷ In his introduction to *Sa'id*, Luqman, writing along the same lines, laid the blame for society's decline, at least in part, on conspicuous consumption:

> Aden was prosperous at the beginning of this century, its Arab inhabitants were tied to the register of commerce they owned tens of thousands of transport animals, cattle, goats and sheep. They did not spend their profits on their leisure and luxuries, saving immense wealth for their sons . . . Today . . . the people of Aden have reached a state that is closer to conditions of poverty, most of the wealthy exhaust their riches on luxuries which leaches [their wealth] abroad [to foreigners]. Costly automobiles and gasoline; electricity

and ice; the cinema, *mila*,[98] and clothes—none [of which] lasts but a few days before it becomes an old fashion—as well as liquor and drugs.

For al-Asnag and Luqman the corruption of society was due in part to what they viewed as the temptations of modern society: alcohol, drugs and the unbridled desire for consumer luxuries. In addition, both argued that a large part of society's problems lie in the lack of modern education for both men and women and their failure to embrace the modern world more responsibly.[99] But, like al-Abbadi, they also believed that the corruption of society was linked to growing impiety. As al-Asnag noted:

> [T]he enemy struts among us morning and night and corrupts the morality of the youth and guides them towards the path of evil and turpitude and with it they are happy and under its power, he who is licentious is damned by God. And if the youth prefer licentiousness they are guided by error and leave the path of Islam and reject the teachings of the Qur'an, and they reach a state of committing every forbidden thing and neglecting everything that is required of a person—every religious obligation and every obligation to the nation.[100]

It was here that al-Asnag and Luqman departed from what is often considered mainstream scripturalist teachings. Al-Abbadi, like many preachers of his day, argued that the root causes of society's decline were erroneous doctrinal practices such as *dhikr* and saint veneration that ultimately led to moral depravity. Like most scripturalist reformers, al-Abbadi and al-Bayhani believed that the faith needed to be cleansed of these as well as other innovations. Al-Asnag and Luqman held a somewhat different perspective. They believed that while doctrinal backsliding was certainly a problem, ignorance, superstition and personal weakness in the face of temptation were the real causes of social decay.

The writers in question roundly condemned superstition as something that held back society. Al-Asnag, for instance, inveighed against numerous "disapproved of customs," promoted by the ignorant. These included the beating of drums and chanting to ward off solar and lunar eclipses, the sacrificing of a sheep on the doorstep of a new bride to protect her against jinn and the consultation of astrologers for important life events, such as business transactions and contracting marriages.[101] Luqman wrote of the "silly practices" of women,

> like Zar, charms and amulets, votive offerings, pilgrimages and tomb visitations . . . to seek remedies for barrenness or hysteria or even from maladies like diabetes and tuberculosis at the tombs of the saints!![102]

While denouncing certain local customs as harmful superstitions, however, Luqman and al-Asnag endorsed others as acts of the pious. Most notably—while there was certainly such a thing as improper tomb visitation, as Luqman notes above—both approved, within certain limits, of the local custom of "visiting the saints." In *Nasib 'Adan* al-Asnag devoted a brief, although important, essay to the subject of *"ziyara al-awliya'."* "Among the benefits of the neighborhoods of Aden," he writes, "is that they each have a saint's festival which is much like an annual exhibition known in Egypt as a *mawlid* and in Aden as a *'ziyara'*."[103] In its ideal form, he noted, one should go to "the place of domes [that is, the tomb of the deceased] on the day of *ziyara* with the intention of visiting the tomb of the pious saint and invoking God as it is said in the *sunna*." While there, "one recalls the good works of the saint during his life which serves as an uplifting lesson or we enter the mosque next to the grave and pray to God as a supplication and read something aloud from the Qur'an."[104]

If anything, Luqman had an even greater affinity for the spiritual benefits of tomb visitation. In his autobiography, he recalled how his mother was a serious devotee of Sayyid Hashim al-Bahr and during a persistent bout of malaria took him to see the *wali*'s sister, Sharifa Aliya, who performed cupping on him as a remedy. He remembered her "as white and pure as crystal . . . very pretty and young and . . . sanctified after her death."[105] It comes as little surprise, then, that the fictional hero Sa'id, as we saw earlier, sought spiritual edification at the tomb of Hashim al-Bahr where he received guidance from the pious Sharifa Aliya.[106] *Ziyarat*, in the estimation of both men, served a valuable spiritual function. The act of visiting the tomb offered the believer the opportunity to reflect on the personal meaning of his or her faith while those associated with the deceased saint (for example, Sharifa Aliya) could provide meaningful moral direction. As al-Asnag noted, the tombs and the saints were overall a "benefit" to society.

Local pilgrimages as practiced, however, were not without their problems. The festivals tended to encourage the kind of conspicuous consumption that Luqman and al-Asnag opposed and, at worst, they promoted depravity. At each *ziyara*, al-Asnag wrote, "people seek to out do one another, men and women, young and old, all of them in new clothes as if for a Ramadan festival."[107] More troubling than people wasting their hard-earned money was the utter wantonness of the surrounding festival. To attend a *ziyara* was to witness, "the decline of morality," where one was forced to observe "ghastly things, such as those who occupy themselves with flirtatiousness and seduction, drunks and debauched libertines . . . and all kinds of gambling that even draw in children . . . as well as dancing with the mixing of men and women [drums] beating with a wantonness that wounds Islam."[108]

Both men were quick to insist that neither opposed *ziyarat* or the veneration of the saints. Al-Asnag stated that when his opponents "ask if I love the saints [I say,] 'who does not love the pious worshippers of God?' and verily I believe of necessity in their honor."[109] Similarly, Luqman noted that "some of those among the rash are of the opinion that I hold extreme views regarding such silliness, but those with even the least reason or awareness know that I am among the lovers of the saints . . . but I do not like placing others next to God."[110]

But the unrestrained activities associated with local festivals made all who attended complicit in one way or another. While no one was forced to take part in such goings on, Luqman related in *Sa'id*, most "foreswear the virtuous and follow carnal desires."¹¹¹ Even those who avoided these activities carried some amount of guilt. "There are a few people," al-Asnag wrote, "who are satisfied with visiting the tomb, but can any among them be satisfied with this practice? No, by God! They are responsible to the Imam of God for what they know." How could one sit by while such things went on? "Would the *wali* approve?" al-Asnag asked. ¹¹²

While willing to make accommodations with local practice, neither al-Asnag nor Luqman saw this as compromising their broader commitment to reformist ideals.¹¹³ In 1938, as President of the Reform Club, al-Asnag arranged scholarships for al-Bayhani and others to study at al-Azhar in Cairo. In 1939, the same year he published *Sa'id*, Luqman delivered a series of lectures to the Reform Club entitled "The Beauties of Islam." As in the novella, these talks denounced "superstition," while at the same time explicitly praising the thought of reformers such as al-Afghani, Abduh and Rashid Rida.¹¹⁴

Reform, empire and local context

The impact of any of these writings on the public at large is difficult to gauge. The Arab Reform Club continued to exist at least through the late 1930s and both al-Asnag and Luqman remained active and important members.¹¹⁵ Al-Abbadi, however, disappeared from the written record after the early 1930s. It is possible that he left the Settlement, passed away or simply retired from preaching to manage the numerous properties he had purchased since arriving in Aden. As mentioned above, Shaykh al-Bayhani continued his studies abroad at the famed al-Azhar in Cairo on a scholarship awarded by the Club.¹¹⁶ He, along with Luqman and al-Asnag, remained prominent fixtures in the Settlement's intellectual life. Luqman, starting with *Fatat al-Jezirah* in 1940, became a major force in local publishing. Al-Asnag continued to write essays and give weekly lectures to the club membership. Al-Bayhani obtained two degrees at al-Azhar, and following his return to Aden in the early 1940s published numerous Salafi tracts. He established an "institute for higher Islamic learning" toward the end of the decade.¹¹⁷ On the other hand, *dhikr* did not cease within the city nor did the various *ziyarat* become less popular. Gambling, dancing and all the other activities associated with the festivals continued, although the British authorities required them to move to the outer edges of the celebrations.

The controversies in Aden do allow us to add nuance to recent scholarship concerning Islamic reform and its trajectory within local contexts outside the highest levels of discourse. Scripturalist reform in Aden, as we have seen, did not sweep all before it gained a foothold in Aden. Instead, significant—one could even say successful—push back by local individuals forced local Salafi proponents to proceed far more carefully when seeking to propagate their teachings. Preachers such as al-Abbadi and al-Bayhani (and their patrons, al-Hindi and Sayyid Ali Isma'il) quickly found that heavy-handed tactics got them nowhere and a subtler approach, as evidenced in the *Hidayat al-murid*, was necessary. Indeed, Sufis were not shy about putting forth their own vision of the faith that subtly impugned the authority of the scripturalists.

Although softening their approach, al-Abbadi and al-Bayhani maintained what are often viewed as mainstream Salafi teachings, namely that the problems of Adeni society were a direct result of various doctrinal shortcomings (particularly *dhikr* and saint veneration) that must be addressed if society were to prosper. Other reformist voices, notably those native to Aden, took a somewhat different tack. Luqman and al-Asnag, both natives of Aden, tended to eschew such issues of doctrine and focused instead on the more readily apparent moral failings of society. They saw *dhikr* and *ziyarat*, in and of themselves, as not only blameless but laudable. The problems in society had less to do with issues of doctrinal interpretation than proper moral conduct and avoiding reprehensible activities such as gambling and drinking, as well as superstitions such as Zar and magical charms, all of which distracted one from a pious life. In effect, Luqman and al-Asnag sought to reconcile Salafism with elements of local belief and practice.

Samira Haj has persuasively argued that while Salafism looked to an ideal of the Islamic past and tradition for inspiration "tradition is not simply the recapitulation of previous beliefs and practices. Instead, each successive generation," uses it to "confront its particular problems via an engagement with a set of ongoing arguments [or problems]"[118] in a process that results in almost constant reinvention. For Haj, Salafism is a fundamental reimagining of early Islamic tradition as a path to dealing with the colonial present. Her own work on Muhammad Abduh is based on an engagement with the highest levels of reformist discourse. Not only can the same process be discerned at the local level, but we can also see that it was not the sole preserve of a single group. Both scripturalist and pro-mystical camps in Aden looked to the founders of the faith as sources of authority and guidance. Preachers like al-Abbadi subscribed to what was by this time a well-established path that looked to the Prophet and the *salaf al-salih* for guidance mediated solely through what was believed to be the latter's textual tradition (the Qur'an and Hadith). The habitués of the saints also looked to Muhammad and the pious ancestors for direction. While they did not eschew the faith as manifest in texts, adherents of Sufism could point to a far more intimate, metaphysical connection through the spiritual genealogies of the *awliya'* (especially Abu Bakr Aydarus al-Adani) that linked them not only with the words of God's Messenger, but the Divine realm proper via Jibril and the "noble cloak." While al-Asnag and Luqman were certainly enamored of Salafi thought, both recognized (consciously or not) elements that were not compatible with these local institutions and beliefs . . . or traditions.

In the end, these two tweaked the message of reform not only in order to make it more palatable but to address what most of their fellow Adenis viewed as the true crux of the problem. Neither subscribed uncritically to the idea of the saints or the *Nur Muhammadiyya* as sources of guidance or authority nor did they deride it. Instead of descending into the morass of doctrine, they pointed to issues that few Adenis would argue were not serious social problems (prostitution, drinking, idleness and gambling). Rather than vilifying local icons and customs, the two natives of Aden made them part of the solution as exemplars of pious behavior and sources of moral guidance. The lives of the saints and the festivals surrounding them provided one with moral focus while their descendants were fonts of advice and direction. Luqman, in particular, held up the saints and their families as paragons of Muslim piety. However, he appeared affected by more than his mother's affection for Sayyid Hashim or nostalgia for the saint's beautiful sister. He also seems to have found resonance in the ideas of Abu Bakr al-Aydraus and his adherents. In a May 1942 edition of *Fatat,* Luqman published a short article by an unnamed reporter on "The *ziyara* of *Sayyid* Aydarus." Rather than an account of the annual festival, the piece was a mini-biography of the saint, outlining his virtues, miracles and reputation for learning, extolling him as "the vanguard of the *awliya'*." In addition to details of his birth and early education, the unknown author focused heavily on the great Shaykh's reputation for learning, noting that verily "every book of hadith, and the roots and branches of the law were on the tip of his tongue."[119] If this phrase sounds familiar, it is because it is drawn directly from the *Jiz al-latif*, as is the entire piece, nearly word for word. While this falls short of an endorsement of a Sufi ontology, it does evince a respect for local intellectual and spiritual endeavor and, by extension, tradition and custom.

In the end, the tempest swirling around religious reform in Aden during the 1930s provides us with an informative window into the spiritual and social life of an imperial Muslim community. In particular, they suggest an avenue of inquiry that takes us beyond the traditional categories of social history, namely individual faith. Certainly, issues of ethnicity, wealth, gender and social standing remain important in any examination of a community's social history. However, as the case of Aden demonstrates, other more personal factors also necessarily come into play when determining an individual's beliefs and how those may become manifest in social discourse. As the episodes discussed here demonstrate, the Muslims of Aden were hardly a monolithic community. Like Muslims around the world, the believers of Aden were divided over how best to engage modernity and the questions of religious practice and belief. An individual's attitudes toward such issues are not easily predicted simply by their membership in a particular socio-economic, educational or ethnic category. While education, profession and social standing certainly played an important role in how one viewed the world, the much fuzzier realm of personal spiritual belief also had its place.

Case in point are the views of al-Asnag and Luqman. It seems unlikely that in co-opting *ziyarat* and the cult of the saints into their own message of reform they were acting purely opportunistically (manipulating images and beliefs simply in order to influence the public). It seems far more probable that, in their effort to address society's problems, both sought to draw on their own stockpile of local traditions that along with the teachings of Salafism offered solutions to the moral quagmire in which they found themselves. In short, they sought to transform Salafi reform by melding the local with the global in an effort to remedy the maladies of their society. The construction of local Muslim space was deeply impacted by currents within the broader Islamic world. Contemporary reformist debates had a clear effect on local intellectual and communal contexts. The emergence of these debates, however, was always shaped by local circumstance via local actors. In the end, while Adeni Muslims were part and parcel of the larger *umma*, the boundaries of their community were constructed through an agency that was wholly their own.

Conclusions

By the late 1930s, Muhammad Ali Luqman noted in his memoirs that he had become increasingly disenchanted with pan-Islamism, most notably because of his South Asian nationalist colleagues whom he considered naïve and petty. Their contempt for the deep attachment Adenis maintained for their town, he declared, pushed him into becoming an Arab nationalist.[1] Indeed, by this point he also increasingly distanced himself from his scripturalist compatriots, endorsing as we saw in the last chapter, tomb visitation while also, in the early 1940s, coming out against the practice of veiling. By this time, Aden, too—under the aegis of British policy—had begun to change significantly. The Settlement was slowly being divorced from India and its fortunes tied to the Arabian hinterland. This was due in large part to the rising tide of nationalist sentiment in India after the First World War and the changing political realities of a post-Ottoman Middle East. In order to protect Imperial interests, British policy determined that the best course of action was to bring Aden increasingly under the direct control of the metropole. In 1932, the town was removed from the control of Bombay and made a "Chief Commissioner's Province," administered directly by the Viceroy in Delhi. By 1937 it was transferred to the Colonial Office becoming the Crown Colony of Aden—a status that it would retain until independence and the creation of the People's Democratic Republic of Yemen in 1967.

The most significant result of this shift was an official emphasis on Aden as an "Arab" town, accompanied by a strategy of rapid "Arabization" of institutions, including the police and local administration. By the late 1930s, the armed and civil police, traditionally a mixture of Arabs, Indians and Somalis, were staffed predominately by the former. As the result of increasing educational opportunities for boys from Aden, as well as the sons of chiefs and princes in the interior, the ranks of Aden's clerks and bureaucrats—the province of Indians, in the past—were increasingly dominated by individuals of Arab descent by the Second World War.[2] The Settlement also grew. From a population of approximately 51,000 in 1931, the town and its surroundings exploded to more than 80,000 by 1945 and more than 225,000 in 1963. The overwhelming majority of these new arrivals, however, were Yemenis drawn from the interior, looking for work in the port, the Colony's ever-expanding military economy or the newly emerging industrial sector. Emblematic of the latter was the opening of an oil refinery in 1955 in the area known as Little Aden, which at the peak of construction in 1953–4 employed more than one in four laborers in Aden.[3]

Furthermore, trade, traditionally the bedrock of the local economy, was now secondary to supplying fuel oil to ships passing from the Suez Canal to the Indian Ocean and vice versa. By 1958, following the expansion and re-dredging of the harbor, Aden was the second busiest port in the world after New York City. This traffic, however, was largely transient, and the once prosperous and cosmopolitan merchant community fell into decline.[4] By the time of the British withdrawal in 1967, Aden was very much an Arab city in population that looked increasingly inland rather than to the sea.

There is a certain irony in the fact that the empire that played such a central role in bringing together the trajectories creating colonial Aden in the nineteenth century would also be instrumental in their disruption in the twentieth. The imperial networks that brought believers to the Southern Arabian port from across the Indian Ocean also introduced nationalist and scripturalist ideologies. The logics of nationalism dictated that Aden's post-colonial fate was ultimately tied to its Yemeni hinterland when it became the capital of the People's Democratic Republic of Yemen (PDRY) in November 1967. This was followed by an unhappy union with the Yemen Arab Republic and Sana'a after 1990.[5] Doctrinaire strains of religious reform gained increasing power in northern Yemen, emerging in the 1990s as the *Islah* party whose militias occupied Aden following the 1994 civil war. Among other things, it was they who were responsible for vandalizing the tomb of Sayyid Abu Bakr Aydarus.[6] Dissecting these legacies requires a separate study. Instead, in these final pages I wish to return to the processes and paths that created a multi-ethnic community of Muslims in imperial Aden.

Trajactories of empire and faith

Over the course of the last six chapters, this book has explored the emergence of Muslim community within the context of British Imperial Aden. The flows of empire undoubtedly tied the fates of believers together in imperial subjecthood. However, the Muslims of Britain's empire were often bound together more tightly by the sinews of their faith. These may be manifest in relatively concrete, or at least observable, institutions, such as mosques, shrines and Sufi orders, but also extended to the more ineffable, such as common understandings of an Islamic multiverse. In order to develop a more nuanced understanding of emergent Muslim community under European imperial rule, it seems critical to appreciate how all of these strands interconnected with one another.

The significance of imperial subjecthood

The importance of imperial subjecthood should not be underplayed. British authority made its presence felt in virtually every facet of life, particularly the spiritual. Furthermore, the structures of empire had a transformative effect on the ways in which believers interacted with one another, with the social contexts of Muslims unremittingly shaped by the imperial state. The emergence of a Muslim community in Aden was the direct result of imperial design and the policies of, first, the British East India Company and, later, the Raj. Believers' movements, personal, political and religious associations, along with their economic and domestic activities were subject to imperial regulation, as well as the colonial surveillance regime.

Even while British officials protested that the state did not interfere in the religious lives of its subjects, the hand of the Company or the Raj was always evident. Frequently, this presence was regulatory or administrative in nature, rationalized on the grounds of health, public order or community interest. As such, Residency officials found themselves involved in local burial practices, regulating the activities of spirit-possession cults, late night *dhikr* and Qur'an recitations or mediating disputes between scripturalist reformers and supporters of Sufism. On occasion, the role of the state may even take on a more spiritual tinge, such as when Bernard Riley, in his role as Resident, presided over the installation of a new *kiswa* covering the grave of Hashim al-Bahr during the saint's annual *ziyara*, while government offices were themselves closed during the festivities.

The networks of transportation and communication that underpinned the Empire similarly served to shape Muslim social and spiritual trajectories. Regular steamship routes and cheap, accessible print allowed for the dissemination of a constantly shifting marketplace of religious ideas. These enabled Muslims in Aden to stay abreast of the most recent intellectual trends, but also allowed them to maintain links across the British imperium, permitting them to play an active role in the social, political and religious discourses of the age. The actions and agendas of bureaucrats, religious scholars and anti-colonial activists were molded by their longstanding connections to the various educational, intellectual and religious networks that traversed (and even transcended) the empire, introducing ideas ranging from post-Enlightenment social theory to scriptural reformism.

Associations with, or access to, the organs of the state also enabled certain individuals to exert influence over the moral direction of society. Western-trained bureaucrats and intellectuals like Yasin Khan and Muhammad Ali Luqman, for instance, were the agents of an approach to the faith infused with European rationalist ideals of law and spiritual probity—ideas that would play decisive roles in the development of important local institutions such as the Wakf Committee and the Arab Reform Club. Religious scholars with a penchant for scripturalist ideas, such as Qadi Da'ud al-Battah, could similarly use their positions to push particular theological agendas like the campaign against spirit possession. By the same token, Sayyid Abdullah Aydarus could use his position and connections to oppose them.

Beyond subjecthood

While pervasive, the structures and influence of the state were not all defining. The community of believers reproduced within the spaces generated by colonial rule depended largely on religious ideals and institutions that formed the core of social and communal life. The existence of these, of course, was not contingent on the state. Mosques and shrines, for instance, underwrote Adeni identity in varying ways. By endowing places of worship or patronizing the tombs of local saints, the wealthy established concrete symbols of their attachment to Aden. Similarly, through participation in communal prayers, annual saints' festivals and spirit-possession rituals, both rich and poor literally performed their membership in community. Although bound up with the state, such institutions were creations of the Muslim community. Moreover, they were critical in fashioning a singular sense of community while at the same time helping establish internal boundaries and relations of authority. The complexities of belonging, however, extend far beyond such performative acts.

While observable institutions served as venues for the mediation of community and belonging, in the final analysis, the negotiation of community in Aden centered on religious ideals and the common—if contested—template of belief created by the discursive tradition. Most often the discursive tradition is imagined as a great body of textual interpretations, shared rituals, norms and values that tie believers to one another across linguistic, ethnic and social differences. However, the tradition includes not just the generally agreed upon tenets of the faith and practice, but far more abstract notions about the nature of being and the structure of God's created universe. As such, it also constitutes an ontological map that represents a critical element of the tradition. To be sure, within this discursive tradition reside a plethora of currents and eddies frequently at odds with one another. It is their intersection, however, that creates the basis for shared community.

Debates surrounding various areas of belief and practice provided platforms for delineating authority and communal boundaries that may playout across multiple levels of society. Disagreements between the *'ulama'* and Muslim registrars regarding marriage, *waqf* properties and the Kamaran mosque extension were ultimately about social authority and who had the right to interpret religious law. Such debates brought conflicting concepts of the law into contact with one another. The Qadis sought to interpret the law as a tool of mediation aimed at finding solutions that best served all parties while the registrars looked to the rules-"heavy" interpretation of *fiqh* known as Anlgo-Muhammadan law. Ultimately, the two sides reached uneasy accommodations with each other that resulted in both retaining significant social authority. The effects of this, however, were felt across society. Individuals from all walks of life, for instance, experienced confusion regarding the proper courses of action related to important social practices—such as marriage and divorce—that marked one as a member of the community. Frequently, this showed itself via not a little rancor toward those who were supposed to provide guidance.

Conflicting trajectories also overlapped in Aden over notions of correct worship and belief in the shape of Sufism and scripturalist reform. The former constituted a critical Muslim institution in Aden that served to not only bind Muslims from different parts of the Indian Ocean to one another, through the veneration of common saints, but also tied them to the port across time as they revived and rebuilt tombs and shrines that dated to the earliest generations of the faith. The latter emerged in the Settlement from the 1920s among individuals who sought to promote specific notions of piety and rectitude within a society they believed had become dangerously corrupt. The collision of these fundamentally different approaches to the faith over issues of correct worship, but also the sources of authority, is unsurprising. More interestingly, both tapped in to imperial networks to support their causes and, in the end, reached accommodations with one another that emerged from local interpretations of Islamic tradition.

The trajectories of tradition that shaped the Muslim community of Aden, however, were not limited to the interpretations of acceptable textual understanding and ritual practice. Just as important were far more abstract elements of belief centering on the shape of the universe. This shared ontology, or understanding of the nature of being, linked Muslims in Aden through the commonality of their faith, but also as inhabitants of an Indian Ocean realm. Understanding God's creation as a complex multiverse that encompassed far more than a dreary temporal world and a distant, inaccessible realm of the Divine was central to the way many believers perceived their connection to Aden. The multiverse and its many dimensions—the earthly, the world of the jinn and the afterlife—regularly impacted the lives of all humanity and was a reality with which all believers must interact.

The power of the multiverse, among Adenis, could most readily be seen in relation to where it was believed to be at its most accessible, the tombs of the saints. As conduits to the *Nur Muhammadiyya*, tombs and the saints interred within them, were natural centers around which the community could gather. Patronage of a tomb, of course, could invest an individual or group with prestige and claims to belonging. But as sites where the membrane dividing the earthly from the Divine was at its thinnest, the tombs of the saints were also where the agency of the unseen could most readily impact the lives of individuals. For many, association with the *ghayb* conferred spiritual and even worldly authority via the "noble cloak" (*al-khirqa al-sharifa*) of the Prophet whose power came directly from the Divine realm. For habitués of the tombs, the cloak was also representative of the immanent nature of the divine reality (*al-haqiqa*) and humanity's everyday contact with it.

Similarly, the positive possession experienced by the tambura *Akils* turned them into physical agents of the unseen and a nexus between this world and the Divine. Given the marginal social status of spirit practitioners in the Settlement, this could be read as an attempt to subvert local hierarchies by claiming power equal to that of their spiritual and social betters. However, the continued support of the head of the Sufi establishment, Sayyid Abdullah Aydarus, and the emphasis that Tambura dancers placed on fulfilling their oaths at the tombs, suggests that the ceremonies served to reinforce the spiritual status quo rather than challenge it. In either case, Tambura dances as well as the annual *ziyarat*, illustrate the impact that the unseen could exert on the existences of everyday believers, in terms of individual lives as well as social relationships. Carving out and defending such practices was not necessarily about concern for membership in society, but represented worries related to one's relationship with the next.

But, people's relationship with, and understanding of, the *ghayb* was not always concerned with the venal matters of the temporal world. The study of Aden provides a variety of examples where the unseen served purposes whose benefits were not readily observable. Burial of one's kin in the proximity of the saints could certainly help solidify a family's claims to being "of Aden." But, at the same time, for the deceased the location of their final resting place had far more to do with a desire to spend the time between death and resurrection in as much tranquility as possible and as close to the *barzakh* as one's soul could get. This could be supplied by the saint and the access his tomb provided to the *Nur Muhammadiyya*. From Ibn al-Mujjawir in the thirteenth century to Hamza Luqman in the 1960s, traditions also circulated widely, portraying Aden as a supernatural lodestone attracting demons, jinn and even the fratricide Cain. These situated the port within a broad spiritual topography encompassing both Arabia and India.

Aden and its connection to dimensions other than the temporal represent a common ontological template that encompassed the Islamic and the pre-Islamic and linked the physical via the metaphysical. Like other elements of the Islamic discursive tradition, these agreed upon notions of the unseen, and their salience in everyday life, served to tie believers to one another within a common framework that transcended ethnic and linguistic differences. Thus, cemeteries become common ground for Muslims, where individual souls may rest closest to God. The story of Hanuman, Alexander's Red Sea excavations and other miraculous events served to collapse and reconfigure physical space connecting Southern Arabia, India and Africa in a literal as well as a figurative sense.

In the final analysis, the communities that emerged within empire were certainly the product of trajectories of the colonial moment that frequently combined in unexpected ways, resulting in novel alliances and unforeseen cleavages. Imperial bureaucrats and religious scholars found common cause via compatible visions of the faith and complementary social agendas. Indian and Arab activists, on the other hand, found themselves going their separate ways, despite their common faith, due to the ascendancy of nationalism. But in creating a community, the Muslims of Aden drew on far more than the networks of empire. More important was the Islamic discursive tradition that they all shared. Encompassing a common epistemology and ontology, the canon of the Islamic faith equipped believers with the tools necessary to generate a vibrant local community from their disparate parts. While visible institutions such as mosques, shrines and the law gave rise to concrete manifestations of community, it was often the less visible that prompted individuals' more intimate engagements. In the end, while empire may have brought subjects together, it was Islam that made them a community.

Notes

Introduction

1. R/20/A/2209 Wightwick to the Chairman of the Settlement March 3, 1911.
2. A source to be discussed in detail in Chapter 3 of this work.
3. R/20/A/2209 Omar Abdalla Sharaf, Kazi of Sheikh Othman and Other Notables of Aden. December 1910. The authorities granted this request with little fanfare or debate.
4. Cemil Aydin, *The Idea of the Muslim World*, Ch. 4.
5. In this vein, I am following the exhortations of Frederick Cooper in the introduction to his book of essays, *Colonialism in Question*.
6. The most important of these include Thomas Metcalf, *Imperial Connections*; Sugata Bose, *A Hundred Horizons;* Tony Ballantyne, "Rereading the Archive and Opening up the Nation-State"; David Lambert and Alan Lester, "Imperial Spaces, Imperial Subjects.".
7. Lambert and Lester, "Imperial Spaces, Imperial Subjects," pp. 13–14.
8. Thomas Metcalf and Sugata Bose are exemplary of the form, as are Tony Ballantyne and David Lambert and Alan Lester.
9. An important exception to this is Sunil K. Amrith, *Crossing the Bay of Bengal.*
10. The work of Nile Green, particularly his book *Bombay Islam*, is an important exception. It and other elements of his work will be discussed below.
11. Muhammad Qasim Zaman, *The Ulama in Contemporary Islam* and *Modern Islamic Thought in a Radical Age*; Samira Haj, *Reconfiguring Islamic Tradition.*
12. Of particular importance in this vein are Asad's *Genealogies of Religion* and *The Idea of an Anthropology of Islam.*
13. In addition to those mentioned above, see Seema Alavi, *Muslim Cosmopolitanism in the Age of Empire*. An important exception to this, of course is, Nile Green's, *Bombay Islam* discussed below.
14. Systemic understandings of the nature of being and existence.
15. R/20/E/5 In S. B. Haines' report on new arrivals, dated September 13, 1839, in which he recorded more than 1,600 new arrivals since the Company take over, the Commander noted that the numbers were almost certainly an under count of the town's actual population for a number of reasons. First, he noted that given the timing of the survey—late February—many of the Indian merchants were away in Bombay stocking up on goods for the trading season. In addition, he cautioned, many among the local Jewish and Muslim population were hesitant to cooperate with the state's attempts at enumerating the population based on "religious scruple." Haines to Malet, March 2, 1849.
16. Figures for the 1839, 1849 and 1871 censuses can be found in the following India Office files: R/20/E/5, R/20/E/34 and R/20/A/400. Figures for the 1931 census are from The Census of India, 1931, vol. VII, pt. II, Bombay Presidency, Aden Report and Tables; R. J. Gavin, *Aden under British Rule*, p. 445.
17. See Chapter 2.

18. See census data.
19. A. S. Bujra, "Urban Elites and Colonialism," pp. 191–2.
20. For instance, while he argued that Somalis always held themselves separate, he also noted the "not insignificant number of Arab marriages to Somali women," which would seem to contradict his assertion of axiomatic separation. Ibid., p. 196.
21. Ibid., pp. 191–2.
22. Among the many works on the pre-Modern Indian Ocean one of the most notable is K. N. Chaudhuri, *Trade and Civilization in the Indian Ocean*.
23. See, for instance, Jeremy Prestholdt, *Domesticating the World* and Johan Mathew, *Margins of the Market*.
24. James Gelvin and Nile Green, eds, *Global Muslims*.
25. E. Tagliacozzo, "Hajj in the Time of Cholera"; and M. C. Low, "Empire and the Hajj."
26. J. Cole, "Printing and Urban Islam in the Mediterranean World."
27. Green, *Bombay Islam*; Alavi, *Muslim Cosmopolitanism in the Age of Empire*; Michael Laffan, *Islamic Nationhood and Colonial Indonesia*.
28. Anne Bang, *Sufis and Scholars of the Sea*; Scott Reese, "The Adventures of Abu Harith."
29. Gavin, *Aden under British Rule*, p. 184. The first submarine cable reached Aden in 1860 but failed almost immediately; a more dependable system was not completed until a decade later.
30. Muhammad Ali Luqman, for instance, worked as a stringer and columnist for several newspapers and magazines in Egypt and India beginning in the 1920s—work that would not have been possible were he not able to file his stories via telegraph. M. A. Lokman, *Men, Matters and Memories*.
31. J. Cole, "Printing and Urban Islam."
32. See, for example, Cole, ibid. Nile Green, *Bombay Islam*; Francis Robinson, "Technology and Religious Change."
33. Scott Reese, "Shaykh Abdullahi al-Qutbi and the Pious Believer's Dilemma."
34. Green, *Bombay Islam*, pp. 10–11.
35. This topic is taken up in detail in Chapters 5 and 6 of this study but had also been amply illustrated by many others, including myself. See, among others, Scott Reese, *Renewers of the Age*; Michael Laffan, *Islamic Nationhood and Colonial Indonesia*; Anne Bang, *Sufis and Scholars of the Sea*.
36. See also, Nile Green, *Terrains of Exchange*.
37. Asad, *The Idea of an Anthropology of Islam*.
38. Most notable among non-Africa works are S. Haj, *Reconfiguring Islamic Tradition*; Mariam Cooke and Bruce Lawrence, eds, *Muslim Networks*; and Muhammad Qasim Zaman, "The Scope and Limits of Islamic Cosmopolitanism."
39. Roman Loimeier, *Between Social Skills and Marketable Skills*, p. 2.
40. Adeline Masquelier, *Women and Islamic Revival*, p. 24.
41. Benedict Anderson, *Imagined Communities*.
42 Jack Hunter, "Spirits are the Problem," p. 80.
43. Dipesh Chakrabarty, *Provincializing Europe,* p. 16.
44. Ibid.
45. Steven Feierman, "Colonizers, Scholars and the Creation of Invisible Histories," p. 198.
46. Ibid., p. 206. Emphasis mine.
47. Ruy Blanes and Diana Espirito Santo, eds, "Introduction: On the Agency of Intangibles."
48. Gavin, *Aden under British Rule*, pp. 253–6.
49. A full account of this episode can be found in R/20/E/209.

Chapter 1

1. Smith, *A Traveller in Thirteenth-Century Arabia*, pp. 133–4.
2. See, for instance, Sugata Bose, *A Hundred Horizons*; Thomas Metcalf, *Imperial Connections*.
3. Although Wilfred Schoff notes in his 1911 translation that it was likely "the Eden" mentioned in Ezekiel XXVII, 3 in the Old Testament. Wilfred H. Schoff, trans., *The Periplus of the Erythraean Sea*, p. 115.
4. Roxani Eleni Margariti, *Aden and the Indian Ocean Trade*, p. 27.
5. Al-Muqaddasi, *Kitab ahsan al-taqasim fi ma'rifat al-aqalim* p. 85, cited in Margariti, *Aden and the Indian Ocean Trade*, p. 27.
6. Successor to the Fatimids.
7. Margariti, *Aden and the Indian Ocean Trade*, especially Chapter 2; In his *Tarikh 'adan*, the local historian Hamza Luqman lists at least six congregational mosques built during the period of the Middle Ages, pp. 264–76.
8. Gavin, *Aden under British Rule*, p. 13.
9. Amitav Ghosh, *In an Antique Land*.
10. Ibid.; S. D. Goitein, *A Mediterranean Society*; S. D. Goitein and Mordechai A. Friedman, *India Traders of the Middle Ages*.
11. Yaqut al-Humawi, *Mu'jam al-buldan*, pt. 4, p. 89; Muhammad Ibn Battuta, *Rihlat*, p. 244.
12. Ibid.
13. Ibn Battuta, *Rihlat*, p. 244
14. Ibid.
15. Ibid.
16. In his recent translation of the *Tarikh*, G. Rex Smith holds that the traditional identification of the author as a certain Yusuf b. Yusuf al-Shaybani al-Dimashqi is a copyist error that has crept in over the centuries. G. Rex Smith, *A Traveller in Thirteenth-Century Arabia*, p. 1.
17. Ibid., pp. 1–3.
18. Ibid., pp. 30, 47.
19. Although as Smith points out, he was hardly a careful historian, muddling dates, people and events with regularity. Smith, *A Traveller in Thirteenth-Century Arabia*, p. 14.
20. See Ibid., Appendix C List of Literary Works Quoted by Ibn al-Mujawir in the Text, p. 301.
21. An apparently no longer extant work by a ruler of the eleventh-century Tihama about whom we will hear more later.
22. Ibid., pp. 125–6.
23. This is something that Ibn al-Mujawir's translator, G. Rex Smith, never tires of pointing out. In his introduction, he refers to Ibn al-Mujawir as "not a reliable historian," due to these deficiencies and points out inaccuracies throughout the translation's footnotes. So, for instance, p. 127 f.n. 5 he writes, "Al-Malik al-Mufiizz could not possibly have been involved during the reign of al-Malik al-Nasir Ayyub."
24. Ibid., p. 124.
25. Ibid., pp. 132–3.
26. Ibn al-Mujawir, in fact, relates this story twice. See, Smith, *A Traveller in Thirteenth-Century Arabia*, pp. 119 and 129.
27. Ibid., p. 119.
28. Ibid., p. 120.
29. Ibid., pp. 130–1.
30. Ibid., p. 133.
31. Ibn al-Mujawir provides a lengthy list of royal prisons and notes that the Fatimids had also used Aden as a place of exile. Ibid., p. 132.

32. Huqqat Bay was the original harbor of Aden located north of Sira Island. Smith speculates that while Jabal al-Manzar does not appear on any modern maps of the region, it may be "one of the peaks to the S. of Crater." Ibid., p. 133 n.1.
33. This reference may, in fact, constitute a further link to the *Ramayana*, as the Sri Lankan demigod Ravana, the principal antagonist in many versions of the myth, is generally portrayed as possessing ten heads. Thanks to Sanjay Joshi for pointing this out. Personal communication, January 29, 2016.
34. Ibid.
35. Paula Richman, ed. *Many Ramayanas*, pp. 5–7.
36. Ibid., p. 4.
37. The name of the demon is, in fact, corrupted in the surviving manuscripts. This is Oscar Löfgren's extrapolation.
38. Smith's translation of this passage differs slightly here from the Arabic passage in Löfgren, *Tarikh thaghr 'adan*, p. 31.
39. Smith notes that the term *al-Qumr* may in this case refer to the Comoros rather than Madagascar. Smith, *A Traveller in Thirteenth-Century Arabia*, p. 137 n.7.
40. Ibid., pp. 137–9.
41. Margariti, *Aden and the Indian Ocean Trade*.
42. G. W. Bowersock, *The Throne of Adulis*. As Travis Zadeh has demonstrated, Ibn al-Mujawir was hardly unique in this adoption of Hellenistic concepts. See Travis Zadeh, "The Wiles of Creation," pp. 21–48.
43. Ibid.
44. The term "inner" here, according to Bowersock, is used to imply "more remote" or "outlying." Ibid. p. 23.
45. Bowersock, *The Throne of Adulis*; Zadeh, "The Wiles of Creation."
46. Compiled by Abu al-Tami Jayyash b. Najah. Smith, *A Traveller in Thirteenth-Century Arabia*, pp. 119–20.
47. Smith, *A Traveller in Thirteenth-Century Arabia*, pp. 132–4.
48. The seriousness with which medieval Muslim writers treated the fantastic and the miraculous as verifiable historical fact is examined at length in Zadeh, "The Wiles of Creation."
49. R. B. Serjeant, *The Portuguese off the South Arabian Coast*.
50. Ibid.
51. Abu Abdullah al-Tayyib Abu Makhrama, *Tarikh thaghr 'adan*, p. 7.
52. Ibid., p. 6.
53. Margariti, *Aden and the Indian Ocean Trade*, pp. 71, 94–105.
54. Abu al-Abbas Ahmad al-Zabidi, *Tabaqat al-khawas*, p. 129. Abu Makhrama, *Tarikh thaghr 'adan*, pt. II, pp. 13–14.
55. Ibid., pp. 21–2; al-Zabidi, *Tabaqat al-Khawas*, p. 108.
56. Ibid., p. 135.
57. Abu Makhrama, *Tarikh thaghr 'adan*, pp. 23–4; Ahmad b. Ali b. Ahmad b. al-Hasan al-Harazi (b. 643 AH) a noted Adeni *'alim*. Ibid., pp. 6–7.
58. Serjeant, *The Portuguese off the South Arabian Coast*, p. 14
59. Barbosa, *Duarte*, pp. 57–8.
60. Ibid., p. 58. The *Tarikh al-shihri* provides a strikingly similar account. Serjeant, *The Portuguese off the South Arabian Coast*, p. 47.
61. Hamza Luqman, "The Egyptian Invasion of Aden," in *Stories from the History of Aden and South Arabia*, pp. 88–9.
62. Giancarlo Casale, *Ottoman Age of Exploration*, p. 46.
63. Ibid.

64. Hamza Ali Luqman, *Stories from the History of Aden and South Arabia*, p. 92.
65. Ibid., p. 43. Citing Qutb al-Din al-Mekki, *Akhbar al-Yamani*, folios 13b–19b.
66. Ibid.
67. Serjeant, *The Portuguese off the South Arabian Coast*, pp. 50–2.
68. Ibid., p. 33; Casale, *Ottoman Age of Exploration*, p. 44.
69. Ibid., p. 46.
70. Serjeant, *The Portuguese off the South Arabian Coast*, pp. 55–6.
71. Casale, *Ottoman Age of Exploration*, pp.
72. Ibid., pp. 47–8.
73. Although Shaykh Amir was not one to throw away all advantage. Al-Shihri notes that most of the Portuguese soldiers ultimately converted to Islam and were dispersed as musketeers among the Shaykh's various forts in the interior. Serjeant, *The Portuguese off the South Arabian Coast*, p. 60.
74. Ibid., pp. 77–8.
75. Casale, *Ottoman Age of Exploration*, pp. 60–1.
76. Serjeant, *The Portuguese off the South Arabian Coast*, pp. 84 and 95; Casale, *Ottoman Age of Exploration*, pp. 60–1.
77. Serjeant, *The Portuguese off the South Arabian Coast*, p. 84.
78. Abu Makhrama, *Tarikh thaghr 'adan*, p. 12
79. Ibid., p. 26.
80. Abu Makhrama, *Tarikh thaghr 'adan*, pp. 43–6, also translated in Luqman, *Stories from the History of Aden and South Arabia*, pp. 48–50. A less prosaic version of the story is also related by Najm al-Din Umarah ibn Ali al-Hakami (d. ca. 1173) in *Kitab tarikh al-yaman* one of the earliest prose works that relates the history of Yemen. Significantly, Umarah, who, although from Yemen wrote his book while living in Egypt, omits many details including Jayyash's disguise and Indian consort. Omarah al-Hakami and Henry Cassels Kay, trans, *Yaman Its Early Medieval History by Najm al-Din 'Omarah al-Hakami*, pp. 154–6.
81. Ibid., p. 46; C. G. Brouwer, "Al-Mukha as a Coffee Port." As Brouwer argues, Jiddah also seemed to play a direct role in this "coffee complex" with coffee coming overland from Yemen.
82. Nancy Um, *The Merchant Houses of Mukha*, p. 40.
83. Douglas Leigh, *Free Yemeni Movement*, pp. 72–3 n. 12.
84. Muhammad Ali Lokman, *Men, Matters and Memories*, a serialized autobiography published in the Aden Chronicle during the early 1960s and republished in book form by his son, Maher (Aden, 2009).
85. Muhammad Ali noted that his father, Ali Ibrahim, married four "Arab wives" in Aden. Ibid., p. 83.
86. R/20/A/2210 Complaint of Shaikh Mahomed Arif and Abdul Kader Suleimanji against the Kadi of Aden June 16, 1916. Among the names of Bohra men married to Sunni women by the Sunni Qadi was Ali Ibrahim Lookman Clerk, residency office, July 13, 1914. List compiled by Sayyid Rustom Ali, July 1, 1916.
87. Lokman, *Men, Matters, and Memories*, p. 83.
88. Ibid., 118. R/20/A/3418, Reception of Gandhi in Aden 1931, Luqman would, in fact, translate Gandhi's speech from Gujarati into Arabic.
89. Ibid., 211–13.
90. The original text of "Kamala Devi" is contained in the collected works of Luqman's *al-Mujahid Muhammad Ali Luqman*, pp. 456–76. The author also included an extensive summary and commentary on this work in his memoir, *Men, Matters and Memories*, pp. 287–90.

91. A place Luqman held was fictitious but may be modeled on Bahawalpur a princely state in colonial Punjab in modern Pakistan. Lokman, *Men, Matters and Memories*, p. 287.
92. Ibid., p. 290.
93. Luqman, "Kamala Devi," p. 457.
94. Lokman, *Men, Matters and Memories*, pp. 159–60, 212.
95. Ibid., p. 82.
96. While it seems that Muhammad Ali's father, Ali Ibrahim, along with his brother Husayn, were the first to settle in Aden, his paternal grandfather maintained commercial interests in the port and owned considerable property. Lokman, *Men, Matters and Memories*, p. 89.
97. The founding and significance of the Arab Reform Club is treated in detail in Chapter 6.
98. Ibid., p. 159.
99. Luqman, in fact, ultimately favored independence for Aden as a city-state along the same lines as Singapore. Unfortunately, British colonial authority supported the integration of Aden into a federation with various South Arabian sultanates that were nominal British protectorates.
100. Most notably, the Indian Registrar M. Yasin Khan, discussed in Chapter 4, was elevated to the newly created Aden High Court in the late 1940s and seems to have remained in Aden following retirement. The last mention of him in the public record is as a member of the Aden Chamber of Commerce in 1959.
101. Shihab Ghanem, *Obituary for Hamza Luqman*, 1919–95, n.d.
102. Ibid.
103. Thanks to Thanos Petouris for finding and sharing what appears to be one of the only extant copies.
104 Luqman, *Tarikh 'adan*, pp. 253ff.
105. Although other stories such as those involving Alexander the Great and the Madagascan immigrants are still missing.
106. Although with certain revisions meant to accommodate the sensibilities of modern readers, so the Indian slave-girl becomes Jayyash's "wife."

Chapter 2

1. With correspondence and passengers heading overland to Alexandria where they would embark, again, for Britain by sea.
2. Gavin, *Aden under British Rule*, p. 21.
3. Ibid., p. 22. Gordon Waterfield, *Sultans of Aden*, pp. 16–17.
4. Dalrymple, *White Mughals*, p. 46.
5. Ibid.
6. Ibid. Coincidentally he was also the brother of the serving Governor-General of India, Richard Wellesley.
7. R/20/E/48 Political Department Aden, 1856, Letter from Commodore Blankett to John Murray, May 8, 1799.
8. Ibid. Report from Lt. Col. J. Murray commanding officer of the Perim Force, May 7, 1799.
9. Neither Murray nor Captain Wilson, commander of the naval squadron, offer an explanation for their cool reception.
10. A small squadron of Company ships were stationed in the Mukha roadstead to provide support for the Perim force if necessary.
11. R/20/E/48 Political Department Aden, 1856, Murray report June 9, 1799.
12. Although unnamed by Murray, this appears to be the Abdali Sultan Ahmad (d. 1827) predecessor of Muhsin bin Fadhl, Sultan at the time of Aden's occupation.

13. R/20/E/48 Political Department Aden, 1856 Murray, October 4, 1799.
14. The Nawab of Arcot was ruler of the princely state also known as the Carnatic located in present-day Tamil Nad.
15. Santosh Kumar Basu, "A Premature Attempt."
16. R/20/E/48 Political Department Aden, 1856 Murray, October 4, 1799.
17. Political Proceedings, March 20, 1800 cited in Basu, "A Premature Attempt," p. 29.
18. Henry Salt, *Voyage to Abyssinia*, p. 106.
19. A Captain Rudland.
20. Salt, *Voyage to Abyssinia*, p. 106.
21. Gavin, *Aden under British Rule*, pp. 23–4.
22. Salt, *Voyage to Abyssinia*, pp. 92–3.
23. Gavin, *Aden under British Rule*, pp. 23–5. It was Gavin's contention that these so-called "Wahhabi pirates," and the Saudi state were motivated by an "anti-commercial" ethic. However, it is far more likely that Arab privateering activities were driven more by a Saudi desire to put pressure on their political enemies, the Sharifs of Mecca, who derived the majority of their revenue from duties on goods imported and exported from Jiddah and the nearly constant flow of Muslim pilgrims intent on visiting the Holy Places of Mecca and Medina.
24. Ibid.
25. Ibid., p. 24.
26. See, Khaled Fahmy, *All the Pasha's Men*.
27. Amir Abdullah was ultimately taken to Istanbul and executed, although most of the remainder of the family was granted clemency for their aggression against the Sublime Porte. See David Commins, *The Wahhabi Mission and Saudi Arabia*.
28. Commins, *The Wahhabi Mission and Saudi Arabia*, pp. 32–7; Jonathan Miran, *Red Sea Citizens*, pp. 55–8.
29. Gavin, *Aden under British Rule*, p. 26.
30. Fahmy, *All the Pasha's Men*, pp. 38–41.
31. Gavin, *Aden under British Rule*, p. 25.
32. The first ship to reach India from Britain was the *Enterprize* in 1825, although it traveled less than one-third of the way on steam power. Beginning in 1830, the *Hugh Lindsay* made several experimental voyages between Bombay and Suez, using Aden and other Red Sea ports as refueling stops, and was the first vessel to demonstrate even the remote possibility of practical steam travel, linking India with Europe via the Red Sea. See Robert J. Blyth, "Aden, British India and the Development of Steam Power."
33. Gavin, *Aden under British Rule*, pp. 26ff.
34. Ibid.
35. Gavin devotes only one short paragraph to the incident while Gordon Waterfield allocates little more than two. Gavin, *Aden under British Rule*, p. 28; Waterfield, *Sultans of Aden*, pp. 38–9.
36. R/20/E/1 no. 692 1837 Political Department, depositions of survivors, Bombay September 20, 1837.
37. The term *Nakhoda* is a notoriously slippery one. It is most often used to refer to a ship's captain, however, in the context of the *Daria Dawlat* it seems to also refer to one who acted as an agent overseeing the affairs of the owner.
38. R/20/E/1 no. 692 1837 Political Department, depositions of Sayyid Nur al-Din, Bombay September 20, 1837 no. 4,098.
39. Ibid.
40. Alappuhza in modern Kerala.

41. R/20/E/1 no. 692 1837 Political Department, depositions of Sayyid Nur al-Din, Bombay September 20, 1837 no. 4,098.
42. Both Sayyid Nur al-Din and Sayyid Tipu treated this matter with great delicacy stating that the women were "brutally insulted," which appears to be a euphemism for sexual assault.
43. One great disadvantage of Mukha as a commercial port is that, unlike Aden, it did not have a good harbor and ships were required to load and off-load goods from off shore.
44. R/20/E/1 no. 692 1837 Political Department, depositions of Sayyid Nur al-Din, Bombay September 20, 1837 no. 4,098; F/4/1778 *Daria Dowlat* No. 8 Minute by the Honorable Mr. Farish. On the Company's use of local agents to oversee its affairs see James Onley, *The Arabian Frontier of the British Raj*.
45. R/20/E/1 Deposition of Syed Tippoo Aldoonebeen August 2, 1837 no. 4,099A.
46. F/4/1778, Charles Malcolm, Rear Admiral to Sir Robert Grant, July 31, 1837; Memorandum by the Chief Secretary, August 7, 1837.
47. Ibid. Haines to Rear Admiral Sir Charles Malcolm, Superintendent of the Indian Navy, July 6, 1837.
48. Sir Robert Gant memorandum, Secret Letters Received from Bombay 1st series, vol. 6, September 23, 1837; Government of India to Bombay, October 6, 1837, Secret Letters from Bombay, 1st series vol. 6 (1830–8) cited in Waterfield, *Sultans of Aden*, pp. 38–9.
49. Gavin, *Aden under British Rule*, p. 31.
50. This despite clear orders from the Governor-General of India to use only peaceful means in gaining control of Aden. Ibid., p. 36.
51. R/20/E/5 Lt. W. L. Western Engineer to Major Thomas Baillie January 25, 1839.
52. J. R. Wellstead, *Travels in Arabia*, v. II, pp. 393 and 394.
53. Ibid., pp. 386–7; R/20/E/10 Haines to Wiloughby, February 28, 1840.
54. J. R. Wellstead, *Travels in Arabia*, v. II, p. 395.
55. R/20/E/11 Substance of a petition from the undersigned Banians inhabitants of Aden to the Honourable the Governor in Council, dated 27th Mohurrum (April 1) and received April 11, 1840.
56. Cited in James Kirkman and Brian Doe, "The First Days of British Aden," p. 195.
57. Although, here these was some room for confusion. The translation provided by the Persian department states, "[M]y sons and my dependents [sic] hold shares in the customs collected at this port, besides which I and Eedroos [sic] are entitled to considerable shares in several other items of income of which Commander Haines is fully aware." We do not possess the original Arabic letter, however, when pressed on this matter, Sayyid Zayn later insisted that there must have been an error in the translation. R/20/E/4 Translation of letter from Seyyid Zine bin Alubee Ediroosee [sic] to the Honourable the Governor, February 1, 1839; R/20/E/5 Aden Affairs, 1839, Note from Baillie, April 4, 1839
58. R/20/E/5 Letter from Mubhechant Mahowejee, Kesowjee Trecunjee, Neerchan Ameerbund, Devchand Nusunrjee, Dhumraj Herruj, Keysowjee Mudhowjee, merchants of Aden, the Honourable Governor, dated 2nd Chutri Mud Savent 1895, April 1, 1839.
59. Ibid., Haines report, August 11, 1839, paragraph 18, "I beg to inform you that the Customs House Accountant Messha died on the first instant [August] and that I have appointed his son Murrahan ben Messha, a steady correct young man, to succeed him having for some years assisted his father in the performance of that duty."
60. R/20/E/5 Secret Consul, March 6, 1839, to Haines.
61. This appointment was made official in October 1839. Waterfield, *Sultans of Aden*, p. 100
62. R/20/E/23 Lt. C. J. Cruttendon note attached to a copy of the treaty with the Sultan to Lahej, 1843. Gavin, *Aden under British Rule,* p. 67.

63. Estimates by the defenders were virtually impossible to verify. See R/20/E/9 and R/20/E/11 Item 2.
64. R/20/E/11 Item 2 Captain Stiles' report on May 1840 attack.
65. R/20/E/10 Letters relating incident in which Captain Stiles was fired upon while riding outside the Turkish wall, July 28 and 29, 1840; R/20/E/17 Ltr from Haines February 1841 regarding the condition of the roads around Aden.
66. R/20/E/11 Bombay to Haines, June 30 1840; Ltr from Haines, September 11, 1841; R/20/E/17 Ltrs Haines to Wiloughby, August 29 and September 11, 1841.
67. R/20/E/9 Haines report on first Abdali attack against Aden.
68. Ibid.; R/20/E/11 various.
69. Kirkman, "The First Days of British Aden," p. 196; R/20/E/10 Haines to Willoughby, February 28, 1840; "Proceedings of a Committee assembled at Aden on the 26th February, 1840."
70. R/20/E/10 Haines to Willoughby, March 31, 1840; R/20/E/11 Persian Department, Substance of a Petition from the undersigned Banians, inhabitants of Aden to the Honourable Governor in Council, April 1, 1840.
71. Who had recently replaced Baillie.
72. R/20/E/10, Court's Opinion, n.d.
73. R/20/E/10 Statement by Lt. Col. Capon the state of the Aden Basar [sic], n.d.
74. R/20/E/17 Haines to Willoughby May 11, 1841.
75. Gavin, *Aden under British Rule*, p. 41.
76. R/20/E/10 Statement by Capon, n.d.
77. R/20/E/9 Report to the Adjutant General regarding the illicit liquor and the defence of Aden, n.d.; R/20/E/10 Statement by Capon, n.d.
78. Ibid., Capon to Haines, February 19, 1840.
79. Most of which was distilled from dates.
80. Ibid. Captain Stiles, Basar Master, to Capon, February 5, 1840.
81. Ibid. Complaints sworn before the Qadi to Haines, n.d.
82. Ibid. Complaint to Haines.
83. Ibid. Government to Haines, March 23, 1840; Gavin, *Aden under British Rule*, pp. 41–3.
84. R/20/E/5 Haines report on new arrivals. This records 1,615 new arrivals since the original census carried out in March 1839, which brought the total population, excluding the garrison, to 2,885 people.
85. R/20/E/25 Political Dept., 1845 v. 2, Lt. Cruttendon's visit to the different Ports in the vicinity of Aden.
86. R/20/E/1 no. 692 1837 Political Department Aden: Wrecks-Daria Doulat. The total value of lost cargo was given as 2 lakhs of rupees. Depositions of Sayyid Nur al-Din and Sayyid Tipu.
87. In the case of Massawa this was temporary as the port was back under Egyptian control by 1846. See Miran, *Red Sea Citizens*; Fahmy, *All the Pasha's Men*.
88. And his various successors through the 1840s.
89. Gavin, *Aden under British Rule*, pp. 72–3.
90. R/20/E/19 Lt. Christopher, commanding the Constance to Sander commander of the Clive, October 2, 1842; R/20/E/23 Rpt by Lt. W. Christopher, commanding the Brig Tigris, on his visit to Massawa, Jiddah and Mocha, 1844; Lt. Adams, commanding the Constance to Haines, May 27, 1850.
91. R/20/E/19 Christopher to Haines, July 9, 1843.
92. R/20/E/23 Extract from Report by Lt. Christopher, commanding the Brig Tigris on his visit to Massawa, Jiddah and Mocha, March 16, 1843.
93. R/20/E/10 Abd al-Rasul to Haines, March 29, 1840. Gavin, *Aden under British Rule*, p. 72.

94. According to Haines, this was accomplished through the machinations of a wealthy patron of Sharif Husayn, referred to as Hajji Yusuf, a merchant in Hodeida. R/20/E/33 Haines to Malet, May 25, 1848.
95. For a full account see Gavin, *Aden under British Rule*, pp. 72–7.
96. At one point, he declared that he would not allow the British flag to be flown at the Company agency in Mukha and in 1845 his forces briefly menaced the Settlement. R/20/E/33 Aden Affairs, 1848; R/20/E/25 Political Department, 1845.
97. R/20/E/17 Aden Affairs, 1841 Haines to Willoughby, February 2, 1841; Gavin, *Aden under British Rule*, pp. 72–6.
98. R/20/E/33 Aden Affairs, 1848, Haines to C. D. Campbell, Lt. commanding the Brig Euphrates, April 22, 1848.
99. Ibid.
100. Ibid.
101. Ibid., Haines additional report, May 6, 1848. Threats to Indian merchant capital in Southern Arabia during this period hardly seem isolated. During a tour of the various ports around Aden in 1845, Haines' assistant, Cruttendon, reported on the continuing efforts to settle the estate of a "Banian" merchant killed during a period of political upheaval in Mukalla in 1832. R/20/E/25 Political Department, Lt. Cruttendon's visit to the different Ports in the vicinity of Aden.

Chapter 3

1. The last of these, spirit possession, was not strictly speaking an "Islamic" institution. However, as we will see, the practices of various cults were at the center of spiritual life and frequently intersected with broader Muslim society.
2. Z. H. Kour, *The History of Aden*, p. 44. Gavin, *Aden under British Rule*, pp. 189–90.
3. J. P. Malcolmson, "Account of Aden," p. 286.
4. F. M. Hunter, *The British Settlement of Aden*, pp. 39–40.
5. For an overview of early Company town planning in Aden, see Kour, *The History of Aden*, especially Chapter 2, "The Growth of the Settlement," pp. 13–62.
6. Hunter, *The British Settlement of Aden*, p. 28. Edward Alpers, "The Somali Community in Aden."
7. Hunter, *The British Settlement of Aden*, p. 40.
8. J.B.F. Osgood, *Notes of Travel*, p. 155.
9. James Kirkman and Brian Doe, "The First Days of British Aden."
10. The incident is not referenced by either R. J. Gavin or Z. H. Kour while Gordon Waterfield makes brief mention of it in *Sultans of Aden*, p. 75.
11. Alexander Knysh, "The Cult of the Saints and Religious Reformism in Hadhramaut."
12. Luqman, *Tarikh 'adan*, pp. 264–76.
13. R/20/E/10 Haines to Wiloughby, February 28, 1840.
14. Ibid.
15. R/20/E/5 Report Haines to Bombay, July 11, 1839.
16. A celebration marking the saint's date of death and "marriage" with the Divine.
17. Hunter, *The British Settlement of Aden*, pp. 174–5.
18. Memons constitute a group of South Asian Sunni Muslims primarily from western India who were widely believed to be made up of communities of Hindu converts.
19. A unit of measure consisting of 100,000.
20. al-Zabidi, *Tabaqat al-khawas*, p. 129.

21. Hunter, *The British Settlement of Aden*, pp. 174–5.
22. al-Zabidi, *Tabaqat al-khawas*, pp. 67–71.
23. Hunter, *The British Settlement of Aden*, pp. 174–5. Al-Zabidi includes an account of a Shaykh Abu al-Abbas Ahmad b. Muhammad al-Haradi in *Tabaqat al-khawas*, pp. 86–7. Like Hunter's notice of the Shaykh's *ziyara*, Zabidi was equally vague. He noted that al-Haradi was a shaykh "famous for his *waliyya*" and "master of miracles," who was widely venerated and of whom disciples recorded his miracles. He does not, however, provide any actual biographical information such as birth dates or place of burial, although he records his death date as 801/1398–9.
24. Hunter, *The British Settlement of Aden*, pp. 174–5.
25. Ibid., p. 175.
26. Hunter, *The British Settlement of Aden*, p. 176.
27. R/20/A/2664 Fairs 1911–36 folios on the *ziyaras* of Shaykh Abban and Shaykh Ahmad al-Iraqi.
28. Sa'id in Luqman, *al-Mujahid Muhammad Ali Luqman*, pp. 423–4.
29. One of several groups in Aden believed to be of servile origins. See Chapter 5 for a fuller description.
30. R/20/A/2664, letter of protest May 7, 1932, outlining complaints of irreligious activity at local *ziyara*s. R/20/A/3471 Shaykh Othman Fair.
31. al-Zabidi, *Tabaqat al-Khawas*, p. 135.
32. Ameen Fares Rihani, *Around the Coasts of Arabia*, p. 328.
33. Ibid.
34. R/20/A/2664, Fairs, 1911–36; R/20/A/2209 File 63/8 1906 Cemeteries and Burials.
35. Rihani, *Around the Coasts of Arabia*, p. 329.
36. R/20/A/2664 Fairs, 1911–36.
37. Ibid.
38. Ibid.
39. R/20/A/2664 Fairs, 1911–36. While important, the British official attitude toward popular piety in Aden is beyond the scope of this article. For an informative discussion of British pragmatic tolerance of local forms of spirituality, see Nicholas Dirks' discussion of "hookswinging" in nineteenth-century India in *Castes of Mind: Colonialism and the Making of Modern India*.
40. Such incidents of posthumous saint making were not unheard of. Perhaps the most famous case was that of Ibn al-Farid in fifteenth-century Cairo, known during his lifetime as an accomplished poet but then sanctified by his descendants after his death. See Th. Emil Homerin, *From Arab Poet to Muslim Saint*.
41. R/20/A/2664 Fairs, 1911–6, Fatima bint Ahmad.
42. See, for instance, R. D. McChesney, *Waqf in Central Asia*; Reese, *Renewers of the Age*; Amira Mittermaier, *Dreams that Matter*.
43. R/20/A/2664 Fairs, 1911–36, No. 1856 of 1922, 25-11-22.
44. Among the many works devoted to examining Sufism in the Indian Ocean among the most notable are: Bang, *Sufis and Scholars of the Sea*; Green, *Bombay Islam*; Laffan, *Islamic Nationhood and Colonial Indonesia*; Engseng Ho, *The Graves of Tarim*.
45. Green, *Bombay Islam*; Reese, *Renewers of the Age*. The friction between scripturalist reformers and supporters of Sufism in Aden will be taken up in Chapter 6.
46. For a non-Islamic example of this penchant see, Feierman, "Colonizers, Scholars and the Creation of Invisible Histories."
47. Curiously, many of the references we find to this in the literary record are denunciations of such beliefs—including Ahmad al-Asnag, *Nasib 'adan*; al-Bayhani, *Hadiyat al-murid*; Luqman, "Sa'id"—all of whom provide numerous examples of what they term "superstitions."

48. Annemarie Schimmel, *And Muhammad is His Messenger*.
49. See Renard, *Friends of God*.
50. Reese, *Renewers of the Age*, p. 191.
51. Quoted in Qassim al-Barawi, *al-Majmu'a al-qasa'id*, pp. 67–8. Emphasis mine.
52. Abdullahi Al-Qutbi a noted that Somali Qadiriyya shaykh of the twentieth century, for instance, spent several months in Aden upon his return from studying at al-Azhar in 1919, while the Oman-Zanzibari *'alim* Abu Harith passed through the port on the eve of First World War as part of the retinue of an Omani prince touring Egypt, Lebanon and Palestine. See Reese, *Renewers of the Age*, and "The Adventures of Abu Harith."
53. The version used here is Abu Bakr al-Aydarus, *al-Jiz al-latif fi al-tahkim al-sharif* published in Cairo in 1936; a lithograph version *Al-Jiz al-latif* appeared earlier as part of an anthology of writings by members of the Aydarus family titled *Majmu'a aydrusiyya al-Shamila l-'arba' kutub al-sunniyya*, printed as a lithograph manuscript by Sultan Shahi on behalf of Sulayman bin Abdullah bin Mara'i in Hyderabad, Deccan in 1904. Abd al-Rahman al-Aydarus, *Risala fi tariqa al-naqshbandiyya* manuscript copy, 1280 AH.
54. The order adhered to by the Aydarus historically appears somewhat disputed. Internal material from Aden implies that, for the most part, the family followed the Naqshbandi way, however, some external sources contend that Abu Bakr Aydarus was in fact a Qadiri.
55. Al-Aydarus, *Risala fi tariqa al-naqshbandiyya*, p. 1.
56. Ibid., p. 4.
57. According to the book's colophon this was the second edition. It seems likely that it is, in fact, based on the lithograph edition published in Hyderabad in 1904. As such, this earlier version was almost certainly known and available in Aden.
58. Al-Aydarus, *al-Jiz al-latif fi al-tahkim al-sharif*, p. 3
59. Al-Adani notes how the lineage of the cloak descends through two lines, that of the Ahl al-Bayt (descendants of the Prophet) via Ali and Husayn and a separate but no less legitimate line traced through Hasan al-Basri. *al-Jiz al-latif fi al-tahkim al-sharif*, p. 4.
60. Emphasis mine.
61. Ibid., p. 28.
62. A matter we will return to in Chapter 6.
63. R/20/A/2209 Omar Abdalla Sharaf, Kazi of Sheikh Othman and Other Notables of Aden. December 1910. The authorities granted this request with little fanfare or debate.
64. R/20/A/2209 Cemeteries and Burials, Anonymous petition, May 1931. The anonymous petition written to the Resident in 1931, which was clearly written using information from the official archive, indicates that all of these moves were met with protests from the population that in at least one instance, in 1881, resulted in a riot.
65. Ibid., 1912 and 1926, respectively. The latter was the source of some controversy within Aden's Muslim community, as we shall see in the following chapter.
66. Ibid.
67. For instance, Sayyid al-Mutawwakil bin Sayyid Ali al-Sanusi and "the wife" of Khan Bahadur Sayyid Hasan al-Mihdar CMG and a notable from the Hadramaut.
68. R/20/A/2209 Petition of Mohamed Mahjoob, November 23, 1928.
69. Ibid. Executive Committee Resolution, No. 639, December 29, 1930.
70. The actual number of burials was likely rather higher given that petitions often refer to other cases where exceptions were made, but that do not appear in the Residency files. For example, in requesting permission for his mother's burial in the Aydarus Cemetery in 1927, Ali Abdullah states that "her son, named Hason Ahmed Maddi" died in 1925 and was interred in the same cemetery. However, there is no record of a petition in the file. Ali Abudlla to Reilly, January 25, 1927. R/20/A/2209.

71. The leader of a powerful family of Sharifs in Aden, Abdullah Aydarus was a direct descendant of sixteenth-century Sufi saint, Abu Bakr al-Aydarus, who was considered by many to be the patron saint of the port. Due largely to the family's political connections throughout Southern Arabia and the local importance of his ancestor's tomb, Sayyid Abdullah was regarded by the British authorities as the "mansab" or head of the Settlement's Muslim community. The Viceroy of India granted him the imperial title "Shams al-'Ulama'" in 1911 in recognition of his service to the government of Aden. R/20/A/1449 "Titles and Honors" Sayyid Aydarous–Shams al-Ulama.
72. R/20/A/2209 Sayed Abdullah Aydarus to Jacob, September 9, 1915; Sayyid Umar b. Hasan to Wood, January 25, 1918.
73. Ibid., Ali Murshid to the Chairman of the Aden Settlement, June 19, 1922.
74. R/20/A/2209, September 30, 1926; October 15, 1928; July 22, 1930; November 5, 1930.
75. Halevi, *Muhammad's Grave,* pp. 201ff.
76. Christopher Taylor, *In the Vicinity of the Righteous,* pp. 47ff.
77. Ibid., pp. 49–50. For example, he writes, "al-Muzani stated near his death that the wished to be laid to rest near the tome of Shayban al-Ra'i because the saint 'was a gnostic of God'." And that "the pilgrimage guides of al-Qarafa cemetery make clear that there were many important tombs in the city of the dead that functioned like great magnets to attract those wishing to pass the *barzakh,* the interval between death and resurrection, near the Baraka of a saint." The tomb of Shafi'i was a particularly sought after spot—while the "tomb of Imam Layth stood in the midst of the Marbarat al-Sadafiyin, surrounded by four hundred tombs."

Chapter 4

1. R/20/A/1395 1/40 Saleh Mohamed al-Makkawi, sub-registrar November 15, 1909.
2. Ibid., Qadi Umar Abdullah to Sayyid Rustom Ali, 1906.
3. Scott Kugle, "Framed, Blamed and Renamed," p. 300.
4. See, for instance, among many others, Samira Haj, *Reconfiguring Islamic Tradition*; Michael Gaspar, *The Power of Representation.*
5. The present chapter examines the interactions of these groups via their interpretations of Islamic law. The next chapter examines the social impact of these same groups through the lens of reformist theology.
6. This title was changed to "Political Resident" in 1856. See Gavin, *Aden under British Rule,* Appendix A, p. 444.
7. This aspect of British Aden is explored in Chapter 2 of this work.
8. IOR R/20E/5 as well as Gavin, *Aden under British Rule,* Appendix B. p. 445.
9. Kour, *The History of Aden,* pp. 78–86.
10. Lauren Benton, *Law and Colonial Cultures,* p. 2.
11. Bombay-Haines: February 24, 1839, Bombay Secret Proceedings 108, in Kour, *The History of Aden,* p. 87.
12. Ibid.
13. Kour, *The History of Aden,* p. 85.
14. R/20/A/148 vol. 184, Correspondence on Aden Police, 1855–6.
15. The earliest mention of Panchayyat in Company records comes from Bombay in 1673. Kugle, "Framed, Blamed and Renamed," 260–1. See also Mitra Sharafi, *Law and Identity.*
16. R/20/A/1395 The continuation of the Qadi's authority in Aden, with Bombay's blessing, is particularly interesting because it coincides with the same period during which the Company began to systematically strip Muslim jurists of independent authority within their Indian possessions reducing them to the status of court advisers and clerks. Kugle, "Framed, Blamed and Renamed," p. 284.

17. It needs to be noted that Haines ultimately gained a reputation as extremely paranoid, seeing enemies everywhere even among his close associates. Such behavior was one reason (corruption another) for his ultimate dismissal. As such, this characterization of the Qadi's actions is not necessarily accurate. See, Gavin, *Aden under British Rule*.
18. Kour, *The History of Aden*, pp. 86–90. I say "theoretically" as there are hints in the contemporary records that the Qadi's position remained influential during this period.
19. R/20/A/1395 notes on the history of Qadis in Aden, 8/12/1907.
20. R/20/A/1395 1/40, Memo from the Magistrate, 20/3/1905.
21. Asim Kumar Dutta, "Why Did the East India Company Recognise Hindu and Muslim Law?" Quote from Sir Charles Fawcett, *The First Century of British Justice in India*, p. 81.
22. James Jaffe, *The Ironies of Colonial Governance*, p. 35.
23. Ibid., p. 45; James Jaffe, "Arbitration and Panchayats in Early Colonial Bombay"; Sharafi, *Law and Identity*, pp. 79–80.
24. Indeed, the committees referred to by Haines may have been *panchayyat*.
25. R/20/A/117. The process was formalized sufficiently that participants were required to fill out a printed form attesting to their willingness to adhere to the committee's decision.
26. All of whom appear literate, signing their names in either Arabic or Gujarati.
27. The exact definition of this title is difficult to determine based on the context. However, it appears to have been a fairly informal civil title given to an individual whose duties included reporting any crimes, disruptions or violent civil disputes to higher authority. R/20/A/4368.
28. R/20/A/4368 Police Correspondence and Depositions.
29. A waterpipe.
30. R/20/A,/4368
31. The title Fakeer may indicate that Muhammad was a local Sufi luminary, however, given his apparent close relationship with the state it seems more likely that it was actually "*faqih*," indicating a person learned in *fiqh* or jurisprudence.
32. R/A/20/4368 A subsequent note in the file indicates that Sayyid Isma'il was suspected of dealing in stolen goods, although the police were never able to prove it and the accusations were based almost purely on hearsay.
33. As James Jaffe points out, in British customary arbitration there were theoretically few restrictions on who could act as an arbitrator. In practice, he notes, things were somewhat different, "[M]ost arbitrators appear to have been 'respectable' people such as prominent businessmen, local notables, and the like . . . (this was also true of Panchayat.)" Jaffe, "Arbitration and Panchayats," p. 57.
34. Other communities, including the Jews, Parsis and Bohra Isma'ilis, mediated disputes via their own designated elites.
35. At least no record of them appears after that period.
36. R/20/A/1395 1/40 1905–21.
37. By the end of his career Shaykh Ahmad was paid 100 Rs/ per month; the salary of his successor Faqih Ali bin Hassan was reduced to 50 Rs. See R/20/A/1395.
38. Kour, *The History of Aden*, pp. 91–5.
39. Kugle, "Framed, Blamed and Renamed," pp. 300–1.
40. R/20/A/1395. See more on this below.
41. Ibid.
42. Including at least six Assistant Residents, various Arabic, Somali, Gujarati and Hindustani interpreters and a legion of clerks and peons.
43. And known in local Arabic as simply "Adan."
44. Gavin, *Aden under British Rule*, p. 189.

45. It should be noted that thus far I have not been able to locate anything approximating a roster of Qadis in the Aden records. As a result, the above is patched together from a variety of notes and memos in the existing files as well as comments in Kour's *The History of Aden*. As such, the list remains tentative and also differs significantly from the list provided by Kapteijns. See Kapteijns, "Government Qadis and Child Marriage in Aden," pp. 401–34.
46. R/20/A/1395 1/40 Memo Sayyid Rustom Ali to the First Assistant Resident, January 5, 1906.
47. Ibid., Saleh Mohamed, sub-registrar, November 15, 1909. As Lidweijn Kapteijns has pointed out, bureaucratically speaking, by the early twentieth century Qadis in Aden had been reduced to little more than clerks. Despite the neutralization of their official authority, however, the Islamic judges as well as others we may term "notables" remained an important element of British rule in Aden.
48. For the prominence of Parsis in the British imperial legal system see Sharafi, *Law and Identity*.
49. In some correspondence he is referred to as Rustomji as well as Rustomali.
50. This estimate of the library's value derives from Rustomji's inventory of his net worth as a result of legal expenses incurred while bringing a case for defamation of character against various Adenis in the Bombay Courts in 1911. R/20/A/1366 Rustom Ali Liable Case, 1911, Rustomali to Political Resident, Aden, 30/12/1911.
51. The proceeding biographical information was gleaned from the *History of Services, Bombay* lists published annually.
52. R/20/A/1395 "Note regarding the status of the Kadhis of Aden and Sheikh Othman with regard to the estates of deceased persons." K. N. Koyaji, March 14, 1905.
53. See, for instance, Leslie Peirce, *Morality Tales* and Loyd I. Rudolph and Susanne Hoeber Rudolph, *Modernity of Tradition*, p. 108.
54. Granted, as Kugle has pointed out, English jurists and Orientalists viewed Muslim jurisprudence as an already codified system—with the supposed closing of the "gate of *ijttihad*"—that simply needed to be streamlined for a modern age. See Kugle, "Framed, Blamed and Renamed, " pp. 270–1, 297.
55. Ibid., 295–7.
56. Ironically, as a bureaucratic expedient, the FAR of the time was in favor of allowing the judges to retain the right to adjudicate at least some inheritance cases. It was the tenacious opposition of the Registrar that ultimately stripped them of this privilege. See R/20/A/1395 1/40.
57. Arabic contained in the English translation.
58. R/20/A/1395 1/40 Affidavit of Qadi Umar Abdullah Sharaf, July 10, 1906.
59. Ibid. No. 1,388 of 1906 E. O'Brien, July 17, 1906.
60. Emphasis mine.
61. R/20/A/1395 1/40 Memo, Sayyid Rustom Ali, July 12, 1906.
62. In a later note, Qadi Umar b. Abdullah accused the Aden Qadi of conspiring to have him dismissed so that al-Hazmi's brother could be appointed to the post.
63. The only other person to include this as part of the case is an undated statement by Zamla. See R/20/A/1395 No. 2 Zamla bint Aid Complainant v. Aboul Gafoor Sulaiman, Defendant, Statement of complainant, undated.
64. R/20/A/1395.
65. Ibid. Sayyid Rustom Ali report, undated.
66. Muhammad Kassim Kamali, *Shari'ah Law*, Chapter 5, "Ikhtilaf" and Wael B. Hallaq, *Shari'a: Theory, Practice, Transformations*.

67. Qadi Umar notes that the above quotes are drawn from pages 188 and 189 of the *Bughayt*.
68. R/20/A/1395 Qadi Umar Abdullah to Sayyid Rustom Ali undated. Emphasis mine.
69. Ibid. Sayyid Rustom Ali to Qadi Umar Abdullah, November 23, 1906, No. 537 of 1906.
70. R/20/A/2210 Complaint of Shaikh Mohamed Arif and Abdul Kader Sulemanji against the Qazi of Aden. June 16, 1916, Sayyid Rustomji's response 26 June 26, 1916.
71. Abd al-Qadir bin Muhammad al-Makki, *The Overflowing River*, p. vii. He notes in the introduction that he had written a shorter version as early as 1886. p. iv.
72. Kugle, "Framed, Blamed and Renamed," p. 273.
73. Ibid. pp. 271–83.
74. Shaykh al-Makki provides a lengthy overview of the text's history. He noted that the first part of the book was written in 1886 and was translated by the German scholar Leo Hirsch soon thereafter. Translated first into German, it met with a certain amount of notoriety in scholarly circles in Germany. In his introduction to the 1899 edition, al-Makki pointed out that in German its usefulness was "limited." Thus, an English translation was commissioned, although when exactly is unknown. Al-Makki, *The Overflowing River*, pp. iv–xiv.
75. Ibid., p. viii.
76. Ibid., p. vii.
77. Ibid., xix–xx.
78. Ibid., pp. 238–40.
79. Ibid., p. 248.
80. Muhammad b. Hasan al-Hazmi's predecessor as Crater Qadi.
81. Al-Makki, *The Overflowing River*, p. xvi.
82. Ibid., p. xvii.
83. Ahmed b. Ali's comment regarding its accessibility to "townsmen and villagers" certainly points to it being perceived by the learned classes as a popular and didactic text.
84. The views of the Hanafis run from page 238 to page 246 and Shafi'i from page 248 to page 256 but while the book is composed of facing-page Arabic and English texts the page numbers are continuous.
85. Like many colonial administrators assigned to Aden, Khan passed most of his career in the Settlement. By the end of the Second World War he had, in fact, been elevated to the newly created High Court of Aden.
86. Sharafi, *Law and Identity*, pp. 85 and 98–9.
87. *Waqf* or the practice of pious endowment is an institution dating to the earliest centuries of Islam in which the revenue from a particular property, which may include agricultural land, shops or market stalls or, as in this case, rental properties, is dedicated to the upkeep of a given institution, such as a mosque, madrasa or hospital.
88. R/20/A/876, Letter of the Waqf Committee to the First Assistant Resident, February 1921.
89. In addition to Sayyid Abdullah Aydarus the original committee included: Muhammad Abd al-Qadir Makkawi, Sayyid Ahmad bin Taha al-Saffi, Ahmad bin Umar Bazara. Sayyid Muhammad bin Hasan, Salih bin Abdullah Khalifa, and' Sa'id bin Abdullah Khalifa.
90. R/20/A/876, Letter of the Wakf Committee to the First Assistant Resident, February 1921.
91. R/20/A/876, Petition Ahmad Abdullah Khayyat, April 14, 1921.
92. Ibid., Petitions Ali Ghalib Noman, April 7, 1921, July 16, 1921.
93. We should note here that Major Bernard Reilly had a long and distinguished career in Aden serving there from before the First World War until 1940 in various posts. Ultimately, he served as both Resident and then Governor when the Settlement became a "Crown Colony" in 1937.

94. R/20/A/876, M. Y. Khan to FAR, September 20, 1921.
95. Ibid. FAR to Wakf Committee, September 30, 1921.
96. Sharafi refers to this as "judicial ethnography," a phenomenon whereby non-European jurists commented extensively on "the history, practices and authority structures" of their communities, their insider status providing them with an air of unimpeachable authority in European imperial circles. Sharafi, *Law and Identity*, p. 250.
97. R/20/A/876, Noman to FAR, October 20, 1920 and appended notes dated October 26, 1921.
98. Ibid, Aydarus to Reilly, April 4, 1922.
99. Ibid.
100. Each petition is worded more or less the same and each contains well over 100 hundred signatures. The text of one reads simply, "WE the undersigned citizens of Aden do hereby declare that our President and Munsab [sic] is Shums al-Ulama Sayed Abdulla Aidross [sic] and our mosques and wakfs administrations are wanted by us to be under his charge and care. We do not want any one else except him therefore we are submitting this for your kind information."
101. R/20/A/876 Letter from Wakf Committee, n.d.
102. Khan's hand can also be discerned in the form of the letter. In addition to a certain "lawyerly" turn of phrase the letter was submitted in both English and Arabic (usually petitions were submitted in Arabic and a translation was made by the Residency translator) and the Persianized form of Qadi, Cazee, was used in the English text rather than the more usual "Kadi." While there is no reason to doubt that al-Battah was the author of the letter, Khan's influence is unmistakable. Such claims to rights as British subjects under the law were becoming increasingly common throughout the Empire during this period. See, for instance, Lynn Hollen Lees' article "Being British in Malaya, 1890–1940."
103. For a detailed overview of quarantine operations at Kamaran see, Tagliacozzo, "Hajj in the Time of Cholera."
104. R/20/A/4216 Civil Administrator, Kamaran Island to FAR, Aden, August 22, 1925.
105. The niche in the wall that indicates the direction of prayer and the pulpit, respectively.
106. R/20/A/4216, Qad Da'ud al-Battah to Registrar Mohamed Yaseen Khan, October 3, 1925.
107. Ibid., M. Y. Khan to B. Reilly, October 9, 1925.
108. Yasin Khan's predecessor, Sayyid Rustom Ali, maintained a particularly contentious relationship with the local *'ulama'* and lobbied successfully to curtail the power of the local Qadis during his long tenure.
109. Doreen Massey, *For Space*, p. 9.
110. David Lambert and Alan Lester, eds, *Colonial Careering*, p. 14
111. As I discuss in Chapter 6, the term "scripturalist reformer" denotes those who subscribe to an ideal of religious reform that looks almost exclusively to the foundational texts of the faith, that is, the Qur'an and the Hadith/Sunna. This term is used in place of the more popular gloss "Salafi" that was only just coming into vogue during this period. See Henri Lauzière, "The Construction of Salafiyya."
112. This differs from the thought of scripturalist reformers of the period in two important ways. First, these pro-imperial reformists looked to Western rationality as the savior of the faith, while the Salafis looked to the moral guidance of "the pious ancestors." Second, the Salafis of Aden ultimately hoped to throw off the colonial yoke, while individuals such as Rustom Ali and Khan saw their communities as evolving within the Empire.
113. Cooper, *Colonialism in Question*, p. 16.

Chapter 5

1. A non-commissioned officer equivalent to the rank of sergeant.
2. R/20/A/2700 Report of Lieut. A. H. E. Mosse to the First Assistant Resident (FAR), April 8, 1906.
3. Chaudhuri, *Trade and Civilization in the Indian Ocean*. Much of this research has focused on the period before 1800. A growing body of work represents a recent and necessary corrective to this trend focusing on the nineteenth and twentieth centuries and the emergent British imperium. See, for instance, Bose, *A Hundred Horizons*; Lambert and Lester, *Colonial Careering*; Thomas Metcalf, *Imperial Connections*; Clare Anderson, *Subaltern Lives*.
4. While this chapter concerns itself with the actions of spirit possession groups, Chapter 6 explores Sufism.
5. See R/20/A/2766.
6. See Chapter 6, "Scripturalism, Sufism and the Limits of Defining Public Religiosity."
7. Descriptions of the urban working classes of British Aden are legion. Among the most comprehensive is that found in Hunter, *The British Settlement of Aden*, pp. 26–36.
8. Although the practical limitations were another matter and may be immense.
9. See, for example, R/20/A/142, R/20/A/508, R/20/A/567 and R/20/A/707.
10. D'Arnaud, "Les Akhdam de l'Yemen," cited in R.L. Playfair, *A History of Arabia Felix or Yemen*, p. 15.
11. Abraha Ashram was the last Aksumite viceroy of Himyar and additionally famous for leading an Ethiopian army against Mecca during the ill-fated Year of the Elephant in 570 just prior to his defeat and expulsion from Arabia at the hands of the Sassanid Persians. See Bowersock, *The Throne of Adulis*.
12. In her insightful article on the contemporary plight of the Akhdam, Huda Seif notes that in Yemen, where local architecture has developed vertically to ensure female modesty through gender segregation, this last restriction is particularly humiliating. Huda Seif, "The Accursed Minority," p. 5. For the Akhdam and prostitution see R/20/A/1289 Private Prostitutes, 1909 and R/20/A/1285 Prostitutes and Venereal Disease.
13. Ibid., p. 16; Seif, "The Accursed Minority," p. 14.
14. Hunter, *The British Settlement of Aden*, p. 33.
15. It is possible that the term "Jabarti" was in fact a popular sobriquet that civilians and officials alike used as a kind of shorthand but not an "officially" recognized category since the term does not appear in any of the Aden census records between the late nineteenth century and 1931.
16. R/20/A/775 Sanitation.
17. J. Spencer Trimingham, *Islam in Ethiopia*, pp. 59 and 150–3. Trimingham cites Enrico Cerulli's edition of *The Harar Chronicle*, p. 40.
18. Ibid. For the etymology of the term Trimingham once again turns to the noted Italian ethnologist Enrico Cerulli, *Oriente Moderno* V, 1925, pp. 614ff.
19. See R/20/A/2766 Tamboora in Aden.
20. See R/20/A/2700 1906–18, Riots Jabarties, Somalis and Arabs.
21. Alexander Knysh, "The Cult of the Saints and Religious Reformism in Hadhramaut."
22. R/20/A/2664, letter of protest May 7, 1932, outlining complaints of irreligious activity at local *ziyara*s. R/20/A/3471 Shaykh Othman Fair. Other entertainments included Sufis performing *majdhib* (from the Arabic *Jadhaba*, meaning "entranced") in which practitioners would cut themselves with knives while twirling in a trance, as well as illicit alcohol and gambling.

23. R/20/A/2664 Fairs, 1911–36. While many local *ziyara*s were major events attracting thousands of participants and onlookers, others were much smaller affairs organized by particular communities such as the *ziyara* of Shaykh Rihan, a one-day festival organized each year by local fishermen. Although it is difficult to determine when many of these *ziyaras* originated many were in evidence by the latter part of the nineteenth century. The former Assistant Resident Capt. F. M. Hunter listed fourteen such festivals in *The British Settlement of Aden*, pp. 173–6. The list, however, is not identical with those cited in the Aden Residency file.
24. Discussed below.
25. G. Makris and Ahmad al-Safi, "The Tambura Spirit Possession Cult"; see also G. Makris and A. al-Safi, *Changing Masters*.
26. Within the context of the Sudan, Janice Boddy has noted numerous deliberate similarities between Zar organization and that of Sufi brotherhoods. Most significantly, public Zar ceremonies bear a striking resemblance to Sufi *dhikr*, while Zar practitioners are accorded the same kind of honor and deference as their Sufi counterparts. As far as we can tell from the colonial record, such affinities were not as marked in Aden. Janice Boddy, *Wombs and Alien Spirits*, p. 278.
27. Although we should note that in the Residency records there is at least one recorded instance of a male practitioner of Zar and one woman who claimed to lead a Tambura "house."
28. Makris and al-Safi, "The Tambura Spirit Possession Cult," p. 132. Although as Janice Boddy notes, in at least some cases in the Sudan, Tambura has, in fact, become absorbed into Zar. Boddy, *Wombs and Alien Spirits*, p. 133.
29. Richard Natvig, "Oromos, Slaves and the Zar Spirits," pp. 669–89.
30. Ibid., p. 669.
31. Archaic term for the Oromo.
32. Krapf, *Journals*, pp. 117–18 cited in Natvig, "Oromos, Slaves and the Zar Spirits," p. 679.
33. See, for instance, Boddy, *Wombs and Alien Spirits*, especially pp. 125–31.
34. Accounts rarely indicate any ethnicity beyond "Abyssinian" when discussing the practitioners of Zar. When they do, however, they are usually identified as "Galla" or Oromo.
35. C. B. Klunzinger, *Upper Egypt*; Emily Ruete (Salma bint Said bin Sultan), *Memoirs of an Arabian Princess*; C. Snouck Hurgronje, *Mekka*.
36. Hurgronje's use of an Arabic term for the leader of local Zar circles in Mecca should not be taken at face value. It must be remembered that he carried out his observations in Mecca primarily among men who may have been unaware of any other term.
37. Hurgronje, *Mekka*, pp. 113–16.
38. Ibid.
39. Ibid.
40. Ruete, *Memoirs of an Arabian Princess*, pp. 158ff.
41. An Amharic wording meaning "leader" or, sometimes, "lieutenant." Terje Ostebo, personal communication, March 27, 2015.
42. R/20/A/2906 Letter from Shaykh Abdullah bin Muhammad to FAR September 19, 1925.
43. A number of petitions refer to Zar being performed for women living in Purdah, or seclusion, which was a custom found only among the town's wealthiest residents.
44. Boddy's *Wombs and Alien Spirits* and I. M. Lewis' *Ecstatic Religion* are among a number of works that have posited a variety of theories intended to explain the social meaning of Zar. Given the nature of the source material, such theorizing is beyond the scope of the current work.
45. Those who supported Zar's ban tended to emphasize more sensationalized practices such as including descriptions of the possessed writhing at the feet of the priestess while supporters of the cult provided much more sober descriptions of chanting and singing.

46. R/20/A/2906 Police Report 7-1-1924. Alcohol and ritual drunkenness may have also been a part of the ceremony but its inclusion in descriptions of Zar ritual seem to depend on whether or not one was lobbying for its prohibition.
47. R/20/A/2906. See, for instance, petition from Shaykh Uthman, January 12, 1924 and petition by Amoon bint Ibrahim et al. January 18, 1924 requesting the lifting of the ban on Zar. Petition by Amina bint. Ali November 9, 1927 mentioned paying a license fee for the performance of Zar in the street "outside her house."
48. Sophie Zenkovsky, "Zar and Tambura," pp. 65–81.
49. Demons, devils and spirits, respectively.
50. Zenkovsky, "Zar and Tambura," p. 73.
51. Boddy, *Wombs and Alien Spirits*, pp. 275–80.
52. Ibid., p. 278.
53. Makris, *Changing Masters*, p. 126.
54. R/20/A/2766 Tamboora in Aden.
55. The term *rababa* does not appear in the Aden records. Instead, the instrument is conflated with the name of cult by British authorities who note that the "Tamboora" is "a large native harp." R/20/A/2766 Deputy Supt. Of Police to FAR, 31/1/25.
56. Zenkovsky, "Zar and Tambura," p. 74.
57. Curiously, *"jariyya"* is an Arabic slang term meaning slave girl but was also the title of an office in Sudanese Tambura groups.
58. R/20/A/2766 No. 680 of 1926 Police Inspector Abd al-Rahim Khan. Zenkovsky held that in the Sudan the names of Rababat were exclusively female. As demonstrated by the use of the name of Salah, a man's name, this convention may not have been so strictly observed in Aden.
59. This particular element is not mentioned in the Aden descriptions of the tambura ritual; however, it is noted in both the Sudan and the Hijaz. See Hurgronje, *Mekka*, pp. 15–16.
60. R/20/A/2766 Tamboora in Aden, but also significantly frequent petitions to perform Tambura at annual ziyarat can also be found in R/20/A/2664 Fairs in Aden, which is a file dealing primarily with the performance of the various annual festivals.
61. R/20/A/2766 Tamboora in Aden,
62. Bilal was a former African slave and one of the Prophet Muhammad's earliest followers. He is believed to have been the first believer to regularly recite the call to prayer.
63. Zenkovsky, "Zar and Tambura," p. 76; Markis and al-Safi provide a similar description.
64. Markis and al-Safi, "The Tambura Spirit Possession Cult," pp. 129–30.
65. Zenkovsky, "Zar and Tambura," pp. 77–8.
66. Ibid., p. 131.
67. R/20/A/2776 Petition of Tambura Akils to Lieut-Col. B. R. Reilly, Chief Commissioner, June 18, 1932.
68. R/20/A/2776 Petition from Mahi Ibrahim and Yusuf Abdi, December 9, 1929.
69. R/20/A3471 "Sheikh Othman Fair," Copy of report No. 316 from the Police Inspector S.O. May 5, 1932.
70. Indeed, one Aden police report from 1931 contends that the practitioners of Tambura seek to become possessed by the spirit of the deceased saint. R/20/A/3471 "Sheikh Othman Fair," Copy of a report No. 316 from the Police Inspector, S.O. May 5, 1932.
71. In fact, several practitioners of Zar held that their cult's presence in Aden predated imperial rule. While in the final analysis this assertion cannot be proved, it is also not implausible. R/20/A/2906 Zar in Aden.
72. R/20/A/2906 Zar in Aden, 1923–34 Petition to the First Assistant Resident regarding Zar. Emphasis in the original.
73. Dirks, *Castes of Mind*.

74. R/20/A/2906 Zar in Aden, 1923–34, Petition of Hasan Khan Mirza to FAR, Aden, June 1931.
75. The complex landscape of religious reform in 1920s Aden is discussed in greater detail in Chapter 6 as well as Scott S. Reese, "Salafi Transformations."
76. Ibid.
77. R/20/A/2906 Aden Residency Memo to Deputy Superintendent of Police, January 14, 1924.
78. Ibid.
79. Ibid. Petition to the First Assistant Resident, 12/24/1923.
80. For a blow-by-blow account of this case see Lidwien Kaptiejns and Jay Spaulding, "Women of the Zar and Middle-Class Sensibilities.".
81. R/20/A/2766.
82. R/20/A/2906 Petition from Amoon bint Ibrahim, Amina Ali, Zainab bint Abdullah and Attiya bint Hasan to FAR, Aden, January 18, 1924.
83. R/20/A/2906 First Assistant Resident report of meeting with Sayyid Abdullah Aydarus January 9, 1924. It will come as little surprise, however, that following the *Alaka*'s petition, his goodwill toward the women appears to have evaporated.
84. Ibid.
85. See Chapter 6.
86. R/20/A/2906, Memo from the Aden Residency 2/2/1924.
87. Other attendees may pay on average 4–8 annas, although it should be noted that 4 rupees for a poor person of Aden in the mid-1920s still represented a considerable sum.
88. R/20/A/2906 petitions to the Resident 31/03/24 and 16/04/24.
89. Ibid. To FAR, Aden from Amoon bint Ibrahim July 5, 1926. It is interesting to note here that this particular petition seems to have been written for Amoon by A. H. Roberts who was most likely Abdullah Roberts, a British convert to Islam who had served as an inspector in the Harbor police but was regarded as a reprobate by authorities who habitually consorted with the "lower sort" of "native."
90. An assertion that was not strictly true since the musicians were often men. See R/20/A/2906 Abd al-Rahman Kadi to FAR, May 15, 1924 and Shaikh Abdullah bin Muhamed, to the FAR, September 19, 1925, both of whom claimed to be Zar musicians requesting permission for ceremonies to resume.
91. R/20/A/2906 July 5, 1926.
92. Ibid. Emphasis mine.
93. Ibid.
94. Ibid. I. J. Sopher Barrister-At-Law to Chief Commissioner Aden, August 2, 1932.
95. Ibid. Note from the District Magistrate, August 11, 1932.
96. Ibid. R. S. Champion, District Magistrate to I. J. Sopher, August 27, 1932.
97. Ibid. Petition to the Chief Commissioner, September 4, 1932; Residency to the Settlement Chairman, October 22, 1932.
98. R/20/A/2664 Fairs 1911–36.
99. R/20/A/2766 Deputy Supt. of Police to FAR, March 31, 1926. Appended to this memo in a different handwriting is the notation, "The tumboora is a Zar in a different form."
100. Ibid, Residency memo, July 27, 1926.
101. Ibid., Petition to FAR Reilly from Man Bayasin, Said Bunda, Khamis Beyrout Muhamed Said and others, 23/3/25; Muhammad Abd al-Rahman and others to Reilly 06/18/32.
102. Ibid. Note from FAR Reilly, 18/3/25.
103. R/20/A/2766 Sayyid Abdullah Aydarus to the First Assistant Resident, October 31, 1925.
104. R/20/A/2766 various petitions from 1926 to 1932. For performing in the sweeper lines see petition of Mahi Ibrahim and Yusuf Abdi, December 9, 1929.

Notes   189

105. R/20/A/2664 Fairs, Petition to FAR Reilly from Mansabs (and others) of the tombs of Hashem al-Bahr and Uthman Damreel.
106. R/20/A/2766 various petitions between 1926 and 1932. For performing in the sweeper lines see petition of Mahi Ibrahim and Yusuf Abdi, December 9, 1929.
107. Lokman, *Men, Matters and Memories*. Serjeant, 'South Arabia and Ethiopia–' n. 28.
108. Ibid.
109. al-Asnag, *Nasib 'adan*, p. 95.
110. Ibid.
111. Ibid., p. 96.
112. The notion of "respectability" will be explored in greater detail in Chapter 6.
113. Literally, "spiritous drinks [*mashrubat ruhiyya*] and opiates [*mukayyifat*]," Luqman, "Sa'id," p. 397.
114. This appears to be the Urdu word for festival. Thanks to John Willis for this clarification.
115. Luqman, "Sa'id," p. 397.
116. Al-Asnag, *Nasib 'adan*, p. 96.
117. R/20/A/2776 Petition of Tambura Akils to Lieut-Col. B. R. Reilly, Chief Commissioner, June 18, 1932.
118. Ibid., Petition from Mahi Ibrahim and Yusuf Abdi, December 9, 1929.
119. R/20/A3471 "Sheikh Othman Fair," Copy of report No. 316 from the Police Inspector S.O. May 5, 1932.
120. R/20/A/2906 Petition of Hasan Khan Mirza, June 1931. Whether or not permission was granted is not recorded.
121. Ibid. Petition of Husayn Fazoo, November 28, 1932.
122. It should be noted, however, that it is possible that Zar in Ehtiopia and Somalia (the regions from which its Aden practitioners hailed) never maintained such associations.
123. The British for their part—the banning of Zar notwithstanding—were generally hesitant to regulate public morality particularly when doing so may lead to volatility.

Chapter 6

1. R/20/A/3465 no. 921 Zikr in Zakariya's mosque Ltr to Resident February 29, 1929. The vast majority of letters and petitions to the state found in the Aden Residency files located in the India Office Library are in the original Arabic.
2. Those subscribing to Salafi ideology, however, hardly held a monopoly on this term. Numerous writers of various ideological stripes used it during the nineteenth century, frequently applying a much broader definition for who should be included in the ranks of the "pious ancestors," regularly including the eponymous founders of the four Sunni law schools—Malik b. Inas, Abu Hanifa, Ahmad ibn Hanbal and Shafa'i—as well as other luminaries such as al-Ghazali. See See Scott S. Reese, "Shaykh Abdullahi al-Qutbi and the Pious Believer's Dilemma: Local Moral Guidance in an Age of Global Islamic Reform," pp. 488–504.
3. Amal N. Ghazal, "The Other Frontiers of Arab Nationalism," p. 106.
4. Ibid.; David Commins, *Islamic Reform*, p. 4. The roots of modern Islamic scripturalism can, of course, be dated even earlier to eighteenth-century thinkers such as South Asian scholars like Sirhindi and Shah Wali Allah al-Dihlawi as well as the Najdi *'alim* Muhammad ibn Abd al-Wahhab; however, an in-depth discussion of the place of these individuals in the history of reformist discourse is beyond the scope of this book. For Sirhindi and Shah Wali Allah see Barbara Metcalf, *Islamic Revival in British India* and Marcia Hermansen, trans. and ed., *The Conclusive Argument for God*. For Ibn Abd al-Wahhab see David Commins, *The Wahhabi Mission and Saudi Arabia*.

5. Lauzière, "The Construction of Salafiyya."
6. Albert Hourani, *Arabic Thought in the Liberal Age*.
7. Oliver Scharbrodt, "The Salafiyya and Sufism."
8. Commins, *Islamic Reform*; Weismann, "Between Ṣūfī Reformism and Modernist Rationalism."
9. Ibid., p. 206.
10. Haj, *Reconfiguring Islamic Tradition*, pp. 6–7. Haj's argument is a good deal more nuanced and complex but the limits of space do not permit a more detailed overview of her important work.
11. This view has recently been strengthened by Henri Lauzière, *The Making of Salafism: Islamic Reform in the Twentieth Century*.
12. Other notable contributions to this growing body of literature include Laffan, *Islamic Nationhood and Colonial Indonesia*; Amal N. Ghazal, "The Other Frontiers of Arab Nationalism"; Alavi, *Muslim Cosmpolitanism in the Age of Empire*; Francis Robinson, "Islamic Reform and Modernities in South Asia."
13. One notable exception is Justin Jones' "The Local Experiences of Reformist Islam."
14. A notion acknowledged by Justin Jones but demonstrated with only circumstantial evidence.
15. Knysh, "The Cult of the Saints and Religious Reformism in Hadhramaut."
16. Although this was hardly the end of the matter as we saw in Chapter 5. For a detailed narrative of this case see Kaptiejns and Spaulding, "Women of the Zar and Middle-Class Sensibilities."
17. The club itself is referred to by a variety of names in both British archival records and local Arabic language publications. It is variously called the Arab Islamic Reform Club, Arab Reform Club, the Islamic Reform Club and the Arab Literary Club—sometimes even within the same text. For the sake of simplicity, we will use *Nadi al-Islah* or Reform Club.
18. R/20/A/3390 Ltr from Muhammad Ali Luqman to Major H. M. Wightwick, Acting Political Resident, Aden, June 24, 1931. Like the organization's varying names, its founders frequently identified different years as the date of the club's founding.
19. For more on the backgrounds of these individuals see Reese, "The Respectable Citizens of Shaykh Uthman."
20. Luqman also spent time at Aligarh Muslim University (AMU) in the 1920s and would go on to obtain a law degree in Bombay in the mid-1930s and established the first of a string of successful Arabic- and English-language newspapers in Aden in 1940. However, his education was not entirely secular. In addition to his Western schooling, Luqman also studied *fiqh* and other elements of the religious sciences with a number of Aden scholars while in his teens, including the pre-First World War Qadi of Aden, Sayyid Muhammad al-Hazmi. Lokman, *Men, Matters and Memories*, pp. 52–4. This recently published work is a compilation of Luqman's serialized autobiography that appeared in his weekly English-language newspaper *The Aden Chronicle* during the early 1960s.
21. Al-Asnag's education is unclear. Judging from his own writings to be discussed below, he seems to have benefited from a mixture of secular and religious education. For information on Muhammad Sa'id al-Asnag (Ahmad's father) see the petition requesting the banning of gambling and other indecent activities at the *ziyara* of Hashim al-Bahr in R/20/A/2664.
22. M. A. Lokman, 'First Literary Club in South Arabia' in *Men, Matters and Memories* p. 136. This piece appeared August 3, 1961. For a brief discussion of al-Thaalibi's involvement with transnational Salafism see Ghazal, "The Other Frontiers of Arab Nationalism."
23. Luqman notes in his autobiography that his first attempt to establish the club in 1924 was something of a false start. While initial interest was strong after a few years the organization had only twelve dues paying members. It was not until 1928 that a revived club began to establish itself on the social scene. Lokman, *Men, Matters and Memories*, p. 136.
24. R/20/A/3452 file no 891 Haslam to Hickinbotham, 23 March, 1932.

25. R/20/A/3390 Luqman to Wightwick, 24 June, 1931 and Laghton to Luqman, 29 July, 1929.
26. Al-Abbadi's education and career is summarized in a number of documents; however, the most comprehensive is the laudatory biography composed by his student and, later, Salafi luminary, Muhammad b. Salim b. Husayn al-Bayhani and included in a collection of al-Abbadi's poetry titled *Hidayat al-murid*, discussed below.
27. Al-Abbadi, *Hidayat al-murid*, p. 1.
28. Until about 1908.
29. Al-Abbadi, *Hidayat al-murid*, p. 1.
30. He is also said to have made shorter sojourns in Persia.
31. Al-Abbadi, *Hidayat al-murid*, p. 2.
32. One police intelligence report contends that he arrived in Lahej as late as 1929 and remained there for only 18 months. R/20/A/3390 Police report on Ahmad bin Ahmad al-Abbadi 5/6/31.
33. Al-Bayhani, in fact, asserts that al-Abbadi founded the Reform Club after his arrival, however, all other sources contradict this assertion.
34. The Shaykh's detractors, such as the former Qadi of Shaykh Uthman, Awadth b. Abdullah Sharaf, would certainly argue that his presence was responsible for the social tensions of the 1930s, however, there is nothing to suggest that al-Abbadi's presence was the sole or even precipitating factor.
35. Lauzière, "The Construction of Salafiyya."
36. Al-Abbadi's unambiguous stance against tomb visitation would certainly place him in this category and was sufficient for his student to refer to him as "the learned Salafi," on the title page of the *Hidayat* in the late 1930s. At least one recent Yemeni author has referred to him as "one of the earliest Salafis in southern Yemen," Ahmad ibn Hasan, *Qaburiyah fi al-Yaman*, p. 232. Similarly, upon his return to Aden, al-Bayhani embarked on a lengthy reform-focused writing career, including most notably a Hadith commentary, *Islah al-mujtama*, that is still in print as well as *al-Sarm al-qirini*, a response to critics of al-Abbadi's poems. The latter, unfortunately, exists only in manuscript form and has never been published. Ahmad ibn Hasan references it in *Qaburiyah fi al-Yaman* as a response to the "tomb worshippers," p. 235.
37. Luqman was personally exposed to a wide range of reformist thought during his youth in both India and the Arab Middle East. He contributed pieces to newspapers in both India and Egypt including the *Bombay Sentinal*, *Bombay Mainland* and *Bombay Chronicle* as well as the Arabic newspapers *al-Jihad, al-Balagh* and *al-Shura* all based in Cairo. Despite receiving his legal education in Bombay and working for a short time at Aligarh Muslim University it was toward the Arab side of reform to which Luqman was drawn. He notes in his autobiography a rather uncomfortable time at Aligarh, making clear his contempt for the Caliphate movement in an invited lecture there in 1936. Furthermore, he maintained a life-long friendship with al-Thaalibi and in a series of lectures delivered to the Reform Club in 1939 he praised al-Afghani, Abduh and Rida as "defenders" of the "fundamental principles and tenets of the Qur'an." Lokman, *Men Matters and Memories*, pp.153, 211–12 and 220. Even as his own path became self-reflexively "pan-Arabist," Luqman's published an editorial in *Fatat al-Jezirah* on November 26, 1944 commemorating al-Thaalibi's death. In this piece, Luqman described al-Thaalibi as a "pillar of Islam and Arab hero," along with al-Afghani, Abduh and Rida. Many of Luqman's *Fatat* editorials are collected in *al-Mujahid Muhammad Ali Luqman, Fatat al-Jazira, ifttahiyah wa maqalat min am 1940–1950,* Ahmad Ali al-Hamdani ed. (2006 privately published.)
38. Such a mixture of intellectual agendas coming together around the notion of a Muslim moral community was hardly unusual during this period. See, for example, Gasper's *The Power of Representation*, especially pp. 48–51 and 119–23.
39. R/20/A/3390.

40. Ibid. A copy of this sermon in the original Arabic was obtained by a police informant present during the Friday prayers. It came to the attention of British authorities because of the inclusion of remarks that denounced atrocities committed by Italian authorities in Libya during the preceding months. The sermon is attributed by association to Muhammad Ali Luqman but while he gave a number of sermons it is not clear that he delivered this particular one.
41. R/20/A/2664 Fairs 1911–36 Petition to Wightwick, First Assistant Resident, May 7, 1931.
42. R/20/A/3465 File no. 921.
43. R/20/A/2664 Petition to Resident, May 6, 1931. It may be noticed that this petition predates Sayyid Ali's petition by a day. In order to gain sufficient signatures such petitions to the authorities generally circulated through various neighborhoods for several days before being sent forward to the Residency. As a result, it is not surprising that those opposed to it had time to put together their own counter petition and send it forward as quickly as their opponents. Dates were frequently assigned to documents as they came in to the Residency Clerk's office and in this case it would appear that the pro-*Ziyara* petition simply passed Sayyid Ali's anti-*Ziyara* one in the bureaucratic queue.
44. Ibid., Ltr to the Resident from Ahmadi Sufis, March 3, 1932; Ltr. To Inspector of Police from Zakariya Muhammad, February 25, 1932; Ltr. to the Magistrate from Zakariya Muhammad, March 10, 1932.
45. "Verily the Almighty and His Angels shower blessings upon His Prophet. Oh Believers! send blessings upon him and salute him with a worthy salutation." Sura 33:56, *The Confederates*. Special thanks to Omid Safi, Ebrahim Moosa and Omer Mozzafer for their help in tracking down this reference.
46. R/20/A/3465 File 921, Note to the Commandant of Police, January 11, 1933. For a more detailed treatment of these events see Reese, "The Respectable Citizens of Shaykh Uthman."
47. See R/20/A/3465 File 921 and R/20/A/3390.
48. R/20/A/3390 "What Kind of Man" article in *al-Shura*, July 1, 1931;IOR R/20/A/3465 File no. 921 Letter from Zakaria Muhammad to the Assistant Resident at Shaykh Uthman, March 15, 1932; IOR R/20/A/3390 Letter from Sayyid Ali Isma'il to Wightwick, July 20, 1931.
49. See various letters and note in IOR R/20/A/3390 and IOR R/20/A/3465 File no. 921. I should add that during the late nineteenth century and early twentieth the label "Wahhabi" was the favorite charge to throw at any individual whose views you did not agree with. As such, it was used more as a swear word than a designator of one's actual theological beliefs.
50. In 1929 Zakaria Muhammad purchased the site of an unfinished mosque from the former Qadi Awadhh Abdullah, for 6,000 Rs., which he then completed for an additional investment of 31,000 Rs. This was what became known as the Zakoo Mosque. He supported the mosque with a *waqf* that generated 100 Rs. of income per month. Built into the endowment was the stipulation that the site should be used strictly for prayer and that activities such as *dhikr*, which seems to have offended his reformist sensibilities, were explicitly forbidden. In addition, he engaged Shaykh al-Abbadi as the imam who used the *minbar* to advocate Salafi-style reforms. Similarly, Sayyid Ali contributed 3,000 Rs. to finish construction on what became known as the Ahl al-Khair Mosque, coincidentally another mosque the former Qadi, Awadhh Abdullah, supposedly started but never finished. See R/20/A/3390.
51. R/A/3390 Confidential note Awadhh Abdullah to Wightwick July 1931.
52. Both Muhammad Ali Isma'il and Ahmad al-Abbadi were educated, but neither was considered to have any local scholarly standing.
53. In particular, al-Abbadi, although from Ibb, is said to have traveled widely and studied in Persia and India.
54. The first three, named as Ali Asef, Ali Ahmad and S. A. Bari, respectively, were signatories of the 1924 anti-Zar petition along with the pro-Salafi Hitaris of Tawahi. The loyalties of the

unidentified police inspector of Crater were demonstrated in a report filed with his superiors on May 6, 1931 in which he praised al-Abbadi and denounced the Shaykh's detractors. A further note was appended to the report by his superiors who worried that the officer had become too closely associated with the pro-Salafi camp. R/20/A/2906 Petition against re-legalization of Zar, September 17, 1932; IOR R/20/A/3390 Confidential report, Police Inspector, Crater, May 6, 1931.
55. For social importance of the cult of the saints and the Yemeni Sayyids see Knysh, 'The Cult of the Saints.' "The Cult of the Saints and Religious Reformism in Hadhramaut,"
56. R/20/A/3390 Letter from Havildar Ali Hussain Murkashee to First Assistant Resident, July 6, 1931.
57. For their own part, the British authorities attempted to affect a position of stunning impartiality in these events. They tended to view the matter as largely one of petty squabbles between various elite factions and their own overriding concern seemed purely the maintenance of authority. As such, in addition to threats they frequently sought compromises between the conflicting parties. They also began to take what were viewed as prudent security precautions, for instance, deploying extra police as well as an armored car or two at the Sayyid Hashim *ziyara* from this time on in order to deter disruptions. R/20/A/2664 Fairs.
58. Gelvin and Green, eds, *Global Muslims*.
59. Tagliacozzo, "Hajj in the Time of Cholera"; Low, "Empire and the Hajj."
60. Bang, *Sufis and Scholars of the Sea*; Reese, "The Adventures of Abu Harith."
61. J. Cole, "Printing and Urban Islam in the Mediterranean World."
62. See, for example, ibid.; Green, *Bombay Islam*; Francis Robinson, "Technology and Religious Change."
63. Reese, *Renewers of the Age*, especially Chapter 5 and Matthews, "Imagining Arab Communities."
64. In addition to being commented upon in international centers of learning such as Cairo and Beirut, Al-Qutbi's work was read and positively remarked upon by more regional figures most notably Muhammad Ali Luqman and Qadi Da'ud al-Battah who reviewed the collection for colonial censors both of whom commented on its positive moral message.
65. Although from this point the Luqmans quickly made up for lost time, establishing at least three other periodicals by the 1950s. These included a literary weekly, *al-Qalam al-'adani* (*The Aden Pen*), and the English-language weekly *The Aden Chronicle*. A short-lived "youth magazine" *al-Mustaqabal* was also published briefly in the late 1940s.
66. See, for instance, Ali Muhammad Salah BaHamish, *Durur al-ma'ani fi al-tahdhir min munthumat al-Abbadi wa ta'liq al-Bayhani*, a commentary on the writings of Abbadi and Bayhani published by the press in 1943.
67. Ami Ayalon, "Arab Booksellers and Bookshops."
68. Although its owners only began to publish their own books in about 1919; see Lauzière, "The Construction of Salafiyya," p. 379.
69. R/20/A/3031 Govt of Bombay Notification, August 30, 1921. See Michael Laffan, "A Sufi Century," pp. 25–39; Bang, "Authority and Piety," pp. 103–4. Halabi & Sons' penchant for publishing anti-scripturalist tracts certainly does not imply any ideological bent on their part. Nor is there any suggestion that like-minded authors necessarily encouraged one another to publish there for any reason other than that they were a reliable operation, that turned out a reasonable product at an affordable price (indeed, word of mouth, was likely everything).
70. *Guidance of the Seeker along the Path of Truth and Doctrine*.
71. In many cases, multiple editions were published with vague references to earlier printings—the dates of which can only be approximated through other references while in others publication dates are missing entirely.
72. Al-Abbadi, *Hidayat al-murid*, p. 5.

73. Ibid., p. 64.
74. Ibid. A second edition was published by the same press in 1969 to which a second work, *Bi-hujat al-qulub bi-tawhid alam al-ghayub*, was attached. Like the *Hidayat* this was a poetry collection by another noted Salafi shaykh, Qadiri b. Ahmad al-Ahdal, but written much later in 1969. I would like to thank Dr. Alan Godlas for the leads that enabled me to track down the history of this work.
75. Literally, *adat mustihajna* or "disapproved of customs," a phrase used liberally by Ahmad al-Asnag but certainly appropriate to the views of al-Abbadi and al-Bayhani.
76. Al-Abbadi, *Hidayat al-murid*, 'On the *Tariqa* and the *Shari'a*' pp. 32-34.
77. Ibid. "On Idolatry and its Types," pp. 24–5.
78. Ibid. "The Verdict on Tomb Visitation,' pp. 47–56.
79. Literally, "O'Shaykh So and So . . ."
80. Emphasis mine.
81. Al-Abbadi, p. 25 n.1.
82. Ibid., p. 14 n.1.
83. Ibid., pp. 7–8.
84. Ibid., pp. 13–14.
85. Ibid., p. 24.
86. Ibid., n. 3.
87. Al-Adani, *al-Jiz al-latif fi al-tahkim al-sharif*, pp. 19–27.
88. Ibid., pp. 6–7.
89. Ibid., p. 34.
90. Ibid.
91. Ibid., p. 50.
92. Al-Bayhani was educated first in the Hadramaut and then came to Aden specifically to study under al-Abbadi. In the late mid-1930s he attended the famed al-Azhar in Cairo under a scholarship provided by the Reform Club. Hasan, *Qaburiyah fi al-Yaman*, p. 234.
93. Ahmad al-Asnag lived to see independence in 1967 but ran afoul of the ruling communist authorities, dying shortly after his release from prison in 1972.
94. *Fatat* was followed by *al-Qalam al-'adani*, a weekly literary paper, and *The Aden Chronicle*, a weekly English-language paper—both of which were founded in about 1950. All of these were published until the end of colonial rule in 1967. According to current conventions of transliteration Luqman's flagship paper's title should be transliterated as *Fitat al-Jazira*, however, on the weekly's masthead the title is printed *Fatat al-Jezirah*, thus we retain the original transliteration.
95. Al-Asnag published another set of essays, *Irij 'adan*, in 1959. These were lectures originally delivered to various local groups between the mid-1930s and late 1950s.
96. For many Adenis today Muhammad Ali Luqman represents their premier intellectual, and, as such, many of his essays, short stories and newspaper editorials have now been published in a number of collections. The novella *Sa'id* can be found in *al-Mujahid Muhammad Ali Luqman al-muhami*.
97. Al-Asnag, *Nasib 'adan*, p. 4.
98. This appears to be a very curious use of the Urdu word for "festival." Thanks to John Willis for this clarification.
99. Luqman, Introduction to *Sa'id,*, pp. 4–9.
100. Al-Asnag, *Nasib 'adan*, p. 5.
101. Ibid., pp. 33, 36 and 40.
102. *Sa'id*, p. 398. Critically, as we shall see below, he did not condemn saint veneration as a whole, but only visiting the tombs of the saints for the wrong reasons.

103. Al-Asnag, *Nasib 'adan*, p. 54.
104. Ibid.
105. Lokman, *Men, Matters and Memories*, p. 67.
106. *Sa'id*, pp. 423–4. See Chapter 4.
107. Al-Asnag, *Nasib 'adan*, p. 54.
108. Ibid.
109. Ibid., p. 56.
110. *Sa'id*, p. 424.
111. Ibid.
112. Al-Asnag, *Nasib 'adan*, p. 55.
113. Al-Asnag and Luqman's views were in fact very similar to the *Effendiya* reformers of the Egyptian middle class during the same period. The difference between them, however, was that the *Effendiya*, like other reformers, sought the abolition of saints' festivals while the two Adenis argued that they could be reformed. See Samuli Schielke, "Hegemonic Encounters."
114. R/20/A/3452 no. 891 report No. C/8, October 3, 1938; Lokman, *Men, Matters, Memories*, p. 220–1.
115. R/20/A/3452 no. 891 report No. C/8, October 3, 1938, Police Inspector, Crater. This report lists Ahmad al-Asnag as the current President of the Club with Muhammad Ali Luqman as its Vice President. He also notes that at the time of writing the Club had about 150 dues-paying members. By the 1940s, however, Luqman seems to have increasingly distanced himself from these reformists and embarked on a more secular, Arab nationalist trajectory.
116. Based on Club records, al-Bayhani traveled to Egypt in 1938 and was resident there for three years according to his biography in the *Qaburiyah*. Hasan, *Qaburiyah fi al-Yaman*, p. 234. See also R/20/B/1531 c. 45/1 1938 Status of the Arab Reform Club in Aden.
117. See n.44.
118. Haj, *Reconfiguring Islamic Tradition*.
119. "Ziyara al-Sayyid al-Aydarus," *Fatat al-Jezirah*, May 17, 1942.

Conclusions

1. Lokman, *Men, Matters, Memories*.
2. Gavin, *Aden under British Rule*, 287–91.
3. Ibid., pp. 320–1. Gavin notes that construction work on the refinery accounted for 11,000 of the Colony's approximately 40,000 manual laborers in 1953–4.
4. Gavin, *Aden under British Rule*, pp. 218–19.
5. Noel Brehony, *Yemen Divided*, pp. xix–xx.
6. Ho, *The Graves of Tarim*, pp. 5–6.

Bibliography

Primary sources

Abu Makhrama, Abu Abdullah al-Tayyib (1991), *Tarikh thaghr 'adan,* Cairo: Maktaba Madbuli.

Aden Residency Records, India Office Library, British Library, especially series R/20/A and R/20/E.

al-Asnag, Ahmad (1934), *Nasib 'adan min al-haraka al-fikriyya al-hadithiyya khatarat wa-muhadarat li-l-adib al-'adani al-ma'aruf al-ustadh Ahmad Muhmmad al-Asnaj, Mudir Nadi al-Islah al-'Arabi al-Islami fi 'adan*, Aden: no publisher.

— (1959), *Irij 'adan, darus min khabir*, Aden: no publisher.

al-Aydarus, Abd al-Rahman (1863), *Risala fi tariqa al-naqshbandiyya,* manuscript copy, 1280 AH.

al-Aydarus, Abu Bakr (1936), *al-Jiz al-latif fi al-tahkim al-sharif*, 2nd edn, Cairo: Mustafa al-Halabi wa ibna'ahu.

BaHamish, Ali Muhammad Salah (1943), *Durur al-ma'ani fi al-tahdhir min munthumat al-Abbadi wa ta'liq al-Bayhani,* no publisher.

al-Barawi, Qassim (1948), *al-Majmu'a al-qasa'id,* Cairo: Mustafa al-Halabi wa ibna'ahu.

al-Bayhani, Muhammad b. Salam, ed. (1969), *Hidayat al-murid ila sabil al-haqq wa-al-tawhid, li-na zamha al-ustadh al-jalil wa-l-alama al-salafi al-nabil al-shaykh Ahmad bin Muhammad bin Awadh al-Abbadi al-Yamani*, 2nd edn, Cairo: al-Matba'a al-Salafiya wa-Maktabatuha.

al-Bayhani, Muhammad b. Salam, ed. (1969), 'On the Tariqa and the Shari'a', in *Hidayat al-Murid ila Sabil al-Haqq wa-al-Tawhid, li-na Zamha al-Ustadh al-Jalil wa-l-Alama al-Salafi al-Nabil al-Shaykh Ahmad bin Muhammad bin Awadh al-Abbadi al-Yamani*, 2nd edn, Cairo: al-Matba'a al-Salafiya wa-Maktabatuha, pp. 32–4.

Burton, Richard (1966) *First Footsteps in East Africa,* edited with an introduction and additional chapters by Gordon Waterfield, New York: Frederick A. Praeger.

Cerulli, Enrico, trans., *The Harar Chronicle* in *Rendiconti della Reale Accademia dei Lincei*, ser. Vi, vol. iv, no. 2, Rome.

Fatat al-Jezirah (1942), Aden: n.p.

al-Hakami, Omarah (1892), *Yaman Its Early Medieval History by Najm al-Din 'Omarah al-Hakami*, trans. Henry Cassels Kay, London: Edward Arnold.

Hickenbotham, Sir Tom (1958), *Aden*, London: Constable and Company Ltd.

al-Humawi, Yaqut (1995), *Mu'jam al-buldan*, Beirut: Dar Sader.

Hurgronje, C. Snouck (2007), *Mekka in the Latter Part of the Nineteenth Century: Daily Life, Customs and Learning. The Moslims of the East-Indian Archipelago*, Leiden: Brill.

Hunter, F. M. (1877), *An Account of the British Settlement of Aden,* London: Trübner & Co.

— (1986 [1909]), *Arab Tribes in the Vicinity of Aden: An Account Compiled by the British Residency in 1886*, London: Darf Publishers.

Ibn Battuta, Muhammad (1968), *Rihlat ibn Battuta,* Beirut: Dar al-Turath.

Ingrams, Harold (1966) *Arabia and the Isles*, 3rd edn, London: John Murray.

Johnston, Charles (1964), *The View from Steamer Point: Three Crucial Years in South Arabia*, New York: Frederick A. Praeger.

Klunzinger, C. B. (1878), *Upper Egypt: Its Peoples and Its Products,* New York: Scribner, Armstrong and Co.

Lokman, M. A. (2009), *Men, Matters and Memories*, compilation and introduction by Professor Ahmed Ali Al-Hamdani, Aden: no publisher.

Luqman, Muhammad Ali (2005) *al-Mujahid Muhammad Ali Luqman al-Muhami (6 November 1898–22 March 1966): Ra'id al-Nahda al-Fikri wa-l-Adabiyya al-Haditha fi al-Yaman*, ed. Ahmad Ali al-Hamdani, no publisher.

— (2005) "Kamala Devi," in *al-Mujahid Muhammad Ali Luqman al-muhami (6 November 1898–22 March 1966): ra'id al-nahda al-fikri wa-l-adabiyya al-haditha fi al-yaman, ed. Ahmad Ali al-Hamdani* , ed. Ahmad Ali al-Hamdani, no publisher, pp. 455–76.

— (2005), "Sa'id," in *al-Mujahid Muhammad Ali Luqman al-muhami (6 November 1898–22 March 1966): ra'id al-nahda al-fikri wa-l-adabiyya al-haditha fi al-yaman,* ed. Ahmad Ali al-Hamdani, no publisher, pp. 395–454.

— (2006), *al-Mujahid Muhammad Ali Luqman, Fatat al-Jazira, ifttahiya wa-maqalat min 'am 1940–1950,* ed. Ahmad Ali al-Hamdani, no publisher.

Luqman, Hamza Ali (1960), *Tarikh Adan wa junub al-jazira al-arabiyya,* Sana'a: Dar al-masir al-matba'a.

— (1985), *Tarikh qaba'il al-yamaniyya,* Sana'a: Dar al-kilmah.

— (n.d.), *Stories from the History of Aden and South Arabia,* typescript.

al-Makki, Abd al-Qadir bin Muhammad (1899), *The Overflowing River of the Science of Inheritance and Patrimony, Together with an Exposition of The Rights of Women, and the Laws of Matrimony*, Cairo: Hajee Abadee Hasan, Proprietor of Arabic Book Depot: Aden.

Al-Makki, Qutb al-Din al-Nahrawali, Clive Smith, trans. (2002), *Lightning over Yemen: A History of the Ottoman Campaign 1569–1571*, London: I. B. Tauris.

Malcolmson, J. P. (1846), "Account of Aden," *Journal of the Royal Asiatic Society*, Volume 8, Issue 15, January, pp. 279–92.

Al-Muqaddasi, Abu Abdullah Mohammed ibn Ahmed (1877), *Kitab ahsan al-taqasim fi ma'rifat al-aqalim, Descriptio imperii Moslemici/autore Schamso 'd-din Abu Abdollah Mohammed ibn Ahmed ibn Abi Bekr al-Banna al-Basschari al-Mokaddasi*, M. J. de Goeje's Classic Edition, Leiden: Brill.

Osgood, J. B. F. (1854), *Notes of Travel: Or Recollection of Majunga, Zanzibar, Muscat, Aden, Mocha, and Other Eastern Ports,* Salem, MA: George Creamer.

Playfair, R. L. (1859), *A History of Arabia Felix or Yemen, from the Commencement of the Christian Era to the Present Time, Including an Account of the British Settlement of Aden,* Bombay: Education Society Press.

— (1859), *Memorandum on the Trade of Aden for 1857–58,* Aden: Printed at the Jail Press.

Rihani, Ameen Fares (1930), *Around the Coasts of Arabia,* New York: Houghton Mifflin.

Ruete, Emily (Salma bint Said bin Sultan) (1888), *Memoirs of an Arabian Princess,* New York: D. Appleton and Company.

Salt, Henry (1814), *Voyage to Abyssinia and Travels into the Interior of that Country Executed under the Orders of the British Government in the Years 1809 and 1810,* London: no publisher.

Schoff, Wilfred H., trans. (1995 [1911]), *The Periplus of the Erythraean Sea: Travel and Trade in the Indian Ocean by a Merchant of the First Century,* New Delhi: Munshiram Manoharlal Publishers Pvt. Ltd.

Serjeant, R. B. (1974), *The Portuguese off the South Arabian Coast: Hadrami Chronicles,* Oxford: Oxford University Press.

Smith, G. Rex, (2008), *A Traveller in Thirteenth-Century Arabia, Ibn al-Mujawir's Tarikh al-Mustabsir,* ser. III, vol. 19, London: Hakluyt Society.

Wellstead, J. R. (1838), *Travels in Arabia,* v. II, London: John Murray.

Secondary materials

Ahmad ibn Hasan (2003), *Qaburiyah fi al-yaman, nasha atuha-atharuha-mawqif al-ulama minha,* Sana'a: Markaz al-kilimah al-tayyibah lil-buhuth wa-al-dirasat al-ilmiyah.

Alavi, Seema (2015), *Muslim Cosmopolitanism in the Age of Empire,* Cambridge, MA: Harvard University Press.

Alpers, Edward (1986), "The Somali Community in Aden in the Nineteenth Century," *Northeast African Studies,* Volume 8, Issue 2/3, pp. 143–68.

Amrith, Sunil K. (2013), *Crossing the Bay of Bengal: The Furies of Nature and Fortunes of Migrants,* Cambridge, MA: Harvard University Press.

Anderson, Benedict (1983), *Imagined Communities: Reflections on the Origin and Spread of Nationalism,* London: Verso.

Anderson, Clare (2012), *Subaltern Lives: Biographies of Colonialism in the Indian Ocean World, 1790–1920,* Cambridge: Cambridge University Press.

Asad, Talal (1986), *The Idea of an Anthropology of Islam,* Occasional Papers, Georgetown University, and Center for Contemporary Arab Studies. Washington, DC: Center for Contemporary Arab Studies.

— (1993), *Genealogies of Religion: Discipline and Reasons of Power in Christianity and Islam,* Baltimore: Johns Hopkins University Press.

Ayalon, Ami (2010), "Arab Booksellers and Bookshops in the Age of Printing, 1850–1914," *British Journal of Middle Eastern Studies*, Volume 37, Issue 1, pp. 73–93.
Aydin, Cemil (2017), *The Idea of the Muslim World: A Global Intellectual History*, Cambridge, MA: Harvard University Press.
Ballantyne, Tony (2003), "Rereading the Archive and Opening up the Nation-State: Colonial Knowledge in South Asia (and Beyond)," in *After the Imperial Turn: Thinking with and through the Nation*, ed. Antoinette Burton, Durham, NC: Duke University Press, pp. 102–24.
Bang, Anne (2003), *Sufis and Scholars of the Sea: Family Networks in East Africa 1860–1925*, London: Routledge.
— (2011), "Authority and Piety, Writing and Print: A Preliminary Study of the Circulation of Islamic Texts in Late Nineteenth-Century and Early Twentieth Century Zanzibar," *Africa*, Volume 81, Issue 1, pp. 89–107.
Barbosa, Duarte, *The Book of Duarte Barbosa: An Account of the Countries Bordering on the Indian Ocean and their Inhabitants/Written by Duarte Barbosa and Completed about the year 1518 A.D.; Translated from the Portuguese Text . . . and Edited and Annotated by Mansel Longworth Dames*, London: Hakluyt Society, 1921.
Basu, Santosh Kumar (1963), "A Premature Attempt by the Bombay Government to set up a Permanent Naval and Military Station at Aden," *Bengal Past and Present: Journal of the Calcutta Historical Society,* Volume 2, pp. 26–30.
Benton, Lauren (2001), *Law and Colonial Cultures: Legal Regimes in World History, 1400–1900*, Cambridge: Cambridge University Press.
Blanes, Ruy and Diana Espirito Santo, eds (2013), "Introduction: On the Agency of Intangibles," in *The Social Life of Spirits*, Chicago: University of Chicago Press, pp. 1–32.
Blyth, Robert J. (2004), "Aden, British India and the Development of Steam Power in the Red Sea, 1825–1839," in *Maritime Empires, British Imperial Maritime Trade in the Nineteenth Century*, eds David Killingray, Margarette Lincoln and Nigel Rigby, Woodbridge: The Boydell Press.
Boddy, Janice (1989), *Wombs and Alien Spirits: Women, Men and the Zar Cult in Northern Sudan,* Madison: University of Wisconsin Press.
Bose, Sugata (2006), *A Hundred Horizons: The Indian Ocean in the Age of Global Empire*, Cambridge, MA: Harvard University Press.
Bowersock, G. W. (2013), *The Throne of Adulis: Red Sea Wars on the Eve of Islam*, Oxford: Oxford University Press.
Brehony, Noel (2013), *Yemen Divided: The Story of a Failed State in South Arabia*, London: I. B. Tauris.
Brouwer, C. G. (2001), "Al-Mukha as a Coffee Port in the Early Decades of the Seventeenth Century According to Dutch Sources," in *Le commerce du cafe' avant l'ere des plantations coloniales; espaces, reseaux societies (Xve–XIXe siecle),* ed. Michel Tuchscherer, Cairo: Cahier des annales islamologiques, pp. 271–91.

Bujra, A. S. (1970), "Urban Elites and Colonialism: The Nationalist Elites of Aden and South Arabia," *Journal of Middle Eastern Studies*, Volume 6, Issue 2, pp. 189–211.
Burton, Antoinette, ed. (2003), *After the Imperial Turn: Thinking with and through the Nation*, Durham, NC: Duke University Press.
Casale, Giancarlo (2011), *The Ottoman Age of Exploration*, Oxford: Oxford University Press.
Chakrabarty, Dipesh (2000), *Provincializing Europe: Postcolonial Thought and Historical Difference*, Princeton: Princeton University Press.
Chaudhuri, K. N. (1985), *Trade and Civilization in the Indian Ocean: An Economic History from the Rise of Islam to 1750*, Cambridge: Cambridge University Press.
Cole, Juan (2001), "Printing and Urban Islam in the Mediterranean World," in *Modernity and Culture from the Mediterranean to the Indian Ocean*, eds Leila Tarazi Fawaz and C. A. Bayly, New York: Columbia University Press, pp. 344–64.
Commins, David (1990), *Islamic Reform: Politics and Social Change in Late Ottoman Syria*, Oxford: Oxford University Press.
— (2006), *The Wahhabi Mission and Saudi Arabia*, London: I. B. Tauris.
Cooke Mariam and Bruce Lawrence, eds (2005), *Muslim Networks: From Hajj to Hip Hop*, Chapel Hill: University of North Carolina Press.
Cooper, Frederick (2005), *Colonialism in Question: Theory, Knowledge, History*, Berkeley: University of California Press.
Dalrymple, William (2002), *White Mughals: Love and Betrayal in Eighteenth-century India*, New York: Viking.
Dirks, Nicholas (2001), *Castes of Mind: Colonialism and the Making of Modern India*, Princeton: Princeton University Press.
Dresch, Paul (2000), *A History of Modern Yemen*, Cambridge: Cambridge University Press.
Dutta, Asim Kumar (1981), "Why Did the East India Company Recognise Hindu and Muslim Law?" in *Western Colonial Policy (A Study on its Impact on Indian Society)*, ed. N. R. Ray, Volume I, Calcutta: Institute of Historical Studies, pp. 173–82.
Fahmy, Khaled (1998), *All the Pasha's Men: Mehmet Ali, His Army and the Making of Modern Egypt*, Cambridge, Cambridge University Press.
Fawaz, Leila Tarazi and C. A. Bayly, eds (2001), *Modernity and Culture from the Mediterranean to the Indian Ocean*, New York: Columbia University Press.
Fawcett, Sir Charles (1934), *The First Century of British Justice in India, An Account of the Court of Judicature at Bombay, Established in 1672, and of Other Courts of Justice in Madras, Calcutta and Bombay, from 1661 to the Latter Part of the Eighteenth Century*, Oxford: Clarendon Press.
Feierman, Steven (1999), "Colonizers, Scholars and the Creation of Invisible Histories," in *Beyond the Cultural Turn: New Directions in the Study of Society and Culture*, eds Victoria Bonnell and Lynn Hunt, Berkeley: University of California Press, pp. 182–216.

Freitag, Ulrike and W. G. Clarence-Smith, eds (1997), *Hadhrami Traders, Scholars and Statesmen in the Indian Ocean 1750–1960s*, Leiden: Brill.
Gaspar, Michael (2009), *The Power of Representation: Publics, Peasants, & Islam in Egypt*, Stanford: Stanford University Press.
Gavin, R. J. (1975), *Aden under British Rule. 1839–1967,* London: Hurst & Co.
Gelvin, James and Nile Green, eds (2013), *Global Muslims in the Age of Steam and Print*, Berkeley: University of California Press.
Ghanem, Shihab (n.d.), *Obituary for Hamza Luqman, 1919–1995*, n.p.
Ghazal, Amal N. (2010), "The Other Frontiers of Arab Nationalism: Ibadis, Berbers, and the Arabist–Salafi Press in the Interwar Period," *International Journal of Middle East Studies,* Volume 42, pp. 105–22.
Ghosh, Amitav (1992), *In an Antique Land—History in the Guise of a Traveler's Tale*, New York: Alfred Knopf.
Goitein, S. D. (1967), *A Mediterranean Society*: *The Jewish Communities of the Arab World as Portrayed in the Documents of the Cairo Geniza, Vol. I: Economic Foundations,* Berkeley: University of California Press.
— and Mordechai A. Friedman (2008), *India Traders of the Middle Ages: Documents from the Cairo Geniza*, Leiden: Brill.
Green, Nile (2011), *Bombay Islam: The Religious Economy of the Western Indian Ocean, 1840–1915*, Cambridge: Cambridge University Press.
— (2014), *Terrains of Exchange: Religious Economies of Global Islam,* Oxford: Oxford University Press.
Haj, Samira (2009), *Reconfiguring Islamic Tradition: Reform, Rationality and Modernity,* Stanford: Stanford University Press.
Halevi, Leor (2007), *Muhammad's Grave: Death Rites and the Making of Islamic Society*, New York: Columbia University Press.
Hallaq, Wael B. (2009), *Shari'a: Theory, Practice, Transformations*, Cambridge: Cambridge University Press.
Hermansen, Marcia, trans. and ed. (1995), *The Conclusive Argument for God, Shah Wali Allah of Delhi's Hujjal Allah al-Baligha,* Leiden: Brill.
Ho, Engseng (2006), *The Graves of Tarim: Genealogy and Mobility across the Indian Ocean,* Berkeley: University of California Press.
Homerin, Th. Emil (1994), *From Arab Poet to Muslim Saint: Ibn al-Farid, His Verse and His Shrine*, Columbia, SC: University of South Carolina Press.
Hourani, Albert (1962), *Arabic Thought in the Liberal Age,* Cambridge: Cambridge University Press.
Hunter, Jack (2015), "Spirits are the Problem: Anthropology and Conceptualizing Spiritual Beings," *Journal for the Study of Religious Experience*, Volume 1, Issue 1, pp. 77–85.
Jaffe, James (2011), "Arbitration and Panchayats in Early Colonial Bombay," *Journal of the K.R. Cama Oriental Institute*, Volume 71, pp. 53–70.
— (2015), *The Ironies of Colonial Governance: Law, Custom and Justice in Colonial India*, Cambridge: Cambridge University Press.

Jones, Justin (2009), "The Local Experiences of Reformist Islam in a 'Muslim' Town in Colonial India: The Case of Amroha," *Modern Asian Studies*, Volume 43, Issue 4, pp. 871–908.

Kamali, Muhammad Kassim (2008), *Shari'ah Law: An Introduction*, Oxford: Oneworld Publications.

Kapteijns, Lidwien and Jay Spaulding (1996), "Women of the Zar and Middle-Class Sensibilities in Colonial Aden, 1923–1932," in *Voice and Power, The Culture of Language in Northeast Africa, Essays in Honor of B.W. Andrzejewski, African Languages and Culture*, Supplement 3, eds R. J. Hayward and I. M. Lewis, pp. 171–89.

— (2004), "Government Qadis and Child Marriage in Aden: Ethnography in the Aden Archives," *International Journal of African Historical Studies*, Volume 37, Issue 3, pp. 401–34.

Killingray, David, Margarette Lincoln and Nigel Rigby eds. (2004), *Maritime Empires, British Imperial Maritime Trade in the Nineteenth Century*, Woodbridge: The Boydell Press.

Kirkman, James and Brian Doe (1975), "The First Days of British Aden: The Diary of John Studdy Leigh," *Arabian Studies*, Volume 2, pp. 179–203.

Knysh, Alexander (1997), "The Cult of the Saints and Religious Reformism in Hadhramaut," in *Hadhrami Traders, Scholars and Statesmen in the Indian Ocean 1750–1960s*, eds Ulrike Freitag and W. G. Clarence-Smith, Leiden: Brill, pp. 199–216.

Kour, Z. H. (1981), *The History of Aden, 1839–1872,* London: Frank Cass.

Kresse, Kai and Edward Simpson, eds (2008), *Struggling with History: Islam and Cosmopolitanism in the Western Indian Ocean*, London: Hurst & Co.

Kugle, Scott (2001), "Framed, Blamed and Renamed: The Recasting of Islamic Jurisprudence in Colonial South Asia," *Modern Asian Studies*, Volume 35, Issue 2, pp. 257–313.

Laffan, Michael (2002), *Islamic Nationhood and Colonial Indonesia: Umma below the Winds,* London: Routledge.

— (2013), "A Sufi Century? The Modern Spread of the Sufi Orders in Southeast Asia," in *Global Muslims in the Age of Steam and Print*, eds James L. Gelvin and Nile Green, Berkeley: University of California Press, pp. 25–39.

Lambert, David and Alan Lester, eds (2006), *Colonial Lives across the British Empire: Imperial Careering in the Long Nineteenth Century* Cambridge: Cambridge University Press.

— eds (2006) "Imperial Spaces, Imperial Subjects," introduction to *Colonial Lives across the British Empire: Imperial Careering in the Long Nineteenth Century,* Cambridge: Cambridge University Press, 2006.

Lauzière, Henri (2010), "The Construction of Salafiyya: Reconsidering Salafism from the Perspective of Conceptual History," *International Journal of Middle Eastern Studies*, Volume 42, pp. 369–89.

— (2015), *The Making of Salafism: Islamic Reform inhe Twentieth Century*, New York: Columbia University Press.
Lees, Lynn Hollen (January 2009), "Being British in Malaya, 1890–1940," *Journal of British Studies*, Volume 48, pp. 76–101.
Leigh, Douglas (1987), *The Free Yemeni Movement*, Beirut: American University of Beirut Press.
Lewis, I. M. (1971) *Ecstatic Religion: An Anthropology of Spirit Possession and Shamanism*, London: Pelican.
Loimeier, Roman (2009), *Between Social Skills and Marketable Skills: The Politics of Education in 20th Century Zanzibar*, Leiden: Brill.
Low, M. C. (2008), "Empire and the Hajj: Pilgrims, Plagues and Pan-Islam under British Surveillance, 1865–1908," *International Journal of Middle East Studies*, Volume 40, Issue 2, pp. 269–90.
McChesney, R. D. (1991), *Waqf in Central Asia: Four Hundred Years in the History of a Muslim Shrine, 1480–1889*, Princeton: Princeton University Press.
Makris, G. and Ahmad al-Safi (1991), "The Tambura Spirit Possession Cult of the Sudan, Past and Present," in *Women's Medicine: The Zar-Bori Cult in Africa and Beyond*, eds Ahmad al-Safi, Sayyid Hurriez and I. M. Lewis, Edinburgh: Edinburgh University Press, pp. 118–36.
— (2000), *Changing Masters: Spirit Possession and Identity Construction among Slave Descendants and Other Subordinates in Sudan*, Evanston: Northwestern University Press.
Margariti, Roxani Eleni (2007), *Aden and the Indian Ocean Trade: 150 Years in the Life of a Medieval Arabian Port*, Chapel Hill: University of North Carolina Press.
Masquelier, Adeline (2009), *Women and Islamic Revival in a West African Town*, Bloomington: Indiana University Press.
Massey, Doreen (2005), *For Space*, London: Sage Publications.
Mathew, Johan (2016), *Margins of the Market: Trafficking and Capitalism across the Arabian Sea*, Berkeley: University of California Press.
Matthews, Nathaniel (2013), "Imagining Arab Communities: Colonialism, Islamic Reform and Arab Identity in Mombasa Kenya, 1897–1933," *Islamic Africa*, Volume 4, Issue 2, pp. 135–63.
Metcalf, Barbara (1982), *Islamic Revival in British India: Deoband 1860–1900*, Oxford: Oxford University Press.
Metcalf, Thomas (2007), *Imperial Connections: India in the Indian Ocean Arena, 1860–1920* Berkeley: University of California Press.
Miran, Jonathan (2009), *Red Sea Citizens: Cosmopolitan Society and Cultural Change in Massawa*, Bloomington: Indiana University Press.
Mittermaier, Amira (2010), *Dreams that Matter: Egyptian Landscapes of the Imagination*, Berkeley: University of California Press.
Naji, Sultan A. (n.d.), *al-tarikh al-'askari lil'yaman*, no publisher.

Natvig, Richard (1987), "Oromos, Slaves and the Zar Spirits: A Contribution to the History of the Zar Cult," *The International Journal of African Historical Studies*, Volume 20, Issue 4, pp. 669–89.

Onley, James (2007), *The Arabian Frontier of the British Raj: Merchants, Rulers, and the British in the Nineteenth-Century Gulf*, Oxford: Oxford University Press.

Peirce, Leslie (2003), *Morality Tales: Law and Gender in the Court of Aintab*, Berkeley: University of California Press.

Prestholdt, Jeremy (2008), *Domesticating the World: African Consumerism and the Genealogies of Globalization*, Berkeley: University of California Press.

Reese, Scott (2004), "The Adventures of Abu Harith: Muslim Travel Writing and Navigating the Modern in Colonial East Africa," in *The Transmission of Islamic Learning in Islamic Africa*, ed. Scott S. Reese, Leiden: Brill, pp. 244–56.

—, ed. (2004), *The Transmission of Islamic Learning in Islamic Africa*, Leiden: Brill.

— (2008), *Renewers of the Age: Holy Men and Social Discourse in Colonial Benaadir*, Leiden: Brill.

— (2008), "The 'Respectable Citizens' of Shaykh Uthman," in, *Struggling with History: Islam and Cosmopolitanism in the Western Indian Ocean*, eds Kai Kresse and Edward Simpson, London: Hurst & Co., pp.189–222.

— (2012), "Salafi Transformations: Aden and the Changing Voices of Reform in the Interwar Indian Ocean," *International Journal of Middle Eastern Studies*, Volume 44, Issue 2, pp. 71–92.

— (2015) "Shaykh Abdullahi al-Qutbi and the Pious Believer's Dilemma: Local Moral Guidance in an Age of Global Islamic Reform," *Journal of Eastern Africa Studies*, Volume 9, Issue 3, Fall, pp. 488–504.

Renard, John (2008), *Friends of God: Islamic Images of Piety, Commitment and Servanthood*, Berkeley: University of California Press.

Richman, Paula, ed. (1991), *Many Ramayanas, The Diversity of a Narrative Tradition in South Asia*, Berkeley: University of California Press.

Robinson, Francis (1993), "Technology and Religious Change," *Modern Asian Studies*, Volume 27, Issue 1, Special Issue: How Social, Political and Cultural Information Is Collected, Defined, Used and Analyzed, pp. 229–51

— (2008), "Islamic Reform and Modernities in South Asia," *Modern Asian Studies*, Volume 42, Issue 2/3, pp. 259–81.

Rudolph, Loyd I. and Susanne Hoeber Rudolph (1967), *Modernity of Tradition: Political Development in India*, Chicago: University of Chicago Press.

Qasimi, Sultan b. Muhammad, (1986), *al-Ihtilal al-britani l'adan*, no publisher.

Scharbrodt, Oliver (2007), "The Salafiyya and Sufism: Muhammad Abduh and his Risālat al-Wāridāt (Treatise on Mystical Inspriations)," Bulletin of SOAS 70, Issue 1, pp. 89–115.

Schielke, Samuli (2007), "Hegemonic Encounters: Criticism of Saints-day Festivals and the Formation of Modern Islam in Late Nineteenth and early 20th-century Egypt," *Die Welt des Islams*, Volume 47, Issue 3/4, pp. 319–55.

Schimmel, Annemarie (1985), *And Muhammad is His Messenger: The Veneration of the Prophet in Islamic Piety*, Chapel Hill: University of North Carolina Press.

Seif, Huda (2005), "The Accursed Minority: The Ethno-Cultural Persecution of al-Akhdam in the Republic of Yemen: A Documentary & Advocacy Project," *Muslim World Journal of Human Rights*, Volume 2, Issue 1. ISSN (Online) 1554–4419, DOI: https://doi.org/10.2202/1554-4419.1029.

Serjeant, R. B. (1966), "South Arabia and Ethiopia: African elements in the South Arabian population," in *International Conference of Ethiopian Studies*, 3rd edn, Addis Ababa, Ethiopia, pp. 25–33.

Sharafi, Mitra (2014), *Law and Identity in Colonial South Asia: Parsi Legal Culture, 1772–1947*, Cambridge: Cambridge University Press.

Tagliacozzo, Eric (2013), "Hajj in the Time of Cholera: Pilgrim Ships and Contagion from Southeast Asia to the Red Sea," in *Global Muslims in the Age of Steam and Print*, eds James Gelvin and Nile Green, Berkeley: University of California Press, pp. 103–20.

Taylor, Christopher (1998), *In the Vicinity of the Righteous: Ziyara and the Veneration of Muslim Saints in Late Medieval Egypt*, Leiden: Brill.

Trimingham, J. Spencer (1965), *Islam in Ethiopia,* London: Frank Cass.

Um, Nancy (2009), *The Merchant Houses of Mukha: Trade and Architecture in an Indian Ocean Port,* Seattle: University of Washington Press.

Waterfield, Gordon (1968), *Sultans of Aden,* London: John Murray.

Weismann, Itzchak (2001), "Between Sufi Reformism and Modernist Rationalism—A Reappraisal of the Origins of the Salafiyya from the Damascene Angle," *Die Welt des Islams*, Volume 41, Issue 2, pp. 206–37.

al-Zabidi, Abu al-Abbas Ahmad (n.d.), *Tabaqat al-khawas ahl al-saddiq wa al-ikhlas*, Sana'a: al-Dar al-yamaniyya lil-nashar wa al-tawzi'a.

Zadeh, Travis (2010), "The Wiles of Creation: Philosophy, Fiction and the 'Aja'ib Tradition'," *Middle Eastern Literature*, Volume 13, Issue 1, pp. 21–48.

Zaman, Muhammad Qasim (2002), *The Ulama in Contemporary Islam: Custodians of Change*, Princeton: Princeton University Press.

— "The Scope and Limits of Islamic Cosmopolitanism and the Discursive Language of the 'Ulama'," in Cooke and Lawrence, *Muslim Networks*, pp. 84–104.

— (2012), *Modern Islamic Thought in a Radical Age: Religious Authority and Internal Criticism,* Cambridge: Cambridge University Press.

Zenkovsky, Sophie (1950), "Zar and Tambura as Practised by the Women of Omdurman (Paper Read before the Philosophical Society of the Sudan in 1948)," *Sudan Notes and Records*, Volume 31, pp. 65–81.

Index

al-Abbadi, Shaykh Ahmad bin Muhammad bin Awad, 142–3, 144–5, 146, 149–53, 154–5
  and Arab Islamic Reform Club, 158–9
Abban, Shaykh al-Hakam ibn, 67, 68, 70
Abd al-Aziz, Sayyid, 104
Abd al-Rahman al-Aydarus, Sharif, 73
Abd al-Rahman Zayla'i, 73
Abd al-Razzaq, 83
al-Abdali, Sultan Ahmad, 43–4, 45, 48, 53–4
al-Abdali, Sultan Muhsin bin Fadhil, 55, 57, 65–6
Abdi, Yusuf, 134
Abdu Muhammad, Sayyid, 70–1
Abduh, Muhammad, 140–1, 148
Abdullah, Awadh, 145
Abdullah bin Hashim, Sayyid, 61
Abu Bakr Aydarus, Sayyid, 65, 66, 68
Abu Makhrama, Abu Muhammad al-Tayyib ibn Abdullah, 20, 24–7, 30–2, 39, 66
Abyssinia *see* Ethiopia
al-Adani, Rihan ibn Abdullah, 26
al-Adani, Sayyid Abu Bakr Aydarus, 73–4, 75, 77, 149, 153–4
al-Adani, Sayyid Aydarus, 26
Aden, 1–2, 3–6, 14, 15–16
  and Abu Makhrama, 24–7
  and administration, 79–80, 81–6
  and Arabization, 162–3
  and attacks, 57–8
  and bazaar, 58–60
  and burials, 75–8
  and community, 106–7, 109–10, 164–5
  and East India Company, 40–1, 43–5, 47–8, 55–6
  and Ibn al-Mujawir, 21–2, 23–4
  and India, 17
  and Luqmans, 33–5, 36–8
  and marginal groups, 110–14, 132
  and Ottoman Empire, 28–30, 32–3
  and Portugal, 27–8
  and print, 147, 148
  and Qadis, 86–9
  and sacred spaces, 65–70
  and Salafism, 158–60
  and settlement, 64–5
  and spirit-possession, 118, 119, 120, 121–2, 136
  and technology, 7–9
  and tombs, 72
  and trade, 18–20, 60–3
  and the unseen, 11
Aden Act (1864), 87
Affan, Abban ibn Uthman ibn, 26
al-Afghani, Jamal al-Din, 140
Africans, 4
Ahmad Ali, Shaykh, 83, 87
Ahmad ibn Alwan, Shaykh, 67
Akhdam, 112–13, 114, 128–9, 129, 132
  and dance, 135, 136
Albuquerque, Afanço d', 27, 28
alcohol, 59
Alexander the Great, 21, 22, 23, 24
Ali b. al-Qom, Husayn ibn, 31–2
Ali Isma'il, Sayyid, 142, 143, 144, 145, 146
Aliyya bint Ali, Sharifa, 1, 74–5
al-Amawy, Khalaf ibn Abi al-Tahir, 31
Ambedkar, Dr. B. R., 35

Anglo-Muhammadan law, 91, 95, 96, 107, 165
anti-colonialism, 37
Arab Islamic Reform Club, 141–2, 143–4, 155, 158
Arabia, 18, 22
arbitration *see Panchayyat*
Arthurs, Lt., 84–5, 86
al-Asnag, Ahmad Muhammad, 133–4, 142, 143, 144, 145, 149
   and Salafism, 154–8, 159–61
Auckland, George Eden, Lord, 54
Aungier, Gerald, 83
awliya' see *wali*
al-Aydarus, Sayyid Abdullah, 76, 125, 164, 180n71
   and Wakf Committee, 99, 100, 101–2, 103
Ayyubids, 19, 24

Badr, Sultan, 29
al-Baghdadi, Isma'il ibn Abd al-Malik, 26
Bahadur, Azim Jah, 54
al-Bahr, Sayyed Hashim, 1, 144
Bailie, Maj T., 65
Banians, 55, 58, 62–3
baraka (blessings), 2
Barbosa, Duarte, 27
al-barzakh, 76, 78, 167
al-Battah, Da'ud, 80, 89, 99, 107–8
   and imperialism, 164
   and Kamaran Island, 104–5
   and Tambura, 129
   and Wakf Committee, 102, 103
   and Zar, 123, 141
BaWazir, Abd al-Latif, 153, 154
al-Bayhani, Muhammad bin Salim, 142–3, 154–5
   and Arab Islamic Reform Club, 158–9
   and print, 149, 150, 151–3
Bin Yiju, 19
Blankett, Adm John, 44
Bohras, 34, 111–12

British Empire, 1–3, 5, 13–14, 33
   and festivals, 70
   and imperial petition, 122, 123–8, 129–31, 136
   and Indian Ocean, 6–7
   and Islam, 163–4
   and the law, 79, 80, 81–2, 96
   and Salafism, 145
   see also East India Company
British Indian Army, 57–8
Bujra, Abdalla, 5–6
BuKhidr, Ahmad, 49, 50–1, 52
burials, 75–8, 167

Cairo, 148–9
Capon, Lt. Col., 58, 59, 60
cemeteries, 6, 75–6
Christianity, 4
Christopher, Lt., 61–2
coal depots, 47, 48, 64
coffee, 32–3, 41
communications, 7, 8, 164
cosmology, 9–10, 72–4, 76–7, 78, 166
Court of the Resident, 87, 90
Cruttendon, Lt. Charles J., 60
customs tax, 61

Daria Dawlat (barque), 47–54, 60–1
Das Sir, 23, 24
demons, 10
dhikr, 67, 139, 144, 156, 158, 159
Dhu al-Qarnayn *see* Alexander the Great
divorce, 91–5
Dohlu, Mancherji Rustom, 89, 90

East Africa, 7
East India Company, 4, 13–14, 33, 38–9, 42–4
   and Aden, 40–1, 44–5, 47–8, 55–61, 64
   and administration, 81, 82
   and Egypt, 46
   and Islam, 163–4
   and shipwrecks, 54

Edoor, Firuz, 49
Egypt, 7, 19, 23, 148–9
  and burials, 77
  and Mehmet Ali Pasha, 45–7
  and Napoleon, 41–2
  and Tihama, 61, 62
  see also Red Sea
elites, 6, 80, 107, 109–10
Ethiopia, 22, 23, 110–11, 112, 113
  and Zar, 115–16, 117, 118
ethnicity, 4–5

Fatamids, 18
Fatat al-Jezirah (newspaper), 148, 155, 158
Fatima bint Ahmad, 70–1
fatwas (legal opinions), 104, 123
Fazoo, Husayn, 134
fiqh (jurisprudence), 80, 91, 96, 165
First World War, 8, 14
France, 42, 45

Gandhi, Mahatma, 35, 36
Grant, Sir Robert, 47

Habib, Ismail, 66–7
Hadim Suleiman Pasha, 30
Haines, Stafford Bettewerth, 5, 40–1, 56, 57, 59
  and administration, 81–2
  and *Daria Dawlat*, 53–5
  and dismissal, 87
  and Islam, 66
  and Qadis, 83
  and trade, 62–3
Hajj, 7, 103, 147
Hanbal, Ahmad ibn, 26
Hanuman, 17, 18, 23, 24, 167
al-Haradee, Shaykh, 67, 69, 70, 72
Hashim al-Bahr, Sayyid, 69–70, 72
al-Hazmi, Sayyid Muhammad bin Hasan, 94, 100
al-Hazmi, Sayyid Yahya bin Muhammad, 88, 97
al-Hidaya (al-Marghinani), 96

Hidayat al-murid (al-Abbadi), 150–3, 158
Hijaz, 46
al-Hindi, Abu Sarrrour Iqbal ibn Abdullah, 26–7
al-Hindi, Salim bin Abdullah, 20
al-Hindi, Zakariya Muhammad, 142, 143, 144–5, 146
Hinduism, 4, 17, 18, 55–6
Hodeida, 61, 62, 63
housing, 64–5
al-Humawi, Yaqut, 19, 20
Hurgronje, Snoucke, 116–17
Husayn bin Ali Haydar, Sharif, 62
Husayn bin Siddiq, 69

Ibn Baksh, 30
Ibn Battuta, 19–20
Ibn al-Mujawir, 17, 18, 19, 20–4, 39
Ibrahim, Mahi, 134
Ibrahim Pasha, 28, 62
ideological trajectories, 106–7, 108
India, 6, 7, 17, 18, 19, 24
  and East India Company, 41, 42, 44, 47–8, 54
  and law, 81, 82, 83, 87
  and Luqmans, 34–7
  and nationalism, 14, 162
  and refuge, 31–2
  and trade, 60–2
Indian Ocean, 2–3, 5, 6
  and Abu Makhrama, 25
  and culture, 109, 111
  and Ibn al-Mujawir, 24
  and shipwrecks, 48–52
Indian Rebellion (1857), 87
inheritance, 96–8
Iran, 5
al-Iraqi, Shaykh Ahmad, 68
al-Iraqi, Shaykh Salim ibn Muhammad, 67, 69
Isenberg, Charles William, 115–16
al-Islah (newspaper), 147
Islah party, 163
Islam, 2, 3, 4–6

and burials, 75–8
and community, 64
and cosmology, 72–4
and imperialism, 163–4
and ontology, 9–11
and printing, 8–9, 147–8
and reformers, 107–8, 122–8, 129–30
and sacred spaces, 65–6, 164–5
and saints, 66–70
and spirit-possession, 119
see also Salafism; Sufism
Islamic law, 79, 80, 82, 91, 96–8; *see also* Anglo-Muhammadan law; *shari'a* law

Jabartis (sweepers), 109, 110–11, 113–14, 120, 132, 135
Jafar, Mulla, 82
Jawhar ibn Abdullah, 67
Jayyash ibn Najah, Abu al-Tami, 31–2
al-Jaza'ri, Abd al-Qadir, 140
Jiddah, 40, 41, 61
jinn, 10, 21, 78, 118; *see also* Tambura; Zar cult
al-Jiz al-latif (al-Adani), 73–4, 153–4, 160
Judaism, 4, 19, 55

Kamala Devi (Luqman), 35–6
Kamaran Island, 103–6, 165
Khayyat, Ahmad bin Abdullah, 100
Koyaji, Nusservanji, 89–90
Krapf, John Lewis, 115–16
Kuvar, Muhammad, 67

laborers, 7, 65
law, 9, 12–13; *see also* Anglo-Muhammadan law; Islamic law; legal pluralism; *Panchayyat*; Qadis
legal pluralism, 81–2
literature, 147
lithographic printing, 8, 147
Luqman, Hamza, 15–16, 34, 37–8, 39, 66

Luqman, Muhammad Ali, 15–16, 34–7, 39, 133
and Arab Islamic Reform Club, 142, 143, 144, 145–6
and imperialism, 164
and print, 148, 149
and Salafism, 154–8, 159–61, 162

Madagascar, 23
Madras, 54
madrasas, 66
al-Makkawi, Saleh Muhammad, 79, 80
al-Makki, Abd al-Qadir bin Muhammad, 96–8, 107
Mamluks, 27, 28
al-Manar (newspaper), 8, 147
Maratha Confederacy, 42
marriage, 80, 91–5, 96–8, 165
Massawa, 41, 61
mawlid (Prophet's birthday), 121
Mecca, 7, 21, 46, 116–18, 133
Medina, 46
Mehmet Ali Pasha, 45–7, 61
Memons, 66–7, 70, 77, 111–12, 177n18
merchants, 5, 7
Middle East, 14, 162
Mirza, Hasan Khan, 134
al-Misri, Muhammad Hasan, 67
Mistry, Pir Muhammad, 49
Mombasa, 7
mosques, 6, 26, 55, 66–7, 164–5
and administration, 99
and Kamaran Island, 103–5
and Salafism, 143–6
Muhammad Ali Pasha, 41
Muhammad bin Hasan, Sayyid, 88
Muhammad, Prophet, 74
Muhammadan Light, 72, 73, 77, 166, 167
Muhsin, Ahmad bin Ali bin, 98
Muhy al-Din Nur Ahman, Sayyid, 103, 104, 105
Mukha, 32, 33, 40, 41, 43, 45
and *Daria Dawlat*, 52–3
and trade, 61, 62–3

multiverse, 10, 72, 78, 163, 166
al-Muqaddasi, 18–19
Murkashee, Ali Husayn, 146
Murray, Lt. Col. J., 42–4
Muslims *see* Islam
al-Musqati, Abdullah, 49, 50, 51
mysticism, 71–3, 153

Nadi al-Islah *see* Arab Islamic Reform Club
Napoleon Bonaparte, 41–2, 45
nationalism, 37, 162, 163
al-Nisa', Begum Ahmad, 48
"noble cloak", 74, 153
Noman, Ali bin Ghalib bin, 100, 101
Nur al-Din bin Jumal, Sayyid, 48, 49–51, 52, 53, 60
Nur Muhammadiyya see Muhammadan Light

O'Brien, E., 91, 92
oil, 162–3
Osgood, Joseph, 65
Ottoman Empire, 27–30, 32–3, 41, 46–7, 61–2
Overflowing River of the Science of Inheritance and Patrimony, The (al-Makki), 96–8, 107

Pakistan, 5
Pan-Arabism, 37
Panchayyat (binding arbitration), 82, 83–6, 106
Parsis, 4
Perim, 42–4
Periplus of the Erythraean Sea, The (manual), 18
Persia, 23
Persian Gulf, 41, 45
petitions, 122, 123–8, 129–31, 136, 144
Playfair, R. L., 83
poetry, 150–3
Portugal, 25, 27–8, 29
prayer, 6
print, 8, 15–16

printing, 147–9
Pursad, Luchmee, 49

Qadis, 6, 79, 80, 82–3, 86–9
  and divorce, 94–5
  and al-Makki, 98
  and mediation, 165
  and Registrars, 90–1, 92–3, 106–7

Ramadan, 49, 87, 119, 121
Ramayana, 17, 23
Rashidi, Shaykh Muhammad, 138, 144
Rasulids, 19
Red Sea, 5, 32, 33, 46, 47, 60–1
  and Alexander the Great, 21, 22, 25, 167
  and East India Company, 41, 42, 44–5
Registrars, 79, 80, 87, 89–90, 106–7
  and *fiqh*, 165
  and al-Makki, 98
  and Qadis, 91, 92–3
Reilly, Bernard, 70, 100–1, 104, 105, 164
religion, 20, 58; *see also* Hinduism; Islam; Judaism
respectability, 133–4, 135, 136–7
Rida, Rashid, 8, 140, 148
Rihan ibn Abdullah, Shaykh, 69
Rihani, Amin, 69–70
Risala fi tariqa al-Naqxhbandiyya (Abd al-Rahman al-Aydarus), 73
rituals, 110–11, 115–22, 130, 133–5
Rustom Ali, Sayyid, 75, 79, 80, 90, 98
  and divorce, 91, 92–3, 94, 95
  and Qadis, 106–7

Safar, 109
Sa'id (Luqman), 68, 155–6, 157–8
saints, 6, 8, 9
  and burials, 75, 76, 166–7
  and mysticism, 71–2
  and Salafism, 156, 157, 160
  and shrines, 11
  and Sufism, 114
  and veneration, 66–71
  see also *ziyarat*

Salafism, 6, 13, 80, 138–41
  and marginal groups, 110–11
  and morality, 159–61
  and mosques, 143–6
  and print, 149–53, 155–6
  and saints, 157–8
  and Sufism, 165–6
  see also scripturalism
Salma bint Said, 116, 118
Salt, Henry, 44, 45
Satan, 25–6
al-Saud, Amir Abudullah, 46
Saudi Arabia, 45, 46
scholarship, 147–8
scripturalism, 133, 136, 137, 139;
  see also Salafism
Second World War, 8
Shaddad b. Ad, 22, 24
Sharaf, Abdullah bin Umar, 89
Sharaf, Awad bin Abdullah, 88–9
Sharaf, Umar bin Abdullah, 88, 91–2, 94–5, 107
shari'a law, 80, 82, 104
shrines, 6, 11, 72, 99, 164–5
Sidis, 112
Singh, Duleep, 15
Sita, 17, 23
slavery, 112
society, 5–6, 75, 76
Solomon, 21, 22–3
Somalia, 7, 110–11, 113
South Africa, 7
spirit-possession, 6, 9, 13; *see also* Tambura; Zar cult
Stace, E. V., 87–8
steamships, 7, 8, 47, 147, 148
Stories from the History of Aden and Southern Arabia (Luqman), 38
Sublime Porte *see* Ottoman Empire
Sudan, 46, 110, 113, 119–20, 135–6
Suez Canal, 7, 41, 42, 147
Sufism, 6, 8, 66, 70
  and mysticism, 71, 73, 120, 121
  and print, 149

  and saints cult, 114
  and Salafism, 139, 140, 150–3, 165–6
Sulayman, Sultan, 29

Taher Rajab, 104
Tahir, Shaykh Amir ibn Da'ud ibn, 29, 30
Tahirids, 19, 24, 28
Tambura, 13, 110–11, 114–15, 119–22, 129–32, 134–7, 166
  and campaigns, 123
Tarikh 'adan wa janub al-jazira al-arabiyya (Luqman), 38
Tarikh al-Mustabsir (Ibn al-Mujawir), 20–1, 66
Tarikh thaghr adan (Abu Makhrama), 24–7, 66
al-Thaalibi, Abd al-Aziz, 142
Tihama *see* Red Sea
Tipu bin Al-Doonebee, Sayyid, 48–9, 50, 51, 52, 53, 60
Tipu Sultan, 42
tombs, 65–6, 67–8, 70, 77–8, 166–7
  and veneration, 72, 156–7
trade, 18–20, 44–5, 58–63
transportation, 7, 8, 147, 148, 164
Turanshah, 19
Turkey *see* Ottoman Empire

Umar bin Abdullah Sharaf, 74–5
Umar ibn Abdullah, 79, 80
Umar, Muhammad, 75
unseen (*ghayb*), 10–12
urban poor, 111–14

Wakf Committee, 99–103, 105, 108
walis, 66, 67, 68, 69, 70–1, 72–3
waqf (pious endowments), 6, 99–103, 165, 183n87
Wellington, Arthur Wellesley, Duke of, 42, 44
women, 110–11, 129
  and Zar, 115, 116, 117–18, 123–9, 132, 133–4, 135

Yasin Khan, M., 90, 99–101, 102–3, 107, 108
  and imperialism, 164
  and Kamaran Island, 104, 105
Yemen, 28, 32–3, 41, 61, 162, 163; *see also* Aden

al-Zafiri, Murjan ibn Abdullah, 27, 28
Zanzibar, 7, 9, 116, 118, 133
Zar cult, 13, 110–11, 114, 115–19, 120, 132, 134–6
  and campaigns, 123–9, 141
  and women, 133–4
Zayn bin Alawi al-Aydarus, Sayyid, 52, 56, 65
ziyarat (saint festivals), 66–9, 70, 73, 114, 166
  and Salafism, 144, 157–8, 159, 160
  and Tambura, 129, 130–1, 134, 136
Zurayids, 19, 21

EU representative:
Easy Access System Europe
Mustamäe tee 50, 10621 Tallinn, Estonia
Gpsr.requests@easproject.com

www.ingramcontent.com/pod-product-compliance
Lightning Source LLC
Chambersburg PA
CBHW051057230426
43667CB00013B/2341